The QUALLS
CONCISE
ENGLISH GRAMMAR

2ND EDITION

With Traditional & QCD Diagramming

EDUARD J. QUALLS, MSBA, BA

DANAAN PRESS™

The cover's satellite image of North America was produced by
NASA. No copyright is claimed on that image.

The image of the seal of the Virginia Company of London (facing the Preface)
was originally produced by the US Government. No copyright is claimed on that image.

The map of the world on page 8 was produced from data supplied by the US
Government and other public domain sources. No copyright is claimed on that image.

The modern and historic flags remain the property of the citizens of the associated nations.

The "New Grand Union" flag is in the public domain because it includes designs drawn from
other public domain flags. This *NGU* flag has the dimensions of the stripes taken from the
current US flag, with the current (2 × 3) Union Flag of the United Kingdom in the
canton, scaled proportionately so that in height it extends from the top of the flag to the
bottom of the seventh stripe (red), as does the star-bearing canton of the US flag.

For the latest information on this volume, visit its website at
www.GrammarExpert.com

Further information about the author may be found at
www.EduardQualls.com

⚥⚭⚲

Library of Congress Control Number: 2018909402
ISBN: 978-1-890-000-18-9
DP-ID: 300-0120-92201-3

Published by Danaan Press, Inc., in the United States of America.

For my 'Grands': Kali, Mallory, Cade, Peyton, Garrett,
Braden, Coby, Aidan & Emma

With special recognition of, and thanks to, my reading, writing
and language teachers in the public-school system of Hot Springs, Arkansas,
for their dedication to teaching and to their students:

Mrs Stewart, Miss Goodman, Mrs Davis, Mrs Francis,
Mr Beard, Mrs Browne,

with special mention of

Carolyn Courteney *for the rich gift of French,*
Mrs Carl Buck *for the rigorous joy of Latin,*
Ruth Sweeney *for Shakespeare and the start of Egyptian and Chinese,*
Elizabeth Sloan Housely *for the mystery of Anglo-Saxon,*

and especially

Verna Dokey,

whose gentle, mellifluent, Tidewater-Southern accent
awoke in a teenager a love for the beauty of North American English

कायस्थस्वर

WRITER'S PREFACE

Pray speak in English. Here are some will thank you
William Shakespeare
Henry VIII, III:1

As a descendent of founding members of the Virginia Company of London, the organization that financed the first successful English settlement, at James-town, Virginia, I am proud to be able to present this documentation of the classic, and now predominant English dialect that we were instrumental in bringing to the New World.

This text was undertaken to provide a grammatical textbook and reference guide that was written to the higher standard of English usage taught before "modern" methods started being forced on teachers during the late 1970's and 1980's. Having been raised in the beauty of that set of texts on which North American English is based — The Book of Common Prayer [1559 & 1662], The King-James Bible [1611] & the works of Shakespeare [1564-1616] — I have used those as the arbiters that establish the very high standard toward which this text is targeted.

I have written those precepts expressed in this text to that standard of English grammar that gave me the ability to handle the English language better than 99% of all U.S. graduate-school candidates of my generation.

Of necessity, this includes the ability to diagram sentences, one of the few ways one may gain true understanding of the deeper structures underlying our language. I have included a large section that encapsulates both the American traditional methods, designed by Reed and Kellogg in the 1880's, as well as my suggestions for correcting that standard's limitations, inconsis-tencies, and tendency toward spaghettification, based on my experience in symbolic representation, communication efficiencies and graphics.

Much of this text incorporates my original concepts, observations and ideas, the results of so many years of study, writing and editing. Other concepts, guides or rules herein presented come from, or date from, the works of Reed and Kellogg and other grammarians of the turn of the twentieth century and before. These are the sources of the criteria needed in order to correct the recent slide of both spoken and written English — of all dialects — into mediocrity.

Copies of the images and diagrams used in the book, as well as information on how to generate other examples using the tools through which the example images were created, will be available on this book's website:

www.grammarexpert.com.

Seal of the Virginia Company of London,
under whose auspices the English Language
was first established in the New World.

This grammar covers **ACE**: ***American-Canadian English***, also known as *General North-American Dialect*, which is the dialect of the majority of native English speakers and is the international standard for business English.

ACE is the most unified, well-documented and standardized form of English. It is also the form truest to its Tudor/Stuart origin, as revealed in its speakers' having maintained their pronunciation by adhering more closely to that of the original, orthographic norms, rather than having allowed the spoken language to fracture, over so large a territory, into a myriad of almost mutually-unintelligible, dialect forms. This unity is both defining and salutary for the language, as *ACE* is the dialect approaching 75% of all native speakers of the English language.

> However, other than issues of pronunciation, those few differences between American-Canadian and British English are primarily centered in minor variations of vocabulary and orthography: there are very few readily apparent differences in standard grammatical usage between these two primary dialects. In this grammar, where needed, notes are added to cover differences between *ACE* and British English. These explanations are accompanied by "*ACE*" or "*BE*" respectively.

This grammar stresses **the protocol of the English language**: the rules specifying the form and order in which items must appear in order to transfer messages successfully: effectively and succinctly. Because of this, some would label it *functional*, others, *proscriptive*.

Some may rail against this proscriptive nature, but the fact is that, once you strip away all the academic minutiæ-obfuscation, **the only basic difference between a descriptive grammar and a proscriptive grammar is the form of the verbs that the authors use in the text**.

> A proscriptive English grammar will state, "The subject and the verb must agree in person and number." A descriptive grammar may say "In English, its speakers make the subject and the verb agree in person and number." These two presentations arrive at the same ultimate effect: *to speak English correctly, do it either as the proscriptive grammar details or as the descriptive grammar describes*.

Each language has rules: **it is the rules that define the language**.

All language exists for communication. **All communication relies on a protocol—a set of rules that provide the mechanism for meaningful exchange**.

In language-studies this is called **_grammar_**, a general term composed of

1. ***morphology***, the rules for word formation, and
2. ***syntax***, how the words are fitted together to create sensible communication.

Grammar is itself coordinated with

1. ***orthophony***, the rules of correct pronunciation, and
2. ***orthography***, the rules of correct writing.

Just as with information transfers between computers, **failure to follow the protocol—the rules of the grammar—causes messages to be garbled, and attempts at communication to fail**.

Communication is a two-way stream.

It is not just a producer, a speaker or writer, but includes consumers, listeners and readers, too.

Only when both sender and receiver know and follow the rules, the protocol, *can communication occur, with the least distortion and the greatest ease.*

The permissive "just speak and write any way you want" attitude too common in today's attitudes and teaching fosters the breakdown of communication: it is the source of **dysglossia**, because it elevates language usage centered within, by and for the individual over the definition of the protocol. It thereby replaces those shared rules, patterns, and paradigms of the language's definition with whatever oddities the individual may quixotically dream up.

The idea that language is an organic entity that arises, independent and in full flower, unencumbered by social interaction, from the mind of each of its speakers is nonsense: all must be taught language the rules of language—even of their *mother tongue*—and those who remain untutored (formally or informally) or unpracticed will never be good at communication.

Indeed, language is, at its root, a tool, first of the community and, thereafter, a tool of the individual within community. Language is not so much *communication* as **communification**, a creation of that held in common: the transformation of personal expression into a common medium, shareable within a broader community, a process that actually serves to establish, unify and augment that community.

Dysglossia also arises when language is used not for communication of the message borne by the words, but for ulterior motives. Whenever the true message is not the words, but is one implied by the surroundings, cultural baggage or affectations of speech, the goal is not communication, but slight: exclusion, denigration, degradation.

> *"The English have no respect for their language, and*
> *will not teach their children to speak it."*
> —George Bernard Shaw
> *Pygmalion* (1916: Preface)

The fact remains that, in order to communicate clearly, precisely, succinctly—to use language with a master's hand for communication—you must know the grammatical, syntactical, and psychological structure of the language, the meanings and cultural auras held within its vocabulary, and the geo-social and historical arena into which you wish your message to fit. This requires that the users of a language share a common set of grammatical rules, a shared lexicon, and the knowledge of how and when to use them.

> **Whoever cannot express a thought logically and clearly**
> **cannot produce a logical and clear thought to express.**

Your medium—your use of language—will either support your message transparently, or derail your message abysmally. Master the rules and they will be your ever-ready helpmate.

You cannot teach a child to dress itself by letting it run around naked till it discover its own fabrics; you cannot teach a child to paint by describing colors; you cannot teach children to work with tools by leaving implements lying about. You must teach them the rules, the techniques, the technology, and then guide their practice.

The very same holds with language.

> *"Every English poet should master the rules of grammar before*
> *he attempts to bend or break them."*
> —Robert Graves

And we are each the poet of our own lives.

CONTENTS

1 Introduction to the English Language

1.1 English is one of ***the Indo-European languages***, a group of related languages that is spoken across the widest geographical extremes, and predominates across the surface of the Earth, physically and electronically.

1.1.1 **The Indo-European languages** are one family uniting several hundred related languages, as revealed by shared vocabulary, grammar and syntax, culture and mythology to have descended from a single parent language spoken by a group whose homeland was centered in that general area stretching from the Caucasus into the plains of south-central Russia and Ukraine several thousand years ago.

There are many families of languages, ancient and modern, within the Indo-European group. The major families, with examples of member languages (with ancient, extinct or currently merely literary ones in italics) are:

1. Hellenic: *Mycenæan, Homeric, Classical, Hellenistic, Medieval* and Modern: Greek
2. Indic: *Sanskrit*, Hindi, Gujarati, Bengali, Rajasthani, Marathi, Sinhala, Nepali, Romani, Kashmiri, Marathi, *et al.*
3. Iranian: *Avestan, Pahlavi, Scythian*, Persian, Pashto, Kurdish, Ossetic, *et al.*
4. Italic: *Latin, Oscan, Umbrian*, Sardinian, Italian, French, Spanish, Portuguese, Romanian, Catalan, Provençal *et al.*
5. Celtic: *Gaulish, Galatian, Celtiberian*, Gaelic, Irish, Welsh, Breton, *et al.*
6. Germanic: *Gothic, Vandalic, Anglo-Saxon, Old Saxon*, German, English, Frisian, Dutch, Yiddish, Icelandic, Swedish, Danish, Norwegian, *et al.*
7. Baltic: *Old Prussian*, Lithuanian, Latvian
8. Slavic: *Old Church Slavonic*, Bulgarian, Russian, Ukrainian, Belorussian, Polish, Czech, Slovak, Serbian, Croatian, Slovenian, *et al.*
9. Albanian: Albanian
10. Armenian: Armenian
11. Tocharian: *Tocharian-A, Tocharian-B*
12. Anatolian: *Hittite, Luvian, Lycian, Carian, Lydian*

1.1.2 **Some of these family groups are quite closely related, and their shared characteristics are expressed using higher group names.** The Indic and Iranian are so closely related linguistically and historically that they are often spoken of as the **Indo-Iranian** languages in linguistic or historical contexts. With less certainty (and less agreement as to usefulness or establishable validity) are the **Balto-Slavic** group and the **Italo-Celtic** group. Although we know that the Indo-Iranian group was unified at one period, the evidence for those other two groups is not so clear, and is based more on implications of vocabulary and grammar than historical evidence. The issue is that these relationships could also have come from those groups' having lived in close proximity rather than their having been earlier, united speech groups.

1.1.3 **The Germanic family** is the most widely-used group of languages in the world simply because it contains both English, today's *lingua franca*, and German, the second most widely spoken or understood language within the European Community. So that, although possibly not the highest in numbers of speakers according to some ways of presenting the data, the Germanic family is the most influential of the Indo-European language groups in modern culture.

1.1.3.1 Most scholars of the history and characteristics of the Germanic languages (of *Germanistik*) hold that there are three branches of this group: the Eastern, the Northern and the Western. This geographic/directional nomenclature corresponds to the placement of the early homelands and origin of the separate groups within the early Germanic settlement areas.

1.1.3.2 The oldest attested is the **Eastern Germanic** branch, represented by texts in dialects of Gothic (Ostrogothic, Visigothic, *etc.*), but is assumed from personal and place names to have included Burgundian, Lombardic, Vandalic, and others. The speakers of the Eastern Germanic languages came originally from Baltic Scandinavia, and their language is remembered in the name of the Swedish island of Gotland. Because of their extensive migrations throughout eastern and southern Europe, this branch was extremely important during the late Roman Empire and early Middle Ages, but has since become extinct. The last known survivor was Crimean Gothic, which appears to have become extinct within only the last 300 years.

1.1.3.3 The **North Germanic** branch is found earliest in the *rune stones* of Scandinavia, and later in the Viking sagas. Its oldest form still in existence is Icelandic, which has remained quite close in written form to the language of the Norsemen, the Viking sagas and that form of North Germanic, Old Norse, which had so great an influence on the development of English. The other principle languages of this family (that are not so close to the early language) are Swedish, Danish and Norwegian.

Some scholars of *Germanistik* hold that the similarities between the languages of the early Northern and the Eastern branches of Germanic suggest that they should be grouped together, as the **Northeastern** branch. However, one most often finds the three-part division, if for no other reason than that it keeps the extinct Germanic languages distinct from the living ones. Yet, based in part on that extinction, more texts are needed from the Eastern group to provide support for such a re-assignment.

1.1.3.4 **Western Germanic** includes the most widely spoken of the Germanic languages, English and German, as well as related tongues, such as Dutch, Flemish, Frisian, Afrikaans, Yiddish, Luxemburgish, Plattdeutsch and Schwyz. Of these, Frisian is the language most closely related to English; the others listed retain forms, sounds and usage closer to historical forms of ancient Germanic. The earliest texts extant for members of this branch are Anglo-Saxon (which formed the basis of modern English), Old Saxon, and Old High German (which evolved into many modern dialects of German, particularly into *Neuhochdeutsch*: today's Standard German).

Man soll alle Tage wenigstens ein kleines Lied hören, ein gutes Gedicht lesen,
ein treffliches Gemälde sehen und, wenn es möglich zu machen wäre,
einige vernünftige Worte sprechen.

*Each day one should, at the least, hear a little song, read a good poem, see
an excellent painting and, if it were possible, speak a few reasonable words.*

—Johann Wolfgang von Goethe
Wilhelm Meisters Lehrjahre (V, 1)

1.1.4   Although belonging to the *Germanic* family of languages, **English** has gone through several evolutionary situations that have differentiated it from the other members of that family: these events have both simplified its grammar tremendously and expanded its vocabulary greatly, by drawing from a widespread mix of sources.

1.1.4.1   **Anglo-Saxon's** having had to share the English countryside with its kindred tongue, **Old Norse**, the language of the Viking invaders, caused a massive simplification of Anglo-Saxon grammatical forms. For, the peasants found that the complexities of inflection were neither necessary nor particularly helpful when an Old English speaker and an Old Norse speaker tried to converse. The fact that the basic forms of so many words were mutually understandable meant that adding language-specific word-endings merely got in the way of communication: it was simpler just to drop them. The results of this common-sense approach were both a tremendous simplification of grammar and the absorption of a sizable part of the Old Norse word-hoard into common English parlance. For example, the source of two common English words is a single Germanic root, but the Anglo-Saxon form of that root, **scyrte**, became the man's **shirt**, and the Old Norse form of the same root, **skyrta**, became the woman's **skirt**. In parallel, the English verb, **beseech**, is from the Anglo-Saxon, **besēcean [be + sēcean**, *be + seek***]**, while the unmodified, **seek**, is from the Old Norse **sækja**, with each word's taking its Middle English and Modern English palatilization, or lack of it, from the source language, just as in **scyrte/skyrta**.

The influence of Old Norse on the course of the English language is unique in the history of English in that it is the only language from which English borrowed not only items of general vocabulary, but also core vocabulary (kinship terms), basic grammatical forms and even personal pronouns, for example:

   sister, although related to the Anglo-Saxon **sweostor** [*cf.* German Schwester], is actually from the Old Norse **systir**;

   the third person present ending of English verbs, **-[e]s**, is the Old Norse ending, which, spreading southwards from the *Danelaw*, gradually replaced the Anglo-Saxon **-[e]þ** [**'þ'** = **'th'**], supplanting it completely by the 17th century (except in formal or religious texts); and

   the Old Norse third person plural pronoun **þeir, þeirra, þeim** became the Modern English **they, their, them**, replacing the Anglo-Saxon **hīe, hiera, him**.

1.1.4.2   After Duke William's conquest, the use of **Norman French** as the language of the royal court and gentry, English received an expanded, dual-level vocabulary, one based on French for the refinements of the lives of the nobility, while the other, the original core of "peasant" Anglo-Saxon, was retained for all the basics.

A well-known example of this layering of vocabulary is how English uniquely has specific words for domestic animals while on the farm, yet another when on the plate—*sheep → mutton, swine → pork, calf → veal, cow → beef*—in which the farmer at work fed it by its Anglo-Saxon name, and the noble at leisure ate it using its Norman French name.

1.1.4.3   By the use of **Medieval Latin** as the language of the Church and education, English was extended with a third level of vocabulary, one based primarily on Latin for things that touched on religious or philosophical matters.

1.1.4.4   As **Middle English** reasserted itself and moved first into the realm held by Norman French, then into that of Latin, it absorbed the specialist vocabulary of those spheres into which it reasserted itself, from the language formerly used in those formal situations. Thus, the borrowing from other languages of vocabulary external to that of the Anglo-Saxon base became quite normal, and ultimately, the usual process for extending the reach and subtlety of our, now huge, English vocabulary.

1.1.4.5   During the *Renaissance*, *the Enlightenment* and *the Scientific Revolution* (which led to that period termed *the Industrial Revolution*), further acquisitions from both **Latin** and **Greek** swelled the lexicon.

Incorporation of scientific vocabulary directly from Latin was augmented by indirect borrowings of words of Latin origin from **Italian** (primarily in Music and Architecture) and **French** (in practically every field of learning and literature).

Ancient Greek as a source for technical vocabulary grew tremendously in importance during the 19th and 20th centuries, a period in which all branches of Science and Medicine exploded in discoveries and understanding, and extended their descriptive labels and nomenclature using the vocabulary of Homer, Socrates, Plato and Aristotle.

1.1.4.6   These have resulted in a language that is extremely simple grammatically, yet extremely rich in vocabulary, and subtle in syntax and contextual nuance.

For example,

As far as grammar is concerned, the two most complicated areas remaining in English are (1) the formation of the plural form of some nouns, and (2) selection of the correct form for the past tense and past participle of verbs.

Compare this with the fact that, while an adjective in English has a single common form (the "positive degree" [§8.12.1]) used in all situations, a Russian or Polish adjective will appear in any of 26 *case-forms* (by change of stem-vowel and/or word-endings)—and a Sanskrit adjective could appear in any of **72** case-forms—forms determined by the gender, number and phrase-role of the noun it modifies or by how it's used independently within a sentence. (And these numbers do not include the comparative and superlative forms!)

At the same time, although most languages have, for example, only one or two simple words (not made up of a phrase) for the color adjective "blue" (*cf.*, Russian *голубой, синий*), English has several, each with its shade of meaning or emphasis: *blue, azure, aqua, aquamarine, cerulean, sapphire, beryl, cobalt, indigo, teal, turquoise, cyan, cyaneous, mazarine, chalybeous*... Although these concepts are expressible in other languages by putting nouns in phrases along the line of "[noun]-*color(ed)*" (*cf.* the Japanese use of 灰色 *hai-iro* [*ash-color*] or 鼠色 *nezumi-iro* [*mouse-color*] for *gray*), English, by-and-large, does not require such circumlocution.

[Japanese is remarkable in that originally it did not have separate words for *blue* and *green*, but had a single word that encompassed both colors: 緑 (み ど り) *midori*. This situation caused problems when three-color traffic signals were introduced to Japan—some drivers saw what they thought was *blue*, but they had been told to wait for *green*... The Japanese have come to use 緑色 (みどりいろ) *midori-iro* or グリーン *g^uriin* exclusively for *green*, while using ブルー *b^uruu* for blue.

However, the original meaning of *midori* is perfect for describing that rich blue-green of the foliage of evergreen forests—in particular both those of northern Japan and those running from northern California into British Columbia—and should be adopted into English for describing that color exactly.]

The fact that many of those English adjectives meaning *blue* started as nouns also shows how its vocabulary is self-enriching because of the ability of words to move, largely unhindered, from one part of speech to another. This process is extremely limited in highly inflected languages because of their requirement of using specific sets of endings with each part of speech: a noun has a set of established, standard endings, that must be replaced by, for example, an acceptable set of endings if that noun is to be used as an adjective, as well.

The limitations on such part-of-speech migrations in analytic languages are largely set by issues of style: the "Hollywood" style of using any noun as a verb is frowned upon in English simply because it usually shows a very limited, shallow and lazy vocabulary—or speaker.

1.1.4.7 Some nations have official committees trying to guard the "purity" of their languages from the "unholy" incursions of foreign phrases. Most well-known among these is the French, whose committee is especially on guard to protect *le français* from the onslaught of English words—despite the fact that so many of those words were borrowed from French into English in the first place.

Since the Renaissance, and particularly during the late 19th century, there were also occasional movements (within England in particular) against the import into and overuse of "foreign" words in English. This produced memorable statements such as *"Protect English! Use terse Anglo-Saxon monosyllables exclusively!"* The laughable aspect to this is that the only two Anglo-Saxon words in that entire slogan are the words *English* and *Anglo-Saxon*! (Except for the one word, *monosyllables*, from Greek, all the other words are ultimately Latin in origin.)

1.2 Modern English is an **analytic language** in structure that retains only a limited set of remnants of its earlier inflections, remnants restricted largely to the possessives and plurals of nouns, the forms of the personal pronouns, and the formation of past tense forms of *strong* (or *irregular*) verbs.

1.2.1 *Inflected* languages, also called *fusional* languages, are those that depend on changing the forms of words, by internal modification or affixes (or by both), to show how each word is used within its sentence. In an inflected language word order is usually free, with placement used to show only emphasis rather than usage.

In **inflected languages**, vowels may mutate according to prescribed patterns, changes that may be supplemented or replaced by the addition of prefixes and/or suffixes. These mutations and affixes will be specific to any of several individual groups of nouns, adjectives and pronouns (*declensions*), or to separate sets of verbs (*conjugations*).

There has been a historical shift from inflection to more analytic structures in most Indo-European family-groups, such as that of the Italic group's evolution into the lesser inflected Romance languages from their highly inflected parent language, Latin.

The most widely spoken, still highly-inflected Indo-European languages are the members of the Slavic group (Russian, Ukrainian, Polish, Czech, Serbian, *etc.*). To those we may add the modern-retained, specialty-usage of ancient languages such as Latin and Sanskrit.

Infected languages are distinct from **agglutinative languages**, which are ones in which affixes (prefixes, infixes or postfixes) are attached to a root word imposing neither phonetic changes (other than vowel or consonant harmonies) nor changes in stress or tone, either on that root word's form or on the form of any affixes. Also, these affixes are general across the entire language rather than being specific to individual groups of words divided into declensions or conjugations. In Japanese, these affixes have been reduced to independent particles, and although much colloquial or slang speech reduces these particles, they are still required for clarity of expression, and allow freer word-particle phrase order than an analytic language would permit.

Most agglutinative languages are marked by their high degree of regularity in grammatical forms. For example, Japanese has only three irregular verbs; Turkish has only one. Compare this to an inflected language such as Sanskrit, which has around 900 irregular verbs.

The Finno-Ugric languages (Finnish, Estonian, Hungarian, *etc.*), the Turkic languages (Turkish, Azerbaijani, Tatar, *etc.*), and Japanese and Korean are among the agglutinative languages of widest parlance.

Fusional and agglutinative languages form a group called **synthetic** languages, because the way a word is used requires that its form be synthesized according to formulas and patterns, using specific values, defined within the rules of the language.

A **non-inflected**, or **analytic**, language is one that depends almost exclusively on the position of the word within its phrase to show its usage, one that does not depend primarily on word forms or the addition of affixes or particles to specify usage.

Thus, in analytic sentences we have the English *"The **dog** bit the **man**."* the French, *"Le **chien** a mordu l'**homme**."* and the Chinese "狗位了男子" [**gǒu** wèi le **nánzi**], sentences that have specific meanings entirely different from their inverted forms *"The **man** bit the **dog**."* *"L'**homme** a mordu le **chien**."* and "男子位了狗" [**nánzi** wèi le **gǒu**]. In these, the forms taken by the subject and object do not vary between the two situations— only the word order determines the difference in meaning.

One may compare these with the situation in two synthetic languages.

In German the simple, word-order swap of *"**Der Hund** hat **den Mann** gebissen."* would be *"**Den Mann** hat **der Hund** gebissen"* (with the case of the nouns still showing their usage: cases specified within the form taken by the definite articles). The word-order swap with the change of meaning as in the other languages would be *"**Der Mann** hat **den Hund** gebissen."*

In Latin they appear as *"**Canis virum** momordit."* and *"**Virum canis** momordit."* **Canis** is the Nominative [subject] form of that noun; the direct object is revealed in the ending applied to the other noun's stem: *-um* is the Accusative singular suffix of second declension nouns like *vir*. Again, the meaning carried by the word-order swap of English would require changing word endings: *"**Vir canem** momordit."* The fact that the placement of the nouns within these sentences does not have to shift in order to commute the meaning is a cardinal attribute of synthetic languages.

The two most widely used analytic languages are English and Chinese. The Romance languages, although the next most widely spoken group, also possessing order as the definer of subject versus object, cannot be labeled properly as analytic because they retain grammatical gender, as well as pervasive, specific sets of verb endings for person and number. These remnants of synthetic Latin create for them the requirement of adjective-noun and pronoun-antecedent gender and number agreement, and of particular and exacting verb conjugation. These aspects are missing in Chinese and are very nearly absent in English.

In synthetic languages, words are moved out of their usual placement into different positions in order to change the emphasis given to specific words. In the following table, the first example is the normal order of the sentence, in which no single word is emphasized. Then, each of the sixteen possible rearrangements shows how Latin may bring shades of emphasis to the words within this small sentence merely by reordering.

Example of differences between synthetic (Latin) and analytic (English) effects of word order:

	Latin: *(emphasis changing with position)*	**English:** *(bold shows [vocal] emphasis)*	**English:** *(using syntax, bolding, and punctuation for emphasis)*
a.	*Puer puellæ rosam dat.*	*The boy gives the girl a rose.*	*The boy gives the girl a rose.*
b.	***Puellæ** rosam dat **puer**.*	***The boy** gives a rose to **the girl**.*	***It's the boy** who gives **the girl** a rose.*
c.	***Rosam** puellæ dat **puer**.*	***The boy** gives **a rose** to the girl.*	***It's a rose** that **the boy** gives to the girl.*
d.	*Puer dat rosam **puellæ**.*	*The boy gives a rose **to the girl**.*	***To the girl** the boy gives a rose.*
e.	*Puer **rosam** dat **puellæ**.*	*The boy gives **a rose to the girl**.*	***To the girl** the boy gives **a rose.***
f.	***Puellæ** puer rosam dat.*	*The boy gives a rose **to the girl**.*	***To the girl** the boy gives a rose.*
g.	***Rosam** dat puer **puellæ**.*	*The boy gives **a rose to the girl**.*	***It's a rose** that the boy gives **to the girl.***
h.	***Dat** puer rosam **puellæ**.*	*The boy **gives** a rose **to the girl**.*	*It's a rose that the boy **gives** to the girl.*
i.	***Dat** puer puellæ **rosam**.*	*The boy **gives a rose** to the girl.*	***It's a rose** that the boy **gives** to the girl.*
j.	***Rosam** puer dat **puellæ**.*	***The boy** gives **a rose to the girl**.*	*A rose, the boy gives it—to the girl.*
k.	***Rosam** dat puer **puellæ**.*	***The boy** gives a rose **to the girl**.*	*A rose—the boy gives it—to the girl.*

Puer is in the **Nominative case** showing that it is the subject; *puella* appears in the **Dative case** (*puellæ*) showing that it is the indirect object; *rosa* has become *rosam* in which the **Accusative case** ending says that it's the direct object; *dat* is the **third person singular** form to agree with the singular *puer* (and is the **present indicative active** of the verb *to give*: *dō, dăre, dătum*). Because of the case forms, moving the Latin words around does not change the usage of the word within the sentence.

However, moving the words around does change the emphasis in the Latin sentence. The order of the Latin words in **a.** is that of the normal or unemphasized version of the sentence: *Subject-Object-Verb*, abbreviated **SOV**, although, as the examples demonstrate, that order is highly flexible. The places of emphasis are the positions at the front of the sentence and at the end of the sentence: any word moved out of the normal *SOV* order achieves at least some increased level of importance.

The normal order for English is, as shown above, *Subject-Verb-Object*, or **SVO**.

SVO and *SOV* are the two sentence orders, common among the Indo-European languages. The sole exception is the modern Celtic languages, whose standard order is *Verb-Subject-Object*, or **VSO**, e.g., Gaelic: ***Chunnaic mi*** *cù aig an doras*, /ˈχuː.nɪk mi ˈkuː ɛk ən ˈdɔ.ʀəs/ literally "***Saw I*** *dog at the door*": "*I saw a dog at the door.*"

1.3 Because of its highly enriched vocabulary, in sharing so large a root-Latin vocabulary with the Romance languages, and by having borrowed so great a number of words from so very many other languages, English is in the unparalleled position of, in large degree, actually belonging to more than just its native speakers.

Unlike those languages that are so jealously and xenophobically guarded, lest they be sullied by foreign expressions, English allows anyone to suggest a word for import into it. If it is found to be useful and to enrich the language, it is granted citizenship with full rights and won't be lightly let go.

English, unique among all languages, acknowledges, nay, celebrates the capabilities of other languages to express concepts in ways that excel its own abilities: the English language treasures *le mot juste.*

From India to the European Union to world commerce, English is the most widely-used support for the **strength in unity** in the world today.

The English language is a legacy shared by the majority of humans today.

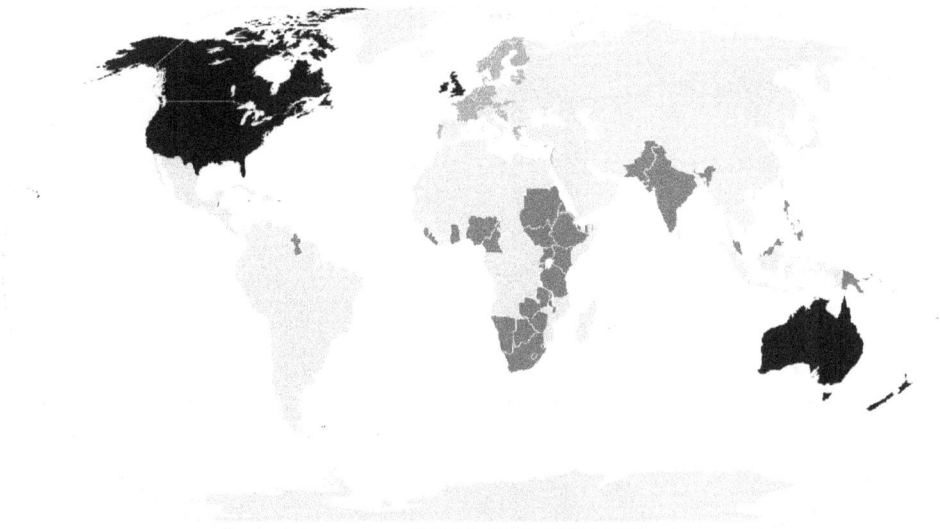

Native English-speaking majorities

English as one of the official languages

30% or more speak English as a second language

*Nations & regions covered by treaties requiring English
    for trade-specific communication (~100%)*

2 English Dialects

2.1 The role of dialects

2.1.1   Dialects have existed throughout the insular life of the English language, but larger, common groups have arisen outside the British Isles because of colonization and the distances those colonies were from the Isles themselves. The dialect groups that developed are differentiated largely by just when the initial colonization took place.

2.1.2   It is a common effect of colonization that colonials will preserve the forms and vocabulary of the original language carried with them, and their dialect will ultimately be truer to earlier forms of the language than will be that of the "mother country". The language involved is taken for granted in the mother country and so continues its organic mutations, but the transplanted form of the language forges a strong, and treasured, bond of identity among settlers in a distant land.

Such ***colonial preservation of language*** has happened not only in the English-speaking colonies, but throughout the Americas. It is true of Québécois and Cajun French, of Brazilian Portuguese and of New World Spanish, each of which preserves an older form of its language than that spoken currently in the locus of its European origin. Even within the British Isles, Gaelic (carried by ancient migration from Ireland into Scotland) preserves an older form of Celtic than does its parent, Erse.

2.1.2.1   Despite its several dialects, English is a remarkably unified language. It shares such a distinction with other European national languages, such as French, Swedish and Russian, all of whose countries were united early in their histories and each of whom had a capital city whose influence included having its dialect predominate over all others.

One need only look at two other modern nations to see how things could happen differently: Germany and Italy.

The standard form of German, *Hochdeutsch* ("High German"), is an originally artificial dialect created from the written style of the Chancellery of the Kingdom of Saxony (also used by Martin Luther in his translation of the Bible [pub. 1535]), partnered with the pronunciation (called *Bühnensprache—stage pronunciation*) of such written material in a manner based on that current in the communities of the Middle Rhine Valley during the 1700's & 1800's. This pronunciation, more closely related to that of *Niederdeutsch* ("Low German"), had already been used throughout the German-speaking states as the standard pronunciation of *Hochdeutsch* texts in performances of stage works before it was adopted as the official pronunciation in the late 1800's. (The words "low" and "high" here refer to the relative altitude of the lands in which these dialects were and are current; it is not a value judgment.)

The German-speaking lands of Europe were a disparate collection of nation-states, principalities, dukedoms and bishoprics, most of whom were, over the span of the past 1200 years, subunits within the loose association called the *Holy Roman Empire*. The result was that, although there was a shared sense of community, or *folkdom*, the regional variations in German were, and to some degree remain, so great that some consider the more extreme colloquial dialects to be separate languages because of the difficulty in mutual intelligibility between those most widely distant dialects: between *Bavarian* and *Berlin* dialects, for example.

However, the Germans had long desired to be united into a single nation, particularly after the nationalism inspired by Napoleon's invasions, and they understood that they needed a shared dialect to foster this unity. German-speakers found that tool in that literary, *Hochdeutsch* dialect, and worked to further its use as a common dialect among the German kingdoms and principalities.

With the formation of the German Empire in 1871, *Hochdeutsch* became the standard form of the national language and was set forth as the language for the growing national, imperial school system. It was also adopted as the standard in the German-speaking regions of the Austro-Hungarian Empire. As an artificial dialect, *Hochdeutsch* was not associated with any locality or population and, so, evoked no regional jealousies and its use was, and has continued to be, a matter of national identity and pride.

However, south of the Alps the situation was very different.

Before it was forcibly united in the 1870's by Garibaldi, using the armies of the House of Savoy, what is now Italy was divided primarily amongst the Kingdom of Piedmont-Sardinia, the Kingdom of the Two Sicilies, the Papal States, the Duchies of Tuscany, Parma, Lucca and Modena, and the Austrian Empire. Each of those regions had a proud history of internationally important independence and separatism, and each had its own variety of Italian, with differences so great that, for example, Italians from Naples speaking their own dialect were (and continue to be) largely incomprehensible to Italians from other regions of the Italian peninsula, even to the Romans, just 115 miles [185 km] to the north of Naples.

Despite (and sometimes because of) that new government's selection of the literary, yet living dialect of Florence as the national language, and because of the slow spread of literacy in 19th century Italy, these differences persisted so that, with the start of World War I—only some 44 years after national unification—the Italian Army found itself forced to hire instructors to teach Standard Italian to the Italians, so that orders could be understood by the troops without requiring the fuss and interruption of constant translation.

Within the past few decades, the situation with dialects within Italy has changed, so that the majority of Italians now list standard Italian, *la bellissima*, as their native dialect, rather than their own, regional dialect.

2.2 The Dialects of English

Area	Nation (with over 2 million Native English speakers)	Native English Speakers (estimates)	Percent of Total Native English Speakers
North America		**246,500,000**	**73%**
ACE Canada		18,500,000	6%
United States		228,000,000	67%
Caribbean		**2,600,000**	**1%**
	Jamaica	2,600,000	< 1%
Europe		**62,600,000**	**18%**
	Ireland	4,400,000	1%
BE United Kingdom		58,200,000	17%
Africa & Oceania		**26,800,000**	**8%**
	Australia	15,600,000	5%
	New Zealand	4,000,000	1%
	South Africa	3,700,000	1%
	The Philippines	3,500,000	1%
Total		**338,500,000**	**100%**

2.2.1 Languages can be dissected *ad infinitum* into dialects from larger into ever smaller groups and designations using a myriad of guidelines, till ultimately one reaches a point at which it can be truly said that each individual has a unique dialect, a dialect that will change with situation, audience and the passage of time.

However, taking the broadest vista, it can be said that there are three main speech groups in Modern English, based on the locations in which English is spoken natively: the dialects of the British Isles, of North America, and of the former British colonies and Commonwealth.

2.2.2 *British Isles dialects*

2.2.2.1 As the original area of the language, the British Isles have long been a patchwork of dialects and sub-dialects, regional variations and differing varieties of speech, stretching all the way back to Anglo-Saxon times. The main dialect areas of modern Britain maintain to some degree the dialects established by the Anglo-Saxon settlement (by c. 850 CE) overlaid by the Viking invasions that ultimately resulted in creation of the Danelaw, stretching from southeast to northwest across England. It was from these northerly regions of the Danelaw that Old Norse exercised its greatest influence on the development of English.

Historically, the village-centered isolation of land-bound peasantry and the difficulty of any mode of travel led to dialect differences within counties, and barely mutually-intelligible dialects between regions.

However, with a strong monarchy, a centralized legal system, the rise in importance of the capital, then the advent of the printing press, an English-only religion, and more recently of mass-communication devices, these differences have been vastly reduced. Although time-honored differences between dialects within England are still far more evident than those between native dialects in any other part of the English-speaking world, they are much less extreme than those experienced within many other countries, such as Germany, Italy and China. This historical proliferation of English dialects has been counter-balanced by the fact that there has long been a single standard for the written form of the language throughout the British Isles.

Well-spoken British English is perhaps the most mellifluous of all the English dialects, in particular that of the great, classic actors and actresses, such as Sir Lawrence Olivier, Sir John Gielgud, Vivien Leigh and Deborah Kerr. The English spoken by Her Majesty the Queen is, to many, as pleasing to the ear as are the best passages from Mozart.

This situation contrasts with the fact that the only widely accepted standard of speech of **Englandic**—the language with its idiosyncrasies specific to the territory of what was once the limited realm of England—has been what was originally called **Received Pronunciation**, or **RP**.

This term has fallen into disrepute largely because of a misunderstanding of the word "received" in that phrase. It means "conventional, standardized" or "generally accepted", yet many in the British population take it to mean "handed down from on-high", *i.e.*, *received* from their social "betters," and so see it as a mark of class, and of social or educational snobbery. Those of this misunderstanding often resort to ostentatious usage of the most local and extreme colloquialisms as their way of protesting against what they see as an imperial imposition. They will also be among the first to claim that "I'm English so what I speak *is* English." (a form of *conceptual derangement*) meaning thereby that their personal dialect and idiosyncrasies—their idioglossias—define the language for all others, not seeing in this the very snobbishness and illogic inherent in why they don't like **RP**.

A term more widely used (and more socially acceptable) than *Received Pronunciation* is **BBC English**. However, there are several versions of English, particularly of English pronunciation, now to be heard over the BBC. These range from an almost **Common English**, merging *BE* and *ACE* aspects in a natural manner, to the beautiful dialect spoken by Her Majesty the Queen, to that form of speech that we may term the **London Pirate Dialect**, from cinema characterizations.

The **London Pirate Dialect** ("**LPD**") is one in that has arisen within England. In this way of speaking (but not writing), *r*'s are appended to words in which they are not original to the language, and as such, do not appear in the orthography. That is, words, ending in an /ɑ/ (or /ə/) sound followed by a word (or a suffix) beginning in a vowel, have that ending sound changed to –*er* /ɚ/, with an *r*- /ɹ/ often also prepended to the following word. (A terminal /ɑː/ sound in this situation is turned into /ɑːɹ/.)

This results in such utterances as, for example, "*in **Asier-rand Africker-refforts** against famine...*", "*frequent earthquakes mean the **magmer is** rising*", "*when Nazi Germany invaded **Rusher-rin** June, 1941...*", "*in one of Turner's preliminary **drawrrings***". The insertion of these *r*-sounds makes this dialect sound like a parody of early movie treatments of Robert Louis Stevenson's **Treasure Island**: this is the reason for the unusual dialect-tag. There are several areal dialects with highly variant pronunciations in all regions of native English speakers, but **LPD** is the only one treated as an acceptable, mainstream degradation of the normal clarity of the language.

In General North American dialect, with its more deliberate, preserving and historical treatment of the language, such insertion of undocumented sounds, or failure to pronounce documented ones correctly, would simply be called a *speech impediment*, and would cause the speaker to be referred to therapy. Or such a speaker might become the inspiration for an animated cartoon character, such as Warner Brothers' characters *Sylvester the cat*—who pronounced every *s* as a *th*: *"Thatth the biggetht mouthe I've ever theen!"*—and *Elmer Fudd*—who pronounced every *r* as a *w*: *"You cwazy wabbit!"*

> *"... but Chiner ritself received nothing."*
> —*World War II in Colour*, Episode 1.
> (*UK-produced television documentary*)

Otherwise, **LPD** maintains the Englandic process of *de-rhoticism*, in which *r*'s are ignored where they appear within a word after a vowel at the end of a syllable (*e.g.*, *rare* /ɹɛɹ/ is treated as if it were *reh* /ɹɛː/ or /ɹɛə/, *rarer* /ɹɛ.ɹəɹ/ is said as if it were *reruh* /ɹɛ.ɹə/, and **the Labour Party** becomes **the Laybuh Pahty**).

Some of the other Englandic dialect features often accompanying the ones given above are failure to maintain the sound of initial *wh* (so that, *e.g.*, **whales** and **Wales** are unmarked); the loss of distinction between adjectival and adverbial forms, such as **unaware** and **unawares**; preference for **unbeknown** over the standard **unbeknownst**; and use of **different _to_** rather than the *Common English* standard **different _from_** (thereby losing the Anglo-Saxon sense of the *ablative of separation*). There are also some spreading, contaminating mispronunciations, such as the inability to pronounce the word **sixth**: saying **sickth** instead.

BE may also divide words into syllables in ways different from that of *ACE*, variations that allow or cause *BE* to assume alternate pronunciations. For example, the word **methane** is a compound of the prefix **meth-** (derived from the word **methyl**, itself found in such a word as **methylene**) plus the suffix **-ane**. *ACE* continues to pronounce the prefix in its original, scientific way: **meth-** + **-ane** /ˈmɛθ.e:n/ while *BE* has split it into the rather self-centered sounding **me** + **thane** /ˈmi:.θe:n/, as if talking in dialectic about one's Scottish *laird*. (The rest of the scientific series, e.g., **hept-**, **pent-**, **hex-**, **oct-**, are not so impaired.)

LPD is heard in the urban south of England, but becomes progressively rarer from Middlesex, through the Midlands and up into Scotland, although its use on the BBC has increased its frequency beyond its core territory. It has also heard in Australia, to a lesser extent, New Zealand, and on occasion pops up in North America, particularly amongst professors aping English university speech.

British English has an additional layer of complexity not found in other forms of English (particularly in *ACE*), in that its dialects present marked differences that are not only geographical but are also used as tools of feudal-remnant, social exclusion, and marks of privilege: overt class differences.

In Britain there is still an amount of deliberate differentiation between the lives of the so-called upper- and lower-classes, where speech patterns introduced at traditional clique-centers of title and wealth privilege, such as the oldest universities, have spread through the dialects of the gentry specifically in order to maintain this separation. Such mechanisms of social distinction have often been copied by other members of English society both in aspiration toward (or subservience to)—and in mocking—the upper classes. In this way *dysglossia*—odd pronunciations, phoneme substitutions, mispronunciations and unusual habits of speech introduced solely for the purpose of marking one version of speech as separate, snobbish or outré—can make its way from those limited locations into general parlance.

One could suggest that this situation is the origin not only of the *London Pirate Dialect* in Britain, and its spread to Australia, but also, although from the opposite societal direction, of *gangsta* or *hiphop* slang in the US (and of such idioglossias there that include substitution of *f* for the 'soft' *th* /θ/ as in "*teef*" (for "*teeth*"), or that fail to pronounce the *t* that ends some word-final consonant groups, such as *st*, *lt* or *ft* [*e.g.,* making "*east*" into "*eass*"]), and of the persistence of variant UK dialects like *Cockney*, or ones that substitute *v* for the 'hard' *th* /ð/ as in "*bruhva*" (for "*brother*"), or those that put a glottal stop in place of *t* or *tt*.

This dysglossic, social-rank differentiation through dialect was a particular target of George Bernard Shaw, most overtly in his *Pygmalion*, and of *Monty Python's Flying Circus* in, among other things, its "The Idiot in Society" sketch (particularly that section dealing with "city idiots") [Episode 20] and the "Upper-class Twit of the Year" skit [Episode 12].

British dictionaries generally still mark forms specific to the gentry as 'U' for "upper class". Such a linguistic situation does not really exist in so pervasive a form outside the British Isles. In the other English-speaking nations such snobbery is usually expressed either in geographically, rather than socially, based dialects, or in baubles: needlessly extravagant houses, jewelry, clothes and automobiles.

2.2.2.2   One of the very few issues of pronunciation that British English has retained that colloquial *ACE* is (unfortunately) losing is the palatalization of long '*u*' sounds in certain words. For example, while everyday *ACE* is coming to pronounce *dew* and *due* almost exactly as it does the word *do*, with only a slight, if any *y*-sound before the vowel, *BE* regularly maintains the pronunciation *dʸew* /dʲuː/ both for *dew* and for *due*. The word *peninsula* in BE is pronounced as *pe.nin.sʸula*, whereas in *ACE* it is now most often heard without the *y*-glide before the *u*. The same is happening with the verb *presume – presʸume* in BE.

At the other extreme, common Australian pronunciation has so emphasized the palatal *y* insertion that the palatal has been obliterated by its transformation of the preceding consonant. There one will hear, for example, *dzhoo* /dʒuː/ instead of the more delicate *dʸew* of BE, and *pe.nin.shula* /ˌpɛˈnɪn.ʃuːlɐ/ and *pre.zhoom* /ˌpɹɪˈʒuːm/ as pronunciations of *dew*, *peninsula* and *presume*, respectively.

2.2.2.3   British English retains some quaint historical, and idiosyncratic spellings, such as using *-ise* or *-ize* (and *-yse* or *-yze*) differentially to mark the presumed source-language of a borrowed word, the former termination proposing to distinguish those Latin-based words and the latter, those from the Greek, although both endings are pronounced as *-ize*]. (Examples would be *civilise* and *privatise versus analyze* or *hypnotize*.)

BE also uses *ae* (*æ*) and *oe* (*œ*), in an attempt to make borrowed forms resemble their source-words more closely—although some, such as *fœtus*, are actually false etymological spellings.

As well, *BE* uses some quasi-French spellings retained from Middle English forms rather than more native spellings of words. Among these are such words as *colour* and *favour* for the French *couleur* and *faveur*, and retaining *-re* instead of using *-er* for words borrowed largely from French, such as *metre* and *centre*.

BE maintains some antique spellings such as *aeroplane*. This word was originally pronounced in four syllables, mimicking its French source (*aéroplane*), *i.e.*, *aëroplane* /ɑ.ˈɛ.ɹo.ˌpleːn/; it was quickly reduced to three syllables /ˈɛ.ɹo.ˌpleːn/ (a pronunciation now sounding rather pretentiously Edwardian upper-class, like pronouncing *envelope* with an initial French nasal /ɑ̃.vɛ.loːp/), and, now may on occasion be heard as two syllables /ˈɛɹ.ˌpleːn/ matching the *airplane* of *ACE*. *BE* also continues to use the insane hieroglyph *gaol*, reflecting a pronunciation that hasn't been current since the mid-1600's.

In these situations, *ACE* has reduced much of this unnecessary complexity by several methods, such as by adopting the unified simplification of *-ize* for the first pair of differences; by re-coining the *aero-* words using the prefix *air-* as in *airplane* (a change presumably patterned after the word *airship*, and matching the Common English *airport* and *airfield*) and retaining the *aero–* prefix specifically for scientific use (*e.g.*, the field of study called *aeronautics*); by using *e* to simplify both *ae* (*æ*) and *oe* (*œ*) in almost all cases [American *fetus* matches both the Latin source, and the pronunciation]; by using *-er* consistently for *BE* *-re* and *-er* (except in pretentious American real-estate development names); by dropping the unnecessary *u* from words ending in *-our*; and by replacing *gaol* with its coeval, British twin spelling *jail*, which reflects the normal pronunciation of both spellings: the pronunciation current since the 1600's.

The standards of *BE* spelling are summarized in a set of rules and data termed *Oxford orthography*. This is termed *International English* in computer usage, although it is "international" only in that it is common to more than one nation: it is **not** the international standard for English, which is **ACE**.

2.2.2.4 **Other British dialects**. The dialects spoken in other parts of the British Isles (known generally from their traditional-county locations) resemble the English spoken in those counties closest to them, varying more as they are farther from London, and are grouped by relative vector from the capital. However, they also show the spread of the London dialect from the growing influence of radio and television's use of *BBC English*. In widest nomenclature, those British dialects outside of England itself are *Scottish English* (as opposed to *Scots*), *Irish English*, *Northern Ireland English* and *Welsh English*.

2.2.2.5 **Scots** is a version of English taken into Scotland by the English and lowland Scots during the Middle Ages. It retains its own style of pronunciation, and preserves unique features of grammar and vocabulary to the point that it might be considered a separate language rather than simply a dialect, although most of the Scots speakers appear content to have it keep its designation as a dialect.

Scots is the form of English found of many of the poems of Robert Burns.

2.2.2.6   **Scottish English** is that dialect of modern English (again, distinct from *Scots*) spoken in Scotland. It has some aspects (some vocabulary items, some ways of phrasing) drawn from Scots or from Gaelic, but it is primarily a variant of standard British English.

It has lately become more important both within Scotland, as it is the working dialect of the Scottish Government, and within Britain, as Scotland has become more economically involved in wider British commerce. Many British businesses have turned to those speaking Scottish English (particularly that of the Glasgow area) for staffing phone centers because this dialect is considered by many to be the warmest, most calming and most friendly of all the British dialects.

Both Scots and Scottish English were carried, along with its cousin dialects from the northern English shires, into Northern Ireland during the Ulster-area settlement efforts of the Stuart governments and during the Commonwealth period. As such, it later exerted some influence on *ACE* with the influx of Ulster Scots into the New World. (In North America, the *Ulster Scots* are often erroneously called the *Scotch-Irish*: other than their temporary residence on the island of Ireland, they are technically not *Irish* at all.)

2.2.2.7   In its basic nature, **Welsh English** is extremely similar to the English dialects spoken in the counties of England nearest its borders, with the admixture of patterns of pronunciation drawn from the Welsh language, *Cymric*, itself. The long association of Wales with England, and the Welsh association with the Royal Family (starting with the success of Henry Tudor: Henry VII) have meant that concourse of English and Welsh has been frequent, particularly in the towns of Wales. J.R.R. Tolkien even proposed that English and Welsh have formed, from Anglo-Saxon times, the heart of a northwestern European *Sprachbund*.

At the same time, the Welsh language itself has survived more successfully than any other Celtic language—of the c. 1.5 million speakers of all Celtic languages, around half speak Welsh. At the same time that the influence of Welsh on the English spoken in Wales continues to be quite strong, Wales has provided some of the greatest actors of the English-language stage, such as Sir Richard Burton, as well as some of the greatest poets of the English language, such as Dylan Thomas.

2.2.2.8   English is one of the two official languages of **Ireland**, having been carried there first during the invasions that the Norman kings of England undertook against the Irish. Despite attempts to revive the native Irish language, *Erse* or *Irish*, only around seventy-thousand of the six million Irish use it now as their daily language (that is, outside of its language classes). This Celtic language has long had an enriching influence on the pronunciation and vocabulary of Irish English, but today's Irish English is moving in some ways closer to the dialects of England, and in others (because of the influence of contemporary culture, and of shared cultural attitudes and family identities) toward American English.

The influence of Ireland and of **Irish English** on *ACE* began with the immigration of Ulster Scots into the North American colonies. In a later wave of emigration from southern Ireland into the United States, this dialect had a noticeable influence on the American English dialects of the eastern urban centers, particularly those of coastal New England and the Mid-Atlantic area.

2.2.3 *North American dialects*

2.2.3.1   ***ACE*—American-Canadian English**—is based on the English carried to the North American colonies, rooted specifically in English as it was spoken in the 16th, 17th and early 18th centuries.

2.2.3.2   Having been the first English colonies—beginning with Jamestown in 1607—the nations of North America still speak a form of English that is older than that spoken in the United Kingdom, or in any other part of the Commonwealth. The English spoken in the United States and Canada—*Standard North American Dialect*—remains truer to its Tudor, Elizabethan and Stuart origins than does the speech of the UK today.

This is revealed from analysis of the disdain some British have for what they call "American bastardisations". Almost all of those complaints are of forms, pronunciations and usages that are actually older, Tudor, or even Anglo-Saxon-retaining items that have been lost in British English as it has itself descended and diverged from the older standard.

A side-effect both of North American distance from the British Isles, and of the influx of so many non-English-speaking immigrants was a reliance on the printed form of the language for teaching English. From that familiarity with books, and the higher general rate of literacy in North America than in Britain during the colonial period, arose a reverence for the language used in the *King James Bible* [1611] and (in the early colonies, in particular) for that of the *Book of Common Prayer* [1559 & 1662]). This has created an emphasis on maintaining the transplanted form of the language by using the written form of the language to preserve and guide speech. While the British in general gave little or no thought to the language or its standards, continued to speak with whatever forms or pronunciations they grew up with or preferred or invented, and never seriously considered English as a subject for teaching, North Americans were schooled in the best usage and pronunciation of the English language by using those texts on hand.

The result of this has been that American pronunciation is, on the whole, closer to the original Tudor, and particularly Stuart form of English brought to the Colonies than is that of present-day British English. Tudor and Stuart forms written into the *King James* translation of the Bible (preserving much from its predecessor, the partial translations done before 1530 by William Tyndale) have played as strong a role in forming North American English as that form of German used by Martin Luther, in his translation of the same volume, has played in creating modern, standard German.

One can truly say that **the three texts composing *the founding corpus of American-Canadian English* are *the 1559 Book of Common Prayer*, *the 1611 Bible* and *the works of Shakespeare, c. 1585–1613*.**

Indeed, it can be proposed that performing Shakespeare's plays in the dialect of modern Britain is an anachronism, for his language was closer to the educated speech of modern Toronto, Chicago, St Louis and Dallas than to that of either current BBC programming or *Received Pronunciation*.

2.2.3.3   Both Canadian and American English can be divided into several dialects, although differences between the dialects, other than exaggerations of diction—often used solely for comic effect—are extremely small.

2.2.3.4   **Canadian English** is, from a high vantage point, largely divided by distance—and Québec—into two dialect regions. Much of the origin and nature of both can be traced back to the Loyalists who left the 13 Colonies as a result of the American Revolution. Because of this, both Canadian and American English are rooted in a common personality, the language and customs of the settlers of the first colonies.

> **The Maritime dialect** is spoken in the Atlantic provinces. Because the Maritime Provinces received a large number of Scottish immigrants as a result of the Highland Clearances, they have an added layer of influence from Scottish English (and to some degree, Gaelic) that was not bestowed on either the western provinces or on the USA.

> **General Canadian dialect** is spoken from Ontario to British Columbia, having had its historical center in the more urbanized areas of Ontario: Toronto and Ottawa. It is the form of English heard most often on broadcasts of the CBC.

> Formal Canadian spelling is largely based on the *Oxford orthography* rules of the British dialect. However, in those items targeted for both a Canadian and US market, American rules are often used, both in recognition of the larger market, and as a favor to their American audience.

2.2.3.5   **American English** has dialects that correspond to the geography of the nation and to the history of settlement across the continent's geographical impediments.

> The **Appalachian dialect** is the oldest of English dialects in British North America, preserving elements of Elizabethan vocabulary, pronunciations and idioms. The language of the earliest English settlers, it was carried into the Appalachian Mountains before further waves of settlement brought newer forms of English from the British Isles, forms that pushed it out of its original tidewater regions. This dialect was later carried from the Appalachians into a sub-dialect area, the Ozark and Ouachita mountain regions of Arkansas and Missouri.
> Of great interest to linguistics, literature, musicology and history has been the number of folksongs of English origin that have preserved their Elizabethan language and melodies, folksongs that are found in both the Appalachian and Ozark/Ouachita mountain dialect regions. [This was the dialect of the author's early years, and the original speech of his grandparents and extended family.]

> The **Southern dialect**, the next oldest, has local variations that range from coastal Maryland and Virginia down to north Florida, then west and northwest into Louisiana, and the Mississippi floodplains of Tennessee and Arkansas.

> **Tidewater Southern dialect** is that associated historically with the plantation-owning society of Virginia, the Carolinas and Georgia. It spread by assimilation through that same economic class across the ante-bellum South, as far west as Mississippi, Louisiana and the Mississippi floodplains of Tennessee and Arkansas. Seldom heard widely or in a pure form now, it is well-known from its appearance in films, such as *Gone with the Wind*, although its characteristics have been exaggerated by Hollywood.

> **Black English** dialects remain numerous. Centered historically in areas of lesser economic development, and varying between regions, these dialects are reflections of several historical and socio-economic limitations placed on Black communities held in servitude (either in slavery or in the virtual slavery of share-

cropping) or in the guiles of depredation excused as segregation. Such economic, racial or education-level based dialects are on the decline in the US, as dialect-levelling continues from the effects of mass media, and education.

Black English, however, has had a marked influence on American English historically, arising during and after the 1920's, primarily from Music: *Blues* and *Jazz*, in particular.

The **Texas dialect-area** is distinguished from the Southern dialect by Texas's historical development from multiple Southern sources and from European influences. The dialect reveals itself in slight differences from the Southern dialect in enunciation and vocabulary, as well as in phrasing and tempo. The oldest German, Czech and Polish settlements in North America are in Texas, and the second largest group of Sorbian speakers outside Germany was in Texas. This European influence is also reflected in Texas's having its own recognized dialect of German: *Texanerdeutsch*. There have also been important influences on its characteristics both from Spanish influence and as a result of Texas's own history and size.

There are approximately seven sub-dialect regions within Texas English: *Northeastern* (Dallas area and eastwards), *Gulf Coast/Eastern* (Houston area, northwards and southwestwards), *Central* (San Antonio and Austin), *German Hill Country* (extending from west of San Antonio to west of Waco, and further north), *Far West* (El Paso area), *Rio Grande* (Brownsville to Big Bend), and *Western/High Plains* (from Midland/Odessa northwards to Lubbock and Amarillo).

The **Middle Atlantic dialect** is a variety with origins in the English spoken or influenced by descendants of the German, Dutch and Swedish immigrants into that area during the 17th and 18th centuries. This area has its own unique dialect of German: *Pennsylvania Dutch*. Historically, this English dialect had several distinct dialect groups, which have now been much diluted because of internal migration within the US after the Civil War, and during and after the World Wars.

New York (City) dialects demonstrate the amount of foreign immigration that this small region experienced during the late 1800 to early 1900's, with varieties changing in some instances from block to block, with the influences of the Italians, the Irish, blacks from the South, and Yiddish-, Slavic- and Cantonese-speaking communities. New Jersey is split between versions of this dialect in its north and its Philadelphia-dominated, Middle Atlantic dialect in the south.

The **Upper Midwest dialect** shows the influence of the extensive immigration of Germans and Scandinavians into the area of Wisconsin, Minnesota, the Dakotas, and the Mississippi Valley region of Illinois in the late 1800's. The most often heard variants from General American Dialect that this dialect demonstrates are found in such things as elision of the object after prepositions of accompaniment: *Are you going with?* for *Are you going with me/us/him/etc.?* from the German: *Gehen Sie mit?*; confusion of *let* and *leave* for permission or command, *Leave it be! Leave me go, too!* instead of *Let it be! Let me go, too!* arising from the fact that *let* and *leave* are a single verb, *lassen*, in German: *Laß [Lass] es sein! Laß mich auch gehen!* and wider use of *the adverbial Genitive* beyond its standard use into such words as *always*: *I would do it anyways* for *I would do it anyway*, a form found in such German adverbs as *wenigstens*, *öfters* and *mehrmals*. (These differences can also be found in both the *German Hill Country* and *Central* sub-dialects of Texas English, and in the *Pennsylvania Dutch* region.)

The **New England dialect** diverged radically from its early, colonial English dialect into its present form after its overwhelming exposure to late 19th century varieties of Insular English, brought to the US particularly by the Irish, but also by immigration of other British dialects. Some Boston-area speech, in particular, can be very close to *London Pirate Dialect* in its pronunciation, and could be termed *Harvard* (or *Hahvad*) *Pirate Dialect*: *"to get a set of drahrrings of this chest of draws…"* (that dialect for *"…drawings of this chest of drawers…"*).

New England sub-dialects range from that of Boston and coastal Massachusetts, to that of the Vermont-New Hampshire-Maine area, to the older sub-dialects of western Massachusetts, Connecticut and Rhode Island.

General American dialect finds its roots in the mixing of those dialects transplanted from the States created from the original, seaboard Colonies into the Midwest, and spoken in the late 1800's to early 1900's from Ohio westward to parts of Michigan and into Indiana, Illinois and Missouri, centering on the great national railroad hub of Chicago. From there it spread throughout the West, across the Great Plains, southward toward Texas and westward into California and the Pacific Coast.

Because of the move of the film industry from the East coast to the West coast in the 1920's, the relocation of the major radio networks' studios to the West coast in the 1930's and 1950's, and the removal of primary television studios from New York City to Los Angeles in the 1960's, this dialect has had nationwide influence for nearly a century.

The geographic proximity of the centers of the two main North American dialects, General Canadian dialect and General American dialect, in the Great Lakes area has resulted in the creation of a North American English-language convergence area, a *Sprachbund*, producing what is essentially a single dialect having only the slightest regional variations across a vast area of North America.

At this point these two dialects have become so similar that the only differences people usually recognize as indicating which is being spoken are the recognizably Canadian variations in pronunciation of the *'ou'* or *'ow'* diphthong as *raised* (/ɛʊ/ or /ʌʊ/ *versus* the Americans' /aʊ/); along with a few differences in words, such as Canadian pronunciation of **schedule** as **shedule**, of **process** as /ˈpɹoːˌsɛs/ (sounding like they're in favor of "cess") rather than rhyming it with **progress** /ˈpɹɑːˌgɹɛs/, and their pronouncing its plural as /ˌpɹoːˌsɛsˈiːz/ *"pro-cess-ease"* [with heavier than normal stress on the final syllable] rather than standard *ACE* /ˈpɹɑːˌsɛsɪz/. To these must be added the well-known Canadian use of the interjection *"eh"* as a sentence-terminal interrogative marker or phrase intensifier.

The differences between North American dialects are very subtle, particularly when contrasted with the disparities between dialects within England itself. This results in North American dialects' being accounted variously by different authors, both as to areas of coverage as well as in number, specification and designation. The presentation given above is concerned primarily with general issues of pronunciation, with the most striking of vocabulary issues, and with widely heard grammatical differences.

The subtleness of the diversity among North American English dialects can be demonstrated by the angry and the frustrated reaction the author witnessed a German writer have to his drive in the late 1970's from Chicago to Austin. As he strode red-faced into the office of the Department of Germanic Studies at the University of Texas he erupted: "A thousand miles—from Oslo to Rome—and there's no difference! It's all the same!"

2.2.3.6 Both Canadian and American English are distinguished from British English in what could be suggested to be a greater amount of respect for words borrowed more recently from other languages, a greater facility for sounds not historically present in English, a greater familiarity or facility with other languages, beyond French. Or it may be simply that a drive on the part of *ACE* speakers to maintain their historically more accurate pronunciation makes them more aware of pronunciation in general. While, particularly in England itself, foreign borrowings are distinguished by spelling-based [mis-]pronunciation, in North America words are usually maintained in forms closer to their pronunciation in the donating language.

Two such words one might hear in the media today are *jaguar* (from Tupi through Portuguese) and *jalapeno* (from Mexican Spanish). In *BE*, *jaguar* is divided into three syllables, with anglicized 'j' [like that in *judge*] and de-rhotacized 'ar': /ˈdʒæ.gʲuː.ˌɑ/ (or /ˈdʒæ.gʲuː.ˌə/) while *ACE* has the disyllabic /ˈdʒæ.ˌgʷɑɹ/, more closely approximating the borrowed /ˌʒɑ.ˈgʷɑr/. For *jalapeno* (whose alternate orthographical form, normal in US English, is the original *jalapeño*), *ACE* has the original /hɑ.lɑ.ˈpeː.ˌɲoː/ while *BE* evinces the bastardized /dʒæ.lə.ˈpiː.no/, which rhymes with *grab a peen-oh*.

It is also apparent from listening to *BE* speakers that they pay more attention to words of relatively recent French origin (or those French words of regular daily usage), and customarily pronounce them in ways closer to their Gallic counterparts. Thus, the word *France* itself is in England regularly pronounced /fɹɑns/, which is a fair approximation of the way it is pronounced in Paris, /frãs/ [or /fʀãs/], while in North America the word continues to be pronounced in its earlier, fully anglicized form /fɹæns/.

Both *BE* and *ACE* have historical retentions. However, while *ACE* has retained more advanced grammatical structures (like the subjunctive), a wider vocabulary and an older pronunciation, *BE* has largely retained less productive elements, like intricacies of spelling, while fostering degradations of pronunciation that take it ever farther from standard orthography.

2.2.4 *Asian, African and Oceanic dialects*

2.2.4.1 The dialects of English spoken in Australia and New Zealand, in South Africa, and in India, Pakistan and Bangladesh are based on very similar starting dialects that were carried there at only slightly different times, and as the result of different purposes, during the height of the British Empire, that is, in the late 18th and the 19th centuries. These dialects are in most ways closer to dialects of *Englandic* than to *ACE*, because of their more recent emigration, or exile, from the Isles.

The English dialect spoken in the Philippines is, however, based on American English.

2.2.4.2 This timing of their involvement with British English is one reason for their dialects' individual characteristics. Other idiosyncrasies came from the nature, professions and goals of the populations that migrated to Australia, New Zealand and South Africa, and who resided in India during the *Raj*.

In **Australia**, the compelled migration of penal inmates from poorer areas of London was significant in starting European settlement there. That early forced migration was followed by the immigration of British farmers and merchants, and gold-seeking adventurers.

New Zealand was first settled by British farmers, merchants and missionaries. Although it shares several aspects with Australian English (because of their having been colonized around the same time), New Zealand English is less extremely different from *BE* than is *AusE*, particularly in issues of pronunciation. And, in comparison to its South Seas cousin, New Zealand English is, to many, softer and more pleasing to the ear.

Early British immigration into the UK colonies within **South Africa** was primarily of miners, farmers, merchants and adventurers from all parts of the British Isles. South African English shares many characteristics with both the Australian and the New Zealand dialects.

The Raj—the British Empire in what was to become India, Pakistan, Bangladesh and Burma—was run first by educated, ambitious or adventurous appointees of the East India Company, later of the British government, while the British troops occupying the vast spread of Imperial India were drawn from a wide spectrum of the British population. The percentage of native English speakers among Indians in particular is quite small, less than one tenth of one percent; however, the estimated number of Indians who speak English as a second or third language is presently over 125 million, making it second only to the US in number of English speakers.

Although Imperial British English is still quite common amongst Indian speakers of English, there is a growing impetus to speak the more common North American English dialect because of its economic and cultural predominance, and because of the growing business and cultural relationships between the United States and India: the US now has the largest Hindu community outside of Asia.

The Philippines adopted English as a result of United States occupation after the Spanish-American War, granting of commonwealth status in 1935 and full independence in 1946. Close relations between the United States and the Philippine governments, and the presence of American businesses and American military bases created and fostered wide-spread use of US English as a second, and often adoption as a first, language among the Filipino people. Although the native language of only around 1% of the population, English is used regularly by almost 60% of Filipinos as a second language.

Filipino English is basically American English with a great deal of influence from Tagalog, and of Spanish, historically, through Tagalog.

2.2.4.3   The aspects of spelling noted for British English [§2.2.2.2], hold particularly for the Australian and New Zealand dialects, except that, in an apparent zeal to be more *English* than the British, these dialects have shifted almost without exception to the *-ise/-yse* ending. Otherwise, they retain all the other idiosyncrasies and complexity of *Oxford orthography*.

3   Schemas

The Sentence

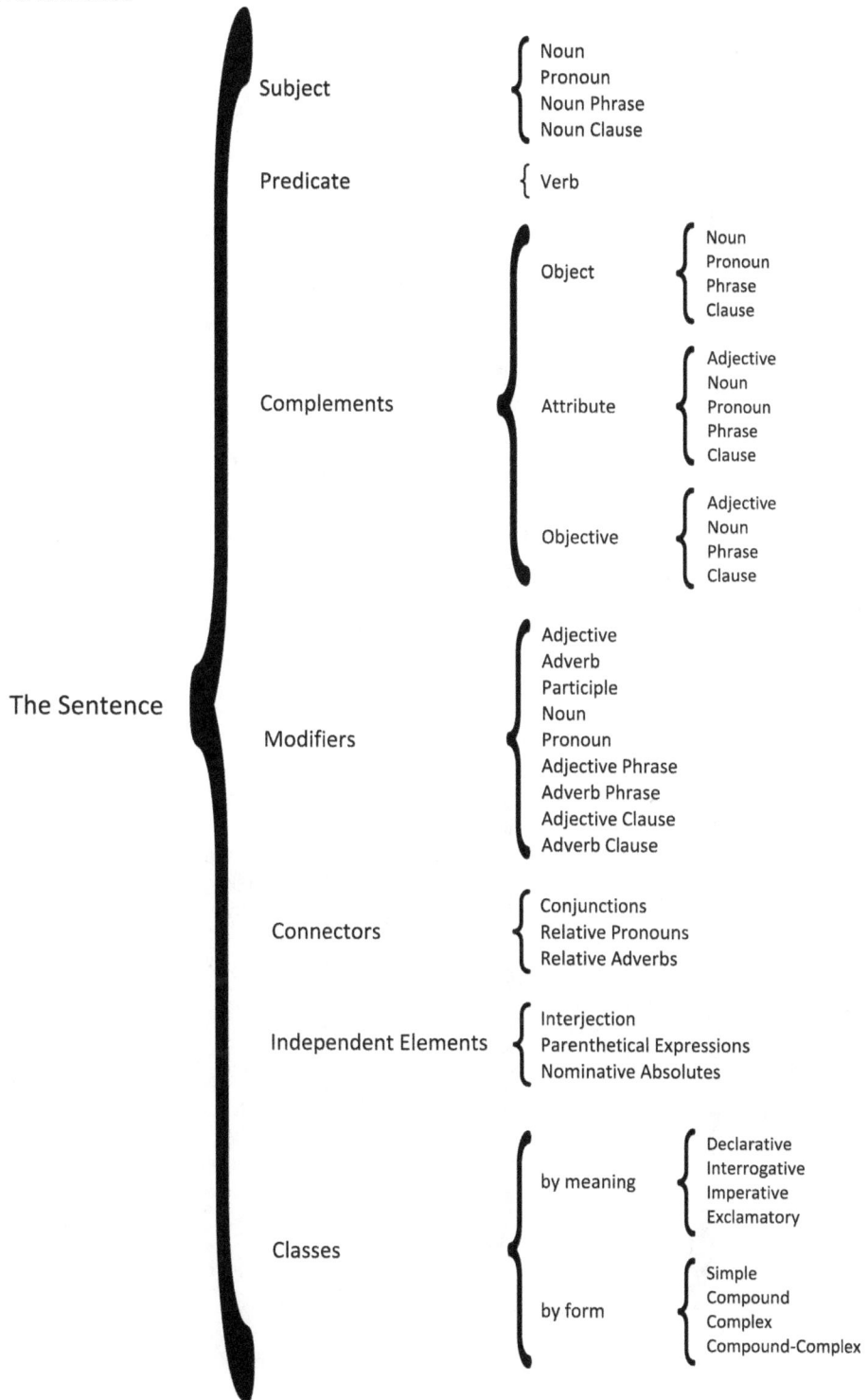

- **Subject**
  - Noun
  - Pronoun
  - Noun Phrase
  - Noun Clause

- **Predicate**
  - Verb

- **Complements**
  - Object
    - Noun
    - Pronoun
    - Phrase
    - Clause
  - Attribute
    - Adjective
    - Noun
    - Pronoun
    - Phrase
    - Clause
  - Objective
    - Adjective
    - Noun
    - Phrase
    - Clause

- **Modifiers**
  - Adjective
  - Adverb
  - Participle
  - Noun
  - Pronoun
  - Adjective Phrase
  - Adverb Phrase
  - Adjective Clause
  - Adverb Clause

- **Connectors**
  - Conjunctions
  - Relative Pronouns
  - Relative Adverbs

- **Independent Elements**
  - Interjection
  - Parenthetical Expressions
  - Nominative Absolutes

- **Classes**
  - by meaning
    - Declarative
    - Interrogative
    - Imperative
    - Exclamatory
  - by form
    - Simple
    - Compound
    - Complex
    - Compound-Complex

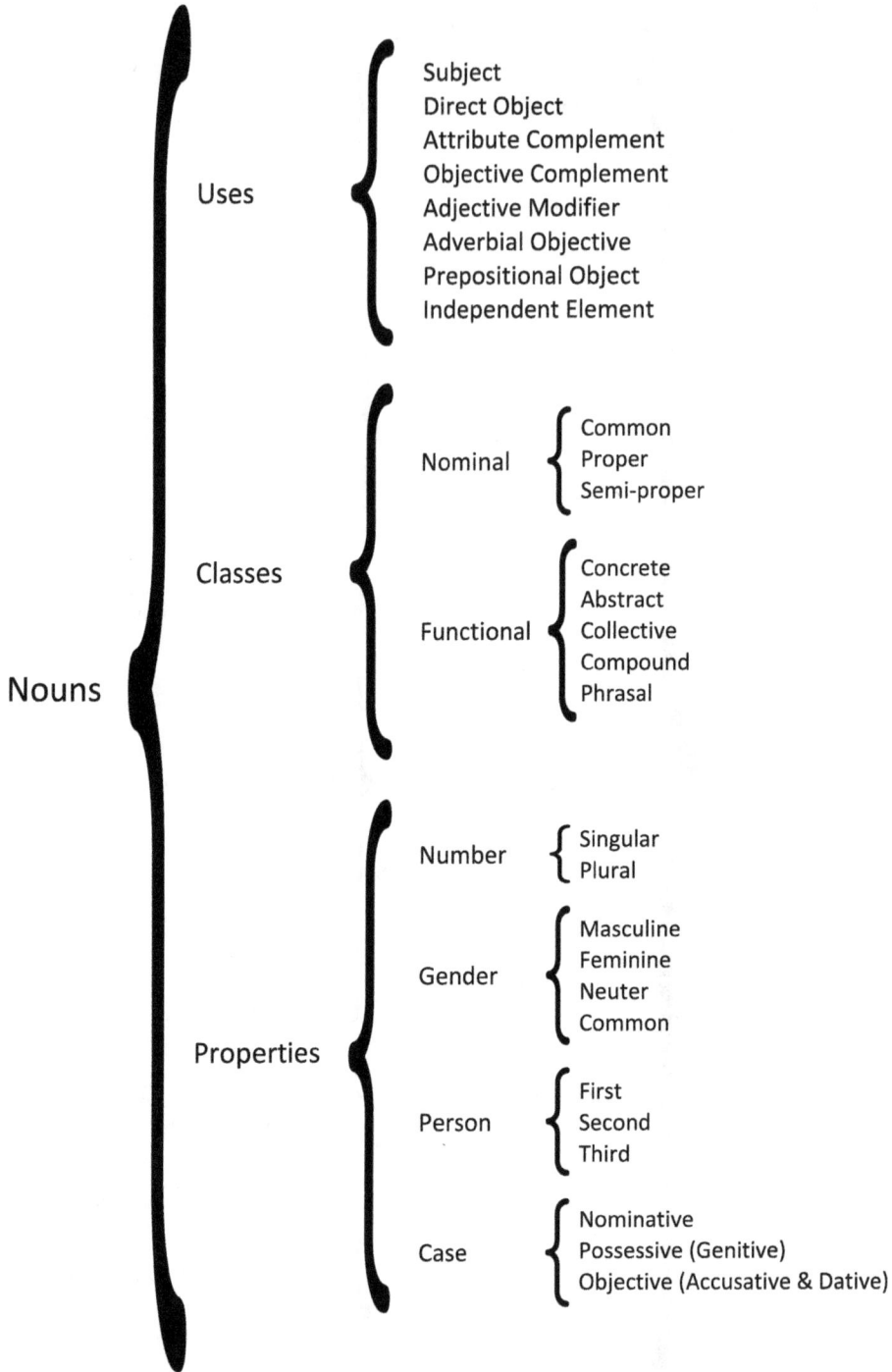

Nouns

Uses
- Subject
- Direct Object
- Attribute Complement
- Objective Complement
- Adjective Modifier
- Adverbial Objective
- Prepositional Object
- Independent Element

Classes

Nominal
- Common
- Proper
- Semi-proper

Functional
- Concrete
- Abstract
- Collective
- Compound
- Phrasal

Properties

Number
- Singular
- Plural

Gender
- Masculine
- Feminine
- Neuter
- Common

Person
- First
- Second
- Third

Case
- Nominative
- Possessive (Genitive)
- Objective (Accusative & Dative)

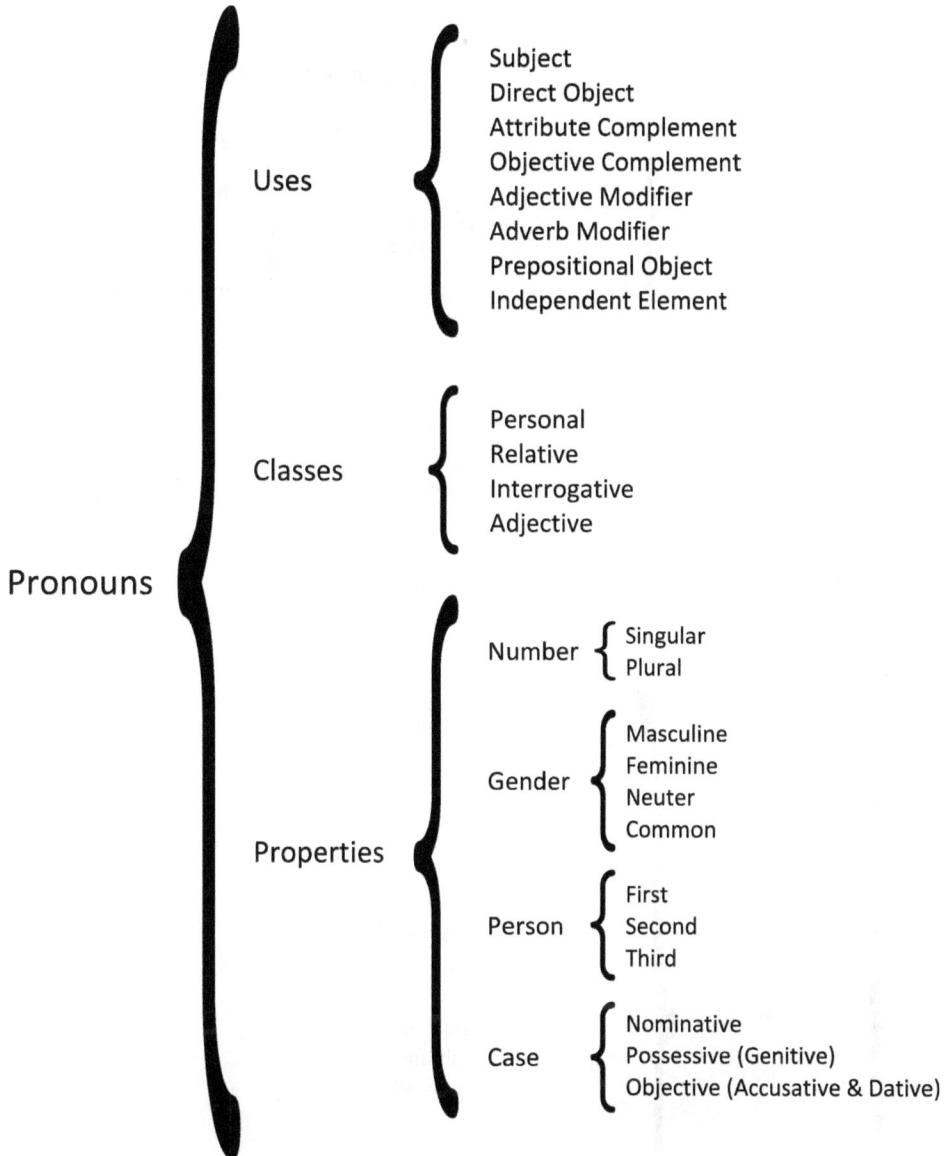

Pronouns

Uses
- Subject
- Direct Object
- Attribute Complement
- Objective Complement
- Adjective Modifier
- Adverb Modifier
- Prepositional Object
- Independent Element

Classes
- Personal
- Relative
- Interrogative
- Adjective

Properties
- Number
  - Singular
  - Plural
- Gender
  - Masculine
  - Feminine
  - Neuter
  - Common
- Person
  - First
  - Second
  - Third
- Case
  - Nominative
  - Possessive (Genitive)
  - Objective (Accusative & Dative)

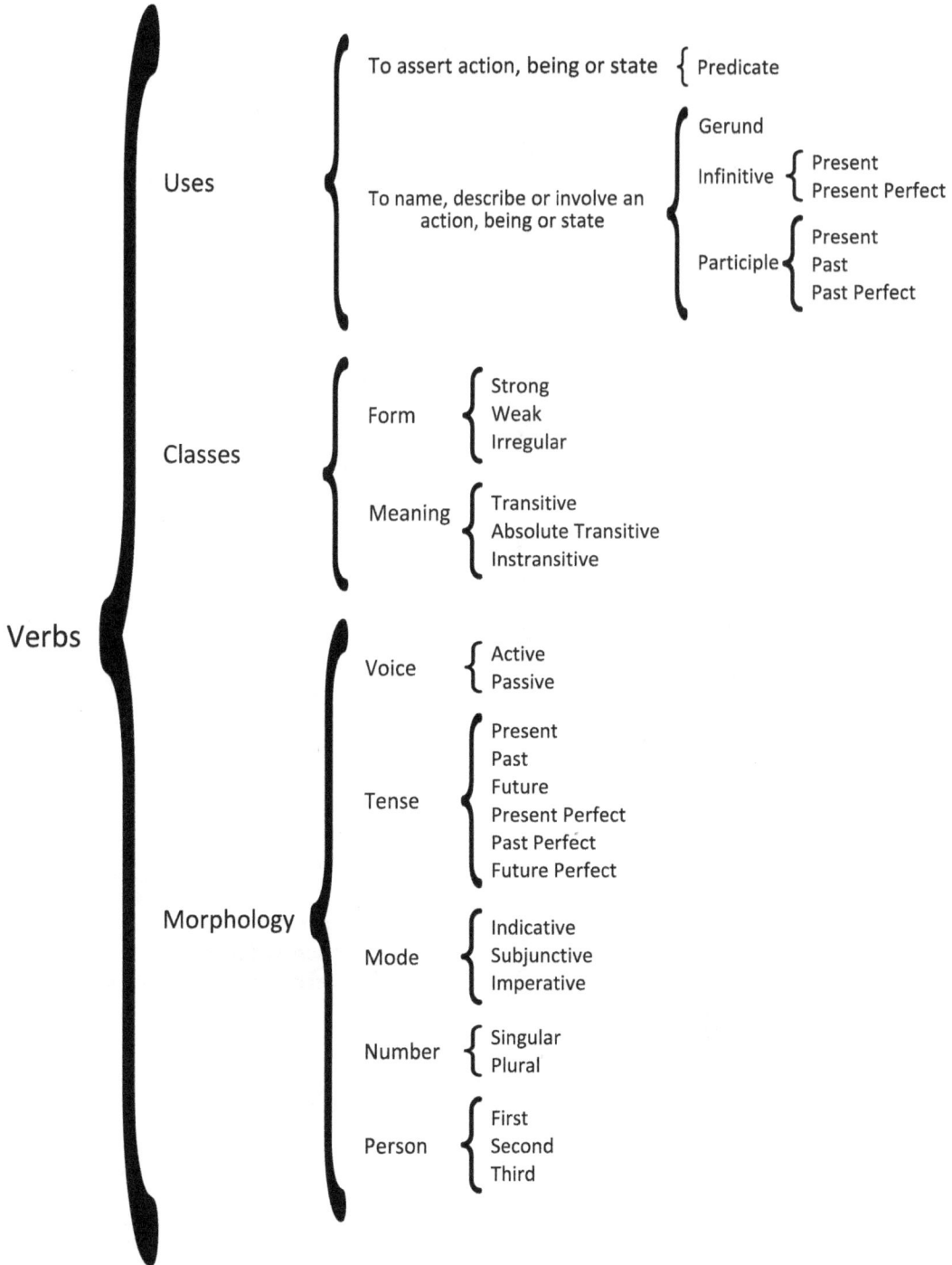

Verbs

Uses

- To assert action, being or state
  - { Predicate
- To name, describe or involve an action, being or state
  - Gerund
  - Infinitive
    - Present
    - Present Perfect
  - Participle
    - Present
    - Past
    - Past Perfect

Classes

- Form
  - Strong
  - Weak
  - Irregular
- Meaning
  - Transitive
  - Absolute Transitive
  - Instransitive

Morphology

- Voice
  - Active
  - Passive
- Tense
  - Present
  - Past
  - Future
  - Present Perfect
  - Past Perfect
  - Future Perfect
- Mode
  - Indicative
  - Subjunctive
  - Imperative
- Number
  - Singular
  - Plural
- Person
  - First
  - Second
  - Third

3.5 ADJECTIVES

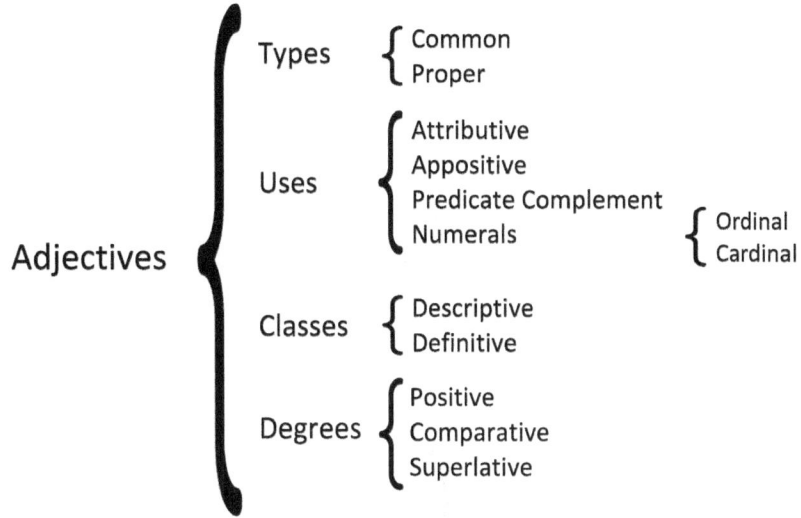

Adjectives
- Types
  - Common
  - Proper
- Uses
  - Attributive
  - Appositive
  - Predicate Complement
  - Numerals
    - Ordinal
    - Cardinal
- Classes
  - Descriptive
  - Definitive
- Degrees
  - Positive
  - Comparative
  - Superlative

3.6 ADVERBS

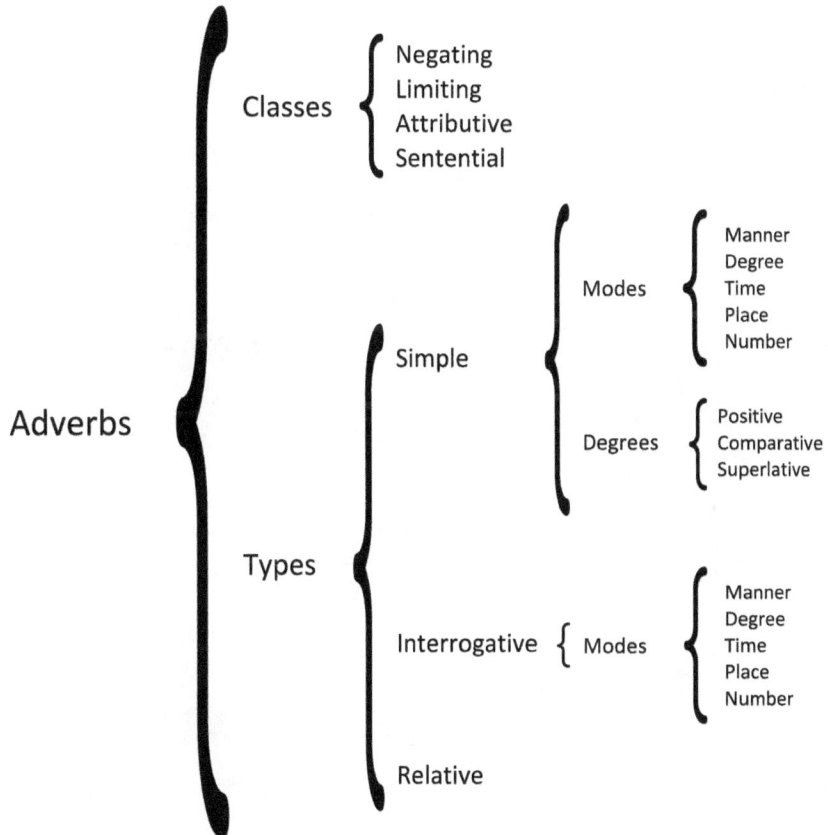

Adverbs
- Classes
  - Negating
  - Limiting
  - Attributive
  - Sentential
- Types
  - Simple
    - Modes
      - Manner
      - Degree
      - Time
      - Place
      - Number
    - Degrees
      - Positive
      - Comparative
      - Superlative
  - Interrogative
    - Modes
      - Manner
      - Degree
      - Time
      - Place
      - Number
  - Relative

3.7   PREPOSITIONS

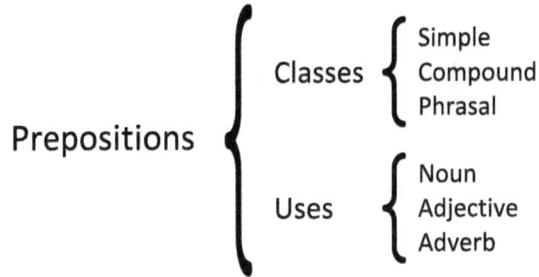

Prepositions
- Classes
  - Simple
  - Compound
  - Phrasal
- Uses
  - Noun
  - Adjective
  - Adverb

3.8   CONJUNCTIONS

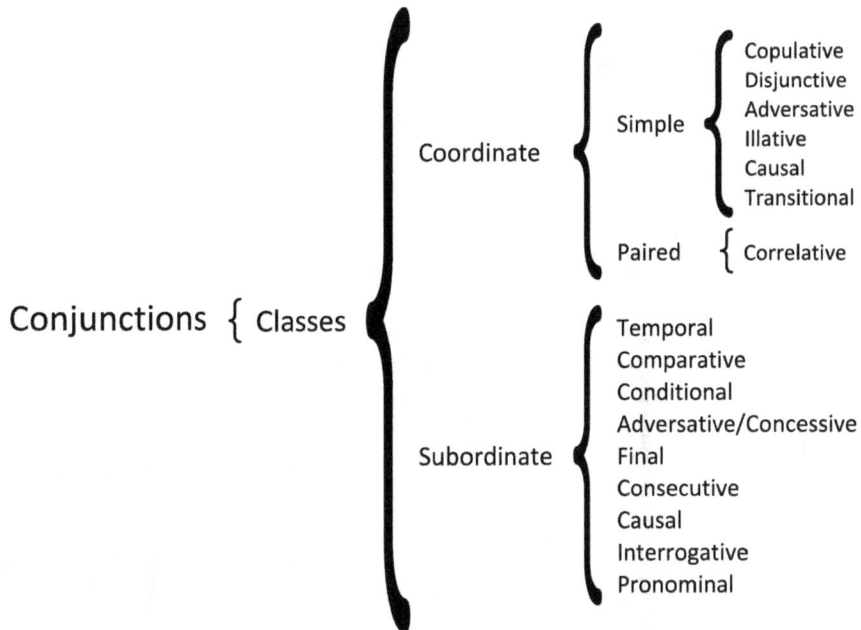

Conjunctions — Classes
- Coordinate
  - Simple
    - Copulative
    - Disjunctive
    - Adversative
    - Illative
    - Causal
    - Transitional
  - Paired
    - Correlative
- Subordinate
  - Temporal
  - Comparative
  - Conditional
  - Adversative/Concessive
  - Final
  - Consecutive
  - Causal
  - Interrogative
  - Pronominal

Independent Elements { Classes {

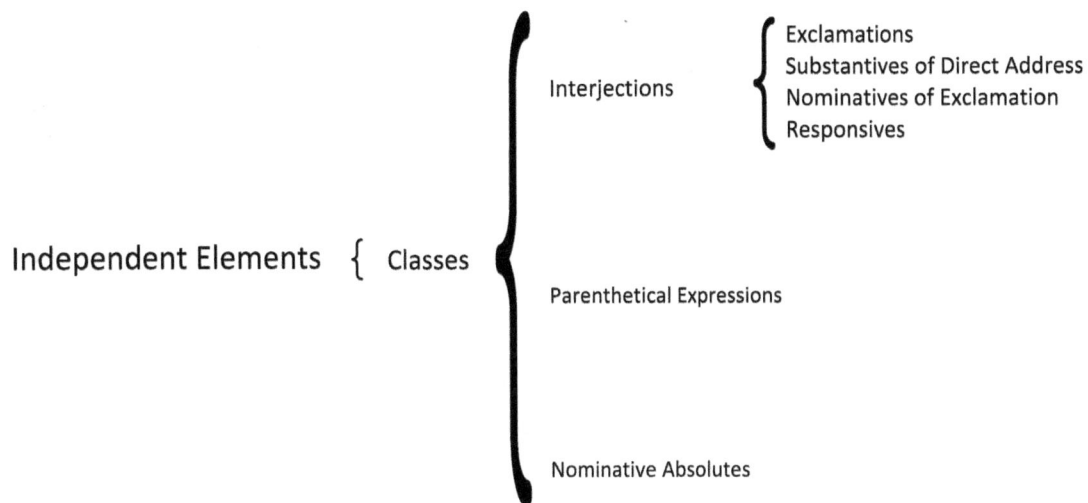

Interjections {
Exclamations
Substantives of Direct Address
Nominatives of Exclamation
Responsives

Parenthetical Expressions

Nominative Absolutes

4 Parts of Speech

4.1   All words in English can be assigned to one of **eight groups**, called ***parts of speech***.

4.2   The group to which a word is assigned is determined by its use in the sentence.

Because classification is determined by use, the same word may appear as any one of several of the parts of speech, depending on its exact use in the particular sentence under consideration.

1. **Noun**:   *a name*

2. **Pronoun**:   *takes the place of a **noun***

3. **Verb**:   *expresses action, existence or state of being*

4. **Adjective**:   *modifies a **noun** or **pronoun***

5. **Adverb**:   *modifies a **verb**, an **adjective**, another **adverb**, a phrase, a clause or an entire sentence*

6. **Preposition**:   *shows the relation between its object and another part of the sentence*

7. **Conjunction**:   *connects words or groups of words*

8. **Interjection**[1]:   *a phrase associated with a sentence, but that has no grammatical relation to the rest of that sentence*

---

[1] More fully: *Independent Element*, but, because of the preponderance of interjections among the *Independent Elements*, that is the more common umbrella term.

5   Nouns

5.1   A *noun* is **the name** of anything.

apple	*Life*
dog	*British Columbia*
honesty	*USS Enterprise*

5.2   There are **three** *nominal classes of nouns*: *common*, *proper* and *semi-proper*.

5.2.1   A *common noun* is the name or label of a general object: person, place or thing.

apple	*the ship*
dog	*a dollar*

5.2.2   A *proper noun* is the name of a specific person, place or thing. These should be capitalized.

Texas	*USS Enterprise*
Mississauga	*the Dollar*

5.2.3   *Semi-proper nouns* are, like **proper nouns**, the names of specific persons, places or things, but because they are common in occurrence, or are not strongly personalized, they are normally not capitalized, unless personalized.

fall	*winter*
north	*southwest*

5.3   There are also **five** *functional classes* into which nouns can be divided:
concrete, **abstract**, **collective**, **compound** and **phrasal**.

5.3.1   A *concrete noun* is the name of a substance or of a physical object. These are not capitalized.

tree	*pigeon*
dirt	*concrete*

5.3.2   An *abstract noun* is the name of a quality rather than a substance. These may be capitalized when the abstract nature or universality of concept is emphasized or potentially personified.

honesty	*hatred*
courtesy	*Life*
Love	*charity*

5.3.3   A *collective noun* is the name of something that is composed of recognized subunits

ACE: these are treated as singular nouns, emphasizing that they are acting as, or are to be treated as, a single unit. They may be treated as plural nouns if the phrase emphasizes individual action or state.

BE: although usually treated as hidden or disguised plurals, that is not always the case, nor is this concept applied consistently: pronouns will often not match either their antecedent nouns or the verbs used in these situations.

This disparity seems to arise from a deeply-rooted difference in outlook based in, or reflected by the more popular of the team sports specific to the locales involved.

In England's apparent *national sport*, the cricket team is a group of individual cricket players who, when at bat, are acting as individuals: other than the two batsmen, there are no members of the batter's team playing a role in the possible scoring of a run, and there is only one member of the team at bat active at a time. Cricket is essentially a series of one-to-one contests between the bowler and the batter. Thus appears the use of the individual-emphasizing plural when speaking of those teams, a usage that has become standard across all teams and groups.

In North America, whether it be baseball, football, basketball or hockey, players come together to form a team; all members of the defense and offense squads on the field are active during any period of the game; and it is the cumulative effort of the entire team that determines success. So, action as a unified, singular unit has been the important concept, rather than focusing on the individual efforts of any single player.

ACE usage is to treat teams and organizations as single units, and if it be necessary to refer to the individuals who compose that team, the phrase "[*the*] ... *members*" or "[*the*] *members of* ..." is inserted to make the meaning unambiguous.

> ACE: *The **team is** ready to play **its** game.*
> BE: *The **team are** ready to play **their/its** game.*
>
> ACE: *The **crew has** gathered to watch the match.*
> BE: *The **crew have** gathered to watch the match.*
>
> ACE: *The **firemen are** here./The **fire department is** here.*
> BE: *The **fire brigade are** here.*
>
> ACE: *The **class has its** pictures taken today.*
> BE: *The **class have their** pictures taken today.*
>
> ACE: *The **class members get their** diplomas today.*
> BE: *The **class get their** diplomas today.*

5.3.4 A *compound noun* is a noun made up of two or more words. These can be separate words, hyphenated words, or have been standardized into a single word.

Note that a *compound noun* does not have a conjunction; such would be a *compound noun phrase*, or possibly a *phrasal noun*.

> *maple syrup*   *newspaper*
> *secretary-treasurer*   *ballpoint pen*
> *attorney general*   *cooking fire*
> *library book*   *Victoria Day*

5.3.5 A *phrasal noun* is a noun made up of a phrase that is complete only when taken as a single expression.

> *Fourth of July*
> *mother-in-law*
> *hue and cry*
> *Duke of Wellington*

5.4 **The *two forms of verbs that are used as nouns* are called verbal nouns**: the *infinitive* and the *gerund*. (These are covered within the Verbs section [§7.23].)

5.5 **Noun Equivalents**: *Substantives*

A **substantive**, or **noun equivalent**, is any word or phrase that is used as a noun.

Examples of substantives are

1. Pronoun: *He is the famous novelist.*
2. Adjective: *The young often do not listen.*
3. Adverb: *Now is the time to get it done.*
4. Gerund: *One excellent exercise is swimming.*
5. Infinitive: *To err is human.*
6. Phrase: *Into the cup is the goal of every golfer.*
7. Clause: *That he was in this movie is a fact.*
8. Quotation: *"Hold the fort! I am coming!" signaled General Sherman.*

5.6 **Properties of Nouns**. There are **four properties** that nouns can demonstrate, each of which may cause a noun to change in form in some way: **gender**, **person**, **number** and **case**.

5.7 **Gender**. In English, gender is a distinction of physical sex, that is, English uses what is termed **natural gender**. This situation is distinct from that in many other languages, who have **grammatical gender**. In grammatical gender, the linguistic history or the time-honored form of the word determines its gender, not the physical sex of the object itself.

Grammatical gender continues to exist, in varying implementations and enforcement, in all Indo-European languages except English. Examples of such distinction can be drawn in comparison with German usage:

The moon shines. It shines. — *Der Mond scheint. Er scheint.* (*masculine gender*)
The sun shines. It shines. — *Die Sonne scheint. Sie scheint.* (*feminine gender*)
The child sleeps. It sleeps. — *Das Kind schläft. Es schläft.* (*neuter gender*)

In contrast, in French, *moon* (*la lune*) is feminine, *sun* (*le soleil*) is masculine and *child* (*l'enfant*) is masculine. At the same time, in Russian, *moon* (*луна*) is feminine, *sun* (*солнце*) is neuter and *child* (*ребёнок*) is masculine.

5.7.1 Because of linguistic natural gender's basis in physical sex, there are **two classifications of gender drawn from the common cases of biology**. There are also **two more that are variations drawn from those original two**. From this come the **four genders** used in English: **masculine**, **feminine**, **neuter** and **common**.

5.7.2 A noun of **masculine gender** denotes a male: *father, brother, uncle*.

5.7.3 A noun of **feminine gender** denotes a female: *mother, sister, aunt*.

5.7.4 A noun of **neuter gender** denotes a non-sexual object: *rock, paper, scissors*.

5.7.5 A noun of **common gender** denotes something that could be male or female, or a group possibly containing mixed sexes: *child, team, teacher, parent, committee*.

5.7.6　There are **three ways of indicating** *specific gender of animate nouns*:

   1.　A difference in gender can be conveyed **by changing the word used**:

man	— *woman*	(*common gender: **human** or **person***)
rooster	— *hen*	(*common gender: **chicken***)
drake	— *duck*	
gander	— *goose*	

   2.　Gender can be relayed **by changing part of a compound**:

grandfather —	*grandmother*	(*common gender: **grandparent***)
manservant —	*maidservant*	(*common gender: **servant***)

   3.　Differences can also be revealed **by adding a suffix**:

actor	— *actress*
host	— *hostess*
hero	— *heroine*

5.7.7　There are discrepancies in gender between English and its source languages, certain variances that have arisen from English-speakers' borrowing of words from languages that have grammatical gender. These disagreements are largely rooted in Americans' close association with, and largely rudimentary knowledge of Latin and the Romance languages, and Americans' erroneous extension of misunderstood characteristics to words borrowed from sources beyond that group.

Because of Americans' predominating exposure to Spanish and Italian, they have learned to hear words ending in *–a* as feminine. Yet when they have borrowed personal names from other languages, they have done so not realizing that those names could actually be masculine.

Thus, for example, in North America we find only girls named *Sasha* and *Misha*, despite the fact that *those are actually masculine nicknames* in the Slavic languages, rarely given to females: *Sasha* comes from *Alexander*, and *Misha* from *Michael*.

5.8　*Person*. Though often thought of as applying only to pronouns, nouns reflect person as well, though to a minimal degree of complexity, as nouns do not change to reflect person: only usage within the sentence determines person. There are **three persons**: *first person*, *second person* and *third person*.

5.8.1　*First person* is the one speaking. (As a noun, this occurs solely as an appositive.):

   *I, **Jane Doe**, swear to tell the truth.*

5.8.2　*Second person* is the one spoken to. (As a noun, this occurs solely as an appositive, or as part of a command or entreaty.):

   *You, **Jane Doe**, will tell the truth.*
   ***Jane Doe**, tell the truth.*

5.8.3　*Third person* is the person or thing spoken of:

   ***Jane Doe** tells the truth? Yes, yes, she does.*

5.8.4　There was a special case in an American election of the late twentieth century in which one candidate was unusually fond of speaking of himself in the third person rather than using the first person. This is a situation of *dysglossia* in which the appositive formation of §5.8.1 is meant, but the third person formation of §5.8.3 is actually used.

Apparently, this was thought to provide extra opportunities for getting the candidate's name into the audience's attention-stream.

However, this usage should be avoided. With its unnatural externalization and objectivization of the speaker, it sounds stilted, forced and not a little fake.

> (*Jane Doe speaking*:) *They say Jane Doe will raise taxes. Well,* **Jane Doe will not raise** *taxes, and that's something that* **Jane Doe promises***.*

5.9　***Number***. Number is whether the noun represents one, or more than one person, place or thing. Therefore, nouns are used in either of **two numbers: singular** or **plural**.

5.9.1　A ***singular noun*** denotes one: ***father, sister, uncle.***

5.9.2　A ***plural noun*** denotes two or more: ***fathers, sisters, uncles.***

5.9.3　**Formation of the plural.**

5.9.3.1　The plural of ***most nouns*** is formed by adding –*s* to the singular

father	—	*fathers*
sister	—	*sisters*
brother	—	*brothers*

5.9.3.2　***Nouns ending in –ch, –s, –sh, –x* or *–z*** form the plural by adding *–es* to the singular

crutch	—	*crutches*
guess	—	*guesses*
ash	—	*ashes*
fox	—	*foxes*
buzz	—	*buzzes*

5.9.3.3　For ***common nouns ending in –y***:

1. If the *–y* is ***preceded by a consonant***, change the *–y* to *–i* and add *–es*:

fly	—	*flies*
spy	—	*spies*

2. If the *–y* is ***preceded by a vowel***, add only *–s*:

journey	—	*journeys*
turkey	—	*turkeys*

5.9.3.4　For ***proper nouns ending in –y***, add *–s*, or add *–es* if the name already ends in *–ch, –s, –sh, –x* or *–z*: **the Marys, the Henrys, the Charleses**

5.9.3.5　For ***nouns ending in –o***:

1. Most nouns ***ending in –o preceded by a consonant*** add *–es* to the singular:

hero	—	*heroes*
tomato	—	*tomatoes*
potato	—	*potatoes*

2. Nouns ***ending in –o preceded by a vowel*** add *–s* to the singular:

radio	—	*radios*
patio	—	*patios*
stereo	—	*stereos*

3. There are **exceptions** to the rule, including several from Music:

  piano — *pianos*
  solo — *solos*
  tempo — *tempos*

5.9.3.6   ***Some nouns ending in* –*f or* –*fe change the* –*f or* –*fe to* –*v and add* –*es:***

  leaf — *leaves*
  loaf — *loaves*
  wife — *wives*
  life — *lives*
  half — *halves*

5.9.3.7   ***Other nouns ending in* –*f or* –*fe simply add* –*s:***

  safe — *safes*
  roof — *roofs*
  fife — *fifes*
  gulf — *gulfs*
  gaff — *gaffs*

5.9.3.8   ***Some nouns change vowels*** within themselves, some also mutate consonants, as well:

  mouse — *mice*
  goose — *geese*
  man — *men*
  woman — *women*

5.9.3.9   ***Two nouns*** add –*en* or –*ren*:

  child — *children*
  ox — *oxen*

5.9.3.10   ***The plurals of compound nouns and phrasal nouns***

  5.9.3.10.1   are usually formed by making the main word in the compound plural

  attorney general — *attorneys general* (*general* is here an adjective)

  Duke of Wellington — *Dukes of Wellington*

  5.9.3.10.2   yet others are formed by making the last word in the compound plural

  ballpoint pen — *ballpoint pens*
  secretary-treasurer — *secretary-treasurers*

  5.9.3.10.3   while others make the first word in the compound plural

  mother-in-law — *mothers-in-law*

  5.9.3.10.4   and still others make every noun in the compound plural

  manservant — *menservants*

5.9.3.11   ***Nouns*** ending in –*ful* add –*s*:

  spoonful — *spoonfuls*

NOTE: a plural form such as *spoonsful* is absolutely incorrect. If you need that phrasing, the correct form is *spoons full*.

A *spoonful* is a unit of measurement; a *spoon full* is a descriptive phrase, detailing the state of a particular spoon.

5.9.3.12 The **plurals of letters, symbols, figures and words treated as topics** form the plural by adding **'s** (apostrophe + s) or, when the word is emphasized with (italic or bold) formatting, or is otherwise understandable, just –s.

> *He got all **A's** on his reports.*
> *No **and's**, **if's** or **but's** about it!* or, less clearly: *No **ands**, **ifs** or **buts** about it!*
> *All the ***s** on the map indicate locations of branch offices.*

5.9.3.13 Some nouns have **the same form in both numbers**: *corps, deer, gross, grouse, moose, series, sheep, species, swine, trout, vermin*.

NOTE: The *s* in *corps* is silent in the singular, but pronounced (as a 'z') in the plural.

NOTE: *fish* has multiple plural forms, used in specific situations. The normal plural is the same as the singular: *one fish, two fish*. However, when referring to two or more fish of more than one species the plural is *fishes*: *red fishes, blue fishes*.

NOTE: *species* is an unusual word in that there is another word that looks as if it would be its regularly formed singular: *specie*. However, the two are completely separate words and must be dealt with correctly:

> *specie*   meaning *coin*, *coins*, or *coinage* has no plural form (and is never used as a plural),

while

> *species*   meaning *a kind*, *a class*, or *a distinct type* has the same form for both singular and plural: *one species, three species*.

5.9.3.14 A limited number of nouns **have no plural**.
Aside from *specie*, mentioned above, others belonging to this group are the word ***information***, and its abbreviation, ***info***, along with the Internet-common words ***hardware*** and ***software***.

Note that, despite their being used on the Internet,
> **there are no such words as** *informations* **or** *infos*; **nor** *hardwares* **or** *softwares*; **nor their made-up abbreviations,** *hards* **and** *softs*.

5.9.3.15 A few nouns have **different plurals depending on meaning**. Examples are

singular	plural	meaning
brother	*brothers*	family members
	brethren	members of a fraternal organization
craft	*crafts*	arts, trades or skills
	craft	transportation units: *aircraft*, *watercraft*, etc.
die	*dies*	forms for making coins, bolts, etc.
	dice	gaming pieces
genius	*geniuses*	those possessing exceptional capabilities
	genii	spirits, demons, or jinns (also: *genies*)

singular	plural	meaning
head	**heads**	the topmost part of bodies
	head	livestock (*e.g., twenty head of cattle*)
sail	**sails**	pieces of canvas
	sail	[sailing] vessels (*e.g., Four sail were at anchor.*)
ware	**wares**	goods, manufactured articles, merchandise held for sale, *etc.*
	ware	specific classes of merchandise: *glassware, hardware, software, silverware*

5.9.3.16   Some nouns are ***plural in form but singular in meaning***, and are used with verbs in the singular number: ***measles***, ***mathematics*** and ***chicken pox***.

Generally, in the case of sciences or fields of study ending in *–ics*, such as ***mathematics***, ***ethics***, ***genetics***, ***statistics***, ***logistics***, ***phonetics***, and ***linguistics***, when used as the name of that science in general or as a course of study, they are singular. However, when dealing with specific instances of the application of that science, they may appear with plural verbs.

However, important exceptions are ***physics*** and the colloquial, shortened form of ***mathematics***—***math***—which are always singular.

> *Statistics **is** not an easy subject.*
> *That group's **statistics are** too often faulty.*
>
> *Ethics **is** studied by too few, too infrequently.*
> *His **ethics are** questionable.*
>
> *Physics **was** his favorite course in college.*
> *The **physics** in your answer **is** incorrect.*
>
> *Mathematics **is** the key to many other sciences.*
> *Math **is** the key to many other sciences.*
>
> *The bank's **mathematics prove** again to be correct.*
> *The bank's **math proves** again to be correct.*

NOTE: The shortened form of ***mathematics*** is ***math***.

There is an almost unpronounceable variant of the abbreviated form used in *BE*, the pseudo-plural ***maths***, that **should be avoided**, as it displays disregard for, or ignorance of, the fact that the word from which it is shortened—***mathematics***—is a singular field of study and, so, **is always singular when abbreviated**.

This slang word, ***maths***, is also too close in pronunciation to the word ***mass*** to avoid easy confusion:

> *"I've always had trouble with maths."*
> *—"Well, I had noticed you've put on weight."*

5.9.3.17   ***Some nouns appear only in plural forms,*** and take verbs in the plural: ***amends***, ***means***, ***odds***, ***pains*** [care, attention, trouble], ***pants***, ***tongs***, ***scissors***, ***chopsticks***. These are essentially plural collective nouns.

5.9.3.18   ***Some nouns of technical or specialist nature*** retain English plurals formed as they were in their original languages.

     5.9.3.18.1   Originally a neuter noun from Latin, the **singular** *bacterium* has the **plural** *bacteria*.

     5.9.3.18.2   Coming from a Greek noun (also of neuter gender in that language), the **singular** *phenomenon* has its **plural** *phenomena*.

     5.9.3.18.3   These are often confused, to some degree because of the influence of singular (feminine) nouns ending *–a* in Latin and the Romance languages (specifically Spanish and Italian). Many people, even scientists, mistakenly use the plural forms as if they were singular, to the point at times of actually inventing and using **false plurals**, *bacterias* and *phenomenas*.

     5.9.3.18.4   In contrast, many nouns, particularly those originally Latin and ending in *-us*, have an optional English-based plural form, in addition to the long-used Latinate plural, *e.g.*, *platypus* can appear in the plural as either *platypi* or *platypuses*, and *hippopotamus* becomes either *hippopotami* or *hippopotamuses* in the plural. The form chosen is largely that which matches the register: the more formal, Latin-derived plural in more technical situations, and the common, English-based plural everywhere else.

                 The name *octopus* is sometimes cited as an example of technical plurals gone wild, and an erroneous history is given for the word, one that says it was borrowed into English directly from Greek. As a result of this misconception, those writers will restate the error that the correct, borrowed plural should be a form taken from the Greek, *octopodes*. However, this suggestion is itself an error, because it puts a Latin plural on the Greek word. The true Ancient Greek form in English orthography would be *octopodia*. (Reflected in the Modern Greek for *octopuses*: τα χταπόδια.)

                 However, the word *octopus* was actually borrowed from Latin, which had borrowed it earlier from Greek, so a Latinate plural, *octopi*, is not incorrect, although the erroneously proposed plural, *octopodes*, is definitely incorrect. The regular, English plural is, of course, *octopuses*.

     5.9.3.18.5   Some words borrowed from French have the option of appearing in either an English-style or in the original French plural. For example, the plural of *milieu* can be either *milieus* or *milieux*.

5.9.3.19   Ultimately, **in case of doubt** about forming a plural, consult an ***ACE*** dictionary.

5.10　**Case**. The case of a noun or pronoun details its relationship to other words in the sentence.

Modern English has three cases: **nominative**, **possessive** and **objective**. For nouns, the nominative and objective have the same form, and these case distinctions are discernible only by usage and placement. The objective case exists in separate forms only in the personal pronouns.

The fact that the pronouns have specific case forms allows us to identify the cases of the nouns, despite the fact that it is the position of the noun or pronoun in the sentence that ultimately determines its usage. This is the reason English can be called an analytic language despite retaining rudimentary usage of case forms.

NOTE: If this situation sounds complicated, rest assured that it isn't, particularly when compared to other languages. German has four cases, Polish and Russian have six, and Sanskrit had eight. Even French, though having a single case for nouns, has four cases in its personal pronouns: *subject*, *direct object*, *indirect object* and *emphatic*.

5.11　The **nominative case** is used for

5.11.1　the **subject of a finite verb**
A **finite verb** is one that can be used as the main verb—the **predicate**—and has both person and number. (Nonfinite forms—the *infinitive*, *participle* and *gerund*—cannot be used as a predicate.)

> **John** *writes well.*
> **Susan** *called her mother.*
> **Mary** *is the girl in the picture.*

5.11.2　the **predicate nominative**
A **predicate nominative** is a noun or pronoun that completes the meaning of the predicate and is essentially the same as the subject. It is also called a **subjective complement** because it completes the meaning of the subject.
In this usage, the verb is a **linking verb**.

> *James is a tall* **boy**.
> *Mary is the* **girl** *in the picture.*

5.11.3　**direct address**
In other languages, particularly when a different form is used for direct address, it's called the **vocative case**. (Although Anglo-Saxon had remnants of word forms specific to this case, Modern English has lost even those distinctions.)

> **Jason,** *get off the couch.*
> *Drop the chalupa,* **Henry***!*

5.11.4　**nominative of exclamation**.
Related to direct address, the nominative of exclamation differs from direct address in that the nominative of exclamation is not targeted directly at a person or object, but is an elided sentence with only the original *predicate nominative* remaining.

> **Fire! Fire!** (for *There is a* **fire***!*)

5.11.5 **nominative absolute**

This is a word or phrase related to the meaning of the sentence, but not directly, grammatically tied to any part of the sentence; it is usually a noun plus a participle, plus any modifiers.

The topic of the absolute phrase, which would be its subject if it were an independent sentence, is never the same as the subject of the sentence in which it appears.

It is separated from the rest of its sentence by a comma.

> **The roof finished,** *we went home.*
> **The day being cooler,** *the dogs ran far and fast.*
> **Mr. Smith being mayor,** *the streetcars will run on time.*
> **Her hair flowing behind her,** *Mary ran across the field.*

This usage is more common in writing; in speaking, a clause or a phrase is usually substituted for the nominative absolute construction.

> **When/Once we had finished the roof,** *we went home.*
> **Because the day was cooler,** *the dogs ran far and fast.*
> **While Mr. Smith is mayor,** *the streetcars will run on time.*
> **With her hair flowing behind her,** *Mary ran across the field.*
> **Her hair was flowing behind her** *as Mary ran across the field.*

5.11.6 **apposition of another nominative**

A word, phrase or clause placed near a substantive to give more information about a substantive is called an **appositive**. An appositive is always in the same case as the word it elucidates, thus nominative when applied to another nominative.

An appositive is always set off by commas from the rest of the sentence.

> *Her boss,* **Dr Rufus,** *has gone to Boston.*
> *Jason,* **my dog,** *loves broccoli.*
> *The cat,* **a sleek and beautiful calico,** *darted across the yard.*

5.11.7 **the complement of the infinitive *to be* when it has no subject**

If **to be** has no subject, the complement is in the nominative case.

(However, the subject of infinitives, including *to be*, is in the objective case: §5.12.8)

> *John wants* **to be a painter.**
> *The visitor was believed* **to be Mary.**
> *It was believed* **to be she.**

5.12   The ***objective case*** is used for

5.12.1   the ***direct object of a verb***

The verb can be ***finite*** (a *predicate*) or ***nonfinite*** (an *infinitive*, a *gerund* or a *participle*). This objective-case usage is also called the ***Accusative case***.

John writes ***essays***.	(direct object)
What *does he write?*	(direct object)
Susan called ***her mother***.	(direct object)
Whom *did Susan call?*	(direct object)
The dog is chasing ***the ball***.	([direct] object of a gerund)
Eric likes ***hamburgers***.	(direct object)
Eating ***hamburgers*** *is his joy.*	(object of a gerund)
To eat a ***hamburger*** *is what he wants.*	(object of an infinitive)
Eating the ***hamburger***, *he drove recklessly.*	(object of a participle)

5.12.2   the ***predicate objective*** or ***objective complement***

Verbs of ***making***, ***naming***, ***calling***, ***choosing***, ***electing*** and ***appointing*** may have ***two objects***: the ***first*** is the direct object and the ***second*** is the predicate objective, which is related to the direct object and completes the meaning of the predicate. This objective complement may be a noun or an adjective.

It may also be an infinitive, with elided ***to***, used as a noun [See §7.24.8].

We elected ***Marcel president***.
Then he appointed ***Jack treasurer***.
But someone called ***Jack lazy***.
Then we saw ***him swim*** *to save the kitten.*

5.12.3   the ***indirect object***

An indirect object may be rewritten as the object of a prepositional phrase constructed with ***to*** or ***for***. (The indirect object is considered to be a special case of **adverbial objective**. [See §5.12.5])

The objective case used as an indirect object is also called the ***Dative case***.

Ellen wrote ***Sharon*** *a letter.*
Ellen wrote ***her*** *a letter.*
Ellen wrote a letter ***to Sharon***.
Ellen wrote a letter ***to her***.
We will do ***Jack*** *a favor.*
We will do ***him*** *a favor.*
We will do a favor ***for Jack***.
We will do a favor ***for him***.

NOTE: Certain verbs are followed by indirect objects rather than direct objects. These noun or pronoun indirect objects are then usually followed an infinitive, which can be complete or partial (*i.e.*, with or without its leading 'to' complement). The infinitive may be elided if this does not cloud the statement; yet even in this case, the object left within the phrase remains an indirect object—it does not convert into a direct object.

The cardinal aspect here is that the infinitive does not act as an adjective nor as an adverb (to express purpose, for example). It is used as a noun, and as such answers the question "What did the verb do?"

These verbs include *to aid, to ask, to benefit, to bid, to command, to entreat, to help, to persuade, to [dis]please, to teach, to tell, to trust.*

> *The scholarship **aided her to go** to college.*
> *They **asked her to send** a letter.*
> *Diagramming **aided them to see** their errors.*
> *He **bids them go** to the city.* or *He **bids them to go** to the city.*
> *He **commanded her to remain**.*
> *She **entreated him to let** her leave.*
> *You **should help me clean** the house.* or *You **should help me to clean** the house.*
> *They **persuaded them to sing** yet another song.*
> *It **displeased me to see** it there.*
> *He **taught them to speak** German.* or *He **taught them German**.*
> *They **told him to return** the money.*
> *She **trusted him to do** it.*

Two of the more common among these are *to help* and *to tell*.

In the earlier forms of the English language, when its nouns and pronouns still possessed cases, the verb *to help* was always followed by a noun or pronoun in the Dative case (as it still does in German); an infinitive often appearing alongside it was the direct object. In Anglo-Saxon, the form of the infinitive (the single-word form ending in *-an*) called *the uninflected infinitive* appeared in this usage.

An example in English translated into Anglo-Saxon and German shows this, as both these two use forms of *you—ēow* and *ihnen*—that are in the Dative case:

> *Can I help you?—Can ic ēow helpan?—Kann ich ihnen helfen?*

The literal implication of using the Dative case is that this means

> *Can I [give/render] help to you?*, viz.,
> *Can I help you cross the street?*, also said (using the complete infinitive) as
> *Can I help you to cross the street?*

What is the actual help rendered?	*to cross the street*	(*direct object*)
What is the actual help rendered?	*to cross the street*	(*direct object*)
To whom was help given?	*[to] you.*	(*indirect object*)

The situation with *to tell* is more easily demonstrable. A usual formation could be something like *Tell me a story!*, which can be restated as *Tell a story to me!* This restatement establishes that *[to] me* is the indirect object and *story* is the direct object.

However, when the sentence is shortened to *Tell me!*, the true nature of the second word is not so readily apparent. This sentence is an elided version of *Tell me it!* or *Tell it to me!*, in which it is obvious that *[to] me* is the indirect object.

> *She told him a bedtime story.*

| What did she tell? | *a story* | (*direct object*) |
| To whom did she tell it? | *[to] him.* | (*indirect object*) |

> *She told him to go home.*

| What did she tell [or say]? | *to go home* | (*direct object*) |
| To whom did she tell it? | *[to] him* | (*indirect object*) |

5.12.4   the ***object of a preposition***

> *The dog is chasing the ball across **the room**.*
> *The dog is sitting in **the chair**.*
> *The dogs ran **into the house**.*
> *The dogs were running around **in the house**.*

5.12.5   the ***adverbial objective***

This adverbial use of a noun modifies a verb, adverb or preposition. The noun (plus any modifiers of its own) expresses length of time, measure, weight, value, location, destination or direction.

> *We waited **three hours**.*
> *They walked **half-a-mile** to the gas station.*
> *The bag of potatoes weighed **twenty pounds**.*
> *But the potatoes cost only **five dollars**.*
> *Let's stay **home** tonight.*
> *Let's go **home**.*
> *Go **north**, then turn **east**.*

In other, synthetic Indo-European languages when the objective is used with units of space or time, it is usually called the *Accusative of duration*. In all these related languages, including English, it represents the complete passage of that amount of space or time.

The noun in the **adverbial objective** can often be restated as the object of a preposition, with that prepositional phrase in some situations requiring insertion of a true direct object for modification:

> *We waited **three hours**.*   —   *We waited **<u>for</u> three hours**.*
> *They walked **half-a-mile** to the gas station.*   —
>   *They walked **a distance <u>of</u> half-a-mile** to the gas station.*
> *The bag of potatoes weighed **twenty pounds**.* —
>   *The bag of potatoes **was <u>of</u> a weight <u>of</u> twenty pounds**.*
> *But the potatoes cost only **five dollars**.*   —
>   *But the potatoes **have a cost <u>of</u> only five dollars**.*
> *Let's stay **home** tonight.*   —   *Let's stay **<u>at</u> home** tonight.*
> *Let's go **home**.*   —   *[Let's go **<u>toward</u> home** / **<u>to</u> the house**.]*
> *Go **north**, then turn **east**.*   —   *Go **<u>toward</u> the north**, then turn **<u>to</u> the east**.*

Those examples using units of time or distance exhibit the *objective/Accusative of extent of space or time*, detailing complete passage of that unit. Those given using "weigh" or "cost" are colloquial circumlocutions, using an idiom with the objective, as will be understood from considering that potatoes, of course, cannot use any measuring-device in order to obtain the weight of themselves, or of anything else.

Note that, of these examples, "*Let's go **home**"* cannot be restated simply by using a prepositional phrase. It is an example of what in the Indo-European synthetic languages would be termed specifically a noun in the *Accusative of place to or toward which*. Latin had this same usage with its word for ***house*** or ***home***, **domus**: *Domum Cæsaris eāmus — Let us go **to** Caesar's **house/home***, in which **domum** is in the *Accusative* case.

NOTE: Some grammars will parse the words **north** and **east** in the first set of examples (along with **south** and **west**) as simple adverbs rather than as adverbial objectives. This is debatable.

Because those words can be replaced, without further edits, with prepositional phrases in which those words appear undoubtedly as nouns—an act that is impossible with true adverbs—**it is more logical and consistent to hold them as nouns used as adverbial objectives**, rather than relabeling them as adverbs in this single situation.

The nouns of the cardinal directions are often used as elided versions of their corresponding adjectives and adverbs of fuller form.

For example, **north** appears in place both of the adjective **northern**, and of the adverb **northward** (or **northwards**). The same situation appears to be involved in the use of **home** for **homeward** (or **homewards**). These facts argue for recognition of the compass directions and **home** as nouns appearing as adverbial objectives in all those situations in which they appear as modifiers.

5.12.6   the **cognate object**

When an intransitive verb (one that does not require a direct object) appears as if it were used as a transitive verb and has an object that contains the same essential idea the verb itself has, that object is called the **cognate object**.

> He **ran** *a tight* **race**.
> We **slept** *a deep* **sleep**.
> She **dreams** *a peaceful* **dream**.

5.12.7   the **retained object**

When a sentence with an active verb that has a direct object is converted into a passive sentence, a situation arises in which the verb cannot take a direct object (because the verb is **passive**), but it still retains that object from its original format. This object is called **the retained object** because it is the object of the verb, as retained from the original **active** formation.

> *John's teacher* **gave** *him* **a good grade**.— *John* **was given** **a good grade** *by his teacher.*

5.12.8   the **objective subject of an infinitive**, as well as the [**objective**] **complement of the infinitive to be, having a subject**

> *Jack believed* **the woman** *to be* **his sister**.   (**the woman** = *objective subject of infinitive;* **his sister** = *infinitive complement*)
>
> *Jack believed* **her** *to be* **his sister**.   (**her** = *objective subject;* **his sister** = *complement*)
>
> *Jack believed* **the woman** *to be* **her**.   (**the woman** = *objective subject;* **her** = *objective complement*)

5.12.9   the **object of an infinitive**

> *James wanted* **to meet the dancer**.   *He wanted* **to meet her**.
> **To see her family,** *she travelled to York.*   **To see them,** *she travelled to York.*
> *He needed* **to have hit the nails** *forcefully.*   *He needed* **to have hit them** *forcefully.*

NOTE: *to be* and all other copulative verbs cannot have either direct objects or indirect objects, but can have objective complements (as in §5.12.8).

*He had hoped **to be home** already.*	*He had hoped **to be there** already.* (**there** *not* **it**, *as a direct object would have to be in this sentence*)

5.12.10 the *object of an active present participle* or *a past participle*

*He saw the man **driving the cars**.*	*He saw the man **driving them**.*
***Having walked the dogs**, he was exhausted.*	***Having walked them**, he was exhausted.*

5.12.11 the *object of a gerund*

*They enjoyed his **playing the old violin**.*	*They enjoyed his **playing it**.*
*She smiled at his **petting the dogs**.*	*She smiled at his **petting them**.*
*Their **eating the melons** created a mess.*	*Their **eating them** created a mess.*

5.13   The *possessive case*.

5.13.1   The *possessive case* is used to show **ownership** or **possession.**
The **possessive case** is also called the *Genitive case*.

> *This is **John's** book.*   (ownership)
> *This is **Mary's** library book.*   (possession; the library is the owner)

5.13.1.1   **Because it modifies a noun, *the noun or pronoun in the possessive case*** may be termed a *possessive adjective*, because it functions in the same way that an adjective or adjective phrase modifies a substantive.

> *This is **John's** book.*   (**John's** modifies **book**)
> *The **dog's** coat is soft.*   (**dog's** modifies **coat**)

5.13.2   The *possessive case* is also used to show *source* (or *origin*), or *producer.*

> *The **tree's** leaves are green.*   (producer)
> ***England's** emigrants founded Jamestown.*   (source)
> *The **carpenter's** bookcases are beautiful.* (producer)

5.13.2.1   *Source* or *origin* may also be shown by using the noun in prepositional phrases. This is the more usual form when expression of location, direction or other adverbial characteristics is emphasized, above source or origin.

> *The pages **in the book** are yellowed.*   (emphasis on location— within this book)
>
> *The leaves **on the tree** are green.*   (emphasis on location—not on the ground)
>
> *Emigrants **from England** founded Jamestown.*   (emphasis on source, or on direction)

5.13.3   The noun in the possessive case can also be used as **an appositive.**
In this situation, the original possessive (that precedes the appositive) loses its possessive ending, relying on that of the appositive. Beginning with two phrases:

> *Mary borrowed her **brother's** book. **John** is her brother.*

with the insertion of the appositive becomes

> *Mary borrowed her brother **John's** book.*

5.13.4   *Possession* or *ownership* may also be shown by using the noun in a prepositional phrase using *of.* This is the form generally used with inanimate nouns, although it is not required.

> ***The book's** pages are yellowed.*   —   *The pages **of the book** are yellowed.*
> ***The tree's** leaves are green.*   —   *The leaves **of the tree** are green.*
> ***The rocks'** weight makes them dangerous.*   —   *The weight **of the rocks** makes them dangerous.*

5.13.4.1   Selection from **an animate group** using *of* may involve what appears to be a doubled possessive—a true possessive within an *of* prepositional phrase.
In such a situation, it is just as correct to say

> *I am **a friend of Mary's**.*

as it is to say

> *I am **a friend of Mary**.*

However, when **inanimate** objects are the ones possessed, the apparent double possessive must be used because

> *This is **a book of Mary's**.*

and

> *This is **a book of Mary**.*

have different meanings: the first sentence means the book is one from among those that *Mary* owns or possesses; the second example means the book is *about Mary, from Mary* or *by Mary*.

5.13.5   An important concept inherited from Indo-European grammar is that of **the part of the whole**. In many Indo-European languages today, that idea is still a required formation, expressed overtly; in English the concept exists and is implied, but is regularly elided. When expressed fully, it appears as the pronoun *some* followed by a prepositional phrase using *of* [*the*] governing the name of the substance or objects; when expressed partially, it has the form of the pronominal adjective *some* followed directly by the noun. Whenever the noun is an uncountable substance, it appears in the singular; if the noun is countable – divisible into distinct units – it is in the plural.

This formation is called the **partitive Genitive**.

*Do you want **milk**?*	(non-partitive: *milk as opposed to tea, water, coffee, etc.*)
*Do you want **some milk**?*	(partitive: *part of the milk on hand, or that exists*)
*Do you want **some of the milk**?*	(*full statement of the partitive concept*)
***Stars** are extremely large.*	(non-partitive: *stars as opposed to planets, moons, etc.*)
***Some stars** are extremely large.*	(partitive: *part of all the stars concerned*)
***Some of the stars** are extremely large.*	(*full statement of the partitive concept*)

5.13.6   *Formation of the possessive*

5.13.6.1   **Singular nouns add 's (*apostrophe* + s).**

> ***John's*** *book*
> *the **dog's** fur*
> *a **moment's** notice*

5.13.6.2   **Singular nouns ending in –s may add only *an apostrophe*.**
This also regularly includes nouns ending in an –s or an s *sound, having two or more syllables*, and *not accented on the last syllable*.

> ***Socrates'*** *philosophy*
> ***Moses'*** *sandals*
> ***Augustus'*** *edicts*
> *Mrs. **Helms'** children*

5.13.6.3   **Singular nouns ending in an –s or an s sound, having *two or more syllables*, and *not accented on the last syllable*** also form the possessive by adding only *an apostrophe*.

However, it is more usual for those multiple syllable nouns to appear in an *of* prepositional phrase rather than in the possessive case, particularly when the possessed noun itself does not begin with an *s* sound.

> *her **conscience'** pangs —   the pangs **of her conscience***
> *for his **reticence'** sake —   for the sake **of his reticence***

> ***NOTE***: Modern usage is not to omit the –s, in either situation given in §5.13.6.2 or §5.13.6.3. This makes formation of the possessive singular much more coherent, and far simpler.

5.13.6.4 **Plural nouns ending in –s add *only an apostrophe*.**

> *the **girls'** books*
> *those **cats'** meow*
> *on a **moments'** notice*

5.13.6.5 **Plural nouns not ending in –s add 's (apostrophe + s).**

> *the **children's** book*
> *some **oxen's** lowing*
> ***men's** shirts*

5.13.6.6 **Compound nouns *make the last word in the compound possessive*.**

> *the **Queen of Sweden's** personal banner*
> *my **mother-in-law's** cooking*
> *her **migraine headaches'** auras*

5.13.6.7 **Compound ownership phrases:**

5.13.6.7.1 **for common ownership**, *put the last word of the compound into the possessive.*

> ***Smith and Brown's** offices*
> ***Texas and Louisiana's** border* (*i.e., their common border*)
> ***Jones and Sons'** shoe sale*
> [*or **Jones and Sons'<u>s</u>** shoe sale, to emphasize the unitary nature of ownership*]

5.13.6.7.2 **for separate ownership**, *make each part of the compound owner possessive.*

> ***Smith's and Brown's** offices*
> ***Texas' and Louisiana's** border* (*i.e., their borders considered separately*)
> ***Jones' and his sons'** shoe sale*

5.13.6.8 For **other common phrases**, such as **someone else** or **everybody else**, the final word is made possessive:

> ***Someone else's** dog ran through the yard.*
> *I looked at **everyone else's** face.*
> ***Nobody else's** car was newer than mine.*

5.13.6.9 **Nouns or pronouns preceding a gerund** (taking the place of the *subject*, if the gerund were restated as a fully formed phrase) are <u>***always***</u> in the possessive case. See §7.26.1.

6 Pronouns

6.1 A *pronoun* is a word used in place of a noun.

6.2 The *antecedent* of a pronoun is the word in whose place the pronoun stands.

> *Jack drove **his** new car.*   (**Jack** *is the antecedent of* **his**.)
> *The **boy who** drove up in a new car parked it there.*   (**boy** *is the antecedent of* **who**.)

   6.2.1   A pronoun agrees with its **antecedent** in *gender*, *person* and *number*.

6.3 A pronoun's *case* depends on its own use within its particular sentence, phrase or clause.

6.4 The *forms a pronoun* can take are the same as those of nouns: *gender*, *person*, *number*, and *case*.

6.5 There are *seven general classes of pronouns*:

1.	**personal**	*I am Spartacus. The Roman army is attacking **us**.*
2.	**possessive**	*This dog is **hers**. **Its** bark is worse than **its** bite.*
3.	**relative**	*I know **whose** house this is.*
4.	**interrogative**	***Whose** house is this? **What** is its address?*
5.	**demonstrative**	***This** is my house. **That** is the new library.*
6.	**indefinite**	***Each** should do his own work, but **many** will not.*
7.	**emphatic**	*Woe is **me**! Officer, that's **him**!*

6.6 **Personal pronouns** take forms specific to whether they are **first**, **second** or **third** person and whether they are **singular** or **plural**, and to their usage within the clause.

6.6.1 Declension of the personal pronouns:
(archaic 2nd person singular is in italics)

	Singular			Plural		
	Nominative	Possessive	Objective	Nominative	Possessive	Objective
1st person	I	my, mine	me	we	our, ours	us
2nd person	*thou*	*thy, thine*	*thee*	*ye*	your, yours	you
	you	your, yours	you	you		
3rd person	he	his	him			
	she	her, hers	her	they	their, theirs	them
	it	its	it			

6.7 **Personal pronouns** take forms specific to whether they are first, second or third person.

6.7.1
The **second person** of the personal pronouns has archaic, historical forms inherited from Anglo-Saxon (and shared throughout the Indo-European family). These forms are largely limited to early Modern English literature. ["Ye" was originally only the Nominative form, but by Shakespeare's time, this distinction had become blurred.] The verb forms matching those singular-number pronouns is covered in §7.21.3.

6.8 The **compound personal pronouns** are formed by adding **–self** or **–selves** to some of the simple personal pronouns, with selection between the two determined by the number of the personal pronoun.

First and second persons of the compound personal pronouns use the possessive case of personal pronoun; third person uses the objective case.

	Singular	Plural
1st person	myself	ourselves
2nd person	*thyself*	yourselves
	yourself	
3rd person	himself	
	herself	themselves
	itself	

6.8.1
A **compound personal pronoun** is used in the predicate as a **reflexive**, referring back to the subject of the sentence:

> *I did it **myself**.*
> ***We** rebuilt the house **ourselves**.*

6.8.2
It can also be used as an **intensive**, positioned (without parenthetical **comma**'s) as an appositive to the noun it augments:

> ***I myself** did it.*
> *The house was rebuilt by **us ourselves**.*

NOTE: Formation of the **compound personal pronouns** is the one situation in Modern English in which there is still a formal difference between the singular and plural forms of the second person pronoun, *i.e.*, the difference between the singular **yourself** and the plural **yourselves**.

NOTE: **There is no such word as *hisself*, *themself*, or *theirself*,** or any other such mixed compound of **–self** or **-selves**.

NOTE: **Do *not* use a compound personal pronoun as a replacement for a normal personal pronoun!**

WRONG:	*Jack rode with Jane and **myself**.*	(**myself** *has no antecedent either to refer to or to intensify*)
CORRECT:	*Jack rode with Jane and **me**.*	

WRONG:	***Myself** and Jim wrote that program.*	(**myself** *has no antecedent*)
WRONG:	*Jim and **myself** wrote that program.*	(**myself** *has no antecedent*)
CORRECT:	*Jim and **I** wrote that program.*	

WRONG: *Jim said that Jack and **himself** wrote the program.*
(**himself** *refers to* **Jack**, *as subject of the subordinate clause*)
CORRECT: *Jim said that Jack and **he** wrote the program.*
CORRECT: *Jim said that **he himself** and Jack had written the program.*
(**himself** *is used here to intensify* **he** *and its antecedent:* **Jim**)

NOTE: **Do not use reflexives, particularly *myself*, unless you are certain that you're using them correctly.**

Misuse of ***myself*** is a particularly easy way to derail the flow of your message by making your communication sound less fully thought-through, as uneducated, or as self-centered.

6.9 ***Emphatic personal pronouns*** are pronouns used in an exclamatory, or an emphatic context. Personal pronouns in emphatic usage appear in their objective case form.

One of the classic phrases in which an emphatic pronoun is found is *"Woe is **me**!"*

Some, less than well-informed authors have tried to use this phrase as a means to ridicule grammatical rules in general. They erroneously point to this phrase in particular as an example of why traditional rules of grammar are largely outdated or just wrong. In this situation, they wrongly cite that the rule that requires that pronouns following a finite form of *to be* appear in the nominative case (resulting in the non-English *"Woe is **I**!"*).

The mistake these authors make is simply that of failing to understand the protocols of English grammar, and how its historical background explains its rules of clear and concise usage.

The use of what looks like the traditional objective case form of the personal pronoun is, in fact, a remnant of an Indo-European grammatical concept: use of a substantive in an objective case, the Accusative or the Dative, to show emphasis, interest or effect.

In Latin the *Accusative of exclamations* occurs, *e.g.*, **"Heu me miserum!"** **"Oh, unhappy me!"** Latin also uses the Dative case, the *ethical Dative*, in the phrase **"Væ mihi"** **"Woe is unto me!"**, and a few other comparable phrases. In Ancient Greek this last phrase appears as **οἴ μοι** **"Oh woe"**: μοι means **"to/for me"** which is the personal pronoun in the Dative case. Those Germanic languages (ancient and modern) retaining cases continue to use the Dative case in this usage, *e.g.*, in the German phrase *"**Weh mir!**" "**Woe is me!**"*, (literally *"Woe* [is] *unto me!"*, as mirrored so often in the English of the *KJV*: *"If I be wicked, woe unto me ..."* [Job 10:15], just as it also has *"Woe is me ..."* [Psalms 120:5]).

This usage is equivalent to what is also called the **emphatic form** of the personal pronouns in French: ***C'est moi!*** "**It's me!**" or ***Ça, c'est lui!*** "**That's** him!" (rather than the disallowed **C'est je!* **Ça, c'est il!* stated with the nominative forms).

WRONG: *Woe is **I**.*   (*pronoun in wrong case; use of nominative instead of the emphatic*)
CORRECT: *Woe is **me**.*

WRONG: *Hello! It's **I**.*   (*pronoun in wrong case; use of nominative instead of the emphatic*)
CORRECT: *Hello! It's **me**.*

In some situations, the subject and verb of the independent clause function almost as **expletives**, merely providing an introductory environment for the important part of the sentence, located in the dependent clause. In these conditions, the personal pronoun takes the case determined by its use within the dependent clause.

WRONG: *Is it **I** you're looking for?*   (*pronoun in wrong case: it is actually the dependent clause's object of the preposition* **for**, *but is also used emphatically within the context of the first phrase*)
CORRECT: *Is it **me** you're looking for?*
LITTERALLY: *Is it [the case] that you're looking for **me**?*
LITTERALLY: *You're looking for **me**, is it?*

However, whenever a phrase such as this is not an independent sentence, but a clause modified by another that is introduced by a relative pronoun, the nominative form is always the correct form to use (accompanied by agreement with that nominative form in person and number within the dependent clause: §6.13.2 and its **NOTE**s):

> *It is **he** who took the necklace.*
> *It is **they** who are painting the spare room.*
> *It is **I** who am opening the window.*
> *It is **I** whom they are talking about.*
> *It was **she** who wrote the winning essay.*
> *It's **you** who will mow the yard, not **I**.*

NOTE: When answering a phone call in which the caller asks to speak to the person who happens to have answered the call, the normal response is *This is **he**.* or *This is **she**.* These phrases are not instances of the emphatic, but are, rather, abbreviations of the full response, *This is **he*** [or ***she**] **who is speaking**. This is shown by the single-word variation on the response: ***Speaking!***
Replacing those nominative case pronouns with emphatic forms, *This is **him**.* or *This is **her**.* is an ungrammatical formation of the response.

6.10   **Personal pronouns appearing in a list** must appear in the correct order.

The standard order is *second person, third person, first person*:

> *He told Jack, "**You, Jill** and **I** will approach the hill from the southwest corner."*
> ***Jim** and **I** wrote that program, but **you** or **I** will rewrite it.*
> *The program was written by **Jim** and **me**, but they're waiting on **you** or **me** to rewrite it.*

Any other order will be taken as inattentive, uneducated, or simply rude.

6.11   **Personal pronouns *must* be used in the correct case, person and number.**

6.11.1   A personal pronoun used as a predicate nominative, or as part of a compound predicate nominative, is in the nominative case.

WRONG:	*It was **him** who called and **them** who answered.*	*(each pronoun is in the wrong case)*
WRONG:	*It was **him** that called and **them** that answered.*	*(pronouns in wrong case; poor choice of relative pronoun)*
WRONG:	*It was **him** what called and **them** what answered.*	*(pronouns in wrong case; error in choice of relative pronoun)*
CORRECT:	*It was **he** who called and **they** who answered.*	

WRONG:	***Me** and **him** went to the store.*	*(the pronouns are in the wrong case and order)*
WRONG:	***Him** and I went to the store.*	*(**Him** is in the wrong case)*
CORRECT:	***He** and I went to the store.*	

6.11.2   A **personal pronoun** appearing *within a compound*, whether *subject of a verb, direct or indirect object of a verb, as a compound object of a preposition*, or as the *appositive* of any of those, must be in the correct case.

Errors in this usage, particularly involving the first and third person *direct objects* or *objects of prepositions*, are extremely common in the lyrics of pop music because of a need to rhyme—constrained by the limitations or failures of teenage language education—and have become common among those who haven't had the training to use pronouns correctly.

One often sees a "flipping" of the cases, in which the nominative is used where the objective is required, and the objective used where a nominative is required.

WRONG:	*It's a new life for **you** and **I**.*	*(compound direct object)*
CORRECT:	*It's a new life for **you** and **me**.*	

WRONG:	*He saw us, **you** and **I**.*	*(compound appositive of the direct object)*
CORRECT:	*He saw us, **you** and **me**.*	

WRONG:	*The teacher gave **her** or **I** an assignment.*	*(compound indirect object)*
CORRECT:	*The teacher gave **her** or **me** an assignment.*	

WRONG:	***Him** and **me** went to the store.*	*(compound subject)*
WRONG:	***Me** and **him** went to the store.*	
CORRECT:	***He** and I went to the store.*	

NOTE: When in doubt as to which form to use in a compound containing a personal pronoun, restate the phrase once with each of the individual nouns or pronouns, then form the compound phrase, with the correct ordering [§6.10], to match the simple phrases:

WRONG:	***Me** and **him** went to the store.*
	1. *I went to the store.*
	2. *He went to the store.*
CORRECT:	***He** and I went to the store.*

> **WRONG:**   *He saw **you** and **I**.*
> 1. *He saw **you**.*
> 2. *He saw **me**.*
>
> **CORRECT:**   *He saw **you** and **me**.*
>
> **WRONG:**   *The teacher gave either **her** or **I** an assignment.*
> 1. *The teacher gave **her** an assignment.*
> 2. *The teacher gave **me** an assignment.*
>
> **CORRECT:**   *The teacher gave either **her** or **me** an assignment.*
>
> **WRONG:**   *It's a new life for **you** and **I**.*
> 1. *It's a new life for **you**.*
> 2. *It's a new life for **me**.*
>
> **CORRECT:**   *It's a new life for **you** and **me**.*

6.11.3   A personal pronoun having a noun in apposition appears in the correct case for the noun's usage in the phrase:

> *Coach gave **us players** a pep talk.*   (**us** *is the direct object;* **players** *is its appositive*)
> *We players needed time to cool off.*   (**We** *is the subject;* **players** *is its appositive*)
> *The cheerleaders rode with **us players**.*   (**us** *is the object of* **with**; **players** *is the appositive*)

6.11.4   A personal pronoun referring to a collective noun is singular or plural depending on whether the members of the collective act in union or severally. See §5.3.3.

6.11.5   ***They*** must have an antecedent, and should not be used impersonally:

> **WRONG:**   ***They*** *say she's a good writer.*   (**They** *has no antecedent: impersonal usage.*)
> **CORRECT:**   ***People*** *say she's a good writer.*   (**People** *gives an exact subject;* **they** *can be used after this*)

6.12   The ***possessive pronoun*** stands in place of both the possessor and the thing possessed.

> *This car is **his**.*   (**his** *stands for the phrase* **his car**)
> ***Mine*** *is the white car.*   (**Mine** *is the equivalent of* **my car**.)

6.12.1   Because the pronoun forms ***my**, **your**, **his**, **her**, **its**, **our**,* and ***their*** are used solely to modify nouns, they are also called ***possessive adjectives***.

6.12.2   **Possessive pronouns are already possessive: they NEVER require addition of the nouns' sign of possession!**

In particular: an ***apostrophe*** + *s* appearing with the third person singular personal pronoun stands for the contraction of that personal pronoun and a present tense form of the verb ***to be*** or ***to have***:

> *I'm here to get **mine** and **he's** here to pick up **his**.*   (**he's** = *he* **is**)
> ***He's** a receipt for **his** order.* [ACE: ***He's** got a receipt for **his** order.*]   (**He's** = *he* **has**)
> ***It's** time to give the bird **its** medicine; luckily, **she's** gotten better today.*
> (**It's** = *it* **is**; **she's** = *she* **has**)

Remember the forms:

> *his, her, its, your, their, whose*
> *vs.*
> *he's, she's, it's, you're, they're, who's.*
> It's just that simple.

NOTE: **There is no such word as _its'_.**

6.13 A *relative pronoun* is both a *pronoun* and a *conjunctive* (or *connector*).

It refers to a noun or noun equivalent in the (independent) main clause while joining a dependent adjective clause to its antecedent. Because they connect a dependent clause to its main clause, relative pronouns are also called *conjunctive pronouns*.

6.13.1 The **relative pronoun** has a specific role in the dependent clause: it may be the subject, the direct or indirect object, or the object of a preposition.

6.13.2 The **relative pronouns** are *which*, *that* and *what*, and the three case forms of *who*.

*She listed the people **who** had written letters.* (**who** is **subject** of the dependent clause)

*She listed the people **whose** responses were still to be written.* (**whose** is a **possessive** modifying **responses**)

*She listed the people **to whom** I will write the responses.* (**whom** is **object** of indirect-object prepositional phrase governed by 'to')

[*awkward: She listed the people **whom** I will write the responses **to**.*]

*She handed me the letters **that** hadn't been posted.* (**that** is subject of the dependent clause)

*She handed me the letters **that** I needed to post.* (**that** is the direct object in the dependent clause)

*She saw **what** she meant.* (**what** is the direct object in the dependent clause)

NOTE: As demonstrated above, whether to use *who* or *whom* is determined by the usage of the word in the **dependent phrase** in which it appears. *Who* is **the subject** of its clause; *whom* is used **wherever it is the object** either of the verb or of a preposition in its phrase; *whose* is **the possessive** within its clause, where it correlates one phrase to the other.

Although the distinction between **who** and **whom** is dying out in the colloquial, using them and getting the forms right demonstrates a higher level of skill in using the language and greater control in expressing one's thoughts.

NOTE: The verb in the dependent clause (which has *who* or *which* as the **subject** of that clause) agrees in number and person with **the antecedent** of the relative pronoun, *who* or *which*. (Agreement in number means that the relative pronouns are singular or plural, as needed.)

*She is one of the few **singers who are** able to reach those notes.*
*Credit for the book was given to **me who am** its author.*
*I cannot thank enough **them who were** here to help.*

6.13.3 Declension of the relative pronoun:

	Nominative	Possessive	Objective: Direct or Indirect Object	Objective: Object of Preposition
who	who	whose	whom	whom
which	which	whose	which	which
that	that	whose	that	which

Singular and Plural

6.13.4 The relative pronoun **who** is generally used to refer to persons, **which** is used to refer to animals and things, while **that** can refer to persons, animals, places or things.

> *This is the professor **who** teaches mathematics.*
> *The porpoise, **which** many adore, is still a wild animal.*
> *We had to move the car **that** was parked by the house.*

6.13.5 **Which**, when used as subject or direct object of a dependent clause, is used to introduce **non-limiting dependent clauses**. This type of clause adds information, but is not essential to the meaning of the sentence.

A *non-limiting dependent clause* is always set off by commas in the same way that an appositive is set apart from the sentence.

For example, in this sentence

> *The porpoise, **which** many adore, is still a wild animal.*

the dependent clause in its center merely adds information to the sentence without changing the essential meaning of the sentence:

> *The porpoise is still a wild animal.*

Whereas in this sentence

> *The porpoise **that** many adore is still a wild animal.*

the dependent clause *that many adore* is a **limiting dependent clause**, pointing out an individual porpoise and limiting the meaning of the sentence to that particular one (potentially among many), and so must be introduced by **that** rather than **which**.

NOTE: Because **which** is also used as the form of **that** when it would appear as the object of a preposition, this situation may become unclear. When this condition arises, see if the dependent clause can be removed from the sentence without changing its essential meaning. If it can be thus removed, set it off with commas to make the meaning more readily apparent.

> *The porpoise **of which** we spoke is still a wild animal.*   (*limiting dependent clause: the sentence refers to a specific animal*)
>
> *The porpoise, **of which** we spoke, is still a wild animal.* (*non-limiting dependent clause: the clause is simply giving more information*)

In speaking, these sentences will be distinguished by the fact that the commas of the second example denote slight pauses during utterance of the sentence as a whole.

NOTE: *Which* is often used instead of *that* to introduce limiting dependent clauses when using *that* would result in two of them occurring together.

> *That which you write must be clear and coherent.*　　(*limiting dependent clause: second* **that** *is replaced by* **which** *to avoid redundancy*)

6.13.6　It is stylistically better not to use **which** to refer to a complete statement. Rather, restate the idea in a more direct, more expressive way.

POOR: *He had skipped breakfast, **which** made him hungry.*
BETTER: *Skipping breakfast had made him hungry.*
BEST: *He had skipped breakfast; he was very hungry.*

6.13.7　The **compound relative pronouns** are the relative pronouns (except for **that**) compounded with *-ever* or *-soever*. (The forms using *-soever* are rather dated or stilted.)

> *I will talk to **whoever/whosoever** shows up.*
> *I will talk to **whomever/whomsoever** she sends.*
> *I will see the people **whosever/whosesoever** responses have not been answered.*
> *I will talk about **whichever/whichsoever** hasn't been mentioned.*
> *I will talk about **whatever/whatsoever** you want.*
> *I will see **whomever/whomsoever** it was sent from.*

6.14　**Interrogative pronouns** are using in asking questions. They are *who, whose, whom, which* and *what*.

> *Who drove his new car?*
> *Which do you mean?*
> *Whose was it?*

6.14.1　The form of *who* to use is determined by the case in which the requested answer would appear in the fully stated answer.

> ***Who** did Jack say has a new car?*　　(*i.e., Jack did say* **John** *has a new car.* **John** *is the* **subject**, *so* **who** *is the form required.*)
>
> ***Whom** did Jack say he would bring?*　　(*i.e., Jack did say he would bring* **Jill**. *Jill is the* **object**, *so* **whom** *is the form required.*)

6.15　**Demonstrative pronouns** (or **adjective pronouns**) indicate, point out or highlight particular persons, places or things: they are **deictic**. The demonstrative pronouns are **this** and **that**, and their plurals **these** and **those**.

> *That is his new car.*
> *She wants **these**, but he wants **those**.*
> *Here, take **this**.*

6.15.1　Whenever one of the demonstrative pronouns is used to modify a substantive, it becomes a **demonstrative adjective** (or **deictic adjective**) and is no longer labeled as a pronoun.

> *That is his car.*　　(**that** *is a pronoun*)
> *But **that** car is newer.*　　(**that** *is an adjective*)

6.16 **Indefinite pronouns** indicate, point out or highlight persons, places or things, but without indicating specific individuals. The more common indefinite pronouns include the pronominal usage of *one, none, no one, some, someone, everyone, anyone, anybody, everybody, nobody, others, another, few, less, both, many, several, all, each, either* and *neither*.

6.16.1 As is the case with demonstrative pronouns, if a word that could be an indefinite pronoun is used to modify a substantive, it is not an indefinite pronoun, but an **indefinite adjective**.

> *Both cars were parked in the yard.*   (**Both** *is an adjective modifying the subject* **cars**.)
> *Both were parked in the garage.*   (**Both** *is a pronoun and is the subject.*)
> *We saw **several doves** in the tree.*   (**several** *is an adjective modifying the direct object* **doves**.)
> *We saw **several** in the tree.*   (**several** *is a pronoun and is the direct object.*)

6.16.2 Forms of two indefinite pronouns may be used together to form a **phrasal indefinite pronoun**. As such, together they are considered to be single units. Among the most common **phrasal indefinite pronouns** are *all other, each other* and *one another*. In the possessive, only the final member is altered: *all other's, each other's* and *one another's*.

6.16.3 A pronoun that refers to a noun that is modified by an **indefinite adjective** or to an **indefinite pronoun** must reflect the implied number of the noun or of the antecedent substantive. In the example list above *one, no one, someone, everyone, anyone, anybody, everybody, nobody, another, less, each, either* and *neither* are singular; the others are treated as plurals, except that *none* is singular when meaning *no one* or *not one*, and plural when meaning *not any* (or *no*) *persons* or *things*.

> *Each car has **its** assigned parking.*
> *Every driver has been given **his** parking-stub.*
> *Neither location is close to **its** assigned parking lot.*
> *All were glad to get **their** awards; **each** rejoiced in **his** own quiet way.*

> *All is gone; **none is** left.*   [*All the pie is gone...*]
> *All are gone; **none** are left.*   [*All my friends are gone...*]
> *All are gone; **not one** is left.*   [*All my friends are gone...*]

NOTE: The phrase *each other* applies to two; *one another* is used for more than two.

> *Jill and Mary talked quietly to **each other** while the other cousins were laughing and joking with **one another**.*

7   Verbs

7.1   A verb conveys action, existence or state of being.

7.1.1   A verb can be *a single word*, a *simple verb*, or *a group of words*, called either a *verb phrase*, which is a root verb with any helping verbs, or a *phrasal verb*, which is a root verb paired with any other words required to convey the singular, desired meaning, or which taken together form an idiom.

I write	(**write** *is a simple verb*)
I shall write	(**shall write** *is a verb phrase*)
I write out the amount on each check.	(**write out** *is a phrasal verb: it is an idiom meaning to convert something into [an alternate] written form, and record it in that form*)
Pick up your socks!	(**pick up** *is a phrasal verb with several meanings, here it means* **retrieve** *or* **collect objects** *from places they are not supposed to be and put them where they do belong*)
Pick up your room!	(**pick up** *here means* **make tidy**, **clear away** *or* **put in good order** *everything that is out of place within* **your room**)
Pick out your socks!	(**pick out** *is here a phrasal verb meaning* **to choose**)

7.1.2   A verb that is used to change the meaning of the main verb with which it appears is called an *auxiliary verb*.
Auxiliary verbs are not used as simple verbs (unless they have homonyms), although they may stand alone when the main verb is elided.

*I **will go** to the park.*	(**go** *is the main verb;* **will** *is the auxiliary*)
***Can** you **help** me with this?*	(**help** *is the main verb;* **Can** *is the auxiliary*)
*Yes, I **can**.*	(**Can** *is the auxiliary;* **help** *is the elided main verb*)
*My grandmothers would **can** vegetables to provide food over the winter.*	(**Can** *here is a different verb, meaning* **to preserve in jars or cans.**)

7.2   The *root form of a verb* (the *present stem*) is found by removing the prefix-particle '*to*' from the verb's infinitive formation.

      to be   —   be
      to write —   write

The infinitive is also used as the *dictionary* or *citation* form of a verb.

7.3   English verbs are described both by *form* and by *usage*.

7.4   Verbs undergo *inflection*, which is modification in form or phrase to convey differences in usage, such as the time, the mood, the subject, etc., to which the verb applies. [See §7.16]

7.5   In *form* English verbs are divided into **weak** (or **regular**) verbs and **strong** (or **irregular**) verbs. This distinction concerns the process involved in distinguishing between the principal parts of the verb.

7.6   English verbs have **three principal parts**: **present**, **past** and **past participle**. These are used to demonstrate and detail the differences between weak and strong verbs, and among strong verbs.

>   NOTE: These are often specified as the **first person singular present indicative** [**active**], the **first person singular past indicative** [**active**] and **the past participle**.
>   However, the first definition is sometimes replaced by **the root form of the verb**, and the second principal part is simply referred to as **the past tense form**.

>   NOTE: **To be** is usually treated separately because it is the one verb whose first person singular present indicative does not match the root form, and because it has more than one form in the past tense. Full presentation of its principal parts is **am, be; was, were; been**.

7.7   **Weak** (or **regular**) verbs form their past tense and past participle **by adding –d, –ed**. Most weak verbs that end in *–t* make no change to the present form in order to form either the past tense or past participle, and so have a single form for all three principal parts.

All weak verbs have a single form for the past and the past participle, for example:

bake	*baked*	*baked*	
listen	*listened*	*listened*	
play	*played*	*played*	
set	*set*	*set*	[*single form in all principle parts*]
hit	*hit*	*hit*	[*single form in all principle parts*]
hear	*heard*	*heard*	
help	*helped*	*helped*	the old, strong forms, **help, holp, holpen**, could still be heard in the Appalachian/Ozark/Ouachita dialect until just a century ago (cf. the Prologue to **The Canterbury Tales**: "that hem hath holpen"):
pass	*passed*	*passed/past*	*passed* is used in verb constructions; *past* is used as an adjective, an adverb, a preposition, or even as a noun

7.8   **Strong** (or **irregular**) verbs form their past tense and past participle **by changing the vowel** of the root form.

Some also change adjacent consonants, or add *–d* or *–t*, or *–n* or *–ne*:

come	*came*	*come*
do	*did*	*done*
drink	*drank*	*drunk*
fly	*flew*	*flown*
lie	*lay*	*lain*
sing	*sang*	*sung*
sink	*sank*	*sunk*
swim	*swam*	*swum*

bring	*brought*	*brought*	
buy	*bought*	*bought*	
think	*thought*	*thought*	

7.9 A few verbs are weak or strong depending on the meaning. (The ability to handle these differences is one thing that shows true mastery of the language.)

lie	*lied*	*lied*	*to tell a falsehood*
lie	*lay*	*lain*	*to recline*
[lay	*laid*	*laid*	*a weak verb: to place in a flat orientation,*
			*must be distinguished from **lie-lay-lain**]*
hang	*hanged*	*hanged*	*to execute by hanging*
hang	*hung*	*hung*	*to attach to a wall, etc.*
prove	*proved*	*proved*	*normal, weak formation of past participle*
[prove	*proved]*	*proven*	*strong formation of past participle*

The strong formation of **proven** in addition to the normal, weak form **proved** is a fairly recent back-formation. **Proven** (along with its negative-sense pair, **unproven**) is best reserved for pure adjectival use; **proved** should be used in all verb formations. **Proved** should also be the form used in all legal situations.

> *In Common Law, one is innocent until **proved** guilty.*
> *The plaintiff **has proved** his case in court.*
> *But the public still believes it an **unproven contention**.*

7.10 In usage, English verbs are divided into **transitive** verbs and **intransitive** verbs. Some verbs can be used only as transitives; some can appear only as intransitives. Others can be used as either, and their usage determines which type of verb each is within a particular phrase.

7.11 **Transitive verbs require both an actor and a recipient of the action.**

7.11.1 When **the actor is the subject** and **the recipient is the direct object**, the verb is in the **active voice**.

> *Jack hit the **ball**.* (**Jack** *is the subject;* **ball** *is the direct object*)
> *Mary parked her **car**.* (**Mary** *is the subject;* **car** *is the direct object*)
> *Jill flew the **kite**.* (**Jill** *is the subject;* **kite** *is the direct object*)

7.11.2 When **the recipient is the subject**, the verb is in the **passive voice**. There is no direct object. The actor appears in a prepositional phrase governed by **by**.

> *The **ball** was hit by **Jack**.* (**ball** *is the subject and recipient;* **Jack** *is the actor*)
> *Mary's **car** was parked by **her**.* (**car** *is the subject and recipient;* **she** [**Mary**] *is the actor*)
> *The **kite** was flown by **Jill**.* (**kite** *is the subject and recipient;* **Jill** *is the actor*)

7.11.3 **The actor does not have to be stated**, yet in that case the verb is still in the passive voice because an actor is required to complete the meaning of the phrase, even if elided: the subject must have been acted upon by someone or something.

> *The **ball** was hit.* (**ball** *is the subject and recipient*)

*Mary's **car** was parked.*	(**car** *is the subject and recipient*)
*The **kite** was flown.*	(**kite** *is the subject and recipient*)

NOTE: A sentence in the passive voice is not as strong a statement as one in the active voice can be. Indeed, using the passive voice can bring an element of implied distancing of the speaker from the description or action, to the point that passive sentences can sound down-right impersonal.

Compare the first lines of the examples above and you'll see that the involvement of the speaker decreases as we move from active voice to passive voice with specified actor to passive voice without actor: each step creates an ever weaker expression.

If you compare this notoriously impersonal sentence from church newsletters

> *And a good time was had by all.*

with its active-voice counterpart

> *And we all had a great time.*

you can discern easily how the passive voice is weaker: an effect created by the passive voice's implied distance between speaker and the message itself.

7.12   ***Intransitive*** verbs **do not require a recipient of the action** for the meaning of the sentence to be complete.

*The **ball** rolled around.*	(**ball** *is the subject and actor*)
*Mary's **cat** sat under the tree.*	(**cat** *is the subject and actor*)
*The **kite** flew over the village.*	(**kite** *is the subject and actor*)

7.12.1   When a verb whose general use is as a transitive verb appears in an intransitive phrase it can be termed an ***absolute transitive*** rather than an intransitive, to distinguish aspects of its meaning.

Two such verbs are ***hit*** and ***bite***: they are used far less often as intransitives, and when they do their usage is keyed toward description of an innate transitive-action quality:

*The cat **bites** me whenever I pet her.*	(*transitive usage: subject actor with direct object*)
*That cat **bites**.*	(*intransitive usage of normally transitive verb: absolute transitive*)
*That kid **will hit** you when he's angry.*	(*transitive usage: subject actor with direct object*)
*That kid **will hit**./That kid **hits**.*	(*intransitive usage of normally transitive verb: absolute transitive*)

7.12.2   A verb that supports both usages may appear as transitive and intransitive in close proximity, or may be ambiguous:

> *She **sang** very nicely, although she **sang** only a few **songs**.*
> (*intransitive usage followed by transitive usage*)
> *When he **flew** the **plane** to Heathrow, the plane **flew** low over Windsor.*
> (*transitive usage followed by intransitive usage*)

*He **flew** into Heathrow.*	([1] *absolute transitive, with "his plane" elided*, or [2] *intransitive, because he was a passenger*)

7.13   Verbs are also classified as being either **complete** or **incomplete**.

7.14   **An intransitive verb is either complete or incomplete**. If it is incomplete, it is called **copulative**.

     7.14.1   A **complete intransitive verb** is one that makes a statement not requiring other words to complete the meaning of the sentence. Additional words may add information (about time, manner, location, duration, *etc.*) but are not required for completeness of meaning.

> *Dogs **bark**.*   *Dogs **bark** at anyone walking past the house.*
> *We **hope**.*   *We **hope** it will rain.*

     7.14.2   A **copulative intransitive verb** requires a *substantive* or an *adjective* in its predicate to complete its meaning. These additional words, called a **complement**, are specifically labeled **predicate nominatives**   (**predicate nouns**) and **predicate adjectives**.

> *He **is sick**.*   (**is** *is the copulative;* **sick** *is a predicate adjective*)
> *She **is Mary**.*   (**is** *is the copulative;* **Mary** *is a predicate noun*)
> *Melville **was** a great **writer**.*   (**was** *is the copulative;* **writer** *is a predicate noun*)
> *I **feel good**.*   (**feel** *is the copulative;* **good** *is a predicate adjective*)
> *The pie **smells delicious**.*   (**smells** *is the copulative;* **delicious** *is a predicate adjective*)

     7.14.3   A **copulative verb** links its subject and a **predicate substantive** or a **predicate adjective**. A copulative, or **linking verb**, stands between two objects that mean the same, or between an object and an adjective (or adjective phrase) that describes, limits or distinguishes the subject. (See the examples above.)

     NOTE: The most common copulative verb is **to be**. However, several other verbs are also used as copulatives; among these are **appear, become, feel, grow, look, prove, remain, seem, smell, sound, taste, turn**. whenever they express the sense of **to be** or **to become**. These predicate adjectives are often the victims of over-correction, when speakers think that, because those verbs are not forms of **to be**, they should be used with adverbs instead of adjectives.

     One of the most common mistakes that one may hear is

> *I feel **badly**.*

     the proper response to which is "Why? What's wrong with your fingers—are they numb? Or are you just clumsy?" The correct phrase is

> *I feel **bad**.*

     The degree of incorrectness can be sensed better, for example, in checking the response to the question "How does sharkskin feel?" For no one would ever say "It feels roughly."

7.15   **Transitive verbs are** (by themselves) **always *incomplete***, because by definition they require a **direct object** (also called **object complement**) or **predicate objective** (also called **objective complement**) to complete their sense.

> *The dog **chased** the **squirrel**.*   (**chased** *requires* **squirrel** [*direct object*])
> *Jack **painted** the **house**.*   (**painted** *requires* **house** [*direct object*])

*They **elected her captain**.*	(**elected** *requires* **her** [*direct object*] *and* **captain** [*predicate objective*])	

7.16   Verbs are **inflected** for

tense	*the time of the action or state*	*present, past, future, etc.*
mood	*the manner of the action or state*	*indicative, imperative, subjunctive*
voice	*whether the subject acts or is acted upon*	*active, passive*
person	*who the actor or topic is*	*first (I/we), second (you) or third (he/she/it/they)*
number	*how many actor or topics are involved*	*singular or plural*

7.17   English has **three simple tenses** and **three perfect tenses**.

7.17.1   The **simple tenses** are **present, past and future**.

7.17.1.1   The **present tense** expresses an action or state occurring at the present time:

*She **sings**.*

7.17.1.2   The **past tense** expresses an action or state completed in the past:

*She **sang**.*

7.17.1.3   The **future tense** expresses an action or state that will occur at a future time:

*She **will sing**.*

7.17.2   The **perfect tenses** are **present perfect, past perfect and future perfect**.

In these names, the word "perfect" retains its original meaning from the Latin **per + factum**: "it has (already) been thoroughly done" (*i.e.*, completed).

The perfect tenses are formed using the simple tense forms of **to have** as an auxiliary verb, plus the past participle of the main verb.

7.17.2.1   The **present perfect tense** expresses an action or state completed at the present time:

*She **has sung**.*

7.17.2.2   The **past perfect tense** expresses an action or state completed before a point in the past:

*She **had sung**.*

7.17.2.3   The **future perfect tense** expresses an action or state that will be completed before a point in the future:

*She **will have sung**.*

NOTE: An alternate, historical formation of the *perfect tenses*, preserved from Anglo-Saxon, can be found in Modern English literature, sacred and common, from its early volumes up through writings of the mid-1800's.

In literature of that period, the perfect tenses of a few, very common intransitive verbs (verbs that don't take a direct object) were often formed by using the corresponding forms of **to be** rather than those of **to have**. (In sacred literature, these often have the aura of a suggested passive sense about them, with the actor implied as the deity within the context.)

Some examples [with editorial emphasis of the specific verbs] are

> Dearly beloved, we **are gathered** here... (*Book of Common Prayer*, 1559 [1662 spelling]:
> *Solemnization of Matrimony*)

> ... and much it joys me too
> To see you **are become** so penitent.   (William Shakespeare, 1593: *King Richard III*:
> I.2)

> That which **is gone** out of thy lips thou shalt keep and perform...
> (*The Bible* [KJV, 1611]: *Deuteronomy* 23:23)

> Pray for me! I must now forsake ye; the last hour
> Of my long weary life **is come** upon me. (William Shakespeare, 1613: *King Henry VIII*:
> II.1)

> We **are met** on a great battle-field of that war.
> (Abraham Lincoln, 1863: *Gettysburg Address*)

This way of forming the perfect tenses with **to be** rather than with **to have** also appears in personal correspondence and in popular literature of that period:

> Lady B---- **is gone** a-visiting, and the rest of us **are come** to Kelly.
> (Andrew Erskine to James Boswell, Sept. 11,
> 1761: *Boswell's Correspondence with the
> Honourable Andrew Erskine, and His Journal
> of a Tour to Corsica*)

> Pray what **is become** of the Cub? Is Dodsley to sell you for a shilling, or not?
> (Andrew Erskine to James Boswell, Nov. 1,
> 1761: *ibid.*)

> "My dear Jane, make haste and hurry down. He **is come**—Mr. Bingley **is come**. He **is**,
> indeed. Make haste, make haste. ..."
> (Jane Austen, 1813: *Pride and Prejudice*)

Forming the perfect tenses of intransitive verbs in this way is still required in several modern Indo-European languages, such as German, French and Italian. For example, *I have gone* always appears in forms similar to its earlier English version, *I am gone*, in those languages: *Ich bin gegangen, je suis allé/allée*, and *[io] sono andato/andata*. (These contrast with the Spanish form, *[yo] he ido*, and with Portuguese, which has *[eu] tenho ido*. Each of these two languages uses its particular auxiliary verb meaning **to have**, as in modern English usage.)

See §7.36 for a demonstration of the formation of this usage of **to be** to form the perfect tenses.

7.17.2.4   When a main clause contains a verb in the *past tense*:

1. the verb in the dependent clause may be in the past tense, or in another tense, as clear expression of the meaning requires

> Mary **said** that she **expected** his call.
> (*general statement of on-going past condition*)

> Mary **said** that she **expects** his call.
>> (*reported current condition; implies immediacy*)
>
> Mary **said** that she **had expected** his call.
>> (*reported past condition; implies completion or termination of expectation*)
>
> Mary **said** that she **will expect** his call.
>> (*report of future condition/promise*)

2. the verb in the dependent clause will be in the present tense when it expresses a general truth because, as a general truth, its state extends into the present

   > *The ancient Greeks **knew** the earth **is** round.*

3. the verb in the dependent clause will be in the past tense when it relays a once-accepted generality now known to be false

   > *Other ancients **thought** the earth **was** flat.*

NOTE: Always use the ***present perfect*** or ***past perfect*** instead of the ***past tense*** where the sense of the phrase (usually established by adverbs) requires. This is especially important **when completion of the act is a requirement for the activity itself or for the subject's state of being.**

WRONG: *Jill **already sang**.*　　**(already** *means that the act has been completed*)
CORRECT: *Jill **has already sung**.*

WRONG: *Mary **did** not **sing** yet.*　　**(yet** *means that completion is expected*)
CORRECT: *Mary **has** not **sung** yet.*

WRONG: *Jack **did** not **finish** the test **before** the rest of us left the classroom.*
CORRECT: *Jack **had** not **finished** the test **before** the rest of us left the classroom.*

NOTE: Be aware of problems that arise while using forms of the auxiliaries *have* and *will* within the parts of a compound sentence.

WRONG: *Jill **has** always **sung** and always **will**.*　　(*implies **will sung***)
CORRECT: *Jill **has** always **sung** and always **will sing**.*

WRONG: *Mary **had** never **sung** and never **would**.*　　(*implies **would sung***)
CORRECT: *Mary **had** never **sung** and never **would sing**.*

The problem, as demonstrated in the examples, arises because the present perfect tense in the first part of the compound requires a different form of the root verb—the past participle—yet the future tense in the second part requires the verb root. Leaving out the verb itself in the second part of the compound sentence implies that the verb form in the first part applies to the second part as well. To avoid this clash of verb forms and assumptions, the needed form of the verb itself must not be left out when the forms of the two clauses are not exactly parallel.

Observe that elision in the following example is OK because the form of the verb needed for the two clauses is the same, *i.e.*, the present root of the verb *to sing* in the following example, so the second instance can be elided with no problem of inconsistency from tense mismatch.

CORRECT: *Mary never **sings**, and never **will**.*

7.17.3   The auxiliaries used in forming the future tense and the future perfect tense, ***shall*** and ***will***, as well as their original past tenses that have come to be used as modal auxiliaries, ***should*** and ***would***, formerly had rules governing which form was to be used with which of the three persons.

Except for #3, below, these rules are not stressed nowadays. However, being able to use them correctly will give your speech or writing a touch of refinement and craftsman-like control.

1.   The forms starting with ***sh-*** are limited to the first person. The forms starting with ***w-*** are limited to the second and third persons.

> *I **shall** sing.*
> ***We should** sing.*
>
> ***You will** sing.*
> ***They would** sing.*

2.   When expressing desire, determination or a promise, the two sets were reversed:

> *I promise **I will** sing.*
> ***You shall** sing!*
> ***She should** sing!*

3.   When asking a question in the first person, the ***sh-*** form is used. When asking in the other persons, use the form from rules 1. or 2. that would be correct in the answer.

> ***Shall I** sing?*   (*the answer will be* **I shall [not] sing**.)
> ***Will I** sing?*   (*the answer will be* **You will [not] sing**.)
>
> ***Should you** sing?*   (*the answer will be* **I should [not] sing**.)
> ***Would you** sing?*   (*the answer will be* **You would [not] sing**.)
>
> ***Will she** sing?*   (*the answer will be* **She will [not] sing**.)

Note that this rule does not apply when ***will*** is used, as implying ***to want to***, rather than being used in its future tense auxiliary role.

4.   In a subordinate clause, always use the ***sh-*** forms:

> *He hoped that **I should** sing.*
> *It is in your contract that **you should** sing.*
> *I promise **that she shall** sing.*

5.   In indirect discourse (indirect quotation or reported speech), use the form from #1 that is correct from the point of view of the speaker:

> *Mary says that **I will** sing.*   from   *Mary says, "**You will** sing."*
> *He said **that he should** sing.*   from   *He said, "**I should** sing."*

7.17.4   The tenses taken by the verbs within the clauses of a sentence in which those clauses form a sequence of actions or events are determined by the sense that the speaker wishes to convey about the state of those events.

Using a simple tense in the dependent, second clause says that that action is considered as a general statement, a simple event, without consideration of its start, finish or completeness.

> *She **sings** after the audience **arrives**.*
> *She **sang** after the audience **arrived**.*

> She **will sing** *after the audience* **arrives**.   (*future usage of the present tense; the future tense itself is never used in this situation*)

Using a perfect tense in the second clause says that the action in that dependent clause is considered as having been completed as a precondition for the action in the first, independent clause.

> She **sings** *after the audience* **has arrived**.
> She **sang** *after the audience* **had arrived**.
> She **will sing** *after the audience* **has arrived**.
> (or *She* **will sing** *after the audience* **will have arrived**.)
>
>   (*emphasizes the completion of* their arrival)

7.18   Verbs have ***three moods***.

7.18.1   The ***indicative mood*** expresses an action or state ***as a direct statement or question:***

> *She* **sings.**
> *She* **sings?**

7.18.2   The ***imperative mood*** expresses an action or state ***as a command or a request:***

> **Sing!**
> **Please sing!**

7.18.3   The ***subjunctive mood*** expresses an action or state as ***a doubt, a wish, a recommendation, a polite imperative or demand, or as a condition contrary to fact:***

> *If it* **be** *true that you are a singer, you will sing.*
> *If it* **were** *true that you were a singer, you would sing.*
> *If it* **be** *true that you will be a singer, you will sing.*
> *I wish I* **were** *a singer.*
> *If he* **were** *you, he would sing.*
> *She demands that she* **be** *heard.*
> *She demanded that she* **be** *heard.*
> *It is important that the song* **be** *sung.*
> *It will be important that the song* **be** *sung.*

NOTE: The **subjunctive** appears only in the ***present, present perfect, past*** and ***past perfect tenses.***

7.18.3.1   In **a wish**, use the past subjunctive or past perfect subjunctive.
In **a real or suggested condition contrary to fact**, use the present subjunctive or past subjunctive.
(There are no future tense usages in wishes or conditions contrary to fact.)

> *If the cat* **be** *in the room, I* **shall see** *it.*
> *If the cat* **were** *in the room, I* **should have seen** *it.*
> *If the cat* **had been** *in the room, I* **should have seen** *it.*
>
> *If the cat* **were** *in the room, Jill* **would feed** *it.*
> *If the cat* **had been** *in the room, Jill* **would have fed** *it.*
>
> *I* **wish** *the dog* **were** *in the house.*
> *I* **wish** *the dog* **had been** *in the house.*
> *I* **wished** *the dog* **were** *in the house.*
> *I* **wished** *the dog* **had been** *in the house.*

*I **will wish** the dog **were** in the house.*
*I **will wish** the dog **had been** in the house.*

7.18.3.2　In **a condition _not_ contrary to fact,** use the indicative instead of the subjunctive:

*If the cat **is** in the room, I **don't see** it.*
*If the cat **is** in the room, **Jill feeds** it.*
*If the cat **is** in the room, **Jill will feed** it.*

*If the cat **was** in the room, I **didn't see** it.*
*If the cat **was** in the room, **Jill fed** it.*

7.18.3.3　When **expressing necessity or command,** use either the subjunctive

*It is important that John **be** present for the exam.*	(**not** is)
*It will be vital that the cat **stay** in the house at night.*	(**not** stays)
*The law requires that your speed not **exceed** a certain limit.*	(**not** exceeds)
***Long live** the Constitution!*	(**not** lives)

or restate the issue in a verb phrase using the future tense or the future perfect tense (both using ***shall*** instead of ***will***), or a modal auxiliary.

*It is important that John **shall be** present for the exam.*	(**not** is **or** will be)
*It will be vital that the cat **shall stay** in the house at night.*	(**not** will stay)
*The law requires that your speed **shall** not **exceed** a certain limit.*	
***May** the Constitution **live long**!*	

The first two restatements imply requirement of specific future compliance rather than a need for present or future fulfillment; the final restatement is simply awkward.

NOTE:　While **ACE** preserves the subjunctive within its Anglo-Saxon, Middle English and Elizabethan heritage, use of the subjunctive has been largely lost in British, Australian and New Zealand English, where it is replaced either with the indicative form of the verb or by using ***should, would*** or ***could*** in a circumlocution.

Unfortunately, this causes a loss of accuracy, subtlety and expressiveness in the language; at times it just sounds wrong (or even illiterate), as in the third example below; at other times failure to use the subjunctive produces unclear, or incorrect, results.

The last example in §7.18.3, compared to its restatement below, shows the problem that arises from substitution of the indicative for the subjunctive. Use of the present tense *"that the song is sung"* puts fulfillment of that statement flatly within the present—indeed, limits it to the immediate present—while that example using the subjunctive does not constrain the fulfillment specifically to the present moment: the *BE* version sounds like a present command rather than a statement of an unlimited or undetermined present or future need or requirement.

Compare the following with their original forms in the examples of §7.18.3:

BE:　*If it **is** true that you are a singer, you will sing.*
BE:　*If it **was** true that you were a singer, you would sing.*
BE:　*If it **would be** true that you will be a singer, you would sing.*
BE:　*I wish I **was** a singer.*
BE:　*If he **was** you, he would sing.*

BE: *It is important that the song **is** sung.*
BE: *It will be important that the song **is** sung.*

Loss of use of the subjunctive results in unclear conditions or requires circumlocutions that destroy the expressive simplicity present in the original language, as retained in **ACE**.

Failure to use the subjunctive makes for a dialect that is less useful, and has lost a great deal of power, of precision and of linguistic sophistication.

7.19 **Transitive verbs** are used in one of **two voices: active** and **passive**.

7.19.1 When **the subject of the verb is the actor**, the verb is in the **active voice**.

Jack carried the water.
Jill accompanied Jack.

7.19.2 When **the subject of the verb is acted upon**, the verb is in the **passive voice**.

The water was carried.
Jack was accompanied.

7.19.2.1 **The actor in a passive sentence** is expressed as the object of a prepositional phrase fronted by the preposition **by**.

*The **water was carried** by Jack.*
*Jack **was accompanied** by Jill.*

NOTE: Avoid shifts between active and passive voices, particularly between clauses in the same sentence.

WRONG: *When **we walked** through the field, **a snake was seen**.* (shift to passive voice in second clause)
CORRECT: *When **we walked** through the field, **we saw** a snake.* (maintain active voice in both clauses)

NOTE: Use the active voice rather than the passive voice unless the passive voice is needed specifically: only if there is an astoundingly good reason to use it that overrides use of the active voice. This is because statements in the passive are inherently weaker in effect—and duller—than active verb phrases. See the **NOTE** with §7.11.3.

7.20 **Intransitive verbs** have **neither active nor passive voice**.

Intransitive verbs are ones that can **never** take an object.

Therefore, the concept either of performing an action (an *active* process, requiring an actor and an object) or of the subject's being the recipient of an action (a *passive* process, also requiring an actor and an object) cannot exist when using an intransitive verb.

7.21 **Verbs** have **three persons** and **two numbers**.

7.21.1 Those *three persons* and *two numbers* of verbs are the same as those of the pronouns: **first person**, **second person** and **third person**, along with **singular** and **plural numbers**. (§6.6.1)

7.21.2 Except for the **third person singular of the present indicative**, modern English no longer uses endings to convey person and number within the form taken by the verb itself. This task is performed by requiring that, where there is no substantive functioning as a subject, the personal pronoun accompany the verb to express person and number.

7.21.3 There are two archaic, Anglo-Saxon derived endings that can be found in modern English texts. However, they ceased to be used by the late 1800's, and even before then had become rare in conversation.

The second person singular, using the personal pronoun *thou*, appears with the verbal ending *–est*. Only two irregular forms occur in the present tense, *thou art* (for **you are**) and *thou hast* (for **you have**), and one form in the past tense, *thou wast* (for **you were**).

One also finds an alternate ending for the third person singular verb in formal, or purposely archaic, writing of the 1800's, largely inspired by its consistent usage in the **ACE Corpus** [§2.2.3.2]. This ending replaces the current standard *–s* with *–(e)th*, (*–th* after vowels; *–eth* after consonants). The sole exception is that there is no *–(e)th* form that replaces the word *is*.

For example, the present indicative of *to sing* is inflected thus:
(*the single required modern verb-ending is underlined; the complete archaic forms of the second- and third-persons singular is in italics*)

	Singular	Plural
1st person	I **sing**	we **sing**
2nd person	you **sing**	you **sing**
	thou sing<u>est</u>	
3rd person	he **sings**	they **sing**
	she **sings**	
	it **sings**	
	he sing<u>eth</u>	
	she sing<u>eth</u>	
	it sing<u>eth</u>	

7.22 There are several *issues of subject and verb agreement in number and/or person*:

7.22.1 Two or more singular subjects connected by *or* or *nor* take a verb in the singular.

Neither **he nor Mary** *was there.*

7.22.2 Two or more subjects of which at least one is plural, and that are connected by *or* or *nor*, have a verb that agrees in number with the noun closest to the verb.

Jill or the boys were on the hill.
Neither the boys nor Jill was at the well.

7.22.3 When one subject is positive and the other negative, the verb agrees with the positive subject.

His humor, not his gifts, was what attracted her.
Her presents and not her presence were unexpected that evening.

7.22.4 When words implying a change of number are connected to the subject by phrases such as *with*, *together with*, *accompanied by*, *as well as*, *including*, *no less than*, the number of the verb is not changed, but continues to agree with the subject itself.

> *Jill, as well as the boys, was* on the hill.
> *The boys, with Jill, were* not yet at the well.

7.22.5 When the phrase *number of* is preceded by the indefinite article *a*, it usually takes a plural verb; but when preceded by the definite article *the*, it requires a singular verb.

> *A number of chickens were* crossing the road.
> *The number of eggs* the farmer gathered *was* not large.

7.22.6 Any phrase that merely modifies the subject does not change the number of the verb.

> *One of the cats is* in the front yard.
> At least *two from my class call* me every day.

7.22.7 The verb of a sentence beginning with *there* or *here* agrees with the number of the substantive following it:

> *There is a problem* with his grammar and *there are errors* in his usage.
> *Here are problems* that must be addressed.
> *There is Jill* and *here are Jack and the boys*. (in the sense of **on one hand**, and then **on the other**)

NOTE: The words *there*, *it* (and sometimes *here*) in this type of phrasing in which they appear as introductory words without intended directional or real pronominal meaning, are called *expletives*.

> *It* is a cold morning.
> *There* was a cat in the tree.

The word *it* may also introduce a sentence in which an infinitive or infinitive phrase appears later in the sentence. In this situation, the infinitive phrase is called an *expletory appositive*, that is, an appositive of the expletive itself rather than of a noun within the sentence.

> *It is too cold to go outside.*　　　(*literally:* **It, to go outside,** is too cold.)
> *It is good to work for your community.*　　(*literally:* **It, to work for your community,** is good.)

7.22.8 For agreement of *collective nouns* with their verb see §5.3.3.

7.22.9 A subject composed of a list (two or more words joined by *and*) takes a verb in the plural.

> *Jill and Jill were* on the hill.
> *Are Jason and the other dogs* outside?

NOTE: A *compound substantive*—one in which, although the words are joined by *and*, the sense is singular—takes a verb in the singular.

> *Bread and butter is* good on a cool morning.
> *Ham and biscuits-and-gravy was* his favorite breakfast.

7.22.10 A subject composed of a list joined by **and**, and in which only one noun is expressed, still takes a plural verb.

> **A red and a blue car were** *parked outside.*
> **Red, green and a black pen were** *still on her desk after class.*

7.22.11 If a phrase governed by *of* modifies **abundance**, **plenty**, **rest**, or **variety**, or **a fraction**, the verb agrees with the noun in the *of* phrase.

> **Plenty of ice cream is** *ready.*
> **Plenty of potatoes were** *cooked and served.*
> **One half of the ice cream was** *later eaten.*
> *Only* **one sixth of the potatoes were** *not from Idaho.*

7.22.12 A noun conveying **a unit of measurement, an amount of money** or **a length of time**, although written in a plural form, takes a singular verb.

> **Two hours is** *too long a time to have to wait; even* **ten minutes is** *bothersome.*
> **Four dollars is** *a bargain for that book.*
> **Six feet is** *his height;* **two hundred pounds is** *his weight.*
> **Ten miles was** *a long walk back to the gas station.*

7.22.13 **Arithmetic expressions** take a singular verb both because numbers used as numerical concepts are taken to be singular, unique items, and because the mathematical operation is perceived as a single action.

> **Two plus two is** *four.* = *"The number two, when two is added to it, becomes four."*
> or **Two plus two equals** *four.*
> or **Two and two is** *four.*
> or **Two and two makes** *four.*
> or **Two incremented by two is** *four.*
>
> **Four minus two is** *two.*
> **Three times three is** *nine.*
> **Ten divided by two is** *five.*

7.23 There are **three Verbals**, verb forms used as other parts of speech: the **infinitive,** the **participle** and the **gerund.**

7.24 The **infinitive** is the form of the verb composed of the particle *to* placed before the root form (the *present stem*) of the verb. In a few, specific cases the *to* is elided.

NOTE: The **infinitive** is *not* "the verb, usually preceded by the preposition *to*".

Such is an incorrect definition of the infinitive. It is as incorrect as it is to say that the gerund is the verb, at the end of which the particle *ing* is attached.

In Anglo-Saxon there were two forms of the infinitive, the **uninflected infinitive** and the **inflected infinitive**.

The uninflected infinitive ended in *-an* [or *-n*] (just as the infinitives of all Modern German verbs end in *-en* [or *-n*]) and was used in those situations in which the elided infinitive is used today, that is, primarily with auxiliaries and with the modal verbs.

The inflected infinitive was a phrase consisting of what was originally the preposition *tō*, **plus the Dative case of a verb-form related to the present participle.** This inflected infinitive was used in all those situations in Anglo-Saxon in which we use the complete, unelided infinitive today: as a noun, an adjective or adverb.

The inflected infinitive was always those two words: the introductory *tō* lost its prepositional usage during that early period and the inflected infinitive was never separated from it thereafter.

During the period of Middle English, the difference between the uninflected infinitive and the verb form within the inflected infinitive was lost. However, the word *to* has never lost its role as the first, and cardinal, part of the complete infinitive.

The first word of the full infinitive, *to*, is here <u>not</u> a preposition, and has not been so for 1200 years. The word has two separate, distinct and unreunitable meanings, just as *bow*, *bow* and *bow* have three unique meanings.

7.24.1 There are *two tenses* of the **infinitive of both transitive and intransitive verbs**: the *present infinitive* and the *perfect infinitive*.

present infinitive	perfect infinitive
to be	*to have been*
to go	*to have gone*
to talk	*to have talked*
to come	*to have come*
to seem	*to have seemed*
to look	*to have looked*

7.24.2 There are also *two voices* for each of the two tenses of the **infinitives of transitive verbs**, creating four forms: the *present active infinitive*, the *present passive infinitive*, the *perfect active infinitive* and the *perfect passive infinitive*.

present active infinitive	present passive infinitive	perfect active infinitive	perfect passive infinitive
to speak	*to be spoken*	*to have spoken*	*to have been spoken*
to see	*to be seen*	*to have seen*	*to have been seen*
to write	*to be written*	*to have written*	*to have been written*
to help	*to be helped*	*to have helped*	*to have been helped*

7.24.3 The *present active infinitive* can also be called the *present infinitive*, but is usually called simply *the infinitive*.

7.24.3.1 Removing the present active infinitive's initial *to* reveals the elided infinitive, which is the *present active root*, or *dictionary form*, of a verb.

7.24.4 The **perfect active infinitive** is usually called more simply *the perfect infinitive*.

7.24.5 **Infinitives** have several usages: as *nouns*, as *adjectives* and as *adverbs*.

7.24.6 As a substantive, an **infinitive** can appear in almost any position in which any other substantive may appear.

1. **subject** of a verb — *To write well is a challenge.*
2. **predicate nominative** — *Flowers are to be seen, not to be picked.*
3. **appositive (punctuated)** — *His job, to paint houses, kept him busy.*

4. **appositive (expletory)**   *It is not easy **to paint** houses both well and quickly.*
*Don't forget your right never **to surrender**.*
5. **object** of a verb   *She loves **to dance**.*
6. **objective complement**   *See Spot **run**.*
7. **objective appositive**   *She enjoys her job, **to speak** before large groups.*

NOTE: The infinitive cannot be used as the object of most prepositions:

WRONG: *This is the train **for to go** to the museum.*   (*the infinitive **to go** cannot be used as the object of **for***)

CORRECT: *This is the train **for going** to the museum.*   (*the gerund, **going**, can be used in place of the infinitive*)

The principle two exceptions are ***about*** and ***except***.

CORRECT: *He had no option **except to relocate**.*
CORRECT: *We were **about to go** to town.*

NOTE: **All tenses and forms of *to try* require the infinitive** (rather than ***and*** plus the elided infinitive):

WRONG: ***Try and go*** *to the store, dear.*
CORRECT: ***Try to go*** *to the store, dear.*
WRONG: *I will **try and go** to the store this afternoon.*
CORRECT: *I will **try to go** to the store this afternoon.*

The incorrect version given in this second example is a compound sentence that literally means "*I **will try**, **and** I **will go*** to the store," which is a nonsense utterance: **you either try to do something or you actually do it.**

As in this example's "***try to go***", this usage of ***to try*** plus a second verb is a unitary concept and must be expressed using an infinitive as the object of ***to try***, not by a compound verb phrase.

Exposition of just how wrong (and completely illogical) the "***try and***" formation actually is can be demonstrated by restating the examples above in other tenses and tense forms, specifically in the *progressive* forms:

WRONG: *I **am trying and go** to the store now.*
WRONG: *I **am trying and going** to the store now.*
CORRECT: *I **am trying to go** to the store now.*

WRONG: *I **tried and go** to the store yesterday.*
WRONG: *I **tried and went** to the store yesterday.*
CORRECT: *I **tried to go** to the store yesterday.*

WRONG: *I **was trying and go** to the store when the phone rang.*
WRONG: *I **was trying and going** to the store when the phone rang.*
CORRECT: *I **was trying to go** to the store when the phone rang.*

7.24.7   The **subject of an infinitive** is in the objective case:

*Mary wants **Jack to write** a play.*
*Mary wants **him to write** a play.*
*He asked **her to sing**.*

7.24.8   The initial component of the infinitive, *to*, is **elided** when the infinitive modifies the object of certain verbs (the ***modal auxiliaries***, along with ***verbs of the senses***, plus ***bid***, ***help***, ***let***, ***make***, ***need***). Their being infinitives is why those truncated verb forms do not change for tense.

Some of these infinitives appear in the role of *objective complements*, in which the direct object of the sentence also appears as the subject of the infinitive. In other situations, they may appear as modifiers.

*We saw **Jack receive** the award.*	— *We saw **Jack ~~to~~ receive** the award.*
*We watched **him receive** the award.*	— *We watched **him ~~to~~ receive** the award.*
*I felt the **house move** during the quake.*	— *I felt the **house ~~to~~ move** during the quake.*
*He smelled the **skunk walk** in the door.*	— *He smelled the **skunk ~~to~~ walk** in the door.*
*You will smell the **skunk walk** in the door.*	— *You will smell the **skunk ~~to~~ walk** in the door.*
*They will make **her go** through security.*	— *They will make **her ~~to~~ go** through security.*

[**Note**, however: *They will force **her to go** through Security.*]

7.24.9   When used ***as an adjective***, the **infinitive** appears **after** the noun it modifies.

*Jack's **article to write** was about the environmental damage from oil spills.*
*She needs to know the color of the **car to buy**.*

7.24.10   When used ***as an adverb***, the **infinitive** appears after the word or phrase that it modifies.

*Jack **went to talk** to the shrimp-boat captains.*   (**to talk** *modifies the verb* **went**)
*Coby **came** over **to spend** some time with his grandparents.*
(**to spend** *modifies the verb* **came**)
*They were **happy to see** him.*   (**to see** *modifies the adjective* **happy**)

7.24.11   The **infinitive** can appear as a ***predicate appositive*** of the subject of a sentence or clause composed of *it* with a form of *to be* followed by a predicate adjective. In this usage, the infinitive functions as an appositive of the subject pronoun.

*It is too cold **to walk** to the store.*   (**It** = **to walk**)
*In big cities, it is common **to hear** several languages.*   (**it** = **to hear**)

7.24.12   If the **infinitive** refers to the same time as, or a time later than, the main verb, use the present infinitive rather than the perfect infinitive.

*He **wanted to read** the book before the semester started.*   (*the action itself, not its completion, is the important aspect*)

Use the perfect infinitive to convey a sense of completeness in the action given by the infinitive.

*He **wanted to have read** the book before the semester started.*   (*completion of the action is an important consideration*)

7.24.13 The **present infinitive** is the contemporary of the main verb; it can be used with a predicate of any tense.

> *He **wants to read** the book.*
> *He **wanted to read** the book.*
> *He **will want to read** the book.*
> *He **has wanted to read** the book.*
> *He **had wanted to read** the book.*
> *He **will have wanted to read** the book.*

7.24.14 Because the **perfect infinitive** refers to time before that of the main verb, it can be used with a predicate of any tense to impart *state before*, or *action completed before* the tense of the main verb.

> *He **wants to have read** the book.*
> *He **wanted to have read** the book.*
> *He **will want to have read** the book.*
> *He **has wanted to have read** the book.*
> *He **had wanted to have read** the book.*
> *He **will have wanted to have read** the book.*

7.24.15 The infinitive is a single logical unit, a single parsing construct and must be kept in a unified state.

NOTE: **The infinitive, although written as two or more words starting with the non-preposi-tional use of the word *to*, is always a single entity. Its parts must never be separated, or *split*, by any words.**

To is not the *sign* of the infinitive, it is *part* of the infinitive, just as *–ing* is part of the gerund and participle. That is, "*to quickly talk*" is as incorrect as "*talk-quickly-ing*" would be.

A *split infinitive* is a grammatical, syntactical and stylistic error.

A split infinitive is a grammatical error because **the infinitive is a single grammatical unit** and should be maintained as a single unit. English is primarily an analytic language, **processed in sequential order**, and units must be maintained in specific places within that order to guarantee the listener's correct identification and easy processing of mean-ing that matches the author's intent.

A split infinitive is a syntactical error because the insertion of a non-verbal unit after the initial *to* means that this small element can be heard as the infinitive particle *to*, the preposition *to* or the adverb *too*. This uncertainty raises a problem with the syntactical ordering of the phrase: it is ambiguous because it is not clear at the point of utterance which word and usage is meant; comprehension must be put on hold until the meaning become apparent. This interferes with correct and rapid analysis and understanding of word usage within phrases, sentences and paragraphs. It's syntactically disruptive.

The syntactical error can be compounded by insertion of words that can be parsed as more than one part of speech. For example, "*to further analyze*" is a multivariate prob-lem because the word "*further*" can be used as an adjective ("*further analysis*"), as an adverb ("*analyzed further*") or as a verb ("*to further our analysis*"). Using it in this infini-tive-splitting phrase (as well as using an **attributive** adverb in the **limiting** adverb position) causes parsing discord that must be resolved by the listener's backtracking to piece the sense of the statement together, which in turn can be done only after the full statement has been completely expressed by the producer and fully retained by the recipient.

A split infinitive is a stylistic error because it interrupts the flow of the phrase, forcing the listener or reader into the 'pause' position, putting part of the infinitive on hold while waiting for the adverb or adverbial phrase to get out of the way. This interferes with the message the speaker is trying to impart. The speaker might as well belch in the middle of the infinitive, for all the good either belching or a split infinitive does in maintaining a smooth flow of information: it takes time for the brain to resolve the ambiguity then patch the phrase back into a decipherable order before it can continue processing the input.

A split infinitive does **_not_** make for clearer expression, nor does it **_ever_** eliminate ambiguity. Rather, **a split infinitive muddies expression; it causes ambiguity**!

A hale infinitive will always be clearer and more concise than a split infinitive: keeping the infinitive as a unit serves to strengthen its expressive presence.

Splitting an infinitive is the equivalent of your putting an adverb between another adverb's root and its —*ly* ending:
if one would ever stoop to writing such a phrase so **unclear-*truly*-ly**.

This is because a *split infinitive* is not an infinitive issue, *per se*, but is, rather, an error in adverb placement.

Adverbs are used for their descriptive, heightening, forceful effects: **hiding the adverb within the body of the infinitive not only weakens the infinitive, but, more importantly, diminishes the effective presence of that adverb, as well.**

Failure to understand the syntactic problems caused by poor placement of adverbs appears to be a growing problem, of which split infinitives are simply the most visible manifestation.

Using **the most notorious split infinitive of our time**, we can see the ambiguity in a rewrite:

To boldly go ...   *Too boldly gone [is too rashly done] ...*

On hearing the first phrase, the listener doesn't know whether the first word is *To* or *Too* until the third word be reached, as is demonstrated in that second phrase.

Using the same egregiously split infinitive, we can see how moving the adverb into its normal place—a place of prominence—takes it from being mere acoustic filler, fluff or noise, and makes it both effective and forceful:

To boldly go ...   ➜   *To go boldly ...*

   How is one to go? **Boldly**!

Keep the rules simple: never split an infinitive.

There are only two split infinitives in all of Shakespeare's works. One is a special case, used in a sonnet for the sake of rhyme. The other is in the play *Coriolanus*, and is apparently a printer's mistake. (Shakespeare died before *Coriolanus* could be published.) There are no split infinitives in the entire *King James Version* of the *Bible*, nor in the *Book of Common Prayer* of 1559. Thus, the founding corpus of North American English demonstrates ably the power and beauty of hale infinitives.

If you feel you have an expression that requires splitting the infinitive in order to state your message, your message is already malformed and needs to be rephrased—you have probably failed to find the clearest, most effective expression. English has many ways of conveying information, so that you are never forced to use an infinitive! Indeed, infinitives are much over-used in all dialects of current English, but they are particularly too common in the over-stuffed, unexpressive, dead, boring language used in spheres of government bureaucracy, in business, and in scientific milieux—in both journals and lectures.

NOTE: **To negate an infinitive, the negating word goes _before_ the complete infinitive, that is, before the infinitive-particle, *to*.**

As Shakespeare demonstrated so ably, and memorably (*Hamlet*: III, 1):

> **To be**, or **not to be**—*that is the question.*

NOTE: **To negate the object or complement of an infinitive, the negating word goes _after_ the infinitive.**

> *It is better* **to be not idle**, *but active.*

This is an elided version of the fuller statement:

> *It is better* **to be not idle**, *but* **to be** *active.*

Examples of both ways of negating the meaning of an infinitive phrase are

> **To be aware** *is your task.*   (*positive infinitive*)
> **Not to be aware** *would be a failure.*   (*negated infinitive*)
> **To be not aware**, *but* **oblivious**, *must be avoided.*   (*positive infinitive with compound complement: a negated complement of the infinitive, then a positive complement of the same infinitive*)

The full statement of the third example, with full statement of the second, previously elided infinitive, is

> **To be not aware**, *but* **_to be_** *oblivious, must be avoided.*

The parallel use of the infinitive is correct only if it can appear in exactly the same form in each location, even if elided as in the original example; this confirms that the complement rather than the infinitive must be negated to produce a truly parallel expression.

If *not* were used to split the infinitive, the parallel would be impossible, because

> **To not be aware**, *but* **oblivious**, *must be avoided.*

in fact (as *not* here modifies the infinitive itself) means

> **To not be aware**, *but* **to not be oblivious**, *must be avoided.*

or, alternately, means

> **_Not to be_** *aware, but* **_not to be_** *oblivious, must be avoided.*

The parallel use of the split negated-infinitive creates a sentence that is the opposite of what was intended.

The location of the negating adverb in the two examples above (creating the ***negated infinitive*** and the ***negated objective complement of the infinitive***) shows how important placement is to an analytic language like English in conveying exactness of meaning: *to be understood clearly* and *not to be misconstrued* must be your ever-present goal.

NOTE: Beware of **dangling infinitives**. A dangling infinitive occurs when an infinitive appears in a sentence, but it lacks a stated or unambiguous subject, for example,

> *To avoid default, austerity measures are now in effect.*

The infinitive phrase in this sentence has no subject, either explicit or unambiguously implied. Although this sentence makes sense, one is left with the questions: *who is the actor? who is it that is **avoiding default?***

A possible subject may have been mentioned in the previous sentences, but it is not apparent in this one. A clearly stated alternative to that sentence would be

> *To avoid default, the government has now put austerity measures into effect.*

This version states clearly that it is **the government** that is acting **to avoid default**.

7.25 The **participle** is a form that **combines the properties of a verb and an adjective.** It is used like an adjective to modify a noun or pronoun, but because it is a verb, it can take an object—if the verb itself allows.

> *The dog **eating** the homework is Jason.*
> *The man **whistling** a tune is walking confidently to work.*
> *Coffee **swallowed** too fast can burn your mouth.*
> ***Having eaten** all the cake, we left the party **hoping** not to be noticed.*

Notice that the phrase must modify the substantive either attributively or in a limiting fashion. Otherwise, the form ending in *–ing* may actually be a gerund acting as an adverbial objective, as the second *–ing* form in the last example above, or in the following example.

> ***Whistling** a tune, he walked confidently to work.*

7.25.1 There are **three tenses** of the participle: the **present participle,** the **past participle,** and the **perfect participle**.

7.25.2 The **present participle** ends in *–ing*. Although called the **present** participle, its action or description occurs **at the same time as that of the main verb.**

*The dog **<u>eating</u> the homework <u>is</u>** Jason.*	(**homework** is object of **eating,** which modifies **dog**)
*The dog **<u>eating</u> the homework <u>was</u>** Jason.*	(**homework** is object of **eating,** which modifies **dog**)
***Whistling a tune,** he **walked** confidently to work.*	(**tune** is object of **Whistling,** which modifies **he**)
***Sitting** alone, I **shall listen** to the song.*	(**Sitting** modifies **I**)

7.25.2.1 The **present participle** is used with forms of *to be* to create progressive verb phrases. (See §7.28.1.)
In the progressive, the *–ing* form is not considered to be a stand-alone participle, but part of the verb itself.

*Jason, the dog, **was eating** the homework.*
*I **was sitting** alone when I listened to the song.*
*He **will be whistling** as he walks confidently to work.*

7.25.3   The **past participle** is the third principle part learned as the definition of verb forms. Its form is determined by the rules of the class of verbs to which each verb belongs, **weak** or **strong**, as described in §7.6ff. For transitive verbs, this verbal is an adjective of passive meaning; for intransitive verbs, it does not (and, by definition, cannot) have a passive meaning. As a passive form, it can be followed by the agent construction used by finite passive verbs, as used in this very sentence: [*passive verb*] **by** + **agent**. The action or description the past participle conveys is always previous in time to that of the main verb.

*The homework **eaten** by Jason is illegible.*
*The dogs **seen** in the park were chasing a soccer ball.*
*A tune **whistled** is lost to the wind.*

7.25.3.1   The **past participle** is used to create the perfect tenses of the finite verb. [§7.17.2]

*Jason, the dog, **has eaten** my homework.*	(*present perfect active*)
*The tune **had been whistled** all the way to work.*	(*past perfect passive*)
*He **will have whistled** the tune all the way to work.*	(*future perfect active*)

7.25.4   The **prefect participle** is formed from the present participle of **to have** plus the **past participle**. Its action or description occurred previous to that of the main verb.

While intransitive verbs have a single form, **transitive verbs** have two forms of the **perfect participle**: the **perfect active participle** and the **perfect passive participle**.

***Having returned** from school, I had homework.*	(*perfect participle:* **to return** *is intransitive here*)
***Having returned** her book, I worked on my math.*	(*perfect active participle:* **to return** *is transitive here*)
***Having eaten** my homework, Jason was full.*	(*perfect active participle*)
*The homework, **having been eaten,** was illegible.*	(*perfect passive participle*)
***Having been at work,** he hadn't whistled all day.*	(*perfect participle:* **to be** *is always intransitive*)

NOTE: Use a **perfect participle** instead of a **present participle** to portray action **precedent to the action of the main verb**:

WRONG: *I **arrived** in Dallas exhausted, **travelling** twenty-three hours from Naples.*
CORRECT: *I **arrived** in Dallas exhausted, **having travelled** twenty-three hours from Naples.*

7.26   **The gerund** is a verbal noun ending in **–ing**. It is also called a **participial noun** because it has the same form as the present participle; however, it is always used as a noun. Because it is a verb, the gerund may have an object, but, unlike the infinitive, it never has a subject. In essence, **the gerund is the name of an action or of a state of being**.

***Singing** is one of Mary's favorite activities.*
*However, Jack likes **running marathons**.*
*Everyone applauded her **dancing**.*

(There are cases in which a gerund has lost the connection with its original verb, has ceased to be considered a gerund and has thereby become a common noun. See the *NOTE* in §7.26.3 for more on this situation.)

NOTE: It can be difficult to distinguish between **gerunds** and **present participles**. The cardinal thing to keep in mind is that if the **–*ing*** form modifies another noun or pronoun in the sentence, it can only be a participle. For example, taking the sentence containing a gerund (which we know is a gerund because it's the name of an action):

> *Jim likes **watching television**.*

and change it to where watching is modifying the subject

> ***Watching television**, Jim is having a beer.*

we know that the second example contains a participle, rather than a gerund.

Also note the usage of the word in question within the phrase, as shown in these two examples:

> ***Having read the book,*** *I was not eager to see the movie.*
> ***After having read the book,*** *I was not eager to see the movie.*

The first sentence contains a participle, because "***Having read the book***" modifies *I*: it details a quality inherent in the subject of its sentence.

In the second example, "***having read the book***" is the object of the preposition ***After***, and because prepositions can take only nouns or pronouns as objects, that phrase must contain a gerund rather than a participle. This sentence's initial phrase is an adverbial clause telling *when* the action of the main clause happened: that phrase modifies the verb in the main clause.

One could also insert ***my*** before the gerund ***having read*** in the second sentence and the sentence would still make sense, a quality the first sentence would not maintain if ***My*** were placed before the participle with which it starts.

7.26.1 **A noun or pronoun preceding a gerund is *always* in the possessive.**
This is simply because **a gerund is a noun, and must be modified by an *adjective* or a *possessive adjective*.** The rationale behind this designation is simple. Take this sentence:

> *His dancing received international acclaim.*

The subject is the noun ***dancing***, not the pronoun, for if it were, the pronoun would have to be the nominative form '***he***':

> ***He*** *received international acclaim.*

and ***dancing*** would be reduced to a mere aside (and a participle modifying *He*, not a gerund) when introduced into such a sentence:

> *He**, dancing,** received international acclaim.*

However, using the original unmodified gerund as subject shows the true sense of the sentence:

> ***Dancing*** *received international acclaim.*

Yet this leaves us with the question "whose dancing?", which can only be answered with the possessive pronoun (also called a *possessive adjective*) modifying the noun:

> *His dancing received international acclaim.*

This shows that the common erroneous form of the statement,

> *Him dancing received international acclaim.*

is nonsense since it would require by its using the objective case form *him* that, somehow, he can be "danced", in a phrase paralleling something like "dish washing". (One could even say that, in this position, it creates the effect of "baby talk": *Him received international acclaim.*)

The same process with the gerund in the predicate shows how great an error in logic is this usage of the objective rather than the possessive. Starting with the correct form:

> *They praised his dancing.*

We see that substituting a simple pronoun for the gerund phrase,

> *They praised him,*

changes the gist of the statement. Then, inserting an *–ing* form, which turns out (again) to be the participle and not the gerund, we get the sentence:

> *They praised him, dancing.*

Using a gerund we have

> *They praised dancing,*

again begging the question, "whose dancing?" Answering this question, we arrive once again at the original, correct form of the sentence:

> *They praised his dancing.*

NOTE: This use of the possessive with the gerund must be differentiated from very a similar situation in which the present participle appears as the remnant of an otherwise elided adjective or adverb phrase:

> *They loved to watch his dancing.*   (gerund: **dancing** *is a noun, the direct object of the infinitive*)

> versus

> *They loved to watch him dancing.*   (participle: **dancing** *is used as an appositive adjective*)

> [more correctly: *They loved to watch him, dancing.*]

In this example the second sentence is actually an elided version of a past progressive phrase

> *They loved to watch him while he was dancing.*

in which the full usage of the participle is manifest and the comma is not necessary since it is not an aside or parenthetical comment, as a previous example showed.

One can hear that the first two sentences are different in intent, as the first emphasizes the act of dancing, while the second emphasizes the person who is dancing.

7.26.2   A ***compound gerund*** is formed *when a (singular) noun is placed in front of a gerund.* This noun would often be the object if the phrase were restated as, for example, a normal gerund, a finite verb or an infinitive. In those restatements the singular noun of the compound gerund appears as an object in the plural:

Stamp collecting is his hobby.	*(compound gerund)*
*He has a fervent interest in **collecting stamps**.*	*(gerund)*
*He **collects stamps** for relaxation.*	*(finite verb)*
*The crowd gathered to protest **fox hunting**.*	*(compound gerund)*
*They think it silly that people continue **to hunt foxes** while calling it sport.*	*(infinitive)*
*There's a great difference between **fox hunting** and actually **hunting foxes**.*	*(1. compound gerund; 2. normal gerund)*

7.26.3 **Gerunds**, because they are nouns, can appear in any position in which a non-gerund noun may appear.

However, unlike nouns, **gerunds cannot be used in the plural**.

1.	subject of a verb	***Writing** well is a challenge.*
2.	predicate nominative	*Life is **living**, not **dying**.*
3.	nominative appositive	*His job, **painting** houses, kept him busy.*
4.	object of a verb	*She loves **dancing**.*
5.	objective appositive	*She enjoys her job, **speaking** to large groups.*

NOTE: A gerund ceases to be considered a gerund *per se* and becomes a pure noun when it becomes more stateful and loses the verbal idea, particularly when it loses the ability to be sensibly restated, using the verbal idea in another verb form.

When this change of identity has occurred, the former gerund can appear **in the plural**, it can be preceded by an article (***the*** or ***a***); or it has become the name of ***a generalized activity***, such as *a specific art, a course of study* or *a general name for a type of exercise*.

> *A **wedding** can be a social event.*
> *Many **weddings** take place in June.*
> *This fall we will teach **reading** and **writing**.*
> *The **running** of the bulls occurs in Pamplona and many other cities.*
> *Some people still think **boxing** is a sport.*

7.26.4 Although gerunds are nouns in usage, they remain forms of the verb.

Because of this, they can take adverbs as modifiers; any such modifiers are placed according to the general rules of placement of verbs and their modifiers.

***Not going** to the wedding would be a social blunder.*	*(negating adverb)*
*This article is about **running rapidly, effectively and efficiently**.*	*(attributive adverbs)*
***By thinking quickly**, he was able to answer her questions without problem.*	*(attributive adverb)*
***By solely thinking** and **reacting**, he was able to avoid the journalist's trick questions.*	*(limiting adverb)*

7.27 The positioning of ***participles*** and ***gerunds***, within the sentence is vital to the meaning conveyed by the sentence.

NOTE: Always express the substantive that is modified by a participial phrase, or is the object of the gerund that is itself the object of a prepositional phrase. Failure to provide something for a modifier phrase to apply to creates a ***dangling modifier***.

WRONG: **Running** at full speed, the race is won.	(participle **Running** has nothing to modify)
CORRECT: **Running** at full speed, Jack wins the race.	(participle **Running** modifies **Jack**)
WRONG: **By writing** clearly, the book sold widely.	(gerund phrase **By writing** has nothing to modify)
CORRECT: **By writing** clearly, he created a book that sold widely.	(gerund phrase **By writing** modifies **he**)
CORRECT: **With its** clear **writing**, the book sold widely.	(gerund phrase **With ... writing** modifies **book**)

NOTE: **Dangling modifiers** have a close cousin in **misplaced modifiers**, in which the modifying phrase is placed away from the word or phrase modified, creating confusion as to which part of the main clause was supposed to have been affected.

WRONG: **By running** at full speed, **we** saw Jack win the race.	(gerund phrase **By running** modifies **we**)
CORRECT: We saw Jack **win** the race **by running** at full speed.	(gerund phrase **by running** modifies **win**)
WRONG: **Whistling loudly**, **we** heard him on his way to work.	(participle **Whistling** modifies **we**)
CORRECT: We heard **him** on his way to work, **whistling loudly**.	(participle **whistling** modifies **him**)

7.28   There are a further **two verbal phrase constructions** specific to the tenses: **the progressive** and **the emphatic**.

    7.28.1   **The progressive construction** is formed with the normal forms of **to be** followed by **the present participle** and exists in all six tenses.

        7.28.1.1   **Present progressive** is used for an action or state going on at the moment:

            *She **is singing**.*

        7.28.1.2   **Past progressive** is used for an action or state going on at a point in the past:

            *She **was singing**.*

        7.28.1.3   **Future progressive** is used for an action or state that will be going on at a point in the future:

            *She **shall be singing**.*

        7.28.1.4   **Present perfect progressive** is used for an action or state that started at a point before the present and is still occurring:

            *She **has been singing**.*

        7.28.1.5   **Past perfect progressive** is used for an action or state that started before some moment in the past and was still occurring at that point:

            *She **had been singing**.*

        7.28.1.6   **Future perfect progressive** is used for an action or state that will have started before some moment in the past and will be still occurring at that point:

            *She **will have been singing**.*

7.28.2 ***The emphatic construction*** is formed using the normal forms of *to do* plus the citation form of the verb, but only in **the present** or **past tense**. *To be.* is the only verb excluded from the present and past forms of the emphatic, appearing only in the **polite imperative** and the **negative imperative**.

7.28.2.1 ***Present emphatic*** is used to emphasize an action or state going on at the moment:

> She **does sing.**

7.28.2.2 ***Past emphatic*** is used to emphasize an action or state going on at a point in the past:

> She **did sing.**

7.28.2.3 **The emphatic** is used to form the normal English interrogative in the present and past tenses by inverting Subject-Verb order:

> She **sings.** — She **does sing.** — **Does** she **sing?** (present tense)
> She **sang.** — She **did sing.** — **Did** she **sing?** (past tense)

7.28.2.4 **The emphatic cannot be used to create any form in the other tenses** because it doesn't exist there.

7.28.2.5 The **interrogative form** of those tenses that do not support the emphatic construction is formed by inverting the subject and the auxiliary used in the normal formation of the tense. (The particular form of the main verb that is required by the tense is also used in the interrogative formation.)

> She **will sing.** — **Will** she **sing?** (future tense)
> She **has sung.** — **Has** she **sung?** (present perfect tense)
> She **had sung.** — **Had** she **sung?** (past perfect tense)
> She **will have sung.** — **Will** she **have sung?** (future perfect tense)

7.28.2.6 **The emphatic** is constructed only from *the finite form of to do* plus *the root form of the second verb*, and only if that verb can be used in the emphatic construction.

> **WRONG**: **Do he has** another girlfriend? (finite and root forms swapped)
> **CORRECT**: **Does he have** another girlfriend?

> **WRONG**: **Did they was/were** at the party? (finite and root forms swapped)
> **WRONG**: **Did they be** at the party? (**to be** is **never** used in the present or past tenses of the emphatic construction)
> **CORRECT**: **Were they** at the party?

7.28.2.7 **The emphatic is used to create the negative imperative of all verbs.**

> **Don't go** up the hill, Jack!
> May I call tomorrow? No, **don't call.** Just **don't.** (the actual verb may be elided if obvious)
>
> Another split infinitive? **Don't be** so inept! (**to be** does appear in the negative imperative)

7.28.2.7.1 Although the emphatic is used to create the negative imperative of the first-person plural in *BE*, in *ACE* a slightly less wordy, non-emphatic form is the normal formation.

Shall we go to town? **Don't let's go** *right now.* (BE usage)
Shall we go to town? **Let's not go** *right now.* (ACE usage)

7.28.2.8 **The emphatic is used to create the polite imperative in the positive.** This normally occurs only as a polite, but emphatic, response to a question.

Shall I write you? — *Please,* **do write.**

Should I be here then? — *Yes,* **do be** *here!* (**to be** *does appear in the polite imperative*)

May we come to visit? — *Yes, please,* **do!** (*the actual verb may be elided if obvious*)

7.29 **Auxiliary** (or **helping**) verbs are used to help establish the complete sense needed by the verb. An auxiliary verb plus the main verb creates a **verb phrase**. The most common auxiliary verbs are **be, do, have, can, may, might, must, shall, will, could, would** and **should**.

NOTE: Use of **to be** as a **copulative verb** must not be confused with its use as an **auxiliary verb**, particularly when forming the progressive tenses. These are usually quite easy to distinguish:

She **is** a **writer**.	(**copulative** verb connecting two nouns)
vs.	
She **is** writing.	(auxiliary verb in an **intransitive** verb phrase; **is writing** is a verb phrase)
vs.	
She **is writing** a letter.	(auxiliary verb in a **transitive** verb phrase; **is writing** is a verb phrase)

7.30 **Modal auxiliary verbs** are auxiliary verbs that extend the meaning or situation of the main verb that follows them: they relay aspects of the mood expressed by the subject. Modal auxiliaries express situations of

possibility or **probability**	**must, may, could, might**
permission or **ability**	**can, could, may, might**
compunction (**direction** or **suggestion**)	**must, should**
uncertainty of state, action or **consequence**	**would, should**, or
question, or **negative statement of attitude or intention**	**dare**.

All **modal auxiliaries** are **followed by the root form of the verb**, identical to the infinitive from which the initial **to** has been removed. There is also **no infinitive form for any modal auxiliary**, although non-modal verbs possessed of modal-like meanings (and used to replace modal verbs in some tenses or situations) all have infinitive forms, for example, the modal **must** and its **causative-verb** twin **to have + infinitive**.

He's gone to Veracruz; now he **must** speak Spanish.	(**modal verb**: compunction)
He's from Veracruz; he **must** speak Spanish.	(possibility: presumed certainty)
He's from Veracruz; he **might** speak Spanish.	(possibility: no presumption of certainty)
I've had lessons, and now I **can** play piano.	(ability)
The cast is off my finger, and now I **can** play piano.	(ability)
Everyone else is out of the house; now I **can** play piano.	(ability)
Everyone else is out of the house; now I **may** play piano.	(permission)
Everyone else is out of the house; now I **might** play piano.	(potential action)
With everyone else out of the house, I **would** play piano.	(potential action)
With everyone else out of the house, I **should** play piano.	(compunction)
May I go to the store now?	(permission)
The car is here; I **may** go to the store now.	(permission)
"**Might** I go to the store now?" I wondered.	(potential: uncertainty of action)

*How **dare** he take the car when was going to the store?* (questioned intention)

*He's gone to Veracruz; now he **has to** speak Spanish.* (**causative** verb: compunction)

*He's gone to Veracruz; now he **is made to** speak Spanish.* (causative verb: compunction)

*He's from Veracruz; he **ought to** speak Spanish.* (causative verb: probability)

*He's from Veracruz; he **has to** speak Spanish.* (causative verb: probability, presumed certainty)

Creation of the non-present tenses of the modal auxiliaries is irregular and for some must be done by using other verbs, verbal formations, or other conditions prevail.

modal verb	present	past	future	present perfect
can	can	can have + *past participle*	*will be able + inf.*	could have + *past participle*
could	could	could have + *past participle*	*could be able + inf.*	*(no form)*
dare	dare	dared	*(no future usage as modal)*	dare have + *past participle*
may	may	may have + past participle	*(use present tense)* *will be allowed + inf.*	might have + *past participle*
might	might	might have + *past participle*	*(use present tense)*	*(no form)*
must	must	must have + past participle	*(no form)*	*(no form)*
		had + *inf.*	will have + *inf.*	had + *perfect infinitive*
should	should	should have + *past participle*	*should be able + inf.*	*(no form)*
would	would	would have + *past participle*	*would be able + inf.*	*(no form)*

NOTE: The modal *can* always refers to *ability*; *may* always means *permission*. In standard usage, **the two are not interchangeable.**

WRONG: **Can** *I take vacation next week?* (there is no question of your <u>ability</u> to take vacation)

CORRECT: **May** *I take vacation next week?* (the question is one of <u>permission</u>)

NOTE: The causative *ought* may elide the *to* prefix of the infinitive when used in a negative phrase. This is optional; use of the full infinitive is more usual in this case, and is required in all other situations.

OPTIONAL: *I **ought not take** vacation next week.*

USUAL FORM: *I **ought not to take** vacation next week.*

7.31 ***Causative verbs*** express compelled, forced or expected actions, and as such are **the non-modal equivalent of modal verbs expressing compunction or probability**. The most important are

> **have** + *infinitive*,
> **make** + *elided infinitive* and
> **ought** + *infinitive*.

7.32   There are two ways of presenting the forms a verb may take: **conjugation and synopsis**.

7.32.1   *Conjugating a verb* means listing or stating the correct forms it takes through its *voices* [§7.11.1*ff*], *moods* [§7.18], *tenses* [§7.17], *persons* and *numbers* [§7.21]. The table this creates is called the verb's conjugation.

7.32.2   *A synopsis of a verb* means listing or stating the correct forms it takes through its *voices*, *moods* and *tenses*, *in only one person* and *number*. A synopsis is a conjugation limited to one person and number, rather than listing all forms; it normally omits all forms that do not pertain to that person, such as infinitives, participles and gerunds, as well as the imperative when second person forms are not required.

7.33   Conjugation of the intransitive verb *TO BE*

(archaic 2nd person singular in italics: replace with 2nd person plural to get the modern form)

INDICATIVE MOOD

Present Tense			Present Perfect Tense	
Singular	*Plural*		*Singular*	*Plural*
1. I am	1. we are		1. I have been	1. we have been
2. *thou art*	2. you are		2. *thou hast been*	2. you have been
3. it is	3. they are		3. it has been	3. they have been

Past Tense			Past Perfect Tense	
Singular	*Plural*		*Singular*	*Plural*
1. I was	1. we were		1. I had been	1. we had been
2. *thou wast/wert*	2. you were		2. *thou hadst been*	2. you had been
3. it was	3. they were		3. it had been	3. they had been

Future Tense			Future Perfect Tense	
Singular	*Plural*		*Singular*	*Plural*
1. I shall be	1. we shall be		1. I shall have been	1. we shall have been
2. *thou wilt be*	2. you will be		2. *thou wilt have been*	2. you will have been
3. it will be	3. they will be		3. it will have been	3. they will have been

SUBJUNCTIVE MOOD

Present Tense			Present Perfect Tense	
Singular	*Plural*		*Singular*	*Plural*
1. if I be	1. if we be		1. if I have been	1. if we have been
2. *if thou be*	2. if you be		2. *if thou have been*	2. if you have been
3. if it be	3. if they be		3. if it have been	3. if they have been

Past Tense			Past Perfect Tense	
Singular	*Plural*		*Singular*	*Plural*
1. if I were	1. if we were		1. if I had been	1. if we had been
2. *if thou wert*	2. if you were		2. *if thou had been*	2. if you had been
3. if it were	3. if they were		3. if it had been	3. if they had been

IMPERATIVE MOOD

Present	
Singular	*Plural*
be	be

VERBALS

INFINITIVES		PARTICIPLES			GERUNDS	
Present	*Perfect*	*Present*	*Past*	*Perfect*	*Present*	*Perfect*
to be	to have been	being	been	having been	being	having been

7.34 Conjugation of the transitive verb *TO SHOW*

(archaic 2nd person singular in italics: replace with 2nd person plural to get the modern form)

ACTIVE VOICE
INDICATIVE MOOD

Present Tense		Present Perfect Tense	
Singular	*Plural*	*Singular*	*Plural*
1. I show	1. we show	1. I have shown	1. we have shown
2. *thou showest*	2. you show	2. *thou hast shown*	2. you have shown
3. it shows	3. they show	3. it has shown	3. they have shown

Past Tense		Past Perfect Tense	
Singular	*Plural*	*Singular*	*Plural*
1. I showed	1. we showed	1. I had shown	1. we had shown
2. *thou showedst*	2. you showed	2. *thou hadst shown*	2. you had shown
3. it showed	3. they showed	3. it had shown	3. they had shown

Future Tense		Future Perfect Tense	
Singular	*Plural*	*Singular*	*Plural*
1. I shall show	1. we shall show	1. I shall have shown	1. we shall have shown
2. *thou wilt show*	2. you will show	2. *thou wilt have shown*	2. you will have shown
3. it will show	3. they will show	3. it will have shown	3. they will have shown

SUBJUNCTIVE MOOD

Present Tense		Present Perfect Tense	
Singular	*Plural*	*Singular*	*Plural*
1. if I show	1. if we show	1. if I have shown	1. if we have shown
2. *if thou* show	2. if you show	2. *if thou have shown*	2. if you have shown
3. if it show	3. if they show	3. if it have shown	3. if they have shown

Past Tense		Past Perfect Tense	
Singular	*Plural*	*Singular*	*Plural*
1. if I showed	1. if we showed	1. if I had shown	1. if we had shown
2. *if thou* showed	2. if you showed	2. *if thou had shown*	2. if you had shown
3. if it showed	3. if they showed	3. if it had shown	3. if they had shown

IMPERATIVE MOOD

Present	
Singular	*Plural*
show	show

VERBALS

INFINITIVES		PARTICIPLES			GERUNDS	
Present	*Perfect*	*Present*	*Past*	*Perfect*	*Present*	*Perfect*
to show	to have shown	showing	shown	having shown	showing	having shown

PASSIVE VOICE
INDICATIVE MOOD

Present Tense

Singular	Plural
1. I am shown	1. we are shown
2. *thou art shown*	2. you are shown
3. it is shown	3. they are shown

Present Perfect Tense

Singular	Plural
1. I have been shown	1. we have been shown
2. *thou hast been shown*	2. you have been shown
3. it has been shown	3. they have been shown

Past Tense

Singular	Plural
1. I was shown	1. we were shown
2. *thou wast/wert shown*	2. you were shown
3. it was shown	3. they were shown

Past Perfect Tense

Singular	Plural
1. I had been shown	1. we had been shown
2. *thou hadst been shown*	2. you had been shown
3. it had been shown	3. they had been shown

Future Tense

Singular	Plural
1. I shall be shown	1. we shall be shown
2. *thou wilt be shown*	2. you will be shown
3. it will be shown	3. they will be shown

Future Perfect Tense

Singular	Plural
1. I shall have been shown	1. we shall have been shown
2. *thou wilt have been shown*	2. you will have been shown
3. it will have been shown	3. they will have been shown

SUBJUNCTIVE MOOD

Present Tense

Singular	Plural
1. if I be shown	1. if we be shown
2. *if thou be shown*	2. if you be shown
3. if it be shown	3. if they be shown

Present Perfect Tense

Singular	Plural
1. if I have been shown	1. if we have been shown
2. *if thou have been shown*	2. if you have been shown
3. if it have been shown	3. if they have been shown

Past Tense

Singular	Plural
1. if I were shown	1. if we were shown
2. *if thou wert shown*	2. if you were shown
3. if it were shown	3. if they were shown

Past Perfect Tense

Singular	Plural
1. if I had been shown	1. if we had been shown
2. *if thou had been shown*	2. if you had been shown
3. if it had been shown	3. if they had been shown

IMPERATIVE MOOD

Present

Singular	Plural
be shown	be shown

VERBALS

INFINITIVES		PARTICIPLES			GERUNDS	
Present	*Perfect*	*Present*	*Past*	*Perfect*	*Present*	*Perfect*
to be shown	to have been shown	being shown	shown	having been shown	being shown	having been shown

7.35 **Synopsis of the transitive verb *TO WRITE* in the third person singular** (using *she* as subject):

ACTIVE	PASSIVE
INDICATIVE MOOD	
Present Tense	
she writes	she is written
Past Tense	
she wrote	she was written
Future Tense	
she will write	she will be written
Present Perfect Tense	
she has written	she has been written
Past Perfect Tense	
she had written	she had been written
Future Perfect Tense	
she will have written	she will have been written

ACTIVE	PASSIVE
SUBJUNCTIVE MOOD	
Present Tense	
if she write	if she be written
Past Tense	
if she wrote	if she were written
Present Perfect Tense	
if she have written	if she have been written
Past Perfect Tense	
if she had written	if she had been written

7.36 Synopsis of the intransitive verb **TO GO** in the third person singular (using **he** as subject), showing the former usage both of the original, Anglo-Saxon 3rd person singular ending, and of **to be** as the auxiliary verb used in forming the perfect tenses (as explained in the **NOTE** to §6.8.1.2):

older usage	*modern usage*	*older usage*	*modern usage*
INDICATIVE MOOD		**SUBJUNCTIVE MOOD**	
Present Tense		*Present Tense*	
he goeth	**he goes**	if he go	if he go
Past Tense		*Past Tense*	
he went	he went	if he went	if he went
Future Tense		—	
he will go	he will go	—	
Present Perfect *Tense*		**Present Perfect** *Tense*	
he is gone *he hath gone*	**he has gone**	*if he be gone*	**if he have gone**
Past Perfect *Tense*		**Past Perfect** *Tense*	
he was gone	**he had gone**	*if he were gone*	**if he had gone**
Future Perfect Tense		—	
he will be gone	**he will have gone**	—	

7.37 Some verbs require more exact usage in order to avoid errors or ambiguities.

7.37.1 *To lie, to lie* and *to lay*.

7.37.1.1 When *to lie* means *to emit a falsehood*, it is a regular (weak) verb, with principal parts *lie lied lied*. (Its present participle is *lying*.)
It never takes an object: it is an intransitive verb.

> Nixon **lied** while president just as he **had lied** while vice president.

7.37.1.2 If *to lie* means *to be or become recumbent*, it is a strong verb, with principal parts *lie lay lain*. (Its present participle is *lying*.)
It never takes an object: it is an intransitive verb.

> **Lie** down—just **lie** on the bed—if you're so sleepy!
> Grandpa sat in his chair; the hound **lay** under the porch.
> He **has lain** on the couch all afternoon watching television
> General Lee's plans for the Battle of Antietam were found **lying** on the ground.

7.37.1.2.1 The idiom *to lie in wait* has the same principle parts as this verb.

> Hannibal **lay in wait** for the Romans at Cannæ.
> After he **had lain in wait** for them, he sprang a trap with his cavalry.

7.37.1.3 **To lay**, meaning *to place something*, *to put something down*, or *to put something in a recumbent position*, is a strong verb, with principal parts *lay laid laid*.
It requires an object: it is a transitive verb.

> **Lay** the book down when you're ready to take the test.
> They **laid** the new carpet in the bedroom yesterday.

7.37.1.4 There are specialty usages of *to lay* meaning, among other things, *to produce* [*eggs*] or *to install* [*flooring, pavement, etc.*]. When meaning *to produce eggs*, the object (*egg* or *eggs*) can be elided, but is always understood. (When the object is elided, *to lay* is called an *absolute transitive*.)

> *That red hen **has laid** in grandpa's old hat!*
> > (*i.e., That red hen **has laid her eggs**...*)
>
> *The old hen has stopped **laying**.*   (*verbal of verb **to lay***)
> *Quail and pheasant build their nests, and **lay**, on the ground.*

   NOTE: Using *to lie* and *to lay*, there are two ways of saying the same thing:
> **Lie** *on your back on the exam table.*
> **Lay yourself** *on your back on the exam table.*

   WRONG: **Lay** *on your back on the exam table.*   (**to lay** *requires a direct object*)

7.37.1.5 *To lay* is used as the root verb to form several idioms of specific meaning. These usages are all transitive, requiring a direct object, because of the transitive nature of the root verb, *to lay*.

To lay low means *to kill, to overcome violently, to overpower*, or, in a slightly different sense, *to cause to fall, to knock down, to force into a prostrate position*.

> *We will attack them and **lay our enemies low**.*

To lay waste means *to destroy, to devastate*.

> *The invaders entered the ancient city and quickly **laid it waste**.*

When the same idiomatic situation stated with those phrases changes into a state of being, the verb *to lay* is replaced with its partner verb *to lie*.

> *In the aftermath of the earthquake and tsunami, northern Japan **lies waste**; her coastal communities **lie low**.*

7.37.2 *To sit* and *to set*.

7.37.2.1 *To sit* means *to be positioned* (*in a chair, on a plot of land, etc.*), and is a strong verb, with principal parts *sit sat sat*. It is an intransitive verb, and is never used transitively.

> *Grandpa **sat** in his chair; the hound lay under the porch.*
> *The old courthouse **sits** in the middle of the town square.*

7.37.2.2 *To set* means *to position something*.
It is a strong verb, with principal parts *set set set*.

> *Grandpa **set** his coffee by his chair before sitting down this morning.*
> *They **will set** the old general's statue in front of the courthouse that sits downtown.*

To set is normally a transitive verb. However, it has a limited number of intransitive uses:

> *The sun rose at 7:24 AM and **will set** at 7:05 PM today.* (*here, parallel with* **rise**, **set** *is a verb of apparent celestial movement*)

> We finally **set off** before dark.
> We must **set out** on the trip before sunset. (*a synonym for* **to leave**, **set** *out and* **set** *off are phrasal verbs here*)

> They cooked the juice too long and it would not **set**. (*a cooking term, used of gelatin, jellies, chocolate, etc., as a synonym for* **to jell**)

NOTE: There are two ways of saying the same thing using **to sit** and **to set**:
> **Sit** *on the exam table.*
> **Set yourself** *on the exam table.*

WRONG: **Set** *on the exam table.* (**to set** *requires an object*)
WRONG: **Sit yourself** *on the exam table.* (**to sit** *cannot take an object*)

7.37.3 *To come, to do, to give, to go,* and *to see.*

7.37.3.1   These five verbs often cause trouble because errors in their forms are heard so commonly that many assume that those errors are the normal forms. Such errors are far more common in certain dialect areas: rock music, hip-hop and rap are some of the predominant sources of errors. The most common misstep is use of the past form instead of the past participle in creating the perfect tenses, except for *to see*, in which the situation is reversed.

The principle parts of those verbs are

come	*came*	*come*
do	*did*	*done*
give	*gave*	*given*
go	*went*	*gone*
see	*saw*	*seen*
[cf. saw	*sawed*	*sawed]*

> We **have come** to seize your berry, not to praise it.
> She **did** it the way she **has done** it before.
> He **gives** at the office, as we **gave**, and as many **have given**.

7.37.4 *To rise* and *to raise.*

7.37.4.1   **To rise** means **to lift (oneself), to move (oneself) to a higher position**, and is a strong verb, with principal parts *rise rose risen*.
It is an intransitive verb, and is never used transitively.

To arise is a variant of **to rise**, with the same meaning and usage, and has the same transitions in its principal parts: *arise arose arisen*.

> Grandpa **arose** from his chair; the hound, however, **did** not **rise**, but stayed under the porch.
> The new courthouse **is rising**, floor by floor, in the middle of the town square.

7.37.4.2   **To raise** means **to lift (something), to move (something) to a higher position**. It is a weak verb, with principal parts *raise raised raised*.

> Grandpa **raised** his coffee to take a sip before rising to go back into the house.
> They **will raise** the old general's statue in front of the new courthouse rising downtown.

NOTE: *To raise* must be distinguished from its homophone *to raze*, which means *to tear down*. Often this distinction is signaled by following *to raze* by the phrase *to the ground*, a prepositional phrase used as a **cognate object** [§5.12.6], although this does raise the issue of redundancy.

> *They finally **raised** the Union Flag over Caen several weeks after Bomber Command unwisely **had razed** the Norman city **to the ground.***

NOTE: There is a pair of phrases that differ between *ACE* and *BE* in the choice between *to raise* and *to rise*.

In *ACE*, one asks for a *pay raise* (based on a verbal form), while in *BE* one seeks a *pay rise* (a noun phrase). This is an interesting situation in how it reveals a basic, different relationship between employer and employee in the two different regions.

The *ACE* usage is based in an active, more straightforward formation: *Hey, boss, raise my pay!* The *BE* usage is formulated from a passive idea (something that happens beyond the speaker's pale of influence, with *pay–rise* paralleling *sun–rise*), and must be stated indirectly, with circumlocution: *Sir, mightn't I receive a rise in my pay?*

7.37.5 *To imply* and *to infer* are often confused.

7.37.5.1 *To imply* means *to suggest* or *to hint*. Most often it carries an air of the suggester's being indirect or veiled about saying exactly what they mean. It appears as the verb in an independent clause that is almost always followed by a dependent clause explaining what that suggestion or hint is.

> *He **implied that** Grandpa was too young just to sit all day on the porch.*
> *The article **implies that** the judge wanted the new courthouse built on the edge of town.*

7.37.5.2 *To infer* means *to form an idea based on something someone else has said*. It is often the report of one's grasping facts beyond the immediate, exact words of the report. It appears as the verb in an independent clause, which is almost always followed by a dependent clause explaining what that idea is.

> *I **inferred that** he meant that Grandpa should be more active.*
> *We **infer that** the judge might own some land out there on the edge of town.*

7.37.6 *To lend* and *loan*.

7.37.6.1 *To lend* is a verb; *loan* is a noun.

WRONG: *Can you **loan** me your truck?*
CORRECT: *Can you **lend** me your truck?*

WRONG: *She **loaned** me enough money for lunch.*
CORRECT: *She **lent** me enough money for lunch.*

"*To loan*" is possibly—marginally—acceptable, but only when dealing specifically with stated quantities of cash, although it will be easier to remember the fact that *loan* **is a noun** by simply adhering to the rule as stated.

Using *loan* in this way is as illogical (and as ugly) as using the noun *repayment* as a verb: *I will gladly **repayment** you next Tuesday.*

VERY POOR: *Loan me twenty bucks.*
CORRECT: *Lend me twenty bucks.*

> *Friends, Romans, countrymen, **lend me your ears!***
> William Shakespeare (*Julius Caesar*: III, 2)

(Notice that Shakespeare did **not** write … *loan me your ears!*)

7.37.7 A *long-lived* mistake in pronunciation.

7.37.7.1 ***Long-lived* is combination of an adjective**, *long*, **followed by a noun**, *life*, with an appended *–d* to create a verbal phrase on the model of the formation of past participles: it means ***having a long <u>life</u>*** or ***having had a long <u>life</u>***. This phrase is not, nor has it ever been, the past participle *lived* preceded by an adverb, *long*: **it has never portrayed the construct** [*something*] *lived* [*a*] *long* [*time*].

This construction process is the same by which we have other *phrasal adjectives* such as ***long-legged*** meaning ***having long <u>legs</u>*** (and not meaning that [*something*] "*legged*" [*a*] *long* [*time*]), as well as other phrases such as ***broad-shouldered***, meaning ***having broad shoulders*** and not the nonsensical "[*something*] ***shouldered broad**[-ly]*".

Long-lived is the pronunciation-adapted spelling of that phrase, ***long-lifed***, where the *f* has taken on the sound, and then the spelling, of a *v*. Its second syllable therefore rhymes with that in the phrase ***long hived***, **not** with that in the phrase ***long hid***.

Long-lived could as well be written ***long-life'd*** or ***long-lifed***. This spelling shows that noun's correct pronunciation.

7.37.8 The *ain't* problem.

7.37.8.1 *Ain't* is always an error; use it only for characterization.

WRONG: *No, your pizza **ain't** ready yet!*
CORRECT: *No, your pizza **isn't** ready yet!*

7.37.8.2 When a request for affirmation is placed at the end of a sentence, the *first person singular of the present tense* has produced two incorrect forms.
Ain't I is definitely incorrect.
Aren't I means literally *are I not*. This is inherently **ungrammatical nonsense**.
Am I not is the only construction that is correct, and is the only one of these three that should **ever** be used.

WRONG: *I'm supposed to bring the food, **ain't I**?*
WRONG: *I'm supposed to bring the food, **aren't I**?*
CORRECT: *I'm supposed to bring the food, **am I not**?*

Alternatively, the sentence-final interjection of the example could just be reworded:

ALTERNATE: *I'm supposed to bring the food, **right**?*
CANADIAN: *I'm supposed to bring the food, **eh**?*

7.37.9 *Got* versus *gotten*.

7.37.9.1 Indicative of its linguistic seniority, **ACE** has retained *gotten*, the original past participle of the verb *to get* alongside the newer form, *got*, while **BE** has lost the older form.

This is unfortunate for **BE** because the two forms do not have the same meaning: use of both forms allows for shades of meaning no longer so easily supported in *Englandic*.

While *got* means "in one's possession" in both dialects, in **BE** it can also mean "just came into the possession of" if surrounded by the appropriate adverbs, a meaning that **ACE** reserves cleanly for **gotten** standing alone.

ACE: *I've **got** a new car.*   (*i.e., I* **possess** *a new car.*)

  BE: *I've **got** a new car.*

ACE: *I've **gotten** a new car.*

  BE: *I've [recently/just/just now] **got** a new car.*

7.38 The **principle parts** of common, important or troublesome verbs:
*Verb forms followed by * are rare or older forms.*

Present Tense	Past Tense	Past Participle	notes
abide	abode	abode	
arise	arose	arisen	
awake	awoke, awaked	awoken	
be [am, is, are]	was/were	been	
bear	bore, bare*	born, borne	*to bring forth, to give birth to*
bear	bore, bare*	borne	*to carry*
become	became	become	
begin	began	begun	
behold	beheld	beheld, beholden	
bend	bent, bended	bent, bended	
bereave	bereft	bereft, bereaved	
beseech	besought	besought	
bet	bet [*BE*: betted]	bet [*BE*: betted]	
bid	bid	bid	*to offer an amount, or enter a bid*
bid	bade	bidden	*to command, order, or summon*
bite	bit	bitten	
bleed	bled	bled	
bless	blessed, blest	blessed, blest	
blow	blew	blown	
break	broke, brake*	broken	
breed	bred	bred	
bring	brought	brought	
build	built, builded*	built, builded*	
burn	burned, burnt	burned, burnt	
buy	bought	bought	
cast	cast	cast	
catch	caught	caught	
chide	chided	chided, chidden	
choose	chose	chosen	
clothe	clothed, clad	clothed, clad	
come	came	come	
cost	cost	cost	
creep	crept	crept	
crow	crowed, crew*	crowed	
dare	dared, durst*	dared	
deal	dealt	dealt	
dig	dug, digged*	dug, digged*	
dive	dived	dived	
do	did	done	
drag	dragged	dragged	
draw	drew	drawn	

Present Tense	Past Tense	Past Participle	notes
dream	dreamed, dreamt	dreamed, dreamt	
drink	drank	drunk	
drive	drove	driven	
drown	drowned	drowned	
dwell	dwelled, dwelt	dwell, dwelt	
eat	ate	eaten	
fall	fell	fallen	
feed	fed	fed	
feel	felt	felt	
fight	fought	fought	
find	found	found	
fit	fit [*BE*: fitted]	fit, fitted [*BE*: fitted]	
flee	fled	fled	
fling	flung	flung	
flow	flowed	flowed	
fly	flew	flown	
forbid	forbade	forbidden	
forget	forgot	forgotten	
forsake	forsook	forsaken	
freeze	froze	frozen	
get	got	got, gotten [*BE*: got]	[see §7.37.9]
gild	gilt, gilded	gilt, gilded	
give	gave	given	
go	went	gone	
grind	ground	ground	
ground	grounded	grounded	*of an electrical circuit & allegorically*
grow	grew	grown	
hang	hung	hung	*to mount on a wall, etc.*
hang	hanged	hanged	*to execute by hanging*
have	had	had	
hear	heard	heard	
heave	heaved, hove	heaved, hove	
help	helped, holp*	helped, holpen*	
hew	hewed	hewed, hewn	
hide	hid	hidden	
hit	hit	hit	
hold	held	held	
hurt	hurt	hurt	
keep	kept	kept	
kneel	kneeled, knelt	kneeled, knelt	
knit	knit, knitted	knit, knitted	
know	knew	known	
lay	laid	laid	[see §7.9]
lead	led	led	

Present Tense	Past Tense	Past Participle	notes
leap	leaped, leapt	leaped, leapt	
leave	left	left	
lend	lent	lent	
let	let	let	
lie	lay	lain	*to recline* [see §7.9]
lie	lied	lied	*to speak falsely*
light	lighted, lit	lighted, lit	
load, lade*	loaded, laded*	loaded, laden	
lose	lost	lost	
loose	loosed	loosed	
make	made	made	
mean	meant	meant	
meet	met	met	
mow	mowed	mowed, mown	
pay	paid	paid	
pen	penned, pent	penned, pent	*to enclose*
prove	proved	proved	
put	put	put	
quit	quit [*BE*: quitted]	quit [*BE*: quitted]	*BE* forms used in *ACE* for *'to leave'*
raise	raised	raised	
rap	rapped, rapt	rapped, rapt	
read /ɹiːd/	read /ɹɛd/	read /ɹɛd/	
rend	rent	rent	
rid	rid	rid	
ride	rode	ridden	
ring	rang	rung	
rise	rose	risen	
rive	rived	rived, riven	
run	ran	run	
saw	sawed	sawed, sawn	
say	said	said	
see	saw	seen	
seek	sought	sought	
seethe	seethed, sod*	seethed, sodden*	
sell	sold	sold	
send	sent	sent	
set	set	set	
shake	shook	shaken	
shave	shaved	shaved, shaven	
shear	sheared, shore	sheared, shorn	
shed	shed	shed	
shine	shined, shone	shined, shone	
shoe	shod	shod	
shoot	shot	shot	

Present Tense	Past Tense	Past Participle	notes
show	showed	shown, showed	
shred	shred	shred	
shrink	shrank	shrunk, shrunken	
shut	shut	shut	
sing	sang	sung	
sink	sank	sunk	
sit	sat	sat	
slay	slew	slain	
sleep	slept	slept	
slide	slid	slid, slidden	
sling	slung	slung	
slink	slunk	slunk	
slit	slit	slit	
smite	smote	smitten	
sow	sowed	sowed, sown	
speak	spoke, spake*	spoken	
speed	sped	sped	
spend	spent	spent	
spill	spilled	spilled, spilt	
spin	spun	spun	
spit	spit, spat	spit, spitten*	
split	split	split	
spoil	spoiled, spoilt	spoiled, spoilt	
spread	spread	spread	
spring	sprang	sprung	
stand	stood	stood	
stave	staved, stove	staved, stove	
steal	stole	stolen	
stick	stuck	stuck	
sting	stung	stung	
strew	strewed	strewn, strewed	
stride	strode	stridden	
strike	struck	struck, stricken	
string	strung	strung	
strive	strove	striven	
swear	swore	sworn	
sweat	sweat, sweated	sweat, sweated	
sweep	swept	swept	
swell	swelled	swelled, swollen	
swim	swam	swum	
swing	swung	swung	
take	took	taken	
teach	taught	taught	
tear	tore	torn	

Present Tense	Past Tense	Past Participle	notes
tell	told	told	
thrive	thrived, throve	thrived, thriven	
throw	threw	thrown	
thrust	thrust	thrust	
tread	trod	trodden	
wake	woke	woken, waked	
wax	waxed	waxed, waxen	
wear	wore	worn	
weave	wove	woven	
wed	wed	wed, wedded [*BE*: wedded]	
wet	wet	wet [*BE*: wetted]	
win	won	won	
wind	wound	wound	
wind	winded	winded	*to work to exhaustion*
work	worked, wrought	worked, wrought	
wring	wrung	wrung	
write	wrote	written	

8 Adjectives

8.1 An adjective modifies a substantive by describing or limiting it.

8.2 A *simple adjective* is one of a single word; a *complex adjective*, is made up of two or more words and appears as either *an adjective clause* or *an adjective phrase*.

> She sings **beautiful** *songs.*　　　　(**beautiful** *is a simple adjective*)
>
> **The** *music* **on the piano** *is* **by Brahms**.　(**The** *is a simple adjective;* **on the piano** *is an adjective phrase;* **by Brahms** *is an adjective phrase modifying an elided predicate adjective*)
>
> **Those** *songs* **that she sings** *are lovely.*　(**Those** *is a simple adjective;* **that she sings** *is an adjective clause;* **lovely** *is a simple adjective used as the predicate adjective*)

8.3 *Proper adjectives* are those derived from a proper noun; or they are proper nouns used as adjectives.
They are regularly capitalized.

> *The foreign students were enjoying the* **American** *experience.*
> *The* **German** *students especially enjoyed* **Texas Southern** *and* **Tex-Mex** *food.*

8.4 *Common adjectives* are all those adjectives not within the class of **proper adjectives**.

8.5 **Adjectives** have three separate usages: *attributive*, *appositive* and *predicate*.

8.5.1 *Attributive adjectives* are direct modifiers of the substantive.
Simple attributive adjectives precede the substantive; *complex attributive adjectives* almost always follow it.

> *She sings* **beautiful** *songs.*　　　(**beautiful** *is an attributive adjective*)
> *The music* **on the piano** *is by Brahms.* (**The** *and* **on the piano** *are attributive adjectives*)
> *Those songs* **that she sings** *are lovely.* (**Those** *is an attributive adjective;* **that she sings** *is an attributive adjective phrase*)

8.5.2 An *appositive adjective* explains or gives more information about the substantive immediately before it; it is not regularly a limiting usage.
The **appositive adjective** or *compound appositive adjective*, is set off from the rest of the sentence by commas.

> *The writer,* **well-versed***, will sell many books.*
> *She could not resist the stranger,* **tall***,* **black-haired** *and* **handsome***.*

8.5.3 The difference between a **attributive participial adjective phrase** and an **appositive participial adverb phrase** is a structural stylistic difference, and can be determined by the presence of off-setting commas.

> *The writer* **sitting on the floor** *read a selection from her work.*　(*attributive*)
> *The writer,* **sitting on the floor***, read a selection from her work.*　(*appositive*)

In the first example, the adjective phrase is one that limits the writer: for example, she is the one sitting on the floor rather than the one standing by the window. Thus, it is an **attributive** usage: it establishes a distinguishing attribute.

The second example describes the writer as sitting on the floor rather than, say, sitting at a desk or standing. Because it simply adds more information about its substantive, this is an **appositive** usage.

> *NOTE:* This phrase, ***sitting on the floor***, could also be an adverbial phrase of location in which (and modifying the verb), if moved into the first position in the sentence.

8.5.4   ***Predicate adjectives*** complete the meaning of the predicate by conveying modification of the subject.

*The film was **boring**.*	(**boring** *completes the predicate* **was**, *and describes the subject* **film**)
*The music on the piano is **by Brahms**.*	(**by Brahms** *completes the predicate* **is**, *and limits the subject* **music**)
*Those songs that she sings are **lovely**.*	(**lovely** *completes the predicate* **are**, *and describes the subject* **songs**)

8.5.4.1   **Predicate adjectives** follow *copulative* (or *linking*) *verbs*, such as *to be* and *to become* (and other verbs, such as *to grow* or *to turn*, when used in the sense of **to become**); they are also used with ***verbs of the senses***. See §7.14.2 for more information on use of predicate adjectives instead of adverbs with this class of verbs.

> *NOTE*: **It is an error to use an adverb where a predicate adjective is required**:

WRONG:	*That smells **nicely**.*	(**nicely** *is an adverb that expresses the capacity, degree or effectiveness with which one smells*)
CORRECT:	*That smells **nice**.*	
WRONG:	*I feel **well**.*	(**well** *is an adverb whose use expresses the manner, mode or ability of* **to feel**)
CORRECT:	*I feel **good**.*	(*this is the usual meaning of the error use of* **to feel well**)
QUESTIONABLE:	*I feel **well**.*	(*a secondary meaning of* **well** *as an adjective, meaning* **no longer ill**, **in good sorts**, **calm**, **safe**, *viz.,* "*Ten o'clock and all is well!*")

8.6   ***Descriptive adjectives*** expose the nature of a substantive ***by revealing something about its qualities***.

> *She sings **beautiful** songs.*
> *We saw a **boring** film.*
> *The **famous** artist gave a **stellar** performance.*

8.7   A *limiting* or *definitive adjective* points out or emphasizes a substantive but ***does not express a quality***.

> *She sings **many** songs.*
> *We saw **that** film.*
> *The **The** Parthenon is in Athens.*

8.8   **Limiting** or **definitive adjectives** include

1.   the ***pronominal adjectives*** (*pronouns used as adjectives*):
   demonstrative adjectives ← **demonstrative pronouns** [§6.15],
   indefinite adjectives ← **indefinite pronouns** [§6.16] and
   possessive adjectives ← **possessive pronouns** [§6.12]

2.   the *numeral adjectives*:
   cardinal numbers [§8.10.2] and
   ordinal numbers [§8.10.3]

3.   the *articles*:
   definite articles [§8.11.1] and
   indefinite articles [§8.11.3]

8.9 **Pronominal adjectives** are distinguished from **demonstrative pronouns** [§6.15], **indefinite pronouns** [§6.16] and **possessive pronouns** [§6.12] by the presence of the substantives that the pronominal adjectives modify.

That dog is a Boxer.	(*pronominal adjective: demonstrative adjective*)
That is a Boxer.	(*demonstrative pronoun*)
Each dog should have its vaccinations.	(*pronominal adjective: demonstrative adjective*)
Each should have its vaccinations.	(*indefinite pronoun*)
Her dog has a new leash.	(*pronominal adjective: possessive adjective*)
Hers has a new leash.	(*possessive pronoun*)

8.9.1 The **pronominal adjectives**, *this, that* **and** *these, those*, are **the only adjectives inflected for number.**

   His are **these four** dogs.
   This cat was in the tree; ***those*** cats were on the veranda.

NOTE: When used with *kind of*, as well as with *kind*, *this, that, these* and *those*, must agree in number with the substantive governed by *of*.

   His dogs are ***this kind of*** dog. (*all are a single variety of dog*)
   His dogs are ***these kinds of*** dogs. (*each is its own variety of dog*)
   That kind of cat was in the tree.
   Those kinds of cats were on the veranda.

8.10 *Numeral adjectives* express number, count or numerical order.

8.10.1 **Numeral adjectives** occur as *cardinal* or *ordinal numbers.*

8.10.2 *Cardinal numbers* are the **counting numbers**.

   He has **four** dogs.
   One cat was in the tree; **two** cats were on the veranda.

8.10.2.1 *Simple cardinal numbers* are the numbers appearing in single words: *one, two, seven, sixteen, twenty,* [*a*] *hundred*, etc.

8.10.2.2 *Compound cardinal numbers* are those made up of two or more simple numbers: *twenty-one, two hundred thirty-seven*, etc.

In compound cardinal numbers between twenty-one and ninety-nine, and ending in a number less than ten, a hyphen is inserted between the multiple of ten number and the final number: *twenty-one, sixty-four, ninety-nine*, etc.

NOTE: There is an old way of forming the compound cardinal (and ordinal) numbers between twenty-one and ninety-nine, inherited from Anglo-Saxon and found now only in older literature and in nursery rhymes. In this, the units number (one through nine) is placed before the tens unit. Rather than being hyphenated, the two parts are connected by *and*.

> *Four and twenty blackbirds were baked in a pie.*
> *They would not pay a farthing over two and fifty guineas.*
> *He had not yet reached his five and thirtieth year.*

8.10.2.3 **Rules for formatting numbers.**

1. Do not begin a sentence with digits.
   > *Twenty-four people have confirmed they will be at the reception.*

2. Write all dates, address numbers, phone numbers and page numbers in digits.
   > *Columbus reached the New World on October 10, 1492.*
   > *The doctor's office is at 1234 Main Street, New Consternation, Texas 75555.*

3. Spell out the number if it can be done in only one or two words.
   > *The kindergartner can already count to a hundred.*

4. When several numbers appear near each other in a text, write them all in digits.
   > *The lottery numbers picked last night were 42, 15, 34, 22, 41, 8.*

5. Except in cases of emphasis, a person's age is spelled out.
   > *He was only 34.*
   > *She earned her master's degree before she was twenty-two.*

6. Individual occurrences of the hour of day are spelled out.
   > *I couldn't sleep again; awaking at three in the morning makes for a long, long day.*
   > *The crew always broke for lunch at exactly eleven-thirty.*
   > *Our test is scheduled for 12:45 to 1:30 next Monday.*

7. Spell out any currency amount that is less than or equal to the principal, working unit of that currency, i.e., don't use "$1" for *one dollar*, "£1" for *one pound*, or "€1" instead of *one euro*. (The unit will vary with time and changes in currency valuation.)

   When an ordinal plus a currency unit are combined into a phrasal adjective, the number and currency unit will be hyphenated.

   > *When I was young, thirty-five cents would buy enough candy to make me sick, and one dollar would have put me in hospital.*

   > *At that time, twelve pence made a shilling, twenty shillings, a pound; and one could still get a filling breakfast for six pence, a good lunch for nine pence, or a four-course dinner for one shilling. So, he ate quite well on a food budget of eighteen shillings a week from his £4'6'2½ [four-pound, six-shilling, two-and-haypny] pay packet.*

8.10.3 *Ordinal numbers* detail the **numerical rank,** or the **order in which** the modified substantive occurs.

> *That is the fourth dog he has adopted.*
> *The first cat climbed the tree; the second and third cats just sat on the veranda.*

The regular formation of **ordinal numbers** is by adding *-th* to the cardinal form of a number ending in a consonant, and *-eth* to a cardinal ending in a vowel, with a final *-y* changing to *-i* before adding *-eth*.

However, several of the lowest ordinal numbers are irregular:

one	***first***	(*from the Anglo-Saxon **fyrest**, **fyrst**, meaning **foremost, far-est [forward]**)*
two	***second***	(*from the Latin **secundus** meaning **following**)*
three	***third***	(*from the northern dialect **þirdda**, form of the regular Anglo-Saxon **þridda**)*
four	***fourth***	(*regular*)
five	***fifth***	(*from the Anglo-Saxon **fifta**)*
six	***sixth***	(*regular*)
seven	***seventh***	(*regular*)
eight	***eighth***	(*irregular: drops final **–t** before **–th**)*
nine	***ninth***	(*irregular: drops final **–e** before **–th**)*
twenty	***twentieth***	(*regular, with change of **–y** to **–i**)*

All other ordinals are formed regularly, based on the above, unitary ordinals whenever necessary.

8.10.3.1   In compound ordinals, made from compound cardinals (those that are combinations of numbers), only the final number is made ordinal: the precedent numbers remain in their cardinal form:

twenty	***twentieth***
twenty-one	***twenty-first***
thirty-two	***thirty-second***
one hundred ten	***one hundred tenth***
two thousand [and] three	***two thousand and third***

8.10.3.2   When position modifiers, such as ***first***, ***next***, ***last***, ***opening***, ***closing***, ***starting***, ***initial*** or ***final***, are **used with numeral adjectives**, they are placed before the numeral, rather than after it.

> *Print the **first ten** and the **last five** pages.*
> *We missed the **opening five** minutes of the performance.*
> *He was very friendly the **next two** times we met.*

The only exception is when the position modifier is part of the noun phrase itself.

> *She conducted the **final three** readings of the score.*
> versus
> *She conducted the **three final readings** of the score.*

where ***final reading*** is a noun phrase with a specific, special meaning of its own.

8.10.3.3   **When used with adjectives in the comparative or superlative degree,** the number comes before the adjective when dealing with a unified group.

> *These were the **ten largest earthquakes** recorded in California.*
> (the **largest earthquakes** *is a unified data group*)
> *These were the **largest ten earthquakes** recorded in California.*
> (**ten earthquakes** *is just a group of that number, whatever the internal data says about each one in the set*)
> *We heard the **loudest five minutes** of the performance.*
> (**five minutes** *is a unified block of time*)
> *We heard the **five loudest minutes** of the performance.*
> (the **loudest minutes** *could be any minute within all the minutes of the performance, taken 1, 2, 3, 4 or 5 minutes at a time*)

8.10.4   **Aggregate nouns**, such as **dozen**, **gross**, **head**, **hundred** and *score*, are always singular, even when preceded by an adjective expressing a number greater than one.

> **Four score** and seven years ago…
> He sold **eighteen head** of cattle today.
> I need to buy only **three dozen** eggs, but she needs **three gross**.

8.10.5   In a **compound adjective** that is created using **a numeral and a noun expressing a unit**, hyphenate the phrase and **always use the singular form of the noun.**

> Mine is a **four-dog** house.   [*Note*: **never** "*dogs*"]
> Cook the pie in a **275-degree** oven.   [*Note*: **never** "*degrees*"]
> She was surprised to have delivered a **nine-pound** baby.   [*Note*: **never** "*pounds*"]
> They left today on a **six-year** assignment.   [*Note*: **never** "*years*"]
> He jumped a **five-foot** fence then took a **half-mile** run.   [*Note*: **never** "*feet*"]

8.10.6   When an **explicitly plural adjective** modifies a noun, the noun should be plural. (This appears to be an erroneous over-application of §8.10.5.)

> We drove **thirty miles**.   (not **mile**)
> He jumped **five feet**.   (not **foot**)

8.11   The **articles** are **attributive adjectives** that occur as either **definite** articles or **indefinite** articles.

8.11.1   **Definite articles** indicate specific persons, places or things.
The noun modified by a definite article can be either singular or plural.

> **The** dog is a Boxer.   (*definite article* [singular])
> **The** dogs are Boxers.   (*definite article* [plural])
> These are **the** dogs that we're adopting.   (*definite article* [plural])

8.11.2   **Definite articles** point out persons, places or things with less particularity or exclusivity, or with less idea of directionality (or location or placement) than do the **demonstrative adjectives:**

> **The** dog is a Boxer.   (*definite article*)
> **This** dog is a Brussels Griffon.   (*demonstrative adjective: particularity or placement*)
> **That** dog is a Dachshund.   (*demonstrative adjective: differentiation or directionality*)

8.11.3   **Indefinite articles** indicate individual, non-specific persons, places or things. These are indefinite, but solo, members of a larger substantive class. The noun modified by an indefinite article is always singular.

> A dog is **a** mammal.   (**dog** is one member of the class of **mammals**)
> A Boxer is **a** dog.   (**Boxer** is one member of the class of **dogs**)

NOTE: The form **a** is used before all consonant sounds; **an** is used before a word beginning with a vowel sound. The important factor is sound, not letter, as shown in the third and fourth examples, below.

> A dog is **a** mammal.
> **An** elephant is also **a** mammal.

*Parsley is **an** herb.*	(*the initial **h** in **herb** is silent in **ACE***)
BE: *Parsley is **a** herb.*	(***BE** pronounces the initial **h**: /hɜːb/ or /hɘːb/, but ignores the **r***)
*A unicorn is **an** imaginary animal.*	(***unicorn** does not begin with a vowel sound, but with a 'hidden' **y** sound: /ˈjuː.nɪ.ˌkɔɹn/*)
*She has written **a** historical novel.*	(*other than in **BE** dialect, **historical** does not begin with a vowel: it is incorrect to use **an***)

NOTE: There is **no plural indefinite article** in English that is formed on the base of the singular. This usage, when required, is usually supplied by the word *some*, or the phrase *some of* [*the*]:

> **Some** *dogs are Boxers.*
> *These are **some of the** dogs we are adopting.*

NOTE: The **indefinite article** *a* is **omitted before** *hundred* when it is preceded by another approximating (indefinite-state-implying) modifier, except in order to emphasize the number itself:

> *This happened **a hundred-fifty** years ago.*   (*use **a** when no emphasis is desired*)
> *This happened **one hundred-fifty** years ago.*
> (*use **one** to emphasize the exact number*)
> *This happened **some hundred-fifty** years ago.*
> (*omit **a** when approximation is provided by another word*)
> *This happened **some one hundred-fifty** years ago.*
> (*insert **one** to emphasize the number, even with approximation*)

8.11.4   When **two or more substantives**, usually connected by *and*, **indicate only one person, place or thing**, place the article only before the first substantive.

> ***A musician, teacher and alderman,** he was appreciated by the entire community.*
> ***The mayor and candidate for governor,** Mr. Smith, will speak at the ladies' luncheon.*

8.11.5   When **two or more substantives**, usually connected by *and*, **indicate individual persons, places or things**, place the article before each substantive.

> ***A priest, a rabbi and a minister** attended the meeting.*
> ***The Mayor and the candidate for governor** were speaking at the ladies' luncheon.*

8.11.6   When **two or more adjectives** modify **one person, place or thing**, place the article only before the first adjective.

> | *He wanted **the blue, red and yellow bird.*** | (*one bird*) |
> |---|---|
> | ***A fast and fuel-efficient** car was on her wish-list.* | (*one car*) |

8.11.7   When **two or more adjectives** modify **individual persons, places or things**, and only the first substantive is stated, place the article before each adjective.

> | *He wanted **the blue, the red and the yellow bird.*** | (*three birds: first two elided*) |
> |---|---|
> | ***A fast and a fuel-efficient** car were on her wish-list.* | (*two cars*) |

8.11.8   After group-defining substantive phrases, such as *kind of* or *sort of*, the indefinite article should *not* be used.

> | *What **sort of** painting were you looking to buy?* | (***NOT**: **sort of a** painting*) |
> |---|---|
> | *He was just that **kind of** man.* | (***NOT**: **kind of a** man*) |

8.12 **Adjectives have three *degrees of comparison*: *positive*, *comparative* and *superlative*.**

8.12.1 The ***positive degree*** is the basic form of the adjective, used as attributive adjective, as predicate adjective or in equal comparisons.

> *That is a **small** dog.*
> *A **large** house is **expensive** to maintain.*
> *Her **young** son is still learning to walk.*
> *Her son is **as young as** my sister.*

8.12.2 The ***comparative degree*** expresses a difference between two persons or things, a difference that is more (or higher, *etc.*) or less (or lower, *etc.*) than the same adjective in the positive degree. Adjectives in the comparative degree are used as attributive adjectives, as predicate adjectives or in unequal comparisons. [For formation: §8.13]

> *That is a **smaller** dog than mine.*
> *A **larger** house is **more expensive** to maintain than is a **less roomy** one.*
> *She has two sons; the **younger** one is still learning to walk.*
> *Her son is **younger than** my brother.*

8.12.3 The ***superlative degree*** expresses the extreme outcome when comparing three or more persons or things. Adjectives in the comparative degree are used as attributive adjectives or as predicate adjectives. [For formation, see §8.13]

> *That is the **smallest** dog that I have ever seen.*
> *The **largest** house is the **most expensive** to maintain.*
> *She has three sons; the **youngest** one is still learning to walk.*
> *Among her children, her son is **the youngest**.*

8.12.4 The **comparative and superlative degrees** are either used attributively, before the word they modify; or they can be used in abbreviated circumstances, in which the actual noun they modify is either replaced by the word "***one***" or (more often in the case of the superlative) by being elided.

> *That is the **smallest** dog that I have ever seen.*
> *That is the **smallest** one that I have ever seen.*
> *That is the **smallest** that I have ever seen.*
>
> *Of all dogs, **the smaller** ones are **better** for apartment living.*
> *Of the two dogs, the **smaller** [one] was **better** in my cramped apartment.*

In these usages, it is best to remember that the adjective forms remain adjectives, and the original, modified word has simply been elided: in Modern English, those forms are not treated as substantives.

8.13 ***Degrees of comparison*** are formed from the positive-degree form of an adjective in one of three ways.

8.13.1 A shorter adjective (of one or two syllables) in the **positive degree** may be extended by *–er* for the **comparative degree** and *–est* for the **superlative degree**. This formation always has the meaning ***more*** and ***most*** in the comparative and superlative; for ***less*** and ***least***, the second way of forming comparisons (using ***less*** or ***least*** explicitly) must be used.

Adjectives ending in *–y* in the positive change it to *–i* before adding the endings.

Single final consonants whose pronunciation would be affected by a following *–e* have those consonants doubled to preserve their original pronunciation.

small	*smaller*	*smallest*
big	*bigger*	*biggest*
young	*younger*	*youngest*
pretty	*prettier*	*prettiest*

8.13.2   In creating the **comparative degree** and the **superlative degree**, the **positive degree** of polysyllabic adjectives can take the prefixes *more* and *most*, for increasing degrees of comparison, or *less* and *least*, for decreasing degrees of comparison.

This construction with *more* and *most* is largely (but not always) limited to multi-syllable adjectives, with the comparative of most monosyllables provided by formation using the –*er* and –*est* endings. Whenever unsure, check a dictionary.

The construction with *less* and *least* can be used with any adjective.

positive	comparative	superlative
costly	*costlier*	*costliest*
costly	*more costly*	*most costly*
costly	*less costly*	*least costly*
sandy	*sandier*	*sandiest*
sandy	*less sandy*	*least sandy*
grateful	*more grateful*	*most grateful*
handsome	*more handsome*	*most handsome*

8.13.3   **Inflected forms**, most inherited from Anglo-Saxon, are used for a very few adjectives, *e.g.,*

positive	comparative	superlative	notes:
[*aft*]	*after*	*aftmost/aftermost*	
bad	*worse*	*worst*	
[*east*]	*eastern*	*eastmost/easternmost*	
far	*farther*	*farthest/farthermost*	
fore	*former*	*foremost/first*	
[*forth*]	*further*	*furthest/furthermost*	
good	*better*	*best*	
[(*be-*)*hind*]	*hinder*	*hindmost/hindermost*	
[*in*]	*inner*	*inmost/innermost*	
late	*later/latter*	*latest/last*	
little	*less/lesser*	*least*	"small amount"
little	*littler*	*littlest*	"small in stature"
many/much	*more*	*most*	
near	*nearer*	*nearest/next*	
[(*be-*)*neath*]	*nether*	*nethermost*	
[*north*]	*northern*	*northmost/northernmost*	
old	*older/elder*	*oldest/eldest*	
[*out*]	*outer/utter*	*outmost/outermost utmost/uttermost*	
[*south*]	*southern*	*southmost/southernmost*	
top	—	*topmost*	

positive	comparative	superlative	notes:
under	*[under]*	*undermost*	
[up]	*upper*	*upmost/uppermost*	
[west]	*western*	*westmost/westernmost*	

8.13.4 **Use the comparative degree in comparing two objects; use the superlative when comparing more than two.**

> *She has two children; the **younger** one is still learning to walk.*
> *She has three children; the **youngest** one is still learning to walk.*

8.13.5 When using the **comparative degree in distinguishing a noun from the class to which it belongs**, use *other*, *else*, or another distinguishing adjective with the name of the class. Otherwise, the distinguished noun is left within the class and you produce an error in logic.

> **WRONG**: *Jack is **taller than any soldier** in his unit.* (**Jack** *is left within the class of* **soldiers in his unit***, which makes this statement illogical, as it says that he's taller even than himself.*)

> **CORRECT**: *Jack is **taller than any <u>other</u> soldier** in his unit.*

8.13.6 On both stylistic and logical grounds, **adjectives expressing absolute qualities—** *absolute adjectives***—should not be compared** because people, places and things can only approach such an absolute: the absolute either applies or it doesn't—there is no *almost* expressible in simple adjective forms.

An easy way to tell which adjectives are included in this group is to ask if something of that quality can be more of that quality, or less of that quality: if it can't, that adjective is an absolute. For example, one cannot be **more alive**—one is either alive or not. People can be **more lively**, but they cannot be **more alive** or **less alive**, nor **more dead** or **less dead**.

Some of these **absolute adjectives** are *alive, dead, endless, finished, infinite, perfect, unique*, as well as **all geometric adjectives**: *square, triangular, perpendicular, parallel, etc*. They cannot be used in the comparative or superlative, but use circumlocution of the adjective or rephrasing using nouns or participles to avoid errors of logic.

> *They used a plumb-line to get the door frame **more nearly square**.*
> *The first window is **less nearly square** than the second.*
> *The first window is **farther from square** than the second.*
> *Although the others' paintings were considered masterful, hers was thought **the most nearly perfect**.*
> *Although the others' paintings were considered masterful, hers was thought **the closest to perfection**.*
> *The apprentice didn't have sufficient time, and his work was considered **the farthest from finished**.*

There are times when usages of these adjectives must be analyzed, to discover how words that were originally absolutes are now used colloquially in ways other than in their original, literal meaning:

> *After running the second marathon I was **deader** than I could remember ever being.*

actually means

> *After running the second marathon I was **more exhausted** than I could remember ever being.*

8.13.7 Use *fewer* and *fewest* when dealing with countable units; use *less* and *least* when dealing with substances or uncountable amounts, including the word ***number***. (In mathematical terms, use *fewer* and *fewest* when dealing with integers; *less* and *least* when dealing with floating point [*real*] numbers.)

> *She has two children; she has **fewer** to feed than Mary does.*   (*i.e., fewer than two children*)
>
> *Jack has a pail of water, but Jill has **less**.*   (*i.e., Jill has less [uncountable] water*)
>
> *Mary has three pails of water, but Max has **fewer**.*   (*i.e., fewer [countable] pails*)

Use the alternate comparative *lesser* when dealing with the word ***number*** itself.

> *Mary has three pails of water, but Max has a **lesser number**.*

8.14 **Comparisons involving adjectives that are in the same degree of comparison** (positive or comparative)   use specific conjunctions.

8.14.1 **Positive comparisons** of adjectives in the **positive degree** use the *as ... as ...* construction.

> *The blues are **as smart as** the reds.*
> ***As smart as** the blues [are], the reds talk faster.*
> *He was **as tall as** his brother.*
> *Jill was **as graceful as** Mary.*
> *She reads **as fast as** he.*

NOTE: Do not omit the second *as* in a comparison; it makes the phrasing complicated and potentially confusing.

WRONG: *She is **as old, if not older than he**.*
CORRECT: *She is **as old as he, if not older**.*

8.14.2 **Negative comparisons** of adjectives in the **positive degree** use the *so ... as ...* construction.

> *The reds are **not so smart as** the blues.*
> ***Not so smart as** the blues [are], the reds just don't listen well.*
> *He was **never so tall as** his brother.*
> *Jill was **not so graceful as** Juliet.*
> *He did **not** read **so fast as** they.*

8.14.3 **All comparisons** of adjectives in the **comparative degree** use *than* as their conjunction.

> *The blues are **smarter than** the reds.*
> ***Not smarter than** the blues [are], the reds have to make things up.*
> *He was **taller than** his brother.*
> *Jill was **more graceful than** Jack.*
> *She wrote **faster than** he.*

NOTE: A personal pronoun following the trailing *as*, or *than* **must be in the correct case**. The correct case can only be determined from the sense of the full statement, or the aim of the speaker or writer.

That last example in each of the previous three sections has the nominative forms, *he* or *they*, because the meaning of each sentence is actually:

> She reads **as fast <u>as he does</u>**.   *She reads **as fast <u>as he</u>***.
> He did **not** read **so fast <u>as they did</u>**.   *He did **not** read **so fast <u>as they</u>***.
> She wrote **faster <u>than he did</u>**.   *She wrote **faster <u>than he</u>***.

It is an **error** to use the objective case in these situations:

> *WRONG*: *She is* **as old as him**.
> *WRONG*: *She did* **not** *read* **so fast as them**.
> *WRONG*: *She wrote* **faster than him**.

The importance of choosing the correct case is made more obvious by considering a pair of statements such as:

> *She likes you more **than me***.
> *She likes you more **than I***.

These two examples have different meanings, meanings made clear only from the case of the final word. Completing the examples with the elided portions of the second clause (and with those elided portions underlined) reveals the extent of the difference between the meanings of the two sentences.

> *She likes you more **than <u>she likes</u> me***.
> *She likes you more **than I <u>like you</u>***.

8.15   Be aware of the effect the ordering of adjectives can have on the meaning, or implications, of phrases. In general, the more specific or important the adjective, the closer it should be to the substantive it modifies.

> *She went shopping for **white women's shoes***.
>   *(confusing; color is the more specific aspect, but implies racism)*
>
>   *or*
>
> *She went shopping for **white, women's shoes***.
>   *(less confusing, but requires diligence to impart meaning)*
>
>   ***vs.***
>
> *She went shopping for **women's white shoes***.
>
> *He wanted a fuel-efficient, fast truck.*
>   *(the order establishes his desire for (1) a **truck**, (2) a **fast** one among all **trucks**, and (3) a **fuel-efficient** one from among the set of **fast trucks**)*
>
>   ***vs.***
>
> *He wanted a fast, fuel-efficient truck.*
>   *(placing **fast** earlier in the sequence of adjectives puts it into a position of emphasis, stating that his desire is for a **fast** one from among the set of all **fuel-efficient trucks**)*

9 Adverbs

9.1 **Adverbs** are words used **to add details, emphasis** or **interest** to **words, phrases** or **sentences.**

It is the **placement of adverbs** that determines which other unit is the target of their modification. In establishing effect and effectiveness when using adverbs, proper placement is paramount.

9.2 **Adverbs** modify

1.	**verbs**	*She writes wonderfully.*
2.	**verbals**	***To write well*** *is a challenge.* ***Not to write well*** *is less so.* ***Sleeping soundly***, *she was difficult to awaken.* ***Eating sloppily*** *was just something that youngster always did.*
3.	**adjectives**	*Some flowers are* ***very beautiful.***
4.	**other adverbs**	*He was hammering* ***very loudly.***
5.	**conjunctions**	***Just before*** *they got home, the storm had blown past.*
6.	**prepositions**	*The cat was* ***almost up the tree*** *when the bird flew away.*
7.	**phrases**	***Not its location***, *but its citizens, made the village prosperous.* ***Not in its location***, *but in its citizens' devotion, lay the village's prosperity.*
8.	**clauses**	*Genius can breathe freely* ***only where the very air is liberty.***
9.	**sentences**	***Frankly***, *it was easier than I had feared it would be.* ***Luckily***, *the train had not yet left.*

9.2.1 **Adverbs** may also be analyzed as modifying larger constructs—clauses, or even the rest of the sentences in which they are used. This often requires changes to the exact placement of the adverb in order to impart clear intention of its usage.

9.3 There are **four general classes of adverbs**: *attributive, limiting, negating* and *sentential*.

9.3.1 The class of an adverb is determined by its placement.

- **Attributive** adverbs *follow* the complete unit they modify.
- **Limiting** and **negating** adverbs *precede* the complete unit they modify.
- **Sentential** adverbs *precede* the complete unit they modify, **or** are placed internally in an adverbial appositive position. They can function as conjunctions when placed between clauses. In either position they are normally offset from the rest of the sentence by commas. **Sentential adverb clauses** in sentence-first position may also be called *adverbial absolutes*.

9.3.2 **Negating adverbs** are limited to the word *not*, and its compound *never* "*not ever*".

9.4 An **adverb** can be a **single word**, a **phrase**, or a **clause**.

Adverbial phrases in which the words must be processed as a single unit—phrases that lose their original meaning when broken into individual parts—are called *phrasal adverbs*.

Phrasal adverbs are always **attributive** and follow the complete unit they modify.

However, when moved into sentence-first position they often become **sentential ad-verbs** (or **_adverbial absolutes_**), modifying the entire sentence rather than any specific part of it.

She writes **wonderfully**.	(**wonderfully** _is a simple adverb modifying the verb_)
She writes **with enthusiasm**.	(**with enthusiasm** _is an adverbial prepositional phrase modifying the verb_)
She writes articles **one by one**.	(**one by one** _is a phrasal adverb modifying the predicate phrase_ **writes articles**)
She writes **because she loves it**.	(**because she loves it** _is an adverbial dependent clause modifying the verb_)
She has learned to write **wonderfully**.	(**wonderfully** _is a simple adverb modifying the infinitive_)
Wonderfully, _she has learned to write._	(**wonderfully** _is a simple adverb modifying the entire sentence_)
She has learned to write her name **wonderfully**.	(**wonderfully** _is a simple adverb modifying the infinitive phrase_ **to write her name**)
She has learned to write **with enthusiasm**.	(**with enthusiasm** _is an adverbial prepositional phrase modifying the infinitive_)

9.5   Adverb placement.

9.5.1   **Attributive adverbs, and all adverbial phrases, go _after the non-adverbs they modify._ _Negating adverbs_ [§9.5.4], _limiting adverbs_ [§9.7] and _sentential adverbs_ [§9.8]** precede the modified or go into specific positions.
Non-phrase adverbs always precede <u>the adverbs</u> they modify.

> _While being worked on, the Gettysburg Address was a **closely guarded** secret._
> _While being worked on, the Gettysburg Address was **guarded closely**._

These examples demonstrate the difference between **limiting adverbs** and **attributive adverbs**. In the first sentence, the limiting adverb _closely guarded_ specifically delimits the meaning of _guarded_. In the second sentence, by its placement, the adverb _closely_ merely states an attribute —a quality or characteristic—of the adjective _guarded_.

9.5.2   **Failure to understand adverb placement** can cause poor phrasing, or placement of an adverb that results in misleading—or even erroneous—consequences. The effect of an adverb is determined by which word is to receive the emphasis, or contrast, within the context in which the adverb is inserted, that is, what appears last in the utterance. This is **_the position of emphasis_**, within the **_adverb + modified_** construct.

Erroneous placement is quite common among messages and prompts seen on computers, for example,

> **Wrong**:   _Your file has been **successfully written**._
> **Correct**:   _Your file has been **written <u>successfully</u>**._

This example demonstrates one principal problem.
The problem is that the writer has made the too common assumption that adverbs

have to go before the verbs they modify. This is incorrect: **limiting adverbs go *before* the verb**, **attributive adverbs go *after* the verb modified**.

In English, the word (or phrase) in the position of emphasis automatically stands in contrast to other possible words of the same class.

Emphasizing ***written*** by placing it at the end of the sentence does not emphasize the success of the act of writing itself (because ***successfully*** has been hidden within the clause), but emphasizes the word ***written***. Such emphasis places that word in comparison with other possible instances of that class of usage (past participles) that could also be placed in this position of emphasis, such as

> *Your file has been successfully **deleted**.*
> *Your file has been successfully **copied**.*
> *Your file has been successfully **eaten**.*

However, this class of comparison was not the goal of the sentence's writer. The user told the program to write the file—it would indeed be an unexpected outcome if the file were somehow deleted instead! The goal of the message is to assure that the user know that the request was fulfilled completely. To do this, the only required construct is that the verb be in the present perfect tense.

"Your file has been written." is indeed all that is actually needed to convey the sense of the message.

However, the goal of the message as presented is to emphasize the completeness, and the reassuringly error-free result of the act of writing the file: *"Your file has been written successfully."* In this sentence, placement of the adverb after the complete verb, at the end of the sentence, places it within a position of emphasis—which is logical since **such emphasis that is exactly why we use adverbs in the first place**!

The complete verbal unit—the predicate—is ***has been written***. This is the unit that needs to be modified; and because that unit is not another adverb, and because a *limiting* (rather than *attributive*) usage of the adverb *successfully* is **not** the goal of the statement, the adverb that modifies that verbal unit attributively **must follow it**.

English is an analytic language: order is *everything*.

Failure to follow the standard protocol produces garbled, unintended messages.

Just consider the differences, or errors, that changes in placement create:

*She **wonderfully** writes.*	(**wonderfully** *incorrectly applies a limiting usage on the verb* **writes,** *setting it in comparison with any other applicable verb, such as* **skis, waltzes, teaches, vacuums,** *etc.*)
***Wonderfully** she writes.*	(*incomplete statement; or stylistic [or poetic] reordering*)
***Wonderfully,** she writes.*	(*statement using sentential adverb to convey writers' estimation of, or exuberance concerning, the fact that she writes.*)
*She writes **wonderfully**.*	(*usual meaning, modifying the verb, in the correct order for that meaning*)

*She **with enthusiasm** writes.*	(**with enthusiasm** *applies a limiting usage on the verb* **writes**; *adverbial prepositional phrases are used attributively, and so must follow what they modify*)
*She writes **one by one** articles.*	(*the phrasal adverb* **one by one** *modifies the verb incorrectly, instead of the entire predicate*)
*She **one by one** writes articles.*	(**one by one** *applies an incorrect limiting usage on the verb* **writes**)
*She writes articles **one by one**.*	(**one by one** *modifies the entire predicate correctly from its position of emphasis*)
Because she loves it, she writes.	(**Because she loves it** *is an adverbial phrase establishing condition or reason; it is emphasized by being moved to the front of the sentence*)
She because it loves writes she.	(**order must be followed correctly to avoid producing nonsense**)

NOTE: The adverb ***very*** is always a ***limiting adverb*** that **modifies only adjectives or other adverbs, and always precedes the modified**.

Very is never used alone to modify a verb directly.

9.5.3 **Whenever adverbs are moved out of place**, they are used deliberately parenthetically and are separated from the rest of the sentence by punctuation (commas or dashes) that sets them off from the baseline phrase. Such parentheses require pauses or changes in pitch or expression when spoken; the punctuation indicates these live, vocal modulations on the static, printed page.

However, unless serving a specific and planned stylistic need, such adverbs and adverbial phrases are often best moved (if positioning for clear attribution allow) either to the front or to the end of the sentence in order to avoid a break in the flow of thought.

*She, **wonderfully** for her age, writes clearly in cursive.*	(*emphasizes* **She** *in contradistinction to someone else; attributive modifier of verb*)
***Wonderfully** for her age, she writes clearly in cursive.*	(*emphasizes the rest of the sentence*)
*She, **with enthusiasm**, writes many letters.*	(*emphasizes* **She** *in contradistinction to someone else; attributive modifier of verb*)
***With enthusiasm**, she writes many letters.*	(*emphasizes* **She writes**; *attributive modifier of verb*)
*She writes many letters, **with enthusiasm**.*	(*modifies entire main clause; attributive modifier of verb, it tells how she writes letters, of which there are many*)
*She writes many letters **with enthusiasm**.*	(*modifies predicate* **writes many letters**; *it implies that not all the letters she writes are written with enthusiasm*)

*She—**only because she loves it**—writes articles for her publisher.*
***Only because she loves it**, she writes articles for her publisher.*
*She writes articles for her publisher **only because she loves it**.*

*She writes—**one by one**—articles for her publisher.*
*She writes articles, **one by one**, for her publisher.*
***One by one**, she writes articles for her publisher.*
*She writes articles for her publisher, **one by one**.*

If you replace ***one by one*** in those last four sentences with ***slowly and deliberately***, you will see, perhaps even more clearly, how adverb placement effects the expressive nature of a sentence, and affects those differences solely by movement between positions.

9.5.4 **Adverb order and adjective order are rarely parallel**.

This is because adjectives and adverbs have different assigned placements within the standard word-order of the English language.

Adjectives, as a rule, always precede the modified item: adjectives are always attributive.

Adverbs can go on either side, or even farther afield, depending on the usage of the adverb itself: whether it's a negating adverb or limiting adverb (on the left of the modified item), or an attributive adverb (appearing to the right of the complete, modified item).

*Very few buildings are **exact matches** of their blueprints.*	*(adjective goes to the left of the complete item it modifies)*
*Very few buildings **match** their blueprints **exactly**.*	*(attributive adverb goes to the right of the complete item it modifies)*

9.6 The ***negating adverbs*** are ***not*** and ***never*** (*"not ever"*).

9.6.1 **When the negating adverb *not* is applied to a finite verb**, the verb must already use, or be restated to use, an auxiliary verb. For the present tense or past tense this involves restating the verb in its emphatic form. In all tenses, ***not*** modifies (and is to the left of) the root verb.

*She **writes**.*	*She **does not write**.*
*She **wrote**.*	*She **did not write**.*
*She **will write**.*	*She **will not write**.*
*She **has written**.*	*She **has not written**.*
*She **had written**.*	*She **had not written**.*
*She **will have written**.*	*She **will not have written**.*
	*(**Never**: She will have **not** written.)*

In older forms of Modern English, the non-emphatic forms *She writes not* and *She wrote not* can be found, principally in works of literature. (There is a continuing preference in English for avoiding this placement, as the present tense 3rd person singular form, combined with rapid enunciation, is too likely to be heard, for example, as *She writes snot*.)

NOTE: When used with a verbal (an *infinitive*, a *gerund* or a *participle*), *not* goes before the complete verbal, always.

She wanted to write a letter.	*She wanted not to write her resignation.*
She loves writing.	*She avoids not writing.*
She is most happy writing.	*She is seldom found not writing.*

9.6.2 **When the negating adverb *not* is used in questions**, its placement changes depending on whether the negation is in a contraction or not. The contraction is applied to the auxiliary verb; the full negator *not* is placed in the same relative position it holds within the declaratory sentence.

Does she write?	*Does she not write?*	*Doesn't she write?*
Did she write?	*Did she not write?*	*Didn't she write?*
Will she write?	*Will she not write?*	*Won't she write?*
Has she written?	*Has she not written?*	*Hasn't she written?*
Had she written?	*Had she not written?*	*Hadn't she written?*
Will she have written?	*Will she not have written?*	*Won't she have written?*

With the modal auxiliaries, the order is much the same as with the non-modal verbs:

May she write?	*May she not write?*	*[no abbreviated form]*
Must she write?	*Must she not write?*	*Mustn't she write?*
Must she have written?	*Must she not have written?*	*Mustn't she have written?*
Might she write?	*Might she not write?*	*Mightn't she write?*
Can she write?	*Can she not write?*	*Can't she write?*
Could she write?	*Could she not write?*	*Couldn't she write?*
Should she write?	*Should she not write?*	*Shouldn't she write?*
Would she write?	*Would she not write?*	*Wouldn't she write?*

9.6.3 **When the negating adverb *not* is applied to a modal auxiliary**, the negating word is placed immediately after the auxiliary verb, just as in the case with the finite verb.

She may write.	*She may not write.*	
She must write.	*She must not write.*	
She must have written.	*She must not have written.*	
She might write.	*She might not write.*	
She can write.	*She cannot write.*	(**can not** *is most often written as a single word*)
	She can't write.	
She could write.	*She could not write.*	
	She couldn't write.	
How dare she write!	*How dare she not write!*	(*required interrogative placement with the modal* **dare**)

9.6.4 **When the negating adverb *not* is used in a statement of a general condition**, put *not* directly before the word or phrase it modifies rather than in a position modifying the verb.

WRONG: *Every player **will not be** team captain.*

CORRECT: ***Not** every player will be team captain.*

The **WRONG** example states that *no one on the team will [ever] be team captain*; the **CORRECT** statement means that *although not every one of them can be selected, the team* *captain will be selected from amongst the team members,* **and** *at least one player will be selected,* **even** *if the honor will not be attained by each in turn.*

9.6.5 **The negating adverb** *not* **can be applied to a phrase**. It is important to recognize the difference between the situations in which *not* modifies a phrase and those in which it negates the word or words starting the phrase.

> *His humor,* **not his gifts,** *was what attracted her.* (**not** *modifies the phrase* **his gifts**)
> *His broccoli,* **not her** *bacon-treat, was what attracted the dog.*
>
> (**not** *modifies the possessive pronoun* **her**)

9.7 *Limiting adverbs* are adverbs that restrict, define or refine the scope of the modified word, such as *always, certainly, completely, just, likely, never, now, obviously, only, often, partially, rarely, seldom, soon,* and are thus so closely connected to the modal nature (specifying aspects of *time, repetition, limitation, completion* or *emphasis*) of the word they modify that they are treated specially.

Limiting adverbs are also often found in degrees other than the positive: *more likely, most likely, more often, most often,* etc., or are themselves modified by other adverbs, such as *very* or *almost*: *very seldom, almost never,* etc. **Limiting adverbs** always appear on the left side of the word or phrase they modify. (See below for more details.)

The modal nature of the limiting adverbs means that they often sound incomplete when they are used in simple sentences. There is an incompleteness in their expression that often implies the need for a completing comparative, defining or contrasting phrase following thereafter. Often, this completing phrase will contain another limiting adverb. For example, *She* **seldom writes** sounds incomplete, whereas the extended

> *She* **seldom writes,** *but* **more often telephones**.

or even

> *She* **seldom writes anymore**.

are heard as complete thoughts.

It is the role of the limiting adverb to place contrastive emphasis on the verb rather than on itself. It does this, in part, by having the verb-unit it is modifying follow it.

Limiting adverbs always appear **before the root verb** in the present and past tenses, and in the same position as that of *not* (*i.e.,* immediately after the primary auxiliary) in all other tenses.

Limiting adverbs do not require use of the emphatic form in the present and past tenses, as can be seen from these examples:

She **writes**.	*She* **seldom writes**.
She **wrote**.	*She* **seldom wrote**.
She **will write**.	*She* **will seldom write**.
She **has written**.	*She* **has seldom written**.
She **had written**.	*She* **had seldom written**.
She **will have written**.	*She* **will seldom have written**.

The limiting adverbs may be moved to the front or the end of a phrase to give added or dramatic emphasis. Often another adverb or adverb phrase is included at the opposite extremity of the sentence for balance.

> **Seldom** *she writes, yet speaks to me* **even less***.*

NOTE: Examples of how much adverb placement, particularly that of the limiting adverbs, can affect the meaning of a sentence are the following:

Mother **just** *wants Jim to go home.*	*means that Mother has no other concerns about Jim. (If the word* **wants** *is accented instead of* **Jim**, *it implies that she can't or won't tell him directly or forcefully to go home.)*
Mother wants Jim **just** *to go home.*	*here, Mother wants Jim not to stop anywhere along the route, or do anything else, but head directly home.*
Mother wants Jim to go **just** *home.*	*Mother wants Jim to go home—not to the garage, not to the barn—but only to that building she calls "home".*

Other possible arrangements,

Just *Mother wants Jim to go home.*	*Mother—and no one else—wants Jim to go home*
Mother wants **just** *Jim to go home.*	*Mother wants Jim—and no one else—to go home*

use *just* as an adjective (meaning *only*) instead of as an adverb.

And another, unusable, unstable arrangement

> *Mother wants Jim to* **just** *go home.*

splits the infinitive; so, this sentence violates the language's protocol. [See §7.24.15]

NOTE: *Limiting adverbs* **precede the word or phrases they modify**. However, it is vital to recognize whether the adverb is actually used as a limiting adverb, and whether the sense of the sentence in fact requires an attributive adverb, instead.

Take, for example, this sentence:

> *He* **only** *runs fast in the early morning.*

Although this is a common way of stating this sentence, it has a problem: it is ambiguous. It is ambiguous because with the adverb in that position it means that he does nothing other than run in the early morning (a meaning that is unlikely because it would not need the adverb *fast*).

Given that the more common sentiment is either (1) that he runs rapidly only at one time of day, or (2) that he restricts his running to a rapid rate at that time, clearer phrasing for each of those meanings would be

> *a. He runs fast* **only** *in the early morning.*
> *b. He runs* **only** *fast in the early morning.*

because in *a.*, *only* modifies the prepositional phrase; in *b.*, it modifies its following adverb.

If we change that first sentence to include an infinitive, in too common parlance it could be heard as something like this:

> *He tries to* **only** *run fast in the early morning.*

This sentence has the same ambiguity as that very first example, on top of the uncertainty introduced by the **split infinitive**. The meanings require it be rewritten thus:

> *a. He tries to run fast **only** in the early morning.* (limiting **when** he runs)
> *b. He tries to run **only** fast in the early morning.* (limiting **how** he runs)
> *c. He tries **only** to run fast in the early morning.* (limiting **what** he does)

Switching to a commonly used intensifier, the limiting adverb **really**, demonstrates a common problem.

> *He tries to **really** run fast in the early morning.*

The problem here is failure to understand the word the adverb is actually trying to modify. It is not modifying the partial phrase **run fast** (created erroneously by splitting the infinitive), but is modifying either the adverb **fast** or the predicate **tries**:

> *a. He tries to run **really** fast in the early morning.*
> *b. He **really** tries to run fast in the early morning.*

Changing the sentence to use a modal auxiliary, **should**, demonstrates another common situation.

> *He should **really** run fast in the early morning.*

The problem here is, once again, failure to understand what the adverb is modifying. As above, it is here also not meant to modify the partial phrase **run fast**, but is meant to modify **either** the adverb **fast**, or the phrasal predicate **should run**, as a limiting adverb:

> *a. He should run **really** fast in the early morning.*
> *b. He **really** should run fast in the early morning.*

Limiting adverbs must directly precede the specific words or phrases they qualify.

> *She had **only baked** three cakes.* (*implies that she had not done anything else, such as prepare the batter or sweep the floor*)
>
> *She had baked **only three** cakes.* (*her past cake output was limited to three*)
> *She needed **to bake only three** cakes.* (*her required cake output was limited to three*)

Understanding what the true modified word or phrase is, then placing the modifier correctly, will remove ambiguity and allow for clean, clear and robust expression.

9.7.1 **Attributive adverbs moved before the word or phrase become limiting adverbs.** If that is not the specifically intended meaning and implication of the adverb, it must be placed **after** the complete unit it modifies.

> *The essay **was written clearly**.* (**clearly** *modifies* **was written**, *and tells the manner or quality of writing*)
> *The essay was **clearly written**.* (**clearly** *modifies only* **written**, *and says that the essay was not produced by mechanical device; in this situation,* **clearly** *could be replaced with another <u>limiting</u> adverb such as* **obviously**)

NOTE: Moving an attributive adverb out of its normal position (after the complete item modified) can change the meaning or implications of the adverb itself. This is because **repositioning an adverb changes what it modifies.**

9.7.2   With modal auxiliaries, **limiting adverbs** are placed *after the modal*.
However, *dare* requires special placement, with the limiting adverb coming after the entire verb.

> *She **write**.*   *She **must seldom write**.*
> *She **must have written**.*   *She **must seldom have written**.*
> *She **can write**.*   *She **can seldom write**.*
> *She **could write**.*   *She **could seldom write**.*
> *How **dare** she **write**!*   *How **dare** she **write seldom**!*
>   (special placement required by modal use of **dare**)

9.8   *Sentential adverbs* **modify the entire sentence** and express the thoughts, attitudes or opinions of the speaker rather than expressing modifications more closely associated with, or derived from the words of the sentence itself. Often these express some quality projected by the speaker onto the subject of the sentence.

Sentential adverbs are normally offset from the rest of the sentence by one or more commas.

There are several types of **sentential adverbs**.

9.8.1   *Complementary* **sentential adverbs** complete the sense or manner of the sentence by expressing a quality of the subject and its action, from the point of view of the speaker.

> ***Wisely**, he dropped the course before he failed it.*
> ***He, wisely, dropped the course** before he failed it.*

Complementary sentential adverbs removed into a position just before the verb, and not separated by commas from the sentence, become limiting adverbs.

> ***He wisely dropped the course** before he failed it.*   (limiting adverb of manner)

9.8.2   *Evaluative* **sentential adverbs** express an evaluation of the sentence or its sentiment from the point of view of the speaker.

> ***He was, surprisingly, allowed to drop the course** before he failed it.*
> ***Surprisingly, he was allowed to drop the course** before he failed it.*
> ***He was allowed to drop the course** before he failed it**, surprisingly**.*

9.8.3   *Modal* **sentential adverbs** express the mood of the speaker in relation to the information given by the sentence.

> ***Evidently, he dropped the course** before he failed it.*
> ***Improbably, he dropped the course** just before he failed it.*

9.8.4   *Domain* **sentential adverbs**. point out the area of concern or field of thought to which the rest of the sentence applies.

> ***Academically, he was allowed to drop the course** before he failed it, but*
> ***emotionally, he will always regret** it.*

9.8.5   *Pragmatic* **sentential adverbs** demonstrate the point of view of the author of the sentence toward the rest of the sentence.

> ***Honestly, I am surprised** that he dropped the course.*

9.8.6   *Environmental* **sentential adverbs** express a general fact about the entire sentence: they do not modify merely one word or phrase within the sentence. These resemble *nominative absolute* phrases that do not contain a verbal.

Often, these are not separated by commas from the rest of the sentence.

> **At the end of the day**, *the work had all been done.*
> **Finally,** *he dropped the course.*

Note that the second example could also be a **modal sentential** adverb or a **pragmatic sentential** adverb, depending on its context.

9.8.7   *Transitional* **sentential/conjunctive adverbs** are adverbs used to join clauses into sentences. These include such adverbs as *consequently*, *furthermore*, *hence*, *however*, *moreover*, *nevertheless* and *therefore*.

> *He had suspected the promotion,* **nevertheless** *he was pleasantly surprised when he got the confirming note from his manager.*
> *"**Furthermore**," she continued, "I can't say that I care for your attitude!"*

9.9   The **adverb of general inclusivity**, *too,*   must follow the final phrase to which it applies, and must be preceded by a comma. If another phrase follow it in the same sentence, a second comma must separate it from any subsequent words.

This inclusive use of *too* must be recognized and handled separately from its use as a normal adverb of manner: of degree or for emphasis.

> *Jack wanted to go up the hill, and Jill wanted to go,* **too**.
> *When Mary finished, John talked about his travels,* **too**, *but we were already* **too** *tired to listen attentively.*

9.10   There are **three types of adverb**, determined by usage: *simple*, *interrogative* and *relative*.

9.11   *Simple adverbs* are divided into **five modes**. These modes reveal how adverbs are used to give life to language.

9.11.1   *Manner*.
Adverbs of manner detail *how* or *why* the action occurs.

> *He walked* **slowly** *along the path.*   (**slowly** *modifies the predicate* [He] **walked**)
>
> *He walked* **with a painful limp** *along the path.*   (**with a painful limp** *modifies the predicate* [He] **walked**)
>
> **Because he was tired**, *he walked slowly.*   (**Because he was tired** *modifies the predicate* [He] **walked**)
>
> *He walked over* **to see** *the stream along the path.*   (**to see** *modifies the predicate* [He] **walked**)
>
> *He walked* **alone** *along the path.*   (**alone** *modifies the predicate* [He] **walked**)
>
> *He walked,* **deep in thought**, *along the path.*   (**deep in thought** *modifies the predicate* [He] **walked**)
>
> *We walked* **together** *to the stream along the path.*   (**together** *modifies the predicate* [He] **walked**)

9.11.2 **Degree**.

Adverbs of degree detail *how much* the action occurs.

He walked **very** slowly along the path.　　　　(**very** *modifies* **slowly** {*which modifies* [He] walked})

He walked with a **quite** painful limp along the path.　(**quite** *modifies* **painful**)

9.11.3 **Time**.

Adverbs of time detail *when* the action occurs.

He walked **early** along the path.　　　　(**early** *modifies the predicate* [He] walked)

He walked **at dawn** along the path.　　　　(**at dawn** *modifies the predicate* [He] walked)

9.11.4 **Place**.

Adverbs of place detail *where* the action occurs.

He walked slowly **along the path**.　　　　(**along the path** *modifies the predicate* [He] walked)

He walked around **outside**.　　　　(**outside** *modifies the predicate* [He] walked)

From the kitchen he walked **outside**.　　　　(*both* **From the kitchen** *and* **outside** *modify* [He] walked)

9.11.5 **Number**.

Adverbs of number detail *how many times* the action occurs.

He walked along the path **twice**.　　　　(**twice** *modifies the predicate* [He] walked)

He will walk **three times** tomorrow.　　　　(**three times** *modifies the predicate* [He] walked)

He walks along the path **once** every morning.　(**once** *modifies the adverbial phrase* every morning)

9.12　**Interrogative adverbs** are used to pose a question. Answers to these questions are most often answered with phrases using instances of the simple adverbs. Some of the most common are *How? Why? When? Where? How much? To what degree? How many times? How often?* The modes into which the interrogative adverbs fall are the same as those of the **simple adverbs**.

How did he walk?	Slowly.
When did he walk?	At dawn.
Where did he walk?	Along the path.
How slowly did he walk?	Very slowly.
How many times did he walk?	Twice.

9.13　**Relative adverbs**, or **conjunctive adverbs**, function as **conjunctions** and are used to connect dependent clauses to the main clause. The clauses introduced by relative adverbs function as nouns or as adverbs. [See §13.17.4] Some words used often as relative adverbs are *after, as, before, how, since, until, when, whence, whenever, where, wherever, while, whither* and *why*.

The wind blew from the north **when it snowed**.　　　(*adverb clause: time*)

Wherever it had snowed, *the birds were roosting on the electric lines.* (adverb clause: place)

I haven't been able to find anything since my secretary went on vacation. (adverb clause: duration of time)

How the dog was able to get on the roof is something I can't imagine! (noun clause: subject)

He told me not whence he had come, whither he was going, nor how he happened to have been here. (noun clauses: direct objects)

9.14 **Adverbs** have *three degrees of comparison*, exactly paralleling those of the adjectives: *positive*, *comparative* and *superlative*.

Not all adverbs are capable of comparison, particularly phrasal adverbs.

9.14.1 The *positive degree* is the basic form of the adverb:

*She writes **clearly**.*
*Walking **briskly,** he soon reached the subway station.*
*Do it **quickly** so we can leave **right away**.*
*We drove **far, late** into the night.*

9.14.2 The *comparative degree* expresses a difference between the states of an adverb, a difference that is more (or higher, *etc.*) or less (or lower, *etc.*) than the same adverb in the positive degree:

*She writes **more clearly** than he.*
*Walking **less briskly,** he reached the subway station after the train had left.*
*Do it **more quickly** (or **quicker**) so we can leave **sooner**.*
*We drove **farther** by travelling **later** into the night.*

9.14.3 The *superlative degree* expresses the extreme outcome when comparing three or more states of an adverb:

*She writes **the most clearly** of anyone in the class.*
*Walking **the least briskly** of the group, only he reached the subway station after the train had left.*
*You can work **the quickest**, so you do it.*
*We drove **the farthest**, and **the latest** of anyone.*

9.14.4 **Adverbs** of one or two syllables in the **positive degree** may be extended by *–er* for the **comparative degree** and *–est* for the **superlative degree**. This includes many (but not all) of those having positive degree forms common to both their adjective use and adverb use, or monosyllable adjectives whose (positive degree) adverb form is created by adding *–ly*.

Some shorter adverbs (such as *clearly*) are compared only by prefixing *more* and *most* in the comparative and superlative. For the negative comparative, using *less* and *least*, those words must be used explicitly.

Other adverbs, if their positive form is not already the same as that of the adjective, switch to the adjective forms of the comparative and superlative. A few adverbs (primarily *adverbs of degree*) do not have comparative or superlative forms.

positive	comparative	superlative	notes
quickly	*quicker*	*quickest*	
quickly	*more quickly*	*most quickly*	
slowly	*slower*	*slowest*	
slowly	*more slowly*	*most slowly*	
slowly	*less slowly*	*least slowly*	
rapidly	*more rapidly*	*most rapidly*	
too	—	—	
very	—	—	
quite	—	—	
rather	—	—	
[near]	*nearer*	*nearest*	
nearly	*more nearly*	*most nearly*	*in more formal English,* **nearer** *and* **nearest** *should not be used as adverbs, but replaced by* **nearly**, **more nearly** *and* **most nearly**

The formation of the adverb from the adjective, and creation of the comparative and superlative forms of both adverbs and adjectives is still an area of English that takes memorization and practice to master fully. When in doubt, consult a reputable dictionary.

9.14.5 **Inflected forms**, inherited from Anglo-Saxon, are used for a very few adverbs, many of which have the same form as their adjective counterparts, *e.g.*,

positive	comparative	superlative	notes
[much]	*more*	*most*	
well	*better*	*best*	
badly	*worse*	*worst*	
little	*less/lesser*	*least*	*"a small amount"* **little**, *meaning "small in stature", does not have an adverbial use*
[north{ward}]	*northerly*	*northmost/northernmost*	
[south{ward}]	*southerly*	*southmost/southernmost*	
far	*farther/further*	*farthest/furthest*	

9.15 **Adverbs are the most used part of speech to which the least amount of attention is paid.**
Several issues need to be raised for general, good usage of adverbs and adjectives.

9.15.1 **Use an adverb rather than an adjective whenever an adverb is required.**

> **WRONG**: *Jill can't carry **near as** much water as Jack.*
> **CORRECT**: *Jill can't carry **nearly so** much water as Jack.*

> **WRONG**: *The car was **most** all within the garage.*
> **CORRECT**: *The car was **almost** all within the garage.*

> **WRONG**: *His mother was **some** better.*
> **CORRECT**: *His mother was **somewhat** better.*

> **WRONG**: *Thanks for holding the door open! —**Sure!***
> **CORRECT**: *Thanks for holding the door open!—**Surely!***

9.15.2 When *too* or *very* modifies a past participle, an additional, intervening adverb, such as ***greatly*** or ***much***, is required, as neither *too* nor *very* should be used to modify a past participle directly.

> **WRONG**: *Your invitation was **very** appreciated.*
> **CORRECT**: *Your invitation was **very much/very greatly** appreciated.*

> **WRONG**: *Her back was **very** sunburned.*
> **CORRECT**: *Her back was **very much/severely** sunburned.*

> **WRONG**: *He was **very** injured in the wreck.*
> **CORRECT**: *He was **very badly** injured in the wreck.*

9.15.3 **Do not use *not* with other negative adverbs or negating adjectives or pronouns**, such as *scarcely*, *hardly*, *neither*, *never*, *no*, *no one*, *nobody*, *nothing*, *none*, *only*.

This creates ***a double negative***. (Just as multiplying two negatives creates a positive result in Mathematics, compounding negative adverbs follows the same logical, mathematical rule.)

The only exception is when creating a characterization that recreates the speech of someone who doesn't know better.

> **WRONG**: *Jill can**'t** carry **no** water.*
> **CORRECT**: *Jill can**'t** carry **any** water.*

> **WRONG**: *The car was **not** in **no** garage.*
> **WRONG**: *The car **weren't** in **no** garage.*
> **CORRECT**: *The car was **not** in **a** garage.*

> **WRONG**: *I'm so tired I ca**n't hardly** move.*
> **CORRECT**: *I'm so tired I can **hardly** move.*

Using a negative adverb with adjectives that are negative in definition does not create a double negative; it creates a *rhetorical positive* for purposes of more emphatic expression, or for deliberate style (for example, to impart a hint of irony or sarcasm).

> *She was **only occasionally friendly** at work.*
> —*She was **not unfriendly** at work.*

*He was **fairly good looking**.*
    —*He was **not unhandsome**.*

*Their writing was **somewhat better than average**.*
    —*Their writing was **not unskillful**.*

9.15.4   **Do not use the noun phrases *kind of* or *sort of* when an adverb is required.** Use ***somewhat*** or ***rather*** instead. ***Kind*** and ***sort*** are nouns of specific meaning; use them only when saying something is a member of a larger class.

WRONG: *Jill was **sort of** thirsty.*
CORRECT: *Jill was **rather** thirsty.*

WRONG: *They reacted **kind of** coolly to his suggestion.*
CORRECT: *They reacted **somewhat** coolly to his suggestion.*

CORRECT: *A giraffe is a **kind of** mammal.*

CORRECT: *A horse is one **sort of** quadruped; a dog is another [sort].*

9.15.5   **Do not use adverbs unnecessarily**.
Extraneous adverbs bloat your message, make it more tedious, and can make less effective any other adverbs you use. [Also see *Errors of Vocabulary* §13.18.9]

POOR: *Jack **stowed** the gear **away**.*
BETTER: *Jack **stowed** the gear.*   (**to stow** *means* **to put away**)

POOR: *Trouble **has started up** in that region again.*
BETTER: *Trouble **has started** in that region again.* (**up** *is unnecessary*)

POOR: *He was about **to dive down** to the wreck.*
BETTER: *He was about **to dive** to the wreck.*   (**down** *is the only way one can* **dive***: it's redundant*)

POOR: *They are ready **to weld** the beams **together**.*
BETTER: *They are ready **to weld** the beams.*   (*you cannot* **weld** *something* **apart***, so* **together** *is redundant*)

9.15.6   **Pay close attention to adverb placement**.
Changes in placement cause changes in the meaning, effect or efficiency of adverbs.

Just because the part of speech's name is ***ad + verb*** does ***NOT*** mean it has to go right in front of what you may think is the verb.

Understanding this entire section on adverbs—§9.5 in particular—is extremely important to attaining clarity and effectiveness of expression.

10 Prepositions

10.1 *Prepositions* are words heading a phrase that expresses the relationship between the object of the preposition and other words in the sentence.

*The cat **on the roof** is a gray tabby.*	(**on** *expresses the [adjectival] relationship between its object,* **roof**, *and the subject,* **cat**)
*The cat went **onto the roof**.*	(**onto** *expresses the [adverbial] relationship between its object,* **roof**, *and the verb,* **went**)
***On the roof** is the cat's own refuge.*	(**on** *expresses the relationship between its object,* **roof**, *and the predicate phrase* [noun usage])

10.2 *Prepositional phrases* function as **one of three parts of speech**:

1. **adjective**   *The dog **under the tree** is Jason.*
2. **adverb**   *We met **in the park** and walked **to the apartment**.*
3. **noun**   ***On the big couch** is Maggie's favorite place to nap.*

10.2.1 **Prepositional phrases** always have at least one object, but may have more than one.

*I was right here **at my keyboard**.*
*I was right here **at my keyboard and mouse**.*

10.2.2 **The objects of prepositional phrases**, like any substantive, may have a single or compound appositive.

*I was right here **with my electronic shovel, my keyboard**.*
*I was right here **with my electronic tools, my keyboard and mouse**.*

10.2.3 **Compound prepositional phrases** may share a modifier, even another prepositional phrase.

*The pioneers built their homes **from the logs**, their roofs **from the bark** and their cooking fires **from the branches** <u>of the trees of the deep forest</u>.*

10.3 **Prepositions fall into three general classes:** *simple, compound* **and** *phrasal.*

10.3.1 *Simple prepositions* are single words.

The most common include ***aboard, about, above, across, after, against, along, amid, amidst, among, amongst, around, at, athwart, before, behind, below, beneath, beside, besides, between, betwixt, beyond, but, by, concerning, despite, down, during, ere, except, for, from, in, inside, into, of, off, on, outside, over, past, round, since, through, throughout, till, to, toward, towards, under, underneath, until, unto, up, upon, with, within*** and ***without***.

Many of the words used as **simple prepositions** can also be found used alone (without an object, in a phrase) as *simple* or as *conjunctive adverbs*.

*I have not seen you **since** college.*	(*preposition*)
***Since** your leaving, I have not seen you.*	(*preposition*)
*I knew you in college, but haven't seen you **since**.*	(*simple adverb*)
*I have not seen you **since** you moved to California.*	(*conjunctive adverb; temporal conjunction*)

*The cat leaps **over the rock**; the mouse crawls **under it**.*　(prepositions)
*The cat leaps **over**; the mouse crawls **under**.*　(adverbs)

*We have stayed **inside the house since the storm**.*　(prepositions)
*We have stayed **inside since**.*　(adverbs)

10.3.2　**Compound prepositions** are prepositions composed of two words heading a single phrase, such as ***according to, along with, as at, as of, as to, as per, because of, due to, except for, from among, from between, from behind, from under, instead of, off of, out of, over against, round about***.

> *According to the GPS, that lake shouldn't be there.*
> *Put the sideboard **over against** that wall.*
> *The floodwaters were suddenly **round about** the house.*

Several of these compound prepositions, particularly those starting with ***from***, ***off***, and ***over***, are actually prepositional phrases imbedded within another. For example, in the sentence

> *The dog came **from under the porch**.*

the prepositional phrase ***under the porch*** can be analyzed as a prepositional phrase acting as a noun (***under the porch*** is a place) that is in turn the object of the preposition *from*.

However, in most situations this fact is of little practical use, so it is ignored in favor of a greater degree of simplicity of expression.

Note that some of these, such as ***as per*** and ***off of***, are needlessly wordy and shouldn't be used, as only one of the words [***per*** and ***off***, in these cases] by itself will convey the meaning without difficulty. [Also see the note to §10.4]

10.3.3　**Phrasal prepositions** are phrases used as prepositions, most of which are composed of a set, leading prepositional phrase followed by a simple preposition, such as ***in accordance with, in addition to, with regard to*** and ***in spite of***.

> *In accordance with the GPS's instructions, he drove into the lake.*
> *The furniture has been moved **with regard to** your instructions.*
> *In spite of the flood, we set off for Grandma's house.*

10.4　**Prepositions** sometimes pose problems of use, or questions of usage, as detailed in the following sections of **NOTE**'s.

NOTE: Avoid insertion of prepositions or the combining of prepositions and adverbs to create needlessly wordy, or pleonastic constructions. In particular, do not use unnecessary additions of ***at***, ***of***, ***on***, ***over***, ***to*** or ***with***.

*Did you read **all of** the book?*	— *Did you read **all** the book?*
***All of** them were there to greet you.*	— ***All** were there to greet you.*
***Where** are you **at**?*	— ***Where** are you?*
***Where** are you going **to**?*	— ***Where** are you going?*
*She will be here **inside of** the house.*	— *She will be here **inside** the house.*
*Will you go **with**?*	— *Will you go? / Will you go along?*
*Will you go **along with** me?*	— *Will you go **with** me?*
***Cover over** the plants against the cold.*	— ***Cover** the plants against the cold.*

NOTE: Differences between certain close-sounding simple, compound and phrasal prepositions, between prepositions and other parts of speech, or between two prepositions are important and must be observed:

- *behind*   vs.   *in back of*
  behind *is a preposition;* **in back of** *is a non-standard, dialect phrase*

  > They parked **behind the building**.
  > **NOT:** They parked **in back of the building**.

- *beside*   vs.   *besides*
  beside *is a preposition of location;* **besides** *means* **in addition to**

  > **Beside the house** an ancient oak tree stood for many years.
  > **Besides the house**, the ancient oak tree is interesting, too.

- *between*   vs.   *from* used with numbers
  between *is always followed by a plural noun;* **from** *takes a singular noun*

  > He answered **from the first to the third question** correctly.
  > But his mind froze **between the third and fourth questions**.

- *into*   vs.   *in to*
  into *always shows direction;* **in to** *states an adverbial location or situation followed by further movement or action*

  > He jumped **into the deeper water**.
  > He went from wading outside **in to dinner**.

- *inside*   vs.   *inside of*
  inside *is a preposition;* **inside of** *is a noun followed by a preposition*

  > We walked **inside the house**
  > We looked at the **inside of each room**.

- *inside of*   vs.   *within*
  inside of *is a location (a noun) followed by a preposition; don't use this phrase when you actually mean* **within**

  > She will be here **within an hour**.
  > **NOT:** She will be here **inside of an hour**.
  > She will be here **inside the house**.

- *near*   vs.   *nearby*
  near *is a preposition or an adverb,* **nearby** *is only an adverb*

  > **Near the pond** was a stand of large pines.
  > From the barn the pond was **near**, and **nearby** was a stand of large pines.

- *on*   vs.   *in*
  on *specifies location close by, near or beside: touching but not part of, ;* **in** *shows location inside or within (the physical bounds of) something else*

  > Her house is **on this street.**   (static location: beside the physical passageway)
  > Her house is **in this street.**   (implies non-static location [e.g., the building is being moved], or that she's living in a vehicle)

*London lies **on the Thames**.* (static location)
*London lies **in the Thames**.* (*used metaphorically: London's life is based on the river's existence, or it's going 'down the river'; or used of a literal change of state: the river has flooded into the city, or part of London is [now, physically] falling into the river*)

- ***on*** vs. ***onto***
- ***onto*** vs. ***on to***

  on *always specifies location;* **onto** *always shows direction;* **on to** *states an adverbial location or situation followed by further movement or action*

  > *He stood **on the ladder**.*
  > *He moved from the roof **onto the ladder**.*

  > *He moved from the roof **onto the ladder**.*
  > *He moved from roofing **on to hanging the doors**.*

- ***since*** vs. ***because of***

  since *applies to the passage of time;* **because** *gives a reason for something*

  > ***Since your early arrival**, have you been comfortable in the waiting room?*
  > ***Because of your early arrival**, you will have to wait to see the doctor.*

  These two prepositional phrases can be restated as clauses using very nearly the same words as conjunctions:

  > ***Since you arrived early**, have you been comfortable in the waiting room?*
  > ***Because you arrived early**, you will have to wait to see the doctor.*

- ***with regard to*** vs. ***with regards to***

  the second phrase is a set construction, an idiom, used as a closing salutation

  > ***With regard to your last letter**, I assure you I'm quite doing quite well.*
  > ***With regards to your family**, goodbye until later.*

  The phrasal preposition ***with regard to*** can be replaced with ***in regard to*** (or in the jargon of business letters, with the Latin phrase ***in re*** or just ***re:***), but ***with regards to*** cannot be replaced by the error phrase, ***in regards to***.

  > ***In regard to your last letter**, I assure you I'm quite doing quite well.*
  > ***In re your previous letter**, we cannot accept your offer for the said assets.*

NOTE: There are preferred usages of prepositions in certain situations, although these preferences may be altered by choices of style:

- ***Be accompanied by** a living being—**be accompanied with** a thing*

  > *Jack was accompanied by Jill.*
  > *Their walk was accompanied with music.*

- ***Agree to** a thing—**agree with** a person or a person's production*

  > *I agreed to his conditions.*
  > *I agree with your conclusions.*

- ***Be angry at** a thing—**be angry with** a person*

  > *He is angry at having to work overtime.*
  > *He is angry with his boss for having required it.*

- **Be anxious about an action—Be eager to undertake an action**

  > *He was anxious about speaking in public.*
  > *She was eager to speak to anyone at any time.*

- **Arrive in a large locale** (*city, country, etc.*)
  — arrive at a small locale (*village, building, etc.*)

  > *We arrived in London on time.*
  > *We arrived at the farm before sunset.*

- **Correspond with a person—Correspond to a compared issue, quality or action**

  > *They corresponded with each other by letter.*
  > *His actions do not correspond to his promises.*

- **Die of a disease** or **condition—die from exposure—die by violence** or **an action**

  > *Jack **died of** crown-inflicted cranial injuries.*
  > *Jill **died from** lying, unattended, at the bottom of the hill.*
  > ***Death by** falling or tumbling is, apparently, not at all unusual in English hill regions.*

- **Differ with someone's opinion**
  — differ from someone or something, or its description, identity or composition

  > *We differ with their conclusions about our product.*
  > *We differ from their company in our level of quality and support.*

- **Be followed by an active entity—be followed with a non-active entity**

  > *She was followed by an angry mob.*
  > *Her picture was followed with a review of her performance.*

- **Part from a person—part with a thing**

  > *We were sorry to part from our friends.*
  > *We were sorry to part with our old home.*

- **Prevent someone from an action**
  — prohibit someone from an action
  — forbid someone + infinitive (*to attempt an action*)

  > *We prevented him from driving in this weather.*
  > *We prohibited him from driving in this weather.*
  > *We forbade him to drive in this weather.*

- **Replace with an object— replace by a person**

  > *The two columns were replaced with an arch.*
  > *The first architect was replaced by a more skillful one.*

- **Succeed in accomplishing an action**
  — succeed to a different office, do something different
  — be succeeded [*as something*] by someone or something

  > *He succeeded in getting his book written.*
  > *Trudeau succeeded to the office of Prime Minister in 1968.*
  > *She was succeeded by the vice-president of Marketing.*
  > *Romulus Augustulus was succeeded as ruler of Rome by Odoacer the Ostrogoth.*

NOTE: **Different** must *always* **be followed by** *from*, **never** *to* (as in some dialects of *BE*), **or** *than* (as in careless *ACE*).

Different followed by *from* is the *Common English* standard. This standard usage is simply a matter of logical correspondence, namely:

As something is ***similar to*** some things,
it is ***different from*** others.

To indicates ***approach***, while *from* conveys ***separation***.

"***Different to***" is as illogical as "***different on***"!

11 Conjunctions

11.1 *Conjunctions* are words that connect words, lists of words or phrases into larger units. Conjunctions can be single words, or phrases termed *phrasal conjunctions*. Conjunctions are also called **connectives**.

Jack **and** Jill went up the hill.	(**and** connects the individual subjects into a compound subject)
Jack fell **while** Jill waited.	(**while** connects its dependent clause with the main clause)
While waiting, Jill saw Jack fall.	(**while** connects the participial clause with the main clause)
Jack **as well as** Jill was on the hill.	(**as well as** is a phrasal conjunction that connects the two subjects)
Jack fell **because** his bucket was heavy.	(**because** connects its dependent clause with the main clause)

11.2 *Conjunctions* fall into two general classes, **coordinate** and **subordinate**.

11.3 *Coordinate* (or *co-ordinate* or *coördinate*) *conjunctions* connect words, phrases or clauses of **equal** usage (or **rank**), that is, of identical construction.

Jack **and** Jill went up the hill.	(**and** connects two nouns)
They went up the hill **and** then they came down.	(**and** connects two independent clauses)
Up the hill **and** down the hill, they walked very far that day.	(**and** connects two prepositional phrases)

The most common coordinate conjunctions are **and, but, for, however, moreover, nor, or, still, then, therefore** and **yet**.

11.4 There are **six classes of coordinating conjunctions**:

11.4.1 *Copulative*: conjunctions of union, such as **also, and, as, as well as, besides, both … and**

11.4.2 *Disjunctive*: conjunctions of separation, such as **or, either … or…, neither … nor…, whether … or …**

11.4.3 *Adversative*: conjunctions of opposition, including **but, else, nevertheless, notwithstanding, on the contrary, rather, still, whereas, yet**

11.4.4 *Illative*: conjunctions of inference, such as **hence, therefore**

11.4.5 *Causal*: conjunctions of cause or purpose (as long as the clause introduced is not a dependent clause), such as **for**

11.4.6 *Transitional*: adverbs used as conjunctions within or between sentences, they provide transition between independent clauses, such as **consequently, furthermore, hence, however, nevertheless,** and **then** [See §9.8.7]

11.5 **Parts of the second member of a coordinate structure may be elided**, particularly when the clause is stated as an alternative, or a negative alternative, idea. For example, in

> *Are you going **or not**?*

the word *or* joins the phrase ***Are you going*** to its elided parallel negative phrase, ***are you not going***.

> *Are you going **or are you not going**?*

Thus, the requirement for paired items of equal rank is satisfied even when one of the pair is only partially expressed.

11.6 *Correlatives* are **paired coordinate conjunctions**. Because they are coordinate conjunctions, the two—and only **two**—words, phrases or clauses that they connect must be of **equal** usage (or *rank*).

One of the pair precedes the first paired element while the second goes between the first element and its matching word, phrase or clause.

The most common are ***both ... and ...***, ***either ... or ...***, ***neither ... nor ...***, and ***not only ... but also ...*** .

> ***Both*** *Jack **and** Jill went up the hill.*
> *They **not only** went up the hill **but also** came down.*
> ***Neither*** *up the hill **nor** down the hill tired them.*

NOTE: Always use *either* with *or* and *neither* with *nor*: they are set pairs and must not be used in any other mix.

> **WRONG**:   *Jack can **neither** go up the hill **or** carry pails of water.*
> **CORRECT**: *Jack can **neither** go up the hill **nor** carry pails of water.*

One may use *or* or *nor* as individual coordinate conjunctions. (Note that *nor* can be used only in a construction that has been negated.)

> **CORRECT**: *Jack **cannot** go up the hill **nor** can he carry pails of water.*

NOTE: **Never use a correlative pair with more than two alternatives.** Either drop the correlative construction, or restate the alternatives.

> **WRONG**:   *Jack can **neither** go up the hill **nor** carry pails of water, **nor** hold onto his crown.*
> **CORRECT**: *Jack can**not** go up the hill **nor** carry pails of water, **nor** hold onto his crown.*
> **CORRECT**: *Jack can **neither** go up the hill **nor** carry pails of water; **neither can he** hold onto his crown.*

NOTE: Be certain that a coordinate conjunction—and each part of a correlative—is positioned correctly to create parallels between the equal-usage units that it joins. If this is not the case, the sentence will be incorrect, illogical, or just sound odd to an attentive fluent speaker. This is a particular problem with correlatives appearing with prepositional phrases or with infinitives in current colloquial speech.

For example, in

> *She wanted **to both write** a letter **and mail** it.*

the correlative ***both ... and ...*** is attempting to join two infinitive phrases. However, the sentence splits the first infinitive, and the second infinitive, written incompletely, is left dangling. The sense of the sentence is both clearer and cleaner, and far more effective, when rewritten correctly:

> She wanted **both to write** a letter **and to mail** it.

The second statement organizes the conjunctions and their phrases into parallel units that are transparent to understand. The structure may be demonstrated by adding punctuation grouping the functional phrases:

> She wanted [**both** (to write a letter) **and** (to mail it)].

The correlative construction (noted within brackets, '[ ]') is the direct object of the verb *wanted*; the parenthesized (to write a letter) and (to mail it) are the parallel phrases, equal in rank, coordinated by the correlative pair **both … and …**.

11.7 **Subordinate conjunctions** connect two clauses of **unequal** usage (or *rank*).

One of the clauses is independent: if it were removed from the sentence, the remaining portion would make a complete statement by itself. The extracted clause is dependent on (or subordinate to) the other clause for completion, or for full expression of its meaning.

The most common subordinate conjunctions are **as, as if, because, before, but that, how, if, like, since, that, till, unless, until, when, whenever, where, wherever, whether, which, who, whoever** and **why**.

The most common subordinate conjunction of all is the word **that**. In English, distinct from most other languages with a like formation, it may be elided. However, sentences are often clearer when it is left at the head of its clause.

Jack has seen the hill **that** he and Jill will ascend.	(**that** introduces the dependent clause)
Jack has seen the hill he and Jill will ascend.	(**that** is elided)
Jack was always healthy, **until** he broke his crown.	(**until** begins the dependent clause)
Jack will go up the hill **if** Jill will go.	(**if** begins the dependent clause)
Jack is going up the hill **whether** Jill goes or not.	(**whether** begins the dependent clause)

When there are two or more verbs following the verb in the independent clause, it is best to include at least one **that**, to clarify the relationship of those subsequent clauses to the main clause.

Mary says Jack fetches well and Jill does, too.	(the status of **Jill** is unclear)
Mary says **that** Jack fetches well **and** Jill does, too.	(**ambiguous:** does **Jill** also **fetch well**, or does she also **say**?)
Mary says **that** Jack fetches well **and that** Jill does, too.	(**Jill** is explicitly reported as fetching well)
Mary says **that** Jack fetches well, **and** Jill does, too.	(**Jill** agrees that Jack fetches well)

11.8 There are **nine classes of subordinating conjunctions**:

11.8.1 **Temporal:**   conjunctions of point in time or duration of time, such as **as, when, as soon as, while, until, as long as, before, after, since**

11.8.2	**Comparative**:	conjunctions of comparing, such as *as, as if, as … as, just as, according as, in comparison to, so … as*
11.8.3	**Conditional**:	conjunctions introducing conditions, including *if, if only, but if, provided*
11.8.4	**Adversative** and **Concessive**:	conjunctions of opposition or concession, such as *although, even if, however much, granted that*
11.8.5	**Final**:	conjunctions of purpose or result, such as *that, in order that*
11.8.6	**Consecutive**:	conjunctions of consequence or result, such as *so that*
11.8.7	**Causal**:	conjunctions of cause, such as *because, inasmuch as*
11.8.8	**Interrogative**:	question-conjunctions in dependent or independent questions, such as *why, whether, whether … or not …*e
11.8.9	**Pronominal**:	the relative pronouns [§11.9]

11.9 **Compound subordinate conjunctions** (a type of correlative [§11.6]) are those such as *as … as …* and *not so … as …*:

> He is *as* old *as* she is.
> He is *as* old *as* she.   (*elision in second clause*)

NOTE: In a comparison, do not omit the second *as*.

WRONG: He is *as old, if not older than she*.
CORRECT: He is *as old as she, if not older*.

11.10 The **relative pronouns** (*which, that* and *what*, and the three case forms of *who*) are also used as **subordinate conjunctions**. See §6.13.

11.11 Several **subordinating conjunctions**—particularly those expressing concepts of time, place, manner or degree—are also adverbs, and are called **relative adverbs** or **conjunctive adverbs**. Common ones are *after, as, before, how, since, until, when, whence, whenever, where, wherever, while, whither* and *why*, as given in §9.13.

11.12 When two or more subordinate clauses are joined, the subordinate conjunction must be repeated with each one in order to make the meaning clear, and to give logical balance to the sentence. (Failure to do so creates a ***dangling clause***.)

WRONG: *Jack said he would climb the hill **and that** he would bring some water back down.*
CORRECT: *Jack said **that** he would climb the hill **and that** he would bring some water back down.*

11.13 Subordinating conjunctions used with participles have a form that looks very much like that of a preposition with its phrase. However, it must be remembered that this is a case of the elision of the subject and verb from a dependent clause, not a prepositional phrase.

ELIDED: *While waiting, Jill saw Jack fall.*
COMPLETE: *While she was waiting, Jill saw Jack fall.*

11.14 **Conjunctions** sometimes pose problems or questions of usage, as detailed below.

11.14.1 Items connected by coordinate conjunctions must be of the same class or usage.

> **WRONG**: *She liked **to write** songs **and singing** them to her friends.* (**and** *connects an infinitive and a gerund*)
>
> **CORRECT**: *She liked **to write** songs **and to sing** them to her friends.* (**and** *connects two infinitives*)
>
> **CORRECT**: *She liked **writing** songs **and singing** them to her friends.* (**and** *connects two gerunds*)

11.14.2 Do not put **and** before **etc.** Because **etc.** is the abbreviation of the Latin phrase **et cetera**, that means "and so forth", prefacing it with another **and** is redundant. On occasion, it is possible to see **etc.** written as **&c.** This is permissible, as the ampersand is a symbol derived from the cursive form of the Latin word **et**, a fact more readily discernible from some fonts (**e.g.**, Book Antiqua Italic's *&*) than from others.

11.14.3 **As** expresses approximation; or it expresses consecutive action or state similarly to **because**. **As** must not be used after verbs of expression, sensation or cogitation, particularly **to say**, **to think** and **to feel**. Use **that**, or **as if**, depending on the targeted meaning.

> **WRONG**: *I do not feel **as** I would be welcome on the trip.*
> **CORRECT**: *I do not feel **that** I should be welcome on the trip*
> **CORRECT**: *I do not feel **as if** I should be welcome on the trip.*

11.14.4 In specialist language, use **as at** for the specific dates or times of the topic's occurrence; use **as of**, when the topic or event commences at that point and continues for a time, whether that length of time is specified or not.

> **CORRECT**: *Total sales was reported as $1000 **as at** December 1, 1964.*
> (*the amount was subject to change almost immediately*)
> **CORRECT**: *The account was in arrears **as of** July 15.*
> (*the account achieved the condition at that time, and continued for an unspecified period*)

11.14.5 Do not use **but what** after a negative independent clause because **what** is not a conjunction, but a conjunctive adjective, and therefore requires a substantive to modify. Use **but that**.

> **WRONG**: *She doesn't know **but what** I bought her a trifle; I bought her a ring.*
> **CORRECT**: *She doesn't know **but that** I bought her a trifle; I bought her a ring.*

11.14.6 Do not use **help but** in the sense of **to avoid**.

> **WRONG**: *When he fell off the chair I could not **help but** laugh.*
> **CORRECT**: *When he fell off the chair I could not **help** laughing.*

11.14.7 When clauses containing verbs of expression, sensation or cogitation, particularly **to say**, **to think** and **to feel**, are followed by a clause starting with an infinitive, never omit the conjunction **that**.

> **WRONG**: *He worked hard because he knew to shirk would cost him the job.*
> **CORRECT**: *He worked hard because he knew **that** to shirk would cost him the job.*

11.14.8 Do not use *except* as a conjunction: it is an adverb. Use *unless* instead.

> **WRONG**: *She sang her songs, **except** her friends objected.*
> **CORRECT**: *She sang her songs, **unless** her friends objected.*

However, *except* may be used to modify a conjunction:

> **CORRECT**: *She sang her songs, **except when** her friends objected.*
> **CORRECT**: *She would have sung her songs, **except that** her friends objected.*

11.14.9 Do not use *if* as a conjunction when a choice limited to alternate actions is implied in the subordinate clause. Use *whether* instead.

> **WRONG**: *I don't know **if** we are still going to be having a sale.*
> **CORRECT**: *I don't know **whether** we are still going to be having a sale.*

However, there is no problem in using *if* when more than one alternative is obviously available:

> **CORRECT**: *I don't know **whether** I will wear the blue suit.* (I will either wear the blue suit, or not.)
> **CORRECT**: *I don't know **if** I will wear the blue suit.* (I don't know what I might wear, of all my choices of clothes.)

11.14.10 *So* is an adverb, **not** a conjunction: use *so that* instead. (This problem is seen most often with *dependent clauses of purpose*.)

> **WRONG**: *Jack worked overtime **so** he could buy some new pails.*
> **CORRECT**: *Jack worked overtime **so that** he could buy some new pails.*

11.14.11 Use *than* after clauses containing a comparative expression.

> *I worked **harder than** I had expected.*

NOTE: A complete second, dependent clause after *than* will avert ambiguity.

> **AMBIGUOUS**: *I worked harder **than expected**.* (expected by whom?)
> **CLEAR**: *I worked harder **than my manager expected**.* (clauses are coeval)
> **CLEAR**: *I worked harder **than my manager had expected**.* (dependent clause precedes independent)
> **CLEAR**: *I worked harder **than I would ever have expected**.*

NOTE: The (positive degree) adjective *different* is **not** a comparative expression: use *from what* to introduce a dependent clause following this adjective. The same thing applies to its adverbial form *differently*.

> *The work was **different from what** I had expected.*
> *The work ended **differently from what** I had expected.*

When *different* is used in the comparative degree, *than* is correct, as it is with all comparatives. Notice, however, the very specific meaning that its comparative usage relays, as expressed within the brackets.

> *The work was **more different than** my previous job [had been different from all the others].*

11.14.12   Use *when* after clauses containing *scarcely* or *hardly*.

> *I had **scarcely** started working **when** the manager showed up.*

11.14.13   In a sentence containing an *if* condition clause followed by a result clause, it is not always necessary to open the result clause with *then*. In modern usage, inserting *then* is done only to emphasize the sentiment of the result clause. Otherwise, *then* is elided.

> ***If** I had started working earlier, I'd already have completed the project.*
> ***If** I had just started working earlier, **then** I would already have completed the project.*

11.14.14   Do not use *where* as a conjunction when location or direction (adverbial usage) is *not* the primary purpose of the subordinate clause.

> **WRONG**:   *I saw in the paper **where** your store will be having a sale.*   (*noun clause?* *adverb clause?*)
> **CORRECT**:   *I saw in the paper **that** your store will be having a sale.*   (*noun clause: direct object*)
> **CORRECT**:   *I saw the store **where** the sale will be.*   (*adverb clause of location*)

11.14.15   Use *while* to join clauses in which the actions occur at the same time. Do not use *while* when contrast is the true meaning; use *although*, *but*, or *whereas* in that situation. Although this may seem a harmless distinction, being consistent in usage will minimize the chance of confusion.

> **UNCLEAR**:   *I read the paper **while** you read the news online.*   (*contemporaneous?* *adversative?*)
> **CONSISTENT**:   *I read the paper, **while** you're reading the news online.*   (*contemporaneous*)
> **CONSISTENT**:   *I read the paper, **whereas** you read the news online.*   (*adversative*)

11.14.16   Do not use *without* as a conjunction: it is a preposition or an adverb. Use *that* instead, with swap of negative for positive.

> **WRONG**:   *She never sang her songs, **without** someone applauded.*
> **CORRECT**:   *She never sang her songs, **that** someone didn't applaud.*

11.14.17   Avoid using *like* as a conjunction: as a word, *like* is trite because it is so horribly overused. Replace *like* with *as*, *as if* or *that*, or the phrase *much like*.

Reserve *like* for use as a conjunction in statements of specific approximation of objects, but not of actions. It were even better if one used *much like* instead of the single word *like*, to break away from all bad uses of that word.

> **POOR**:   *Write the letters **like** he showed you.*
> **CORRECT**:   *Write the letters **as** he showed you.*
>
> **POOR**:   *Try to act **like** you care.*
> **CORRECT**:   *Try to act **as if** you care.*
>
> **PASSABLE**: *One breed of cat is **like** the others.*
> **CORRECT**:   *One breed of cat is **much like** the others.*

As a test for how to replace *like* with a better conjunction, insert the appropriate form of the verb *to approximate* in place of the verb (if one is involved), and of the conjunction *like*: if the statement still makes sense, *like* is OK to be used there.

> **SOURCE**:   *Write the letters [**like?**] he showed you.*
> **TEST**:   *Write the letters **approximate** he showed you.*
> **CORRECT**:   *Write the letters **as** he showed you.*   (**like** *should **not** be used here*)

> **SOURCE**:   *The letters you wrote [**are like?**] the ones he wrote.*
> **TEST**:   *The letters you wrote **approximate** the ones he wrote.*
> **CORRECT**:   *The letters you wrote **are like** the ones he wrote.*   (**like** *is OK to be used here*)

Meaningless, and often repetitive, use of the word *like* and usage of the phrase "*to be [so] like*" <u>must be avoided</u>. The word should be replaced with a real verb or other word, and that phrase with a completely different phrase, in order not to sound juvenile, ignorant or anxiety-ridden.

Like has three, and only three, possible uses. It conveys

    ① affection: *I like my teacher.*

    ② want or preference: *I'd like another apple, please.*

    ③ comparison: *That dog is like one I used to have.*

This author once heard a teenage girl, sitting with a teenage boy on the subway seat behind him, say the word *like* 73 times within three minutes. Apparently, her nervousness at being on what appeared to be a first date had overwhelmed both her vocabulary and her ability to hear just how vapid she sounded.

> **SOURCE**:   *And I [**was so like?**] Huh? And they [**were like?**] Yeah!*
> **TEST**:   *And I **so approximated** Huh? And they **approximated** Yeah!*
> **CORRECT**:   *And **I thought**, "What?" And they **replied**, "Yes!"*
> (*And I am so like,* **like** *is* **like so wrong** *to be like used here!*)

NOTE: *like* is also used as a preposition, specifically meaning *approximation* or *emulation*, and is often found governing prepositional phrases after verbs of the senses.

> *What does this drawing **look like**?*   (*With rearrangement, this parses as "<u>Like what</u> does this drawing look?"*)

> *This spice **smells like** rich chocolate.*   (*Here,* **like** *governs an adverbial prepositional phrase modifying the verb* **smells**.)

12 Interjections

12.1 Interjections are independent words or phrases added to the basic sentence to express further emotional content or information, or to add color to the utterance. They do not have any effect on the grammatical structure of the sentence to which they are attached.

12.2 An interjection that is the name of the person addressed, a situation called **direct address**, may be said to be in the **Vocative** case. Although some languages have alternate forms for nouns in the Vocative, in English the addressed name has the same form as the **Nominative case**, and is said to be in that case rather than in the Vocative.

> **Jason,** *get off the couch.*
> *Drop the chalupa,* **Henry***!*

12.3 Some nouns may be used as interjections in order to direct others' attention to a particular topic or item of concern. This is the function of the **nominative of exclamation**.

> **Fire! Fire!** (elided expression for **There is a fire!**)

12.4 **Exclamations** are other words or phrases used as interjections added to sentences; or they may be stand-alone phrases. Having no connection (other than emotional) to any sentence around them, these are often **idioms**, or even phrases borrowed from other languages.

These are often expressions of emotional or physical responses to conditions, and use of dialect forms is often used to give color to the expression, or just for fun:

> **Hey!**
> **Ouch!** *That hurts!*
> *You want what on your bagel?* **Oy, gevalt!**
> **Oh!** *They said that?* **Get outta here!**
> *What is the answer?* **Why,** *I don't know!* – **Why?**

NOTE: In this last example the first **why** is, in *ACE*, pronounced differently from its second occurrence in the same example. In its first use, as an interjection, the 'h' is ignored and the word is pronounced as if spelled **wy**, /waɪ/, while in its other uses (including as an interrogative pronoun, as here) the 'h' is pronounced correctly, as spelled: /hwaɪ/.

12.5 A **responsive** is a **yes** or **no** added to a sentence:

> **No,** *I can't come to the phone right now.*
> *If you want,* **yes,** *I'll read you a story now.*

13 The Sentence

13.1   The framework on which meaningful utterances are formed is ***the sentence***. Words do not exist by themselves, as floating dictionary entries, but rather are joined into phrases that constitute sentences.

13.1.1   A sentence contains ***a complete thought***.

13.1.2   A sentence is made up of ***a subject and a predicate***.

13.2   The ***subject*** is a substantive with any modifiers: it is a word or a phrase.
The **subject** of a sentence is ***the topic***, about which information is conveyed, or ***the actor*** performing the remainder of the sentence.

> ***Dogs*** *bark.*
> ***Apples*** *are red.*
> ***Clouds*** *block the sun.*
> ***The sun*** *is blocked by clouds.*
> ***His singing*** *is annoying.*
> ***I*** *can't abide his singing.*

13.2.1   The ***simple subject*** is the subject without any accompanying modifier.

> *Young **Jack** went up the hill.*
> ***They*** *both should have come down by now.*

13.2.2   The ***complete subject*** is the subject with all its accompanying modifiers.

> ***Young Jack*** *went up the hill.*
> ***They both*** *should have come down by now.*

13.2.3   A ***compound subject*** is one made up of two or more simple subjects joined by a **conjunctive**.

> *Young **Jack and Jill** went up the hill.*
> ***He or she*** *came down.*

13.3   A ***predicate*** is a verb and any modifiers: it can be a single word or a phrase.

The predicate of a sentence is the information—an action or a state—that is ***caused by*** or ***descriptive of*** the subject.

> *Dogs **bark**.*
> *Apples **are red**.*
> *Clouds **block the sun**.*
> *The sun **is blocked by clouds**.*
> *His singing **is annoying**.*
> *I **can't abide his singing**.*

13.3.1   The ***simple predicate*** is the **predicate** without any accompanying modifier. It can be a single verb or a verb phrase—a verb along with all its auxiliaries.

> *Young Jack and Jill **went** up the hill.*
> *They both **should have come** down by now.*
> *Jack **must have been wearing** his crown.*

13.3.2   The **complete predicate** is the predicate with all its accompanying modifiers.

> *Young Jack and Jill **went up the hill**.*
> *They both **should have come down by now**.*
> *Jack **must have been wearing his crown**.*

13.3.3   A **compound predicate** is one made up of two or more simple predicates.

> *He **fell** down **and broke** his crown.*

NOTE: The word **predicate** is most often used specifically to mean **simple predicate**. and this meaning should be assumed unless the context of its usage involves contrasts between a **simple predicate** and either **complete predicates** or **compound predicates**.

13.4   An **elliptical sentence** is one in which either the subject or predicate has been omitted.

subject elided: [**You**] *Read this sentence!*   (*The subject is elided, leaving the predicate phrase.*)

predicate elided: *Who reads? You* [**read**].   (*The predicate is entirely elided.*)

subject and verb elided: *What do you read?* [**I read**] *Sentences.*   (**Sentences** *is the direct object remnant of that sentence's predicate phrase.*)

13.4.1   The subject or the predicate may be elided (or omitted) and understood from context, but at least some part of either the subject or the predicate must be expressed.

13.5   The word or phrase that receives the action of the verb is the **direct object**. Only an **active verb** can govern a **direct object**.

> *The dog chases **cats**.*
> *I ate **apples**.*
> *You read **sentences**.*

13.6   The other kind of verb, besides an **active verb**, is a **state of being**, or **linking verb**. **State of being verbs** include **to be** as well as any verb that does not act, but merely conveys the state of the subject, or a simple change of state not caused by the verb itself.

> *The dog **is** happy.*
> *I **feel** good.*   (*i.e., I am healthy, happy, in a good mood, etc.*)
> *I **feel** well.*   (*i.e., I am no longer sick.*)
> *I **feel** bad.*   [*never "I feel badly" unless the nerves in your fingers have stopped working!*]
> *The weather **grows** cold.*   (*i.e., The weather is becoming cold.*)

13.6.1   The state expressed by the word or phrase following a state of being verb is called a **predicate nominative**, or **subjective complement**.
[Note: comp**le**ment, not comp**li**ment]

13.7 A *transposed sentence* is one in which the normal order of words, particularly of the subject and predicate, are reversed from their normal sequence, in order to express a greater level of sentiment—stronger feeling, force or importance.

*Sorrowful **appeared** his **visage.***   (*His **visage appeared** sorrowful.*)
Pass** the test **I** certainly **shall!   (***I shall** certainly **pass** the test.*)
*One good push and down **came the wall.***   (*One good push and the **wall came** down.*)

Now is the winter of our discontent
Made glorious summer by this sun of York
William Shakespeare (*Richard the Third*: I, 1)

13.8 A word or group of words that changes or refines the meaning of another word is a **modifier**. Examples of modifiers are **adjectives**, **adverbs** and **prepositional phrases**.

13.9 A **phrase** is a group of related words that has neither a subject nor a predicate.

13.10 A **clause** is a group of related words that has a subject and a predicate.

13.10.1 Either the subject or the predicate of a clause may be elided.

13.11 An **independent clause** is a clause that can stand alone as an independent sentence: a **simple sentence** is also an independent clause.

13.12 A **dependent clause** is a clause that can stand alone as an independent sentence because it does not make complete sense. Dependent clauses are always accompanied by an independent clause that determines the meaning of the entire sentence.

13.12.1 **Dependent clauses** can function as

1. **nouns:**   *Where he had been was a secret.*
What the dog had eaten was what the vet needed to know.
2. **adjectives:**   *She who had asked never got a clear answer.*
3. **adverbs:**   *When he gave his answer she didn't believe him.*

13.12.1.1 *Noun dependent clauses* can be used wherever a noun may appear.

13.12.1.2 *Adjective dependent clauses* are used, like adjectives, to modify nouns or pronouns.

13.12.1.3 *Adverb dependent clauses* are limited in that they do not modify the full range of types that simple adverbs may modify, but instead modify only verbs.

13.12.2 **Dependent clauses** can be either *limiting* or *non-limiting.*

13.12.2.1 A **non-limiting dependent clause** is not essential to the meaning of the sentence, but merely adds information, making the sentence more descriptive.

13.12.2.2 A **limiting dependent clause** is essential to the meaning of the sentence.

Removing a limiting clause either changes the meaning of the sentence, or reduces its sensibility.

13.13 **Connectives** are used to join parts of a sentence. These include both conjunctions and prepositions. Connectives are made up of words, phrases or clauses.

13.14 **Independent elements** are Words, phrases or clauses that have no grammatical connection to the sentence in which they appear, or that modify the sentence (or major clauses within it) rather than acting as appositives of individual units. They are set off from the rest of the sentence by parentheses, or by other separating punctuation.

There are several classes and subclasses of **independent elements**:

1. **Interjections**
   a. **Exclamations** — *Hey! Ouch!*
   b. **Substantives of direct address** — *Drop the chalupa, **Henry**!*
   c. **Nominatives of exclamation** — *Tornado!*
   d. **Responsives** — *Yes, I will be there this morning.*
2. **Parenthetical expressions** — *The answer, **I've heard**, is 42.*
   *Independence Day **(July 4th)** is usually hot.*
3. **Nominative absolutes** — ***The day being cooler,** the dogs ran far and fast.*

13.15 The four **classifications of sentences** are:

- **declarative**   sentences that make a statement

  I didn't hear you say that.

- **imperative**   sentences that state a command or strong request

  Don't say that!

- **interrogative**   sentences that ask a question

  Did you say that?

- **exclamatory**   sentences that express strong emotion, or convey a statement forcefully

  Surely you didn't say that!

13.16 As explained in §1.2.1, the **standard order**, or "natural order", of the English sentence is **subject**, then **verb**.

After the verb may come

(1) **direct objects** and **indirect objects** of transitive verbs, or

(2) **predicate nouns** or **predicate adjectives** of linking or state of being verbs, or

(3) **predicate adverbs** of intransitive verbs.

13.16.1 Any words or phrases that follow a verb and complete its meaning are called a **predicate complement**.

13.17 The ***three types of sentences*** are

- **simple**
- **compound**
- **complex**

13.17.1 In a ***simple sentence***, there is a single independent clause and no dependent clause.

> *The dog barks.*
> *The cat meows.*
> *The boy plays cards.*
> *Linda sings.*
> *Marsha dances.*

A **simple sentence** may have a ***compound subject***, a ***compound predicate***, or ***both***.

> *The dog **barks and chases** the ball.*   (compound predicate)
> ***The cat and the bird*** *are watching each other closely.*   (compound subject)
> ***Linda and Pat are playing*** *cards **and talking** about toys.*   (compound subject and compound predicate)

13.17.2 A ***compound sentence,*** is **two or more simple sentences** connected by a **word**, **words** or **punctuation**.

> *The dog barks **and** the boy chases the ball.*
> *I've eaten dinner, **and yet** I am still hungry.*
> *The cat meows**;** the bird looks nervous.*

13.17.3 A ***complex sentence*** is one that contains **a single independent clause** and **one or more dependent clauses**.

> *The dog barks **while** the boy chases the ball.*
> ***When*** *the wind blew, the cat meowed **as** the bird looked around nervously.*

13.17.4 The ***dependent clauses*** appearing in **complex sentences** can be ***noun clauses***, ***adjective clauses*** or ***adverbial clauses***.

13.17.5 A ***noun clause*** fills the role of a noun.

> ***That the hills are steep*** *was already well known to the hikers.*
>   (the dependent clause is the subject)
>
> *They knew **that the hills are steep.***   (the dependent clause is the direct object of the verb)

13.17.5.1 A noun clause can be restated in any one of several manners, depending on the words used in the clause, and the logical sense they themselves permit.

> ***Cheerfulness*** *helps with every task.*   (noun)
> ***To be cheerful*** *will make every task lighter.*   (infinitive phrase)
> ***Being cheerful*** *makes every task go faster.*   (gerund phrase)
> ***That we are cheerful*** *makes our every task easier.*   (noun clause)

13.17.5.2 Much like the infinitive [§7.24.11], a noun dependent clause can appear as a **predicate appositive** to the subject of a sentence or clause composed of *it* with a form of *to be* followed by a predicate noun. In this usage, the clause functions as an appositive of the subject pronoun, *it*.

> *Given the heavy snowfall, it was a wonder **that we could walk** to the store.*
>
> (**it** = **that we could walk**)

13.17.5.3 When an adverbial conjunction is used to introduce a **noun dependent clause**, that adverb modifies only the predicate of the dependent clause.

This stands in contrast to the situation with **adverbial dependent clauses**, in which such an adverb connector will modify the predicates of both the dependent clause and the independent clause to which it is attached.

> ***When the man entered the store*** *can be determined from the security cameras.*
>
> (**when** *modifies only* **entered the store**)
>
> ***When the man entered the store*** *the security cameras were active.*
>
> (**when** *modifies both* **entered** *and* **were active**)

13.17.6 An ***adjective clause*** modifies a noun or pronoun, or functions as a **predicate adjective**.

> *The fact **that the hills are steep** was well known to the hikers.*
>
> (the dependent clause modifies the subject)
>
> *The hikers **who knew the hills well** dreaded their steepness.*
>
> (the dependent clause modifies the subject)

13.17.7 An ***adverb clause*** modifies any part of speech that a simple adverb can modify.

> *They knew the path's steepness **before they ever started hiking**.*
>
> (the dependent clause modifies the verb; it restricts the meaning of the verb in time)

13.17.7.1 An adverb clause is, like all adverbial phrases, set off from the rest of the sentence by commas unless it follows and restricts the meaning of whatever it modifies.

> ***Before they started hiking***, *they sat and talked about the hill's steepness.*
>
> (the dependent clause modifies the verb; it restricts the meaning of the verb)

13.17.8 ***A complex sentence*** can have several dependent clauses, mixing the types of clauses whenever needed.

> ***Before they had even started hiking***, *they knew **that the hills are steep**.*
>
> (the first, adverb dependent clause modifies the verb; the second, noun dependent clause is the direct object of the verb)

13.17.9 ***A compound-complex sentence*** is one that has more than one independent clause, each of which can have several dependent clauses, of whatever types are required.

> *The water in the rivers flowing across the surface of the Earth obeys the rules of fluids; the shallow surface flows faster than the depths; and the wide center flows faster than the bank-hugging sides.*
>
> [See No. 59, p. 305, in the Advanced Diagramming Examples for an example of the complexity involved in a compound-complex sentence.]

13.18 *Common mistakes to avoid in sentence construction*

In writing that is not specifically for style or characterization (*i.e.*, specifically for poetry or characterization in a novel), avoid these common mistakes.

13.18.1 Do not use a ***fragment*** in place of a complete sentence.

> *While the boy chases the ball.*
> *As the bird looked around nervously.*

13.18.1 Do not place two (or more) independent statements (whether their ideas are related or not) within what appears to be a single sentence. This is called a ***run-on sentence***. This is a serious blunder, but it is usually caused by haste (and failure to proofread) rather than lack of skill or understanding.

Use the punctuation that is appropriate to your aim: either use a semicolon to divide the statements, or separate them into two sentences.

Do not use a comma in place of the semicolon; reserve the comma for its own usages.

WRONG: *The dog barks the boy chases the ball.*   (***run-on sentence***)
CORRECT: *The dog barks. The boy chases the ball.*

WRONG: *The wind blew the cat meowed, the bird looked around nervously.*
CORRECT: *The wind blew; the cat meowed; the bird looked around nervously.*

13.18.2 ***Personal pronouns*** must be clear in their usage.

13.18.2.1 The ***antecedent of a personal pronoun*** must be clear. It is often necessary to replace such a personal pronoun with nouns or verb phrases to remove the ambiguity.

WRONG: *The book criticized his prose, but he ignored it.*
> The pronoun ***it*** has nothing definite to serve as its antecedent: does it refer to **the book**, the **criticism**, or even to **his prose**?

CORRECT: *The book criticized his prose, but he ignored **that text**.*
> (*refers to* **the book**)

CORRECT: *The book criticized his prose, but he ignored **such petty responses**.*
> (*refers to* **criticized**)

CORRECT: *The book criticized his prose, but he **refused to edit his writing**.*
> (*refers to* **his prose**)

13.18.2.2 The ***reference of a personal pronoun*** must be clear.

WRONG: *The priest told Alexander that he was the son of a god.*
> It is unclear whether **he** refers to **the priest** or to **Alexander**.

WRONG: *The priest told Alexander that he himself was the son of a god.*
> ***Himself*** refers to **he**, and it is still unclear whether **he** refers to **the priest** or to **Alexander**.

CORRECT: *The priest told Alexander that he, Alexander, was the son of a god.*
> The appositive defines and clarifies the reference.

CORRECT: *Alexander was told that he was the son of a god by the priest.*
> Use of the passive allows positioning of **he** so that it refers clearly to ***Alexander***.

(Note that moving the prepositional phrase of the agent into the wrong position does not fix the problem: *Alexander was told by the priest that he was the son of a god.* is still ambiguous.

CORRECT: *The priest told Alexander, "You are the son of a god."*
Rephrasing as a direct quote results in removal of the ambiguous pronoun.

13.18.2.3 The **reference of a relative pronoun** must be clear.

WRONG: *The dog chased the ball on the carpet that the boy had thrown.*
The dependent clause is confusing. In its position it modifies **on the carpet**, and implies that the carpet had been thrown; yet, in sense it probably modifies **the ball**.

CORRECT: *The dog chased the ball that the boy had thrown on the carpet.*
This indicates where the ball had been thrown: on the carpet rather than, say, on the couch.

CORRECT: *The dog chased the ball on the carpet, the one that the boy had thrown there.*
This sentence could mean either that the ball had been thrown by the boy rather than by someone else, or that there could have been another ball that he had, for example, rolled somewhere instead of thrown. This is because the dependent clause is parallel, with the substantive **one** matching the noun **ball**, and the adverb **there** matching the adverbial prepositional phrase **on the carpet**.

13.18.2.4 Do not use the relative pronoun **which** to refer to an entire clause.
Replace this construction with one that emphasizes the central idea of the sentence, or with phrases of greater descriptive power.

WRONG: *The dog chased the ball across the carpet, which made the boy laugh.*
CORRECT: *The boy laughed when the dog chased the ball across the carpet.*
CORRECT: *The dog chased the ball across the carpet; the boy cackled with laughter.*

13.18.3 Do not use **and** or **but** to connect unequal phrases, unrelated ideas, or just to string clauses together.
Use of either conjunction inappropriately makes an utterance puerile.

WRONG: *The dog chased the ball on the carpet and it made the boy laugh.*
CORRECT: *The boy laughed when the dog chased the ball on the carpet.*

WRONG: *The dog chased the ball on the carpet and the boy laughed and we saw a cat in a tree.*
CORRECT: *The boy laughed when the dog chased the ball on the carpet; then we saw a cat in a tree.*

13.18.4 Do not speak or write in **monotonous, short sentences**. These **primer sentences** produce the impression of writing done for those just learning to read.

WRONG: *The dog chased the ball. The boy laughed. We saw a cat.*
CORRECT: *The boy laughed when the dog chased the ball on the carpet; then we saw a cat perched in a tree.*

13.18.5 Avoid **mishandled modifiers.**

Because English is an analytic language, statements are recognized and understood in their sequential order. Things out of order cause changes in meaning or confusion modifying or blocking understanding.

13.18.5.1 Avoid **dangling modifiers**. These are phrases in which the modified item is not expressed: the modifier is left dangling with no connection, or an incorrectly implied connection, to the main clause.

> **WRONG**: **On starting to read** Moby Dick, an interesting phrase **is found**.
>> (**phrase** does not do the **starting**)
>
> **CORRECT**: **On starting to read** Moby Dick, **one finds** an interesting phrase.
>> (**one does** do the **starting** as well as the **finding**)
>
> **WRONG**: **At seven years of age his father died**, leaving him destitute.
>> (the **father** died at seven)
>
> **CORRECT**: **When he was seven years of age, his father died**, leaving him destitute.
>> (**he** was seven when it happened)

13.18.5.2 Avoid **misplaced modifiers**.

> **WRONG**: Scarlet saw drapes hanging in a window **that she liked**.
>> (the clause modifies **window**)
>
> **CORRECT**: Scarlet saw drapes **that she liked** hanging in a window.
>> (the clause modifies **drapes**)
>
> **WRONG**: To **quickly** make a dress, Scarlet used the material of the drapes.
>> (**split infinitive**)
>
> **CORRECT**: To make a dress **quickly**, Scarlet used the material of the drapes.
>> (**quickly** modifies **to make a dress**, not just the word **make**)
>
> **POSSIBLE**: He **almost** walked ten miles.
>> (this means that he was stopped before having started; it needs context)
>
> **CLEAR**: He walked **almost** ten miles.
>> (i.e., he walked eight or nine, but not ten, miles)
>
> **CLEAR**: Before I stopped him, he **almost** walked ten miles.
>> (i.e., he was stopped just before undertaking the walk)
>
> **CLEAR**: Before I stopped him, he had walked **almost** ten miles.
>> (i.e., he was stopped before he had walked the full ten miles)
>
> **UNCLEAR**: He died at home after a long and painful illness **on May 4, 1925**.
>> (this seems to give the date as a modifier of the illness)
>
> **CLEAR**: He died at home **on May 4, 1925**, after a long and painful illness.
>> (this is clearer because it groups the verb with its modifying date, and saves the additional information for later in the sentence)

13.18.6 Avoid **needless shifts**.

13.18.6.1 Do not shift between **disparate constructs** for like ideas. **Use parallel structures for parallel thoughts**.

> **WRONG**: **Speaking** English is easier than **to write** it.
>> (**Speaking** is a gerund; **to write** is an infinitive)

CORRECT: *Speaking* English is easier than *writing* it. *(both constructs are gerunds)*

CORRECT: *To speak* English is easier than *to write* it. *(both constructs are infinitives)*

13.18.6.2   Avoid **needless shifts in person.**

WRONG: *You* can speak English before *one* is able to read it.
(You *is second person,* **one** *is third person)*

CORRECT: *You* can speak English before *you* are able to read it.
(second person in both clauses)

CORRECT: *One* can speak English before *one* is able to read it.
(third person in both clauses; second **one** *could be replaced by* **he** *or* **she** *[but not* **he or she**])

13.18.6.3   Avoid **needless shifts in number.**
This has invaded almost all of English, like fire ants in the American South, because of a desire to appear politically correct by not using what has been portrayed as sexist, that is, the (actually gender-indeterminate) use of *he* in referring to a demonstrative, indefinite or relative pronoun antecedent.

WRONG: *Each* can speak English before *they* are able to read it.
(Each *is singular,* **they** *is plural)*

CORRECT: *Each* can speak English before *he* is able to read it.
(singular in both clauses; gender neutral)

CORRECT: *Each* can speak English before *she* is able to read it.
(singular in both clauses; gender specific)

CORRECT: *All* can speak English before *they* are able to read it.
(plural in both clauses)

13.18.6.4   Avoid **needless shifts in subject.** This is often related to the shifts in person and/or number mentioned above.

WRONG: *His novels* are good, and *he* writes them well.   *(shift in subjects)*

CORRECT: *His novels* are good, and *they* are well-written.   *(single subject)*

CORRECT: *His novels* are good; *he* writes well.   *(separation into multiple clauses)*

13.18.6.5   Avoid **needless shifts in tense.**

WRONG: *He* **couldn't speak** *English, but then he* **is able** *to.*
(past tense shifts suddenly to present tense)

CORRECT: *He* **couldn't speak** *English, but then he* **was able** *to.*
(both are in the past tense)

WRONG: *We* **walked** *down the street when we* **come** *upon a wallet on the sidewalk.*

CORRECT: *We* **were walking** *down the street when we* **came** *upon a wallet on the sidewalk.*

13.18.6.6   Avoid **needless shifts in voice.**

WRONG: *You can speak* English before *it can be read*.
(can speak *is in the active voice,* **can be read** *is in the passive voice)*

CORRECT: *You can speak* English before *you are able to read it*.
(both are in the active voice)

CORRECT: *English can be spoken* before *it can be read*.
(both are in the passive voice)

13.18.7 Learn the differences between parts of speech and how each one is used.

> **WRONG**: *This will really **impact on** the way I work.*
> > (**impact** *as a **verb** never requires a preposition*)
> **CORRECT**: *This will really **impact** the way I work.*
> **CORRECT**: *This will have a major **impact on** the way I work.*
> > (**impact** *as a **noun always** requires a preposition in this usage*)

> **WRONG**: *The cat's springing from behind the couch took me **back**; it caught me **unaware**.*
> > (**to take aback** *is an idiom and requires* **aback**)
> > (**unawares** *is an adverb that means* **by surprise, unexpectedly, suddenly.** *To use the adjective* **unaware** *here would require further information, such as* **unaware of its having hidden there**, *or restatement, such as "It caught me while I was unaware", which actually differs in meaning from the original example.*)
> **CORRECT**: *The cat's springing from behind the couch took me **aback**; it caught me **unawares**.*

13.18.8 **Use the Subjunctive** wherever it is called for.

> **WRONG**: *I just wish Jack **was** here to see this.*
> > (*but* Jack *isn't there, so use the subjunctive, or risk sounding puerile*)
> **CORRECT**: *I just wish Jack **were** here to see this.*

13.18.9 **Avoid errors of vocabulary.**

13.18.9.1 **Avoid redundancy.**

A particularly common redundancy is the **overuse of the word** *together*.

> **WRONG**: *They **joined** the steel beams **together**.*
> > (*you cannot* **join** *objects* **apart**, *so* **together** *is redundant*)
> **CORRECT**: *They **joined** the steel beams.*

> **WRONG**: *They **welded** the steel beams **together**.*
> > (**welding** *involves joining two items, so* **together** *is again redundant*)
> **CORRECT**: *They **welded** the steel beams.*

> **WRONG**: *They **riveted** the steel beams **together**.*
> > (*same issue as with* **weld**: **riveting** *is one way of* **joining** *items*)
> **CORRECT**: *They **riveted** the steel beams.*

> **WRONG**: *They **fused** the steel beams **together**.*
> > (*same issue as with* **weld**: **to fuse** *cannot be but* **together**)
> **CORRECT**: *They **fused** the steel beams.*

> **WRONG**: *Then they **mix** the chemicals **together**.*
> > (*you cannot* **mix** *things* **apart**, *so* **together** *is redundant*)
> **CORRECT**: *Then they **mix** the chemicals.*

> **WRONG**: *In the cyclotron, the atoms will **collide together**.*
> > (**together** *is the only way things can* **collide**: **together** *is redundant*)
> **CORRECT**: *In the cyclotron, the atoms will **collide**.*

13.18.9.2 Avoid tautology. This is the repetition of the same idea in different words within the same construction.

WRONG: Jack saw a **big giant** walking toward him.
(**big** is part of the definition of **giant**)
CORRECT: Jack saw a **giant** walking toward him.

WRONG: Aunt Sadie had been a **widow woman** a long time.
(a **widow** is defined to be a **woman**)
CORRECT: Aunt Sadie had been a **widow** a long time.

WRONG: We'll be able **to see visually** what had happened.
(In this sense, there is no other way to see.)
CORRECT: We'll be able **to see** what had happened.

WRONG: The seacoast town was hit by a **tsunami wave**.
(a **tsunami** is a specific type of **wave**)
CORRECT: The seacoast town was hit by a **tsunami**.

WRONG: The truck crossed the **center median** into oncoming traffic.
(a **median** is by definition in the **center** of the lanes of traffic)
CORRECT: The truck crossed the **median** into oncoming traffic.

The most flagrant acts of tautology and redundancy practiced by today's writers and speakers involve the word *time*.

Its tautological misuse is found in the phrase *time period*; and its redundant usage appears in prepositional phrases that restate *time* or its units.

Unfortunately, all these tautologies and redundancies are now widespread in scientists', bureaucrats', television-scriptwriters' hyper-wordiness, coming apparently from the speakers' and writers' misconception that they are being more specific, more descriptive. They aren't—they are merely creating new clichés and making their statements less effective because of the needless surfeit of words.

WRONG: Several notable things happened **during this time period**.
WRONG: Several notable things happened **during this period of time**.
CORRECT: Several notable things happened **during this time**.
CORRECT: Several notable things happened **during this period**.
(a **period** is **a span of time**, so incorporating the word **time** is naught but redundant:
time period = "time span-of-time",
period of time = "span-of-time of time")

WRONG: Only **during a fleeting moment in time** was the storm severe.
CORRECT: Only **during a fleeting moment** was the storm severe.
(a **moment** is a non-specific unit of time, so adding the phrase **of time** is redundant: "during a fleeting unit-of-time in time")

WRONG: This happened **within ten seconds of time**.
CORRECT: This happened **within ten seconds**.
(a **second** is a specific unit of time, so adding the phrase **of time** is redundant: "**within ten units-of-time of time**"; the original statement is comparable to saying "**within ten feet of distance**")

Note that tautological and redundant usages of the word *time*, such as these, are distinct from its use in situations in which its statement is subsequently defined more precisely.

CORRECT: *The **time** in which this happened, **within ten seconds**, was wholly unexpected.*

13.18.9.3 **Avoid monotonous repetition.**
This can involve identical words, or the same words appearing as different parts of speech.

WRONG: *I **enjoyed** the vacation; it was most **enjoyable**.*
BETTER: *I **enjoyed** the vacation; it was most **pleasurable**.*

This is a rule that English, compared to all other languages, makes the most use of, and takes most advantage of. English vocabulary is so huge, varied and rich in expression that it has the luxury of being minimally repetitive. In other languages this rule is not emphasized, or, indeed, cannot exist because the more general situation of constrained lexicons, as demonstrated in §1.1.4.6.

13.18.9.4 **Avoid wordiness.**
Avoid artificial expressions.

WRONG: *I enjoyed the vacation; it was **a most refreshing interlude of carefree bliss**.*
BETTER: *I enjoyed the vacation; it was **most pleasant**.*

WRONG: *The athlete walked **in a painful manner**.*
BETTER: *The athlete walked **painfully**.*

13.18.9.5 **Avoid triteness**, as they make your message sound like you're trying to be "hip", or "with it", and your message will ultimately sound dated or childish.

WRONG: *They had a **ginormous** wedding cake.*
BETTER: *They had an **enormous** wedding cake.*
BETTER: *They had a **gigantic** wedding cake.*

Being called, or referred to, by the word *dude* is rude for men, overtly offensive for women. The synonyms for this word include *dandy, fop, clotheshorse*, and in the American Southwest, *accident prone greenhorn*: an irritating novice.

WRONG: *Hey, **dude**!*
BETTER: *Hey!, Hi!, Hello!,* or be polite and use the individual's name!

The trite overuse of the ungrammatical misuse of "like", particularly in the phrase "so like", is the most common ignorant and childish utterance afflicting modern English. Please extend and use your vocabulary instead of inflicting this.

WRONG: *And I **was so like** "huh?"*
BETTER: *And I **thought**, "What?"*

Avoid using "um" or "uh".

WRONG: ***Um**, I'm not sure.*
BETTER: ***Well**, I'm not quite sure.*

Both the childish misuse of "like", and the use of "um" or "uh" create the impression of indecision, insecurity or unpreparedness. [See #17 in §11.14]

13.18.9.6 **Avoid clichés**, as they dilute the effectiveness of communication. They add words, but not meaning, wherever they appear. Use of clichés is often a sign of an insufficiently developed vocabulary.

Clichés are particularly undesirable when they are, in fact, internally redundant or inconsistent.

      BAD: *We wanted to know **the why and the wherefore**.*   (**wherefore** means **why**)
CORRECT: *We wanted to know **why** it had happened.*

      BAD: *She was angry, so she avoided him **like the plague**.*
  BETTER: *She was angry, so she avoided him **strenuously**.*

13.18.9.6.1 Remember that adding the suffix **-wise** to another word to create some sort of general, environmental or spatial adverb or adjective is a cliché, and is the hallmark of the poor speaker and of the hack writer. It does not matter whether it's hyphenated or not: it's a cliché.

      BAD: ***Weather-wise**, our temperatures should moderate in the next week.*
POSSIBLE: ***In our weather**, the temperatures should moderate in the next week.*
      (however, *as the temperatures spoken of do not involve anything like feverish persons, baking, firing pottery or such—and talking about the weather is already your topic, or your job—putting the word* **weather** *in the sentence is also redundant, unless you are specifically drawing attention to a change of topic.*)
  BETTER: *Our temperatures should moderate in the next week.*

      BAD: ***Support-wise**, that department has always been difficult.*
POSSIBLE: ***For those of us providing support**, that department has always been difficult.*
POSSIBLE: ***In terms of support**, that department has always been difficult.*
  BETTER: *That department has always been difficult to support.*

13.18.9.7 Unless you are specifically creating technical terms that do not already exist, and you are trained in proper creation of lexical items, **do not make up your own words**—you will just sound pretentious or uneducated: your audience either will not understand, or will presume you don't know what you're doing.

    WRONG: *They were a **warfaring** people.*   (*There is no such verb as **to warfare**, so there can never be a participle **warfaring***)
CORRECT: *They were a **warlike** people.*
CORRECT: *They were a people **given to war**.*

13.18.9.8 **Don't use words in senses opposite to, or at odds with, their actual meaning.**

    WRONG: *The Kanto region was **decimated** by the 1923 earthquake and fire.*
      (**to decimate ONLY** means **"to reduce by 10%"**; it does not now, nor has it ever meant **"to reduce by 90%"**, or **"to destroy utterly"**)
CORRECT: *The Kanto region was **devastated** by the 1923 earthquake and fire.*
CORRECT: *The Kanto region was **destroyed** by the 1923 earthquake and fire.*
CORRECT: *The Kanto region was **laid waste** by the 1923 earthquake and fire.*

WRONG: *This chicken salad is very **healthy**.*

> (*in reality, it is not **healthy** at all; to be so, the chicken would have to be running around, still alive, and the vegetables would yet be growing in the field*)

CORRECT: *This chicken salad is very **healthful**.*

13.18.9.9 **Make sure your use of vocabulary makes sense in context.**

If mistakes in vocabulary aren't seen as momentary lapses—or as evincing a lack of education—they will most often be taken to be comical, as demonstrated in the technical name for such a misstep: a *malapropism*, taken from the name of the character, *Mrs Malaprop*, in *The Rivals*, a play of 1775, written by Richard Sheridan. (Her name was coined from the adjective *malapropos*, an English word formed from the French phrase *mal à propos*, "ill [suited] to/for the purpose".)

Examples of the lexical missteps of *Mrs Malaprop*:

*"... she's as headstrong as an **allegory** on the banks of the Nile."*
> (*for* "an **alligator**")

*"Sure, if I **reprehend** any thing in this world it is the use of my **oracular** tongue, and a nice **derangement** of epitaphs!"*
> (*for* "**if I apprehend**", "**my vernacular**", *and* "**a nice arrangement of epithets**")

Note that observation of this rule is much loser in poetry than in prose. In poetry such bending, extension or fading of definitions can be used to great effect.

13.18.9.10 Unless done specifically for comic effect, **make sure the vocabulary within the context of your statements is both logically consistent and used correctly.**

Failure to do so will raise the specter of misunderstanding, of second-guessing, or of comical disbelief in your audience.

"Egypt was surrounded on all sides by desert, with the Mediterranean Sea in the north."
> — Ancient Discoveries, "Egyptian Warfare" [television series: Episode 17]
> (*Egypt cannot possibly be both surrounded by desert "**on all sides**" **and** have **a sea on one side**.*
> *Also, Egypt's geological situation has been constant over historical time, so the verb should be in the present tense.*)

"I don't know whether there is anything particularly exciting about the air in this particular part of Hertfordshire, but the number of engagements that go on seem to me to be considerably above the proper average that statistics have laid down for our guidance."
> — Oscar Wilde, The Importance of Being Earnest [1895]
> (*Statistics does not issue statements "**for guidance**"; it merely produces descriptions of observations, with possible derivations from those observations in the form of forecasts, probabilities and estimates.*
> ***Statistics** is also a singular noun when used as the name of a field of study, as it is here, so the character is confusing the science with the data used or produced by that science: the verb should be in the singular.*)

13.18.10 Present-day television programs are rife with extremely poorly written, presented and spoken English. Here are just a few of those noted [with this author's marks of explanatory emphasis], without reference to source because these ineffective or incorrect ways of expression are so very common across multiple presentations:

- *"**restore** the artifacts **back** to their former glory"*
  redundant: back is part of the definition of **restore**
  > *"**restore** the artifacts to their former glory"*

- *"the skull shows an injury **sustained by** a sword or an axe"*
  wrong preposition: as given, this phrase states that **the sword or axe was injured, not the skull**; the phrase should be
  > *"the skull shows an injury **sustained from** a sword or an axe"*

- *"they blast the paper with **hot steam**"*
  tautological: if it isn't hot, it isn't steam—
  > *"they blast the paper with **steam**"*

- *"beneath the Phlegrean Fields is a reservoir of **hot magma**"*
  tautological: magma is by definition, **hot**
  > *"beneath the Phlegrean Fields is a reservoir of **magma**"*

- *"they **spin** the dish **around** on an old turntable"*
  tautological: around is part of the definition of **spinning something on a central axis—**
  > *"they **spin** the dish on an old turntable"*

- *"it **connects** us **into** our customers"*
  wrong preposition: into is used exclusively for motion:
  > *"it **connects** us **to** our customers"*

- *"the wood could **catch on fire**"*
  incorrect phrasing of idiom
  > *"the wood could **catch fire**"*
  [on fire is a state of **having already caught fire]**

- *"this finding **heralds in** a new era"*
  incorrect usage: to herald does not take a preposition:
  > *"this finding **heralds** a new era"*

- *"this makes **a polyhedra**"*
  incorrect form: polyhedra is the plural of **polyhedron**:
  > *"this makes **a polyhedron**"*

- *"if you **never saw** the show **before**"*
  incorrect verb tense with adverb of prior-time:
  > *"if you **have never seen** the show **before**"*

- *"I've never **sang** before so many people"*
  incorrect past participle of verb **to sing**:
  > *"I've never **sung** before so many people"*

- *"at that **point on** [sic] **time**"*
  wrong preposition, *along with* **redundant use of phrase point [of] time***:*
    - *"at that **point**" or "at that **time**"*
- *"we could get a surgeon **to cleanly and quickly separate**"*
  infinitive horribly split by a modifying compound phrase*, one that is, in meaning, more of an adverbial after-thought:*
    - *"we could get a surgeon **to separate, cleanly and quickly,** …"*
- *"**to repeatedly and accurately fire a handgun**"*
  infinitive horribly split by a modifying compound phrase*, a phrase that modifies the entire infinitive, not just the verbal root within the infinitive:*
    - *"**to fire a handgun repeatedly and accurately**"*
- *"The dry cleaners **switched my clothes with some goth girl.**"*
  incomplete phrase*: stating that the merchant somehow substituted clothes for a person:*
    - *"The drycleaners **switched my clothes with those of some goth girl.**"*
- *"**As a damsel in distress, I** have to help you."*
  incorrect modifier/modified sequence*: this says that the subject of the main clause, "I", is the damsel. It literally means, "As I am a damsel in distress, I…"*
    - *"**As you're a damsel in distress, I** have to help you."*
- *"we have designed the controls to be **simplistic**"*
  incorrect word*:* simplistic *means* **overly simplified, naïve, incompletely thought through or executed** *(certainly not the description a designer would hope for):*
    - *"we have designed the controls to be **simple**" or*
    - *"we have designed the controls to be **easy to understand**"*
- *"Do you want **to permanently delete** this file?"*
  utterly ineffective use of split infinitive:
    - *"Do you want **to delete** this file **permanently?**",*

  and

  simplistic use of the word permanently *as* **deletion (like death) is, by its standard definition, permanent.** *Such abusage (and verbal inflation) has become commonplace on computer systems because users – invariably – delete first, regret later.*
    - *"Do you want **to delete** this file?" or*
    - *"Do you want **to delete** this file? **(It will be irretrievable.)**"*

  This should be counter-balanced by the contrasting, optional process that would ask
    - *"Do you want **to mark** (or **to send**) this file **for deletion?**"*

  *which would be obvious both in its ultimate target, yet in its **not** being a permanent action, would establish that the file would be at least temporarily retrievable. (Using "recycling" or "trash cans" are poor analogies for this process because they depend in the first case on someone's familiarity with recycling, and in the second case on the user's sanitary perceptions of the acceptability of pulling something* *out of the trash. Both cultural conceits have arisen from the fact that the designers of these programming analogies live in highly urbanized and self-centric areas of Western culture.)*

- *"highway **speeds will go** around forty miles per hour"*
  incorrect word: **speeds don't go anywhere**; **speed** is a measurement
    *"highway **speeds will be at** around forty miles per hour"*

- *"I was so **nauseous** after riding the roller coaster."*
  incorrect word: nauseous means **causing nausea**, so unless the roller-coaster ride resulted in the subject's unfortunate physical degradation, this is not the correct word
    *"I was so **nauseated** after riding the roller coaster."*

- *"The **flooding will let up after the rains stop**."*
  incomplete statement: unless you add further timing details, this is a tautology that is just the result of TV presenters' need to fill airtime.
    *"The flooding will let up **this afternoon**, after the rains stop."*

- *"the area can expect a **rain event** overnight"*
  a clichéd tautology/pseudo-technical jargon: everything that happens is an event, so calling it an event is simply adding unneeded wordiness. Weather reports and geology presentations are rife with this silly overstatement: *rain event, snow event, severe weather event, earthquake events...*
    *"the area can expect **rain** overnight"*

- *"the shark had bitten into its **prey item**"*
  tautology/pseudo-technical jargon: **prey** can be either specific or the generic name of a class. When it is specific, it is already an item, so adding the word **item** is, in that situation, redundant because it is part of the definition of **prey**.
    *"the shark had bitten into its **prey**"*

- *"Thales was the first person **in recorded history to successfully predict** an eclipse."*
  ① **a clichéd tautology: there is no other kind of history**—history is the set of recorded events. This has become so hackneyed a tautology that it is now a cliché, too.

  ② **a split infinitive**: the adverb is fatally weakened by being hidden within the body of the infinitive

  ③ **wrong tense of the infinitive**: the adverb, **successfully**, implies completion (and testing) of the prediction, so the perfect infinitive is required

    *"Thales was the first person **in history to have predicted** an eclipse **successfully**."*

14 Rules of Capitalization

Capitalize *(make the first letter of a word a capital):*

14.1 the first word of each sentence

> ***This*** *is a sentence.*

14.2 the words *I*, and *Oh* or *O*

> ***Oh****, that is a sentence **I** wrote.*
> *That is not a sentence **I** wrote; **Oh**, yes, it is.*

14.3 every proper noun and every adjective derived from a proper noun

> ***France, French; Moscow, Muscovite; Texas, Texan; Nova Scotia, Nova Scotian***

14.4 the names of the days of the week, the months, and special holidays

> *This **Tuesday**, **June** 14ᵗʰ, is **Flag Day**.*

However, the names of the seasons are not capitalized, except when strongly personalized.

> *School is out during the **summer**.*
> *Now torrid **Summer** stumbles off as **Autumn** sneaks in with cooling shadows.*

14.5 the names of the points of the compass are capitalized when they refer to the regions at those points

> *The **South** suffers from heat as the **Northeast** does from frost.*

14.6 the initials of a person's name

> ***J. S. Bach*** *was not as famous during his lifetime as he is today.*

14.7 the first word of a direct quotation

> *Then she yelled, "**Don't** forget to call me, Ishmael!"*

14.8 important historical events

> *The **Anglo-Saxon Invasion**; the **Battle of Normandy**; the **Irish Potato Famine***

14.9 titles used with proper names, or alone when used in direct address, but not when the title is not used as part of a specific personal name

> *Yes, the winning armies were led by the **Duke of Wellington**, **Prime Minister**.*
> *Who was **president** at that time?*
> *The **representatives** couldn't agree on a budget within the time required.*

14.10 terms for family members when referring to a particular person, except when preceded by a possessive

> ***Mother** and **Father**'s 50ᵗʰ wedding anniversary was several years ago.*
> *Jack went home to see his **mother**.*

14.11 names of particular groups and associations, and proper names of members of those associations

> ***Unitarian-Universalism, Unitarians; Rotarian; Danaan; Methodism, Methodist; Democrat***

14.12 classes, schools and colleges when referring to particular units

> The **Senior Class** had its prom last night.
> As a **senior**, Mary attended **Oakville High School**; to attend **college**, she matriculated at **Greenburg College**.

14.13 numbered school courses

> She went from **introductory mathematics** to **Calculus 201**.

14.14 school subjects when derived from proper names (otherwise they are not capitalized)

> He studied **Chinese** as well as Indo-European **linguistics**.

14.15 the first word of a formal statement or resolution following the word declaring its formality or resolution

> **Resolved**, **That** these United Colonies are ...

14.16 most abbreviations of names or specific substantives

> **P.O. Box**; **MSS**; **BCE**; **CE**

14.17 traditionally, every line of poetry, as in these famous lines from Chaucer:

> **Whan** that aprill with his shoures soote
> **The** droghte of march hath perced to the roote ,
> **And** bathed every veyne in swich licour
> **Of** which vertu engendred is the flour ...

14.18 common nouns used in a personalized setting

> The cold, dark **Forest** Primeval made him shudder with dread.
> The **Sea** has always been a stern **Mistress**.

14.19 common nouns that are part of a proper name

> Lakeview **Park** is very near Sunny View **Acres** and Meadowland **Center**.
> University **Avenue** crosses Duboce **Street** at the northwest corner of the university.

14.20 the titles of books, articles, chapters of books, poems, plays, tales/stories, magazines, newspapers, as well as pictures and musical compositions. Secondary words (articles, prepositions, conjunctions and auxiliary verbs) are not capitalized unless they initiate the title. However, if the name of a newspaper or magazine begins with **the** or **a**, those are not capitalized unless they are exposed at the start of a sentence, or are in a title cited by itself, or are always capitalized as part of the official name of the publication.

> Beethoven's **Opus 123 in D Major** is known as **Missa Solemnis**.
> We studied **the Canterbury Tales** in the original Middle English.
> He liked to watch **the Cowboys of Rooster Creek** when he felt nostalgic.
> She was reading "**Our Friend, Cornbread**", the featured article in **The Sick & Shut-Ins' Golden Hearth** magazine.
> They were reporters for **The Paris Picayune & ArkLaTex Times**.

15 Rules of Punctuation

15.1 *The Period*
*BE: **full stop***

15.1.1 In English, as in the scripts used by the Western European languages, a period is a round dot placed at the level of the baseline of the letters (such as all those in example 1., below) that do not have descenders.

15.1.2 Place a period

1. at the end of a declarative sentence

    This is a declarative sentence.

2. at the end of an imperative sentence, when there is no exclamation, or high emotion, involved

    Pass your exams to the front of the class.

3. at the end of a polite request (or imperative) stated as a question

    Will you please pass your exams to the front of the class.

4. at the end of an elliptical sentence.

    Yes. Jack, you, too.

5. after initials and most abbreviations

    J. S. Bach sent his manuscript C.O.D.

6. between the integer and fractional portions of a real number

    In calculations, pi is often shortened to 3.14159.

15.1.3 If a period is called for in a single position in the text by more than one rule, only one period is required. (This is shown at the end of the example for rule 5, above.)

15.1.4 A sentence used parenthetically within the body of the main sentence is neither capitalized nor followed by a period.

Jackie Smith (she was Dad's intensive care nurse) will be at his birthday party.

15.2 *The Ellipsis*

15.2.1 An ellipsis is formed from what appear to be three periods without spaces between them. Most modern fonts provide a specific character for this usage, and having an ellipsis created by three separate periods is not required.
It is also advisable to use that character rather than the three periods because the ellipsis is designed within the style of the font, and with some fonts its use can produce a better, often more legible—albeit subtle—effect.

"..." *vs.* "..."

15.2.2 The ellipsis is used to show where material has been omitted on purpose. This may appear anywhere within a sentence, or at its beginning or end.
This contrasts with the standard use of brackets to show material that has been lost from the physical transmission of the message, whether aural or written, or text that has been removed or made illegible on purpose by a third party, such as a censor.

> *I am Mrs. … your substitute teacher.*
> *I am Mrs. Smith your teacher here at … High School.*

15.2.3 An ellipsis at the end of a sentence or phrase is also used to show the position at which the author thinks the reader can continue the sense of the phrase by drawing conclusions from what or how the previous text has been presented.

> *He actually thought he was helping …*

15.2.4 An ellipsis may also be used to show where an author wishes to note a pause.

> *Well … I'm just not sure … What do you think?*

15.3 *The Question Mark*

15.3.1 The question mark, looking vaguely like an incomplete number '2' with a period beneath, is used to end interrogative sentences.

> *Are you certain? Yes, yes, I am.*

15.3.2 A question mark within parentheses is an expression of editorial doubt or uncertainty.

15.3.3 Do not use a question mark after a statement beginning with a relative adverb [§9.13].

Dreadfully common on the Internet, these phrases are actually adverbial noun clauses used as the subject of an elided predicate, which would usually be something along the lines of "follows".

WRONG: *How to complete the entrance form?*   (*This is a statement, **not** a question.*)
CORRECT: *How to complete the entrance form.*

WRONG: *Where to find us?*   (*This is a statement, **not** a question.*)
CORRECT: *Where to find us.*

15.4 *The Exclamation Mark*

15.4.1 Looking like a line above a period, the exclamation mark is used at the end of exclamations and forceful or direct imperatives.

> *Jason! Get in the house!*

15.4.2 An exclamation mark within parentheses is an expression of editorial agreement, excitation, or ironic disbelief.

15.5 *The Comma*

15.5.1 The comma is a small curve that starts at the same position as the period, and descends in a half-arc clockwise. In some fonts it looks like a period with a curl, or a short tail.
The comma is the most common of any of the punctuation marks, and its use can provide quite subtle nuances.

15.5.2 Use a comma to set off interjections or nouns of direct address.
If the interjection appears in the midst of a sentence, the commas must be paired.

> *Were they there? Yes, they were.*
> *I had forgotten, alas, to stir the soup. Well, is it burnt?*
> *Oh, where have the minutes gone?*

15.5.3 Parenthetical items are set off by commas; two commas are necessary when the parenthesis occurs within the sentence. These parentheses include appositives, vocatives, items within dates or addresses, independent clauses and non-sentence phrases.

> *Jack, my clumsy cousin, fell down the hill.*
> *Did you tumble after, Jill?*
> *They lived in Chicago, Illinois, until June 12, 1943, when they moved.*
> *They are replacing, I think, all the old, broken sidewalks in the neighborhood.*

This does not apply to appositives that are part of a proper name or that are closely connected to the word it modifies.

> *Alfred the Great translated Latin texts into Anglo-Saxon for his people.*
> *My brother John is flying to Frankfurt to see my niece Gretchen.*

15.5.4   Commas are used to separate numbers at or above ten thousand into groups of threes.

Whether numbers between one thousand and ten thousand are thus segmented is up to the writer, and should be based on clarity and ease of comprehension.

Year numbers less than ten thousand never have a comma.

> *Xenophon wrote his Anabasis about the **10,000** Greek mercenaries hired by Cyrus the Younger.*
> *In **1812** Napoleon invaded Russia with an army of **690,000** men, of whom he lost around **563,000**.*
> *The **9000** Athenians, with a thousand Platean allies, routed the Persians at Marathon.*

15.5.5   Commas are used to separate the items of a list or series of words, phrases or clauses.

> *We bought milk, eggs and broccoli at the store.*
> *She bought shirts, shopped for drapes and exchanged her shoes at the store.*
> *Charles XII, Napoleon and Hitler all learned the perils of invading Mother Russia.*

Whether there is a comma preceding the conjunction before the final member of the list may depend on the need for clarity, on whether a previous part of the list functions as a compound unit, or on the writer's decision as to whether that final item is to be taken as more distinct from the rest of the list. (This level of distinction is often reinforced by choice of a more powerful conjunction than **and**, or adverbs may be introduced that modify the conjunction.)

William, Mary and Anne were the last Stuart monarchs.	(*simple list*)
William, Mary, and Anne were the last Stuart monarchs.	(*simple list with* **Anne** *slightly distinguished from sequence*)
William and Mary, and Anne were the last Stuart monarchs.	(**William and Mary** *set forth as single, distinct unit*)
*William, Mary, **and then** Anne were the last Stuart monarchs.*	(**Anne** *emphasized as final item*)

15.5.6   Adjectives of the same nature in a series modifying the same substantive are separated by commas, unless they are joined by conjunctions. The final adjective does not have a comma between it and the noun.

This arrangement also applies to adjective sequences used in predicate nominatives.

*This has been a **long, hot** summer.*
*The terrier was **restless, pacing, barking**, until he was taken for a walk.*

NOTE: When the final adjective is conceptually part of the noun, that adjective is not preceded by a comma.

*He was a very **ambitious young man**.* (**ambitious** *modifies* **young** man)

*New York is a very **noisy, crowded, big city**.* (**New York** *is a* **city: noisy, crowded** *and* **big**: *city contrasts with* **non-city**)

*New York is a very **noisy, crowded big city**.* (**New York** *is a* **big city: noisy,** *and* **crowded**: *big city is a specific label and implies comparison with other* **big cities**)

15.5.7 A direct quotation (used in reporting *direct discourse*) is usually set apart from the sentence by a comma. However, this is not always the case. See §15.15 for information on formatting direct quotations.

NOTE: Be certain to differentiate between quotation marks used to set off direct discourse and those that enclose titles of articles, short poems or stories, or chapters of books. These require commas only if and when used appositively.

The chapter in the book is "How to enjoy your summer".
(the chapter's name does not require separation from the rest of the sentence)
The second chapter, "How to make every day count", is quite short.
(*the chapter's name appears as an appositive to* **chapter**)

NOTE: Do not use commas to set indirect quotations apart from the sentence.

On the front page he read, "Water rationing has been implemented because of the drought." (*direct quotation*)
*On the front page he read **that** water rationing had been implemented because of the drought.* (*indirect quotation*)

15.5.8 The clauses forming a compound sentence are separated by a comma placed just before the conjunction.

The comma may be omitted if the clauses are short and removing the comma does not decrease the clarity of the sentence. Use of the comma in this situation may imply a degree of separation, in idea or timing, or contrast between the ideas of the two clauses, or it may reflect a pause.

*She walked to school **and** I rode my bike.*
(*short, simple clauses; no contrast implied; could imply simultaneous actions*)

*She walked to school, **and** I rode my bike.*
(*short, simple clauses; some contrast implied*)

*She walked to school, **but** I rode my bike.*
(*short, simple clauses; explicit contrast*)

*New York is a very noisy, crowded big city, **and** is an international transportation hub.*
(*longer, more complicated clauses require a comma before the conjunction*)

NOTE: For clarity, use a semicolon instead of a comma when either of the joined clauses contains commas within itself.

*New York is a very noisy, crowded big city; **and**, more importantly, is an international transportation hub.*

NOTE: Always use a semicolon instead of a comma whenever the conjunction between independent clauses is omitted.

> *She walked to school; I rode my bike.*

15.5.9 Commas & dependent clauses

15.5.9.1 **Nonrestrictive clauses** must be separated from the rest of the sentence by a comma, or pair of commas. (A nonrestrictive clause is one that could be omitted without diminishing the meaning, sense or value of the main clause.)

> *Abraham Lincoln, **who was our sixteenth president**, wrote the Gettysburg Address in 1863.*
>> (**who was our sixteenth president** *is a nonrestrictive clause: it simply adds information to the sentence that is not needed for the core expression*)

> *The professor **who teaches French** went to Europe last summer.*
>> (**who teaches French** *is necessary for the meaning of the main clause: it is a restrictive clause, modifying* **professor** *directly*)

15.5.9.2 **Participial phrases** and **nominative absolutes** are separated from the rest of the sentence by commas.

> ***Having just returned from Italy,*** *the professor was radiant about her visit to Florence.*
>> (**Having just returned from Italy** *is a participial phrase; it requires a comma*)

> ***The German class being over,*** *we headed to the Biergarten of the Singverein for some cold refreshment.*
>> (**The German class being over** *is a nominative absolute; it requires a comma*)

15.5.9.3 An adjective or adverbial clause that precedes the rest of the sentence is set off by a comma, unless it is very short. Whether to insert a comma is determined by how its absence will affect clarity of expression.

When the subject of the clause is not the same as the subject of the main clause, it is more effective to insert a comma to signal that break in subject.

> ***When he went to France*** *he made sure to visit the memorial at Oradour-sur-Glane.*   (*no comma necessary*)

> ***If you want to travel,*** *your family must plan for it.*   (*comma necessary*)

NOTE: The comma is almost always omitted when the dependent clause follows the main clause.

> *Your family must plan **if you want to travel**.*   (*comma not necessary*)

15.5.10 Commas may be used to divide sentences or clauses for clarity.
But be aware also that overuse of commas actually decreases clarity by introducing extra clutter.

15.6 *The Semicolon*

15.6.1 A semicolon is used between two independent clauses of a compound sentence whenever they are not joined by a conjunction.
However, if the clauses are very short, they may be separated by commas.

> *He brought up several points, and a lot of data; he would not quit trying to convince me. I hear you, I see the data, I am not convinced.*

15.6.2 Independent clauses that are joined by conjunctions that are long or have commas within themselves are separated by a semicolon for clarity. [See the first note of §15.5.8.]

15.6.3 A semicolon usually precedes the conjunctions *as*, *namely*, *such as* or *thus* when they are used to introduce a list of non-limiting examples.

> *She liked a lot of subjects she had in school; such as algebra, biology and Latin.*

15.6.4 A semicolon is used between the independent clauses of compound sentences when they are united by those conjunctions such as *accordingly*, *hence*, *however*, *nevertheless*, *then*, *therefore*, *thus*.

> *The dogs had been in their kennels all morning; however, I couldn't rush home at that moment.*

15.6.5 A semicolon can be used in place of a comma wherever the replacement would make the phrasing of the sentence, or intent of the author, more clear.

15.7 *The Colon*

15.7.1 A colon is used as formal introduction of a single word, a list or a quotation. The list may be a sequence of individual words, of statements or questions.
The expression *as follows* or *the following* may serve as preparation for a list.

> *The dogs we have for adoption are **the following**: a dachshund, two terriers and a German shepherd.*
> *He mentioned Shakespeare's most famous quotation: "to be, or not to be".*

15.7.2 A colon is used after the salutation of a formal announcement or a business letter.

> *Dear Sir:*
> *To whom it may concern:*

15.7.3 A colon is used to separate the hours, minutes and seconds units within a specific time value.
Fractional seconds use a period, as is normal for representation of fractional values.

> *Her flight came in at **11:34** a.m.*
> *The ending chronometer reading was **2:17:53.82**.*

15.8 *The Apostrophe*

15.8.1 The apostrophe denotes the omission of one or more letters from a word or a contraction of two words; it is inserted at the point of elision.

> *****Don't** put your feet on the coffee table!*   (**Don't** *stands for* **do not**, *with the apostrophe for the missing* **o**)
>
> *I **can't** see over the fence.*   (**can't** *stands for* **can not** [*or* **cannot**], *with the apostrophe for the missing* **n** *and* **o**)

15.8.2 The apostrophe is used in forming the possessive (the *Genitive case*) of nouns. [See §5.13.6]

This use of the apostrophe comes from a misunderstanding current in the 16th and 17th centuries of the origin of the original *s* marking the possessive singular. At that time, it was erroneously thought that the *s* was the result of the contraction of a noun with the following possessive adjective **his**, so that one may see broadsheets or musical scores of the period using the mistaken uncontracted form, saying something like "*Mr. **Handel His** Water Musick*", whose (as they thought) contracted (or elided) version would have been notated using the **apostrophe + s**: "*Mr. **Handel's** Water Musick*".

15.8.3 The apostrophe is used in forming some plurals. [See §5.9.3.]

15.9 *The Hyphen*

15.9.1 The hyphen is used to mark a word division at the end of a line of text, when only part of the word will fit on that line, and the rest transferred to the start of the next. This is more common in text that is *justified*, or that is arranged in narrow columns, to avoid unpleasantly large blank spaces between words within a line.

Such a division hyphen must be made only between syllables, and placed at the end of the line. Correct division of a word may not be obvious, so use of a dictionary or a good software package is vital.

15.9.2 A hyphen is used to join words combined into a single adjective modifier.
However, many of these compounds, particularly those made of an adverb and an adjective, are not hyphenated when used as a predicate adjective or as an appositive.

> *He thought the Gettysburg Address a **well-written** speech.*
> > *(compound adjective: adverb + adjective)*
> *The Gettysburg Address is **well written**.*
> > *(predicate adjective: adverb modifying an adjective)*
> *Since its presentation, the Address has had **wide-ranging** effects.*
> > *(compound adjective: adjective + adjective)*
> *Since its presentation, the Address's effects have been **wide-ranging**.*
> > *(compound adjective)*
> *Lincoln's **brother-in-law** was a surgeon in the Confederate army.*
> > *(compound noun: noun + prepositional phrase)*

NOTE: Adverbs ending in *–ly* are not used to create such compound modifiers.

> *While being worked on, the Gettysburg Address was a **closely guarded** secret.*
> *While being worked on, the Gettysburg Address was **guarded closely**.*

These examples also demonstrate the difference between limiting adverbs and attributive adverbs. [See §9.5.1]

15.9.3 Also use a hyphen

1. to join prefixes or suffixes to proper nouns

> *His thesis was on the economy of the **post**-Civil War South.*
> *This summer was horrible, with its Sahara-**like** heat and dryness.*

2. to separate a prefix or suffix from a common noun to which it is applied, if joining the two would create double or triple letters

> *This is an important **anti**-inflammatory treatment.*
> *The plant has petal-**like** appendages at the growing ends of its branches.*
> *The dry summer created a fall-**like** shower of leaves.*
> *compare:*
> *It is better for your health, and for the planet, not to use **anti**bacterial soap.*

NOTE: this rule is not applied to most cases of *e*'s coming together, and is optional with many *o*'s that adjoin. [In older texts, such a second *o* may be marked with a dieresis (German: *Umlaut*) instead of being preceded by a hyphen, *e.g.*, *co**ö**rdination*.]

> *Management decided to **reevaluate** the branding of the current product line.*
> *While we are **coordinating** operations, the **cooperation** of members of the*
> **Co-op** *will be very much appreciated.*

3. whenever leaving out the hyphen would cause confusion with another word

> *After Jill **recovered** from her tumble, she **re-covered** the couch.*

4. within compound numbers ending in values from ***twenty-one*** to ***ninety-nine.***

5. whenever fractions are spelled out

> ***Seven-eighths*** *of the population don't know what a verb is.*

6. whenever joining the prefix *ex–* to a word to create the "previous, but no longer" version of that word

> *Teddy Roosevelt quickly became bored with being an **ex**-president.*

15.9.4   Multi-word compounds are usually hyphenated when first coined, but may be joined into a single word after they have been accepted into general parlance, or when their non-hyphenated spelling becomes mainstream.

A widely accessible example of this is the word that is now spelled *today*, as it was, up until around the time of World War II, regularly spelled *to-day*. (Its original form lies in the Anglo-Saxon prepositional phrase **tō dæg** "on [this] day"—in which **dæg** is pronounced essentially the same as its modern counterpart.) This same sequence of events happened with *tonight* (*to-night* – **tō niht, tō neaht**), and with *tomorrow* (*to-morrow* – **tō morgenne**), as well.

NOTE: Use hyphens to join the words of a compound to avoid ambiguity. Unless one specifically wants to use the uncertainty of meaning as a literary device, clarity is served best by inserting explicit punctuation rather than relying on the possible vagaries of placement or capitalization.

> **AMBIGUOUS**: *There was an **End of Season Savings** sign in the window.*
> (*Does it announce savings during a particular time of year, or the end of a specific type of savings?*)
>
> **POSSIBLE**: *There was an **End of Season-Savings** sign in the window.*
> (*end of a specific type of savings*)
> **POSSIBLE**: *There was an **End-of-Season Savings** sign in the window.*
> (*savings during a particular time of year*)

15.9.5   When *half* and *quarter* are used as prefixes, they are joined to the following word by a hyphen.

> That candy bar was once priced at just a **quarter-dollar**.
> Australia has just announced a new **half-dollar** coin.
> The collector was searching for pre-Victorian era florins, **half-crowns** and sovereigns, so the coin dealer noted the man's name and address, then scribbled alongside it quickly "pre-1837: 2s, 2/6, £1".

15.10 *The Dash*

15.10.1   The dash is distinct from a hyphen in its having a greater length. On a typewriter, a dash was represented by two hyphens with no space between them. Luckily this double character has been replaced with the ***Em-dash*** [Unicode U+2014], a dash with the width of the 'm' in the font with which it's formatted. By standardizing on this, most text-editing software programs now have the ability to replace a typed double-hyphen with a real dash automatically. (There is also an *En-dash* [Unicode U+2013], which some word processing applications will use in special or specific situations.)

15.10.2   A dash can be used before a summarizing, or result, clause at the end of a sentence; it can be used alone or in pairs for emphasis, or in a pair to replace the parentheses that enclose a parenthetical remark.

> The parking ticket was for going three minutes—just three minutes—over the limit.
> (*emphasis*)

> Lincoln wrote on the speech, travelled to Pennsylvania, and gave the speech—then the audience didn't know quite what to make of it!   (*summary/result*)

> The address—and all its symbolic meaning—was only understood later.
> (*parenthetical phrase*)

15.10.3   A dash can show a sudden break in thought or action within a sentence.

> I'd like to go to the concert tomorrow—now what did I walk in here for?

15.10.4   In older texts one may see the dash used to indicate the omission of letters or words, particularly when the author didn't want to use someone's complete name.

> How goes it with the elegant gentle Lady A—? the lovely sighing Lady J—? and how, O how does that glorious luminary Lady B— do? You see I retain my usual volatility.
> (James Boswell; *Letter to Erskine, Aug. 25, 1761*)

15.10.5   One does not usually place a space between a dash and its attached letter, word or phrase. However, some web browsers and web utilities cannot parse dashes correctly when they are not surrounded by spaces. This is a problem of non-standard implementation that must be tested for.

15.11 *Quotation Marks*
BE: *inverted commas*

15.11.1   Use quotation marks to set off reported direct discourse. [See §15.15 for details.]

15.11.2   The titles of articles, of short poems and stories, and of chapters of books are placed within quotation marks.

The titles of longer poems and of books or periodicals should be in italics rather than within quotation marks.

> *I'd like to re-read **"Jabberwocky"** and **Beowulf** when I can find the time.*
> *She needs to answer the questions at the end of **"The Jacksonian Era"** before her history test.*

15.11.3 A specific letter, word or phrase that is the topic of discourse should be either within quotation marks or italicized.

> ***"To be"** is an infinitive.*
> *He writes his **"a"** a little differently from the way she does.*
> *No **if's and's** or **but's** about it.*

15.11.4 Nicknames and hypocorisms, as well as words or phrases used in irony, should be within quotation marks.

> *He rarely used her name, but always called her **"Baby"**.*
> *Their **"guard dog"** turned out to be a large and particularly unfriendly house cat.*
> *My manager called me **"Cowboy"**, but the others nicknamed me **"Travis"**.*

15.11.5 Quotations from other texts should be in quotation marks.
If more than one paragraph is quoted in a single reference, opening quotation marks go at the start of each paragraph, but only the final paragraph gets the closing quotation marks.

> *"When I started the job fresh out of graduate school, I couldn't have imagined the conditions under which I would have to work. However, I was soon exposed to all the limitations faced by a very small company in a very large city.*
> *"Because of the business' solitary incoming phone-line, the receptionist had to announce over the intercom each call we received as it came in. The owner and I had the same first name, so I had the honor of picking my own phone-call nickname.*
> *"Travis, y'all got a call," she would often giggle in a faked drawl, echoing across the workstations and into the server room. Ugh—Californians."*

15.12 *Parentheses*

15.12.1 Parentheses are used to separate incidental words, phrases or even sentences—items not directly part of the sentence, but adding information, reaction or opinion to it. These additions are termed *parenthetical* remarks, statements or questions.
Sentences used parenthetically don't require capitalization. Normal statements do not require termination with a period, although question marks and exclamation marks are used for parenthetical questions and exclamations.
Punctuation marks that apply to the base sentence must be placed outside the parentheses.

> *He rarely used her name **(did he even remember it?)**, but always called her "Baby".*
> *Their "guard dog" turned out to be a large **(at least I thought so)** and particularly unfriendly house cat.*
> *My manager called me "Cowboy" **(Oh, those ever-present boots)**, but the others **(they got tired of hearing about Austin!)** had their fun by nicknaming me "Travis".*

15.13 *Brackets*

15.13.1 Use brackets "[ ]" to enclose explanatory matter when editing another's work, or to enclose editorial or informational directions or comments within your own work.

> *"Their "guard dog" turned out to be a large and paticularly* **[sic]** *unfriendly house cat* **[mentioned in his letters]**.*"*
>
> *The apostrophe is used in forming the possessive (the Genitive case) of almost all English nouns.* **[See §5.13.6.]**

15.13.2 Brackets are used, particularly when containing an ellipsis, to mark where source material is no longer legible, or has been physically lost from disintegration or destruction of medium, such as paper, papyrus, clay tablet or stone inscription.

15.14 *Braces*

15.14.1 Braces "{ }" enclose references to sources of information.

> *Its form comes from the Anglo-Saxon prepositional phrase, tō dæg.* **{Bright's Anglo-Saxon Reader, 1917; p. 360}**

15.14.2 Braces may also be used to enclose informational, opinion or parenthetical statements when they are fairly large or discursive.

15.14.3 Braces may also be used in place of parentheses or brackets to imply a greater degree of conceptual separation of their contents from the running text in which they appear.

15.15 *Notes on direct quotations*

15.15.1 If the direct quotation is so constrained in meaning that it forms a true unit of the sentence, no separating punctuation should be used.

> *Our physics professor always started his lectures with "People, prepare to be amazed!"*

15.15.2 A comma is the normal punctuation used to separate quotations from the rest of the sentence.

> *On the front page he read,* *"Water rationing has been implemented because of the drought."*
>
> *"Oh, well, there goes,"* *he paused and sighed,* *"the garden."*

15.15.3 However, other separating punctuation should be used whenever necessary.

> *"Oh, well,"* *he sighed.* *"There goes the garden."*
>
> *"What?"* *she snapped.* *"But, we must have a garden!"*
>
> *She added,* *"Vegetables from the store are never as good as our own!"*
>
> *"Wait a minute!"* *he said after taking a sip of coffee.* *"I may have an idea."*

15.15.4 A pair of quotation marks must be placed surrounding each quotation, or around each part of a quotation whenever it is broken into more than one unit. [See examples above.]

15.15.5 Exclamation marks and question marks are placed inside the quotation marks if they apply to the quote, or outside if they apply to the sentence itself.

If either mark applies both to the quotation and to the sentence, place a single mark within the quotation marks; a duplicate outside the quotation marks for the sentence is unnecessary.

15.15.6 When a quotation appears within another quotation, single quotation marks should be used around the internal one. If another quotation were to appear within *that* internal quotation, double quotation marks would be used around it.

This switching of double and single quotation marks would continue, however many levels of quotation the text might require.

15.15.7 Whenever possible, use shaped quotation marks, " and " [Unicode U+201C & U+201D] rather than the old typewriter-style, unshaped " [Unicode U+0022]. The directionality inherent in the angles of the shaped marks—their embrace—gives greater clarity to the text.

NOTE: The quotation marks used in English, those two-stroke marks floating high in the letter space, are not used by the scripts of many other languages. For example, in other languages you may find symbols such as these, used in various configurations:

> „quotation" »quotation« ›quotation‹ 「quotation」
> „quotation" »quotation» ‹quotation› 『quotation』
> «quotation» ›quotation›

The British term for the quotation mark, "inverted commas", derived solely from English-language usage, should be avoided both because of its cultural specificity and limitation, and because its attempt to describe the punctuation graphically means that its usage in other languages or situations is inherently illogical and misleading.

15.16 *Italics*

15.16.1 The titles of books, periodicals, paintings and longer poems, and the names of ships should appear in italics. [See §15.11.2.]

15.16.2 A specific letter, word or phrase that is the topic of discourse should be either within quotation marks or italicized. [See §15.11.3.]

15.16.3 Italicize foreign terms that have not become naturalized, such as *"e.g."*, *"etc."*, *"viz."*, *"cf."*, *"ibid."* and *"sic"*.
When in doubt, consult a good dictionary.

15.16.4 If the name of a city appear in the title of a magazine or newspaper, italicize it along with the rest of the title, because it is an inseparable part of the complete designation of the publication.

Do not italicize a leading definite article unless it is a part of the full, legal name of the periodical.

> She liked to read ***The London Times***, ***The New York Times*** and the ***Los Angeles Times***.
> That was yesterday's lead article in the ***Austin American-Statesman***.
> Norman Rockwell did several famous magazine covers for ***The Saturday Evening Post***.

15.16.5 Italicization can be used to set words or sections of text apart as items requiring emphasis, attention, or that provide auxiliary information.

15.16.6 **Never use underlining instead of italicization** when working in text-processing software—unless required to by specific project instructions, or as an additional, ultimate method to draw attention to text selections.

Underlining was created as a temporary solution to notating italicized *printed* text on a typewriter, because of the typewriter's technical limitation to a single font. So, its use has become of only limited importance ever since text-processing computer software, capable of multiple fonts and font lay-outs, has taken over the role of text input, formatting and output.

15.16.7 Do not italicize punctuation whose context is the primary text itself.

This provides a means of distinguishing cited punctuation from the active author's own, or editorial punctuation.

> He writes, "*This is the houre* [*sic*] *toward which I have been striving.*"
> ([*sic*] *was added by the reporting author*)
> He writes, "*This is the houre [sic] toward which I have been striving.*"
> ([*sic*] *had been used by the cited author*)

16 Sentence Structure and Analysis: Parsing and Diagramming

16.1 *Structural analysis.*

Structural analysis is the process of taking a sentence, identifying its parts and their relationships to each other, and to the sentence as a whole, and describing orderly those parts and relationships.

Each word in a sentence can be described both as to its grammatical form, and its usage.

There are two ways of analyzing a sentence into these two functional parts. One may talk one's way through the sentence, first giving the details of its organization and then the grammatical form and usage within its clause of each word.

The other is to use structural drawings – diagrams – to elucidate these properties visually rather than verbally.

There are few activities more productive for the student of any language – not only English – than to practice structural analysis and be able to complete analytical puzzles successfully.

16.2 *Parsing.*

Parsing is a method that allows the textual display of the results of the dissection of a sentence for the discovery, analysis and description of its functional parts.

The following are examples of the **parsing** process, using examples given in the previous sections of this text.

16.2.1 *He is the famous novelist.* [§5.5, ex. 1]

16.2.1.1 This is a simple sentence.

16.2.1.2 *He* is the subject, and is the third person masculine nominative singular personal pronoun.

16.2.1.3 *is* is the predicate, and is the third person singular present indicative form of the verb *to be*.

16.2.1.4 *the* is the definite article modifying *novelist*.

16.2.1.5 *famous* is a positive-degree attributive adjective that modifies *novelist*.

16.2.1.6 *novelist* is the predicate complement, completing the meaning of [*He*] *is*, and is a singular common noun in the nominative case.

16.2.2 *The young often do not listen.* [§5.5, ex. 2]

16.2.2.1 This is a simple sentence.

16.2.2.2 *The* is the definite article modifying *young*.

16.2.2.3 *young* is the subject of the sentence, and is a substantive adjective.

16.2.2.4 *often* is a limiting adverb that modifies the predicate *do listen*.

16.2.2.5 *not* is a negating adverb, and modifies the predicate *do listen*.

16.2.2.6   ***do listen*** is the predicate; it is the third person plural present emphatic indicative of the verb ***to listen***.

16.2.3   *Now is the time to get it done.* [§5.5, ex. 3]

16.2.3.1   This is a simple sentence.

16.2.3.2   ***Now*** is a substantive adverb used as the subject.

16.2.3.3   ***is*** is the predicate, and is the third person singular present indicative form of the verb ***to be***.

16.2.3.4   ***barks*** is the predicate, and is the third person singular present indicative form of ***to bark***.

16.2.4   *One excellent exercise is swimming.* [§5.5, ex. 4]

16.2.4.1   This is a simple sentence.

16.2.4.2   ***One*** is the definite article modifying ***exercise***.

16.2.4.3   ***excellent*** is an attributive adjective in the positive degree; it modifies ***exercise***.

16.2.4.4   ***exercise*** is the subject of the sentence, and is a singular common noun in the nominative case.

16.2.4.5   ***is*** is the predicate, and is the third person singular present indicative form of the verb ***to be***.

16.2.4.6   ***swimming*** is a predicate noun, and is the gerund of the verb ***to swim***.

16.2.5   *To err is human.* [§5.5, ex. 5]

16.2.5.1   This is a simple sentence.

16.2.5.2   ***To err*** is a present infinitive and is the subject.

16.2.5.3   ***is*** is the predicate, and is the third person singular present indicative form of the verb ***to be***.

16.2.5.4   ***human*** is an attributive absolute adjective; it is the predicate adjective.

16.2.6   *Into the cup is the goal of every golfer.* [§5.5, ex. 6]

16.2.6.1   This is a simple sentence.

16.2.6.2   ***Into the cup*** is a prepositional phrase used as a noun; it is the subject.

16.2.6.2.1   ***Into*** is the preposition governing the phrase.

16.2.6.2.2   ***the*** is the definite article modifying ***cup***.

16.2.6.2.3   ***cup*** is a singular common noun that is the object of the preposition ***into***.

16.2.6.3   ***is*** is the predicate, and is the third person singular present indicative form of the verb ***to be***.

16.2.6.4   ***the*** is the definite article modifying ***goal***.

16.2.6.5   ***goal*** is the predicate nominative, and is a singular common noun in the nominative case.

16.2.6.6   ***of every golfer*** is a prepositional phrase used as an adjective to modify ***goal***.

16.2.6.6.1   ***of*** is the preposition governing the phrase.

16.2.6.6.2   ***every*** is an indefinite adjective modifying ***golfer***.

16.2.6.6.3   *golfer* is a singular common noun that is the object of the preposition *of*.

16.2.7   *That he was in this movie is a fact.* [§5.5, ex. 7]

    16.2.7.1   This is a simple sentence.

    16.2.7.2   *That he was in this movie* is a noun clause; it is the subject.

        16.2.7.2.1   *That* is the conjunction introducing the dependent clause.

        16.2.7.2.2   *he* is subject of the dependent clause, and is the third person masculine nominative singular personal pronoun.

        16.2.7.2.3   *was* is the predicate of the dependent clause, and is the third person singular past indicative form of the verb *to be*.

        16.2.7.2.4   *in this movie* is an adverbial prepositional phrase; it is the predicate adverb.

            16.2.7.2.4.1   *in* is the preposition governing the phrase.

            16.2.7.2.4.2   *this* is the definite article modifying *movie*.

            16.2.7.2.4.3   *movie* is a singular common noun that is the object of the preposition *in*.

    16.2.7.3   *is* is the predicate, and is the third person singular present indicative form of the verb *to be*.

    16.2.7.4   *a* is the indefinite article modifying *fact*.

    16.2.7.5   *fact* is the subject of the sentence, and is a singular common noun in the nominative case.

16.2.8   *"Hold the fort! I am coming!" signaled General Sherman.* [§5.5, ex. 8]

    16.2.8.1   This is a simple sentence in inverted order.

    16.2.8.2   *"Hold the fort! I am coming!"* is a direct quotation used as the direct object of the sentence.

        16.2.8.2.1   *Hold the fort!* is a simple imperative sentence.

            16.2.8.2.1.1   *[you]* is the elided subject of the verb *hold*.

            16.2.8.2.1.2   *Hold* is the imperative form of the verb *to hold*; it is the predicate of this quoted sentence.

            16.2.8.2.1.3   *the* is the definite article modifying *movie*.

             16.2.8.2.1.4   *fort* is a singular common noun that is the direct object of the verb *hold*.

        16.2.8.2.2   *I am coming!* is a simple exclamatory sentence.

            16.2.8.2.2.1   *I* is subject of this quoted sentence, and is the first person nominative singular personal pronoun.

            16.2.8.2.2.2   *am coming* is the first person singular present indicative of *to come*; it is the predicate of this quoted sentence.

    16.2.8.3   *signaled* is the predicate, and is the third person singular past indicative active of the verb *to signal*.

    16.2.8.4   *General Sherman* is the subject, and is a proper noun.

16.2.9 ***The dog barks.*** [§13.17.1]

    16.2.9.1   This is a simple sentence.

    16.2.9.2   ***The*** is the definite article modifying ***dog***.

    16.2.9.3   ***dog*** is the subject of the sentence, and is a singular common noun in the nominative case.

    16.2.9.4   ***barks*** is the predicate, and is the third person singular present indicative form of ***to bark***.

16.2.10 ***This is John's book.*** [§5.13.1]

    16.2.10.1   This is a simple sentence.

    16.2.10.2   ***This*** is a singular demonstrative pronoun in the nominative case; it is the subject.

    16.2.10.3   ***is*** is the predicate, and is the third person singular present indicative form of the verb ***to be***.

    16.2.10.4   ***John's*** is a proper noun in the possessive case, modifying ***book***.

    16.2.10.5   ***book*** is the predicate complement, completing the meaning of [***This***] ***is***, and is a singular common noun in the nominative case.

16.2.11 ***Mary parked her car.*** [§7.11.1]

    16.2.11.1   This is a simple sentence.

    16.2.11.2   ***Mary*** is the subject and is a proper noun in the nominative case.

    16.2.11.3   ***parked*** is the predicate, and is the third person singular past indicative active form of the verb ***to park***.

    16.2.11.4   ***her*** is the third person feminine possessive singular personal pronoun used as an adjective modifying ***car***.

    16.2.11.5   ***car*** is the direct object of the verb and is a singular common noun in the objective case.

16.2.12 ***The ball was hit by Jack.*** [§7.11.2]

    16.2.12.1   This is a simple sentence.

    16.2.12.2   ***The*** is the definite article modifying ***ball***.

    16.2.12.3   ***ball*** is the subject and is a singular common noun in the nominative case.

    16.2.12.4   ***was hit*** is the predicate, and is the third person singular past indicative passive form of the verb ***to hit***.

        16.2.12.4.1   ***was*** is the third person singular past indicative form of the auxiliary verb ***to be***.

        16.2.12.4.2   ***hit*** is the past participle of the verb ***to hit***.

    16.2.12.5   ***by Jack*** is an adverbial prepositional phrase of *agent*, modifying the passive predicate.

        16.2.12.5.1   ***by*** is the preposition governing the phrase.

        16.2.12.5.2   ***Jack*** is the agent of the passive action, object of the preposition ***by***, and is a proper noun in the objective case.

16.2.13 *He and I went to the store.* [§6.11.2]

    16.2.13.1   This is a simple sentence with a compound subject.

    16.2.13.2   *He and I* is the compound subject

        16.2.13.2.1 *He* is the first subject, and is the third person masculine nominative singular personal pronoun.

        16.2.13.2.2 *and* is a conjunction joining the two subjects, *He* and *I*.

        16.2.13.2.3 *I* is the second subject, and is the first person nominative singular personal pronoun.

    16.2.13.3   *went* is the predicate, and is the third person plural past indicative form of the verb *to go*.

    16.2.13.4   *to the store* is an adverbial prepositional phrase of *direction*, modifying the predicate *went*.

        16.2.13.4.1 *to* is the preposition.

        16.2.13.4.2 *the* is the definite article modifying *store*.

        16.2.13.4.3 *store* is the object of the preposition *to*, and is a singular common noun in the objective case.

16.2.14 *She listed the people who had written letters.* [§6.13.2]

    16.2.14.1   This is a complex sentence with one dependent clause.

    16.2.14.2   *She listed the people* is the independent clause

        16.2.14.2.1 *She* is the subject

        16.2.14.2.2 *listed* predicate, and is the third person plural past indicative form of the verb *to list*.

        16.2.14.2.3 *the* is the definite article modifying *people*.

        16.2.14.2.4 *people* is the direct object, and is a plural common noun in the objective case

    16.2.14.3   *who had written letters* is the dependent clause

        16.2.14.3.1 *who* is the conjunction, and a relative pronoun that functions as subject of the dependent clause.

        16.2.14.3.2 *had written* is the predicate of the dependent clause; it is the third person plural past perfect indicative of the verb *to write*.

        16.2.14.3.3 *letters* is the direct object in the predicate of the dependent clause, and is a plural common noun in the objective case.

16.2.15 *Mary said that she expected his call.* [§7.17.2.4]

    16.2.15.1   This is a complex sentence with one dependent clause.

    16.2.15.2   *Mary* is the subject and is a proper noun in the nominative case.

    16.2.15.3   *said* is the predicate and is the third person singular past indicative active of the verb *to say*.

    16.2.15.4   *that she expected his call* is a noun clause, the direct object of the verb *to say*.

        16.2.15.4.1 *that* is the relative pronoun introducing the dependent clause.

16.2.15.4.2   *she* is third person feminine nominative singular personal pronoun and is the subject of the dependent clause

16.2.15.4.3   *expected* is the predicate of the dependent clause; it is the third person singular past indicative active form of the verb **to expect**.

16.2.15.4.4   *his* is the third person masculine possessive singular personal pronoun, used as a possessive adjective modifying *call*.

16.2.15.4.5   *call* is a common noun in the objective singular, the object of the dependent clause's predicate **expected**.

16.2.16 *I wish I were a singer.* [§7.18.3]

16.2.16.1   This is a complex sentence with one dependent clause.

16.2.16.2   *I* is the first person nominative singular personal pronoun, and is the subject of the independent clause.

16.2.16.3   *wish* is the predicate, and is the first person singular present indicative active of the verb **to wish**.

16.2.16.4   *I were a singer* is a noun dependent clause, the direct object of the verb **wish**.

16.2.16.4.1   [*that*] is the elided relative pronoun introducing the dependent clause.

16.2.16.4.2   *I* is the first person nominative singular personal pronoun, and is the subject of the dependent clause.

16.2.16.4.3   *were* is the predicate of the dependent noun clause; it is the first person singular past subjunctive form of the verb **to be**.

16.2.16.4.4   *a* is indefinite article modifying the noun **singer**.

16.2.16.4.5   *singer* is the predicate nominative of the dependent clause, a common noun in the nominative singular.

16.2.17 *Mary wants Jack to write a play.* [§7.24.7]

16.2.17.1   This is a simple sentence.

16.2.17.2   *Mary* is the subject, and is a proper noun.

16.2.17.3   *wants* is the predicate, the third person singular present indicative active form of the verb **to want**.

16.2.17.4   *Jack to write a play* is a noun infinitive phrase, the direct object of the verb **wants**.

16.2.17.4.1   *Jack* is the subject of the infinitive **to receive**, and is a proper noun in the objective case.

16.2.17.4.2   *to write* is a present active infinitive, the infinitive of the phrase.

16.2.17.4.3   *a* is the indefinite article modifying **play**.

16.2.17.4.4   *play* is a common noun in the objective singular, and is the object of the infinitive **to write**.

16.2.18 *We saw Jack receive the award.* [§7.24.8]

16.2.18.1   This is a simple sentence.

16.2.18.2   *We* is the subject, and is the first person nominative plural personal pronoun.

16.2.18.3   *saw* is the predicate, the third person singular past indicative active form of the verb ~~to receive~~.

16.2.18.4 *Jack* is both the direct object of the verb *saw*, and the subject of the infinitive *to receive*, and is a proper noun in the objective case.

16.2.18.5 *receive the award* is the predicate complement phrase modifying the verb *saw*.

    16.2.18.5.1 *t̶o̶ receive* is a present active infinitive with elided *to*, and is the predicate complement.

    16.2.18.5.2 *the* is the definite article modifying *award*.

    16.2.18.5.3 *award* is a common noun in the objective singular, and is the object of the infinitive *to receive*.

16.2.19 *His humor, not his gifts, was what attracted her.* [§7.22.3]

16.2.19.1 This is a simple sentence with a compound subject.

16.2.19.2 *His humor, not his gifts* is the compound subject.

    16.2.19.2.1 *His humor* is the first of the compound subjects.

        16.2.19.2.1.1 *His* is the third person masculine singular possessive personal pronoun, used as a possessive adjective modifying *humor*.

        16.2.19.2.1.2 *humor* is the first subject, a singular common noun in the nominative case.

    16.2.19.2.2 *not his gifts* is the second of the compound subjects.

        16.2.19.2.2.1 *not* is an adverb, negating the phrase *his gifts*.

        16.2.19.2.2.2 *his* is the third person masculine possessive singular personal pronoun, used as a possessive adjective modifying *gifts*.

        16.2.19.2.2.3 *gifts* is the second subject, a common noun in the nominative plural.

16.2.19.3 *was* is the predicate, the third person singular past indicative form of the verb *to be*.

16.2.19.4 *what attracted her* is a predicate nominative dependent clause

    16.2.19.4.1 *what* is the relative pronoun introducing the dependent clause as its subject.

    16.2.19.4.2 *attracted* is the predicate of the dependent clause, the third person singular past indicative active form of the verb *to attract*.

    16.2.19.4.3 *her* is the third person feminine objective singular of the personal pronoun, acting as the direct object of the dependent clause's predicate *attracted*.

16.2.20 *He walked with a quite painful limp along the path.* [§9.11.2]

16.2.20.1 This is a simple sentence.

16.2.20.2 *He* is the subject, and is the third person masculine nominative singular personal pronoun.

16.2.20.3 *walked* is the predicate and is the third person singular past indicative of the verb *to walk*.

16.2.20.4 *with a quite painful limp* is an adverbial prepositional phrase of manner.

    16.2.20.4.1 *with* is the governing preposition.

16.2.20.4.2   *a* is the indefinite article modifying **limp**.

16.2.20.4.3   *quite* is an adverb modifying **painful**.

16.2.20.4.4   *painful* is a positive-degree adjective modifying **limp**.

16.2.20.4.5   *limp* is the object of the preposition, and is a common noun in the objective singular.

16.2.20.5   *along the path* is an adverbial prepositional phrase of location.

16.2.20.5.1   *along* is the governing preposition.

16.2.20.5.2   *the* is the definite article modifying the noun **path**.

16.2.20.5.3   *path* is the object of the preposition, and is a common noun in the objective singular.

16.2.21   ***She wanted both to write a letter and to mail it.*** [*Note* of §11.6]

16.2.21.1   This is a simple sentence with a compound direct object.

16.2.21.2   *She* is the subject, and is the third person feminine nominative singular personal pronoun.

16.2.21.3   *wanted* is the predicate and is the third person singular past indicative active of the verb **to want**.

16.2.21.4   *both to write a letter and to mail it* is the compound direct object.

16.2.21.4.1   *both* is the first part of the paired correlative **both ... and ...** .

16.2.21.4.2   *to write a letter* is a noun infinitive clause, and is the first direct object.

16.2.21.4.2.1   *to write* is a present active infinitive.

16.2.21.4.2.2   *a* is the indefinite article modifying **letter**.

16.2.21.4.2.3   *letter* is the object of the infinitive **to write**, and is a common noun in the objective singular.

16.2.21.4.3   *and* is the second part of the paired correlative **both ... and ...** .

16.2.21.4.4   *to mail it* is a noun infinitive clause, and is the second direct object.

16.2.21.4.4.1   *to mail* is a present active infinitive.

16.2.21.4.4.2   *it* is the object of the infinitive **to mail**, and is the third person neuter objective singular personal pronoun.

16.2.22   ***This fall we're teaching reading and writing.*** [*Note* of §7.26.3]

16.2.22.1   This is a simple sentence with a compound direct object.

16.2.22.2   *This fall* is an adverbial phrase of time modifying the predicate **are teaching**.

16.2.22.2.1   *This* is a singular demonstrative adjective modifying the noun **fall**.

16.2.22.2.2   *fall* is a singular semi-proper noun in the nominative singular.

16.2.22.3   *we* is the subject, and is the first person nominative plural personal pronoun.

16.2.22.4   *are teaching* is the predicate, and is the third person plural past progressive indicative active of the verb **to teach**.

16.2.22.5   *reading and writing* is the compound direct object.

16.2.22.5.1   *reading* is the first direct object, and is a common noun (a course of study: derived from a gerund) in the objective singular.

16.2.22.5.2 *and* is the conjunction joining the two direct objects.

16.2.22.5.3 *writing* is the second direct object, and is a common noun (a course of study: derived from a gerund) in the objective singular.

16.2.23 *Not going to the wedding would be a social blunder.* [§7.26.4]

16.2.23.1 This is a simple sentence.

16.2.23.2 *Not going to the wedding* is a gerund phrase used as the subject.

16.2.23.2.1 *Not* is a negating adverb modifying the gerund *going*.

16.2.23.2.2 *going* is the gerund of the verb to go.

16.2.23.2.3 *to the wedding* is an adverbial prepositional phrase of *place to which*.

16.2.23.2.3.1 *to* is the governing preposition.

16.2.23.2.3.2 *the* is the direct article modifying the noun *wedding*.

16.2.23.2.3.3 *wedding* is a singular common noun and is the object of the preposition *to*.

16.2.23.3 *would be* is the predicate.

16.2.23.3.1 *would* is a modal auxiliary modifying the main verb *to be*.

16.2.23.3.2 *be* is the main verb, and is the root form of the present infinitive *to be*.

16.2.23.4 *a social blunder* is the direct object phrase.

16.2.23.4.1 *a* is the indefinite article modifying *blunder*.

16.2.23.4.2 *social* is a positive-degree adjective modifying *blunder*.

16.2.23.4.3 *blunder* is the direct object, and is a common noun in the objective singular.

16.2.24 *She will have been singing.* [§7.28.1.6]

16.2.24.1 This is a simple sentence.

16.2.24.2 *She* is the subject, and is the third person feminine nominative singular personal pronoun.

16.2.24.3 *will have been singing* is the predicate, it is the third person singular future perfect progressive indicative of the verb *to sing*.

16.2.25 *She is writing a letter.* [*Note* of §7.28.2.7]

16.2.25.1 *She* is the subject, and is the third person feminine nominative singular personal pronoun.

16.2.25.2 *is writing* is the predicate and is the third person singular present progressive indicative active of the verb *to write*.

16.2.25.3 *a* is the indefinite article modifying *letter*.

16.2.25.4 *letter* is the direct object and is a singular common noun in the objective case.

16.2.26 *Lie down—just lie on the bed—if you're so sleepy.* [§7.37.1.2]

16.2.26.1 This is a simple sentence into which an interjection has been inserted.

16.2.26.2 [*you*] is the elided subject of the imperative verb *to lie*.

16.2.26.3 *Lie down* is the predicate phrase of the main, independent clause.

   16.2.26.3.1 *lie* is the predicate and is the [second] person singular/plural imperative of the verb *to lie*.

   16.2.26.3.2 *down* is an adverb of place/direction, modifying the verb *lie*.

16.2.26.4 *if you're so sleepy* is an adverbial dependent clause of condition.

   16.2.26.4.1 *if* is the conjunction introducing the dependent clause.

   16.2.26.4.2 *you* is the subject of the dependent clause; it is the second person nominative singular/plural personal pronoun.

   16.2.26.4.3 *are* is the predicate of the dependent clause; it is the second person singular/plural present indicative of the verb *to be*.

   16.2.26.4.4 *so* is an adverb modifying the adjective sleepy.

   16.2.26.4.5 *sleepy* is a positive-degree adjective used as a predicate adjective.

16.2.26.5 *just lie on the bed* is an interjection restating the imperative main clause.

   16.2.26.5.1 *just* is a limiting adverb modifying the verb *lie*.

   16.2.26.5.2 *lie* is the predicate and is the [second] person singular/plural imperative of the verb *to lie*.

   16.2.26.5.3 *on the bed* is an adverbial prepositional phrase of place.

      16.2.26.5.3.1 *on* is the governing preposition.

      16.2.26.5.3.2 *the* is the direct article modifying the noun *bed*.

      16.2.26.5.3.3 *bed* is the object of the preposition *on*, and is a singular common noun in the objective case.

16.2.27 *They laid the new carpet in the bedroom yesterday.* [§7.37.1.2.1]

16.2.27.1 This is a simple sentence.

16.2.27.2 *They* is the subject, and is the third person nominative plural personal pronoun.

16.2.27.3 *laid* is the predicate and is the third person plural past indicative active of the verb *to lay*.

16.2.27.4 *the* is the direct article modifying the noun *carpet*.

16.2.27.5 *new* is a positive-degree adjective modifying *carpet*.

16.2.27.6 *carpet* is a singular common noun and is the direct object of the predicate.

16.2.27.7 *in the bedroom* is an adverbial prepositional phrase of location.

   16.2.27.7.1 *in* is the governing preposition.

   16.2.27.7.2 *the* is the definite article modifying the noun *bedroom*.

   16.2.27.7.3 *bedroom* is the object of the preposition *in*, and is a singular common noun.

16.2.27.8 *yesterday* is an adverb of time modifying the predicate *laid*.

16.2.28 *The pioneers built their homes from the logs, their roofs from the bark and their cooking fires from the branches of the trees of the deep forest.* [§10.2.3]

16.2.28.1 This is a simple sentence with compound direct object.

16.2.28.2 *The* is the definite article, modifying *pioneers*.

16.2.28.3 *pioneers* is the subject, and is a plural common noun.

16.2.28.4 *built* is the predicate and is the third person plural past indicative active of the verb *to build*.

16.2.28.5 *their* is the third person plural possessive personal pronoun modifying the noun *homes*.

16.2.28.6 *homes* is a plural common noun and is the first member of the compound direct object of the predicate.

16.2.28.7 *from the logs* is an adjectival prepositional phrase modifying *homes*.

    16.2.28.7.1 *from* is the governing preposition.

    16.2.28.7.2 *the* is the definite article modifying the noun *logs*.

    16.2.28.7.3 *logs* is the object of the preposition *from*, and is a plural common noun.

16.2.28.8 *their* is the third person plural possessive personal pronoun modifying the noun *roofs*.

16.2.28.9 *roofs* is a plural common noun and is the second member of the compound direct object of the predicate.

16.2.28.10 *from the bark* is an adjectival prepositional phrase modifying *roofs*.

    16.2.28.10.1 *from* is the governing preposition.

    16.2.28.10.2 *the* is the definite article modifying the noun *bark*.

    16.2.28.10.3 *bark* is the object of the preposition *from*, and is a singular common noun.

16.2.28.11 *and* is a coordinating conjunction joining the compound direct object.

16.2.28.12 *their* is the third person plural possessive personal pronoun modifying the noun *roofs*.

16.2.28.13 *cooking fires* is a plural phrasal noun and is the third member of the compound direct object of the predicate.

16.2.28.14 *from the branches* is an adjectival prepositional phrase modifying *cooking fires*.

    16.2.28.14.1 *from* is the governing preposition.

    16.2.28.14.2 *the* is the definite article modifying the noun *branches*.

    16.2.28.14.3 *branches* is the object of the preposition *from*, and is a plural common noun.

16.2.28.15 *of the trees* is an adjectival prepositional phrase modifying the compound prepositional phrase group *from the logs, from the bark and from the branches*.

    16.2.28.15.1 *of* is the governing preposition.

    16.2.28.15.2 *the* is the definite article modifying the noun *branches*.

    16.2.28.15.3 *trees* is the object of the preposition *of*, and is a plural common noun.

16.2.28.16 *of the deep forest* is an adjectival prepositional phrase modifying the noun *trees*.

    16.2.28.16.1 *of* is the governing preposition.

    16.2.28.16.2 *the* is the definite article modifying the noun *forest*.

    16.2.28.16.3 *deep* is an adjective modifying the noun *forest*.

    16.2.28.16.4 *forest* is the object of the preposition *of*, and is a singular common noun.

16.2.29 *The music on the piano is by Brahms.* [§8.2]

    16.2.29.1 This is a simple sentence.

    16.2.29.2 *The* is the definite article, modifying **music**.

    16.2.29.3 *music* is the subject, and is a singular common noun.

    16.2.29.4 *on the piano* is an adjectival prepositional phrase modifying **music**.

        16.2.29.4.1 *on* is the governing preposition.

        16.2.29.4.2 *the* is the definite article modifying the noun **piano**.

        16.2.29.4.3 *piano* is the object of the preposition **on**, and is a singular common noun.

    16.2.29.5 *is* is the predicate and is the third person singular present indicative of the verb **to be**.

    16.2.29.6 *by Brahms* is an adjectival prepositional phrase used as a predicate adjective.

        16.2.29.6.1 *by* is the governing preposition.

        16.2.29.6.2 *Brahms* is the object of the preposition **by**, and is a proper noun.

16.2.30 *The writer sitting on the floor read a selection from her work.* [§8.5.3] Compare with §16.2.31, below.

    16.2.30.1 This is a simple sentence.

    16.2.30.2 *The* is the definite article, modifying **writer**.

    16.2.30.3 *writer* is the subject, and is the third person masculine nominative singular personal pronoun.

    16.2.30.4 *sitting on the floor* is an **adjectival participial phrase** modifying **writer**.

        16.2.30.4.1 *sitting* is the present participle of the verb **to sit**; it modifies **writer**.

        16.2.30.4.2 *on the piano* is an adverbial prepositional phrase of location, modifying **sitting**.

            16.2.30.4.2.1 *on* is the governing preposition.

            16.2.30.4.2.2 *the* is the definite article modifying the noun **floor**.

            16.2.30.4.2.3 *floor* is the object of the preposition **on**, and is a singular common noun.

    16.2.30.5 *read* is the predicate and is the third person singular past indicative active of the verb **to read**.

    16.2.30.6 *a* is the indefinite article, modifying **selection**.

    16.2.30.7 *selection* is the direct object; it is a singular common noun.

    16.2.30.8 *from her work* is an adjectival prepositional phrase modifying **selection**.

        16.2.30.8.1 *from* is the governing preposition.

        16.2.30.8.2 *her* is the third person singular feminine possessive pronoun, used as a possessive adjective modifying the noun **work**.

        16.2.30.8.3 *work* is the object of the preposition **from**, and is a singular common noun.

16.2.31 *The writer, sitting on the floor, read a selection from her work.* [§8.5.3] Compare to §16.2.30, above.

> **16.2.31.1** This is a simple sentence.
>
> **16.2.31.2** *The* is the definite article, modifying **writer**.
>
> **16.2.31.3** *writer* is the subject, and is a singular common noun in the nominative case.
>
> **16.2.31.4** *sitting on the floor* is an **adverbial participial phrase** of *location*, modifying **read**.
>
> > **16.2.31.4.1** *sitting* is the present participle of the verb **to sit**; it modifies **read**.
> >
> > **16.2.31.4.2** *on the piano* is an adverbial prepositional phrase of location, modifying **sitting**.
> >
> > > **16.2.31.4.2.1** *on* is the governing preposition.
> > >
> > > **16.2.31.4.2.2** *the* is the definite article modifying the noun **floor**.
> > >
> > > **16.2.31.4.2.3** *floor* is the object of the preposition **on**, and is a common noun in the singular objective.
>
> **16.2.31.5** *read* is the predicate and is the third person singular past indicative active of the verb **to read**.
>
> **16.2.31.6** *a* is the indefinite article, modifying **selection**.
>
> **16.2.31.7** *selection* is the direct object; it is a singular common noun.
>
> **16.2.31.8** *from her work* is an adjectival prepositional phrase modifying **selection**.
>
> > **16.2.31.8.1** *from* is the governing preposition.
> >
> > **16.2.31.8.2** *her* is the third person singular feminine possessive pronoun, used as a possessive adjective modifying the noun **work**.
> >
> > **16.2.31.8.3** *work* is the object of the preposition **from**, and is a singular common noun.

16.2.32 *Where he had been was a secret.* [§13.12, #1, example 1.]

> **16.2.32.1** This is a complex sentence with an independent clause and one dependent clause.
>
> **16.2.32.2** *Where he had been* is a noun dependent clause; it is the subject of the independent clause.
>
> > **16.2.32.2.1** *Where* is the relative adverb introducing the clause.
> >
> > **16.2.32.2.2** *he* is the subject of the dependent clause, and is the third person masculine nominative singular personal pronoun.
> >
> > **16.2.32.2.3** *had been* is the predicate of the dependent clause and is the third person singular past perfect indicative of the verb **to be**.
>
> **16.2.32.3** *was a secret* is the predicate phrase of the independent clause.
>
> > **16.2.32.3.1** *was* is the predicate of the independent clause and is the third person singular past indicative of the verb **to be**.
> >
> > **16.2.32.3.1** *a* is the indefinite article, modifying **secret**.
> >
> > **16.2.32.3.2** *secret* is the predicate noun of the independent clause and is a singular common noun in the nominative case.

16.2.33 *What the dog had eaten was what the vet needed to know.* [§13.12, #1, example 2.]

> **16.2.33.1** This is a complex sentence with an independent clause and two dependent clauses.

16.2.33.2 *What the dog had eaten* is a noun dependent clause; it is the subject of the independent clause.

    16.2.33.2.1 *What* is a relative pronoun introducing the clause; it is the subject of the clause and is in the nominative case.

    16.2.33.2.2 *the* is the definite article, modifying **dog**.

    16.2.33.2.3 *dog* is the subject of this dependent clause, and is a singular common noun in the nominative case.

    16.2.33.2.4 *had eaten* is the predicate of the dependent clause and is the third person singular past perfect indicative of the verb **to eat**.

16.2.33.3 *was* is the predicate of the independent clause.

16.2.33.4 *what the vet needed to know* is a noun dependent clause; it is the predicate nominative of the independent clause.

    16.2.33.4.1 *what* is a relative pronoun introducing the clause; it is the subject of the clause and is in the nominative case.

    16.2.33.4.2 *the* is the definite article, modifying **vet**.

    16.2.33.4.3 *vet* is the subject of this dependent clause, and is a singular common noun in the nominative case.

    16.2.33.4.4 *needed* is the predicate of the dependent clause and is the third person singular past indicative of the verb **to need**.

    16.2.33.4.5 *to know* is the direct object of the predicate of the dependent clause and is the present active infinitive of the verb **to know**.

16.2.34 *She who had asked never got a clear answer.* [§13.12, #2]

16.2.34.1 This is a complex sentence with an independent clause and one dependent clause.

16.2.34.2 *She* is the subject of the independent clause, and is the third person feminine nominative singular personal pronoun.

16.2.34.3 *who had asked* is an adjective dependent clause modifying the pronoun **She**.

    16.2.34.3.1 *who* is the relative pronoun introducing the clause; it is the subject of the dependent clause and is in the nominative case.

    16.2.34.3.2 *had asked* is the predicate of the dependent clause and is the third person singular past perfect indicative of the verb **to ask**.

16.2.34.4 *never* is a negating adverb modifying the predicate of the independent clause.

16.2.34.5 *got* is the predicate of the independent clause and is the third person singular past indicative of the verb **to get**.

16.2.34.6 *a* is the indefinite article, modifying **answer**.

16.2.34.7 *clear* is an adjective in the positive degree, modifying **answer**.

16.2.34.8 *answer* is the direct object of predicate of the independent clause; is a singular common noun in the objective case.

16.2.35 *When he gave his answer she didn't believe him.* [§13.12, #3]

16.2.35.1 This is a complex sentence with an independent clause and one dependent clause.

16.2.35.2   *When he gave his answer* is an adverbial dependent clause, modifying the predicate of the independent clause.

    16.2.35.2.1   *When* is a relative adverb introducing the clause; within the clause it modifies its own predicate, *gave*.

    16.2.35.2.2   *he* is the subject of the dependent clause, and is the third person masculine nominative singular personal pronoun.

    16.2.35.2.3   *gave* is the predicate of the dependent clause and is the third person singular past indicative of the verb *to give*.

    16.2.35.2.4   *his* is the third person masculine singular possessive personal pronoun; it modifies *answer*.

    16.2.35.2.5   *answer* is the direct object of the predicate of the dependent clause, and is a singular common noun in the objective case.

16.2.35.3   *she* is the subject of the independent clause, and is the third person feminine nominative singular personal pronoun.

16.2.35.4   *didn't believe* is the predicate of the independent clause.

    16.2.35.4.1   *did believe* is the predicate of the independent clause and is the emphatic form of the third person singular past indicative of the verb *to believe*.

    16.2.35.4.2   *n't* is the contraction of the negating adverb *not*, modifying the predicate.

16.2.35.5   *him* is the object of the independent clause, and is the third person masculine objective singular personal pronoun

16.2.36   *The dog barks and the boy chases the ball.* [§13.17.2]

16.2.36.1   This is a compound sentence.

16.2.36.2   *The dog barks* is the first independent clause.

    16.2.36.2.1   *The* is the definite article, modifying *dog*.

    16.2.36.2.2   *dog* is the subject, and is a singular common noun in the nominative case.

    16.2.36.2.3   *barks* is the predicate and is the third person singular present indicative of the verb *to bark*.

16.2.36.3   *and* is the conjunction joining the two independent clauses.

16.2.36.4   *the boy chases the ball* is the second independent clause.

    16.2.36.4.1   *the* is the definite article, modifying *boy*.

    16.2.36.4.2   *boy* is the subject of the second clause and is a singular common noun in the nominative case.

    16.2.36.4.3   *chases* is the predicate and is the third person singular present indicative active of the verb *to chase*.

    16.2.36.4.4   *the* is the definite article, modifying *ball*.

    16.2.36.4.5   *ball* is the direct object of the verb *chases*, and is a singular common noun in the objective case.

16.3 *Diagramming.*

Diagramming is a method of textual analysis that breaks a sentence into its pertinent parts, then arranges those parts in a graph-like structure.

This graphical arrangement allows the individual units, and the units to which they in turn belong, to be displayed in a way that very often makes the structure clearer than that provided by other methods of analysis. This can be a great aid both to teachers in explaining and to students in understanding the concepts of grammar by clarifying the nature of the units composing the sentence and the relationships between the various parts of which it is composed.

There are two principle types of diagramming in use nowadays.

In current textbooks, a method of diagramming (from X-bar theory) has pushed its way from the rarefied academic study of linguistics and transformational grammar into pedagogical texts for high school, or even younger, students. Being made up of inverted tree-structured tent-posts carrying English-based abbreviations, it requires that the student learn not only the grammar underlying the exercise, but the concepts, their names, and their correct abbreviations required for graphing before they may even start to parse a sentence, well before being able to fill in the branches and leaves. Yet even with the completed structures, the diagrams themselves do not easily reveal the roles or relationships of or between words, phrases and clauses. Although such loftily conceived layouts may have their place in college-level investigations or in graduate-level flights of theorization, in terms of pedagogy and the exacting, quality-oriented teaching of grammar, X-bar diagrams are about as useful as a tapioca piano.

The other principal method of diagramming, one that has long been used in the schools of the United States, was first formalized by Alonzo Reed and Brainerd Kellogg in the decades between 1870 and 1920. Their manner of diagramming was used in grammar instruction in pre-college institutions between its first publication until the early 1970's, and it has seen a revival of interest (particularly among home-schoolers) as it has become so painfully apparent that the various attempts to "modernize" methods of education with error-pandering "self-actualization" begun in the 1970's have failed so miserably.

The Reed/Kellogg method as they defined it was necessarily adapted or extended by teachers of English and textbook writers during those many years of practice and ex-perience. There is now no central or exhaustively defining "standard" of that method, apart from the original, long-ago published Reed/Kellogg methodology. Those books form the basis of a group of diagramming descriptions that have been adapted into what may now be termed simply *traditional diagramming*. Traditional diagramming in practice has made some changes to the R/K method, attempting to fix problems that were early perceived in their original designs and conventions.

However, there are some obvious problems with traditional diagramming that often make it more complicated to use and harder for students to remember than it should be. Its biggest problems are its lack of consistency of representation; its use of dis-jointed layouts of clauses, often creating "spaghetti" diagrams [*viz., p. 305*]; unnecessarily difficult, obtuse or simply wrong layouts of more advanced formations; and its use of single symbolic arrangements (or insufficiently distinct structures) to represent multiple, disparate usages (*e.g.*, the traditional layouts for prepositional phrases, infinitives and adverbial complements are all the same). Compounding its structural weaknesses is its failure to use standard mathematical symbols for like concepts, but its reliance on designing new ones, an act that just creates more work for both students and teachers.

To remedy those problems, an improved method, called **Qualls Coherent Diagramming**—"**QCD**"—will be presented here, with details showing how it corrects problems within the traditional methods by building on them or by redesigning them, or by choosing one traditional method over other traditional variants. The changes are labeled as they are dealt with, so that the emendations will be readily apparent, and either the new method or a traditional method may be chosen and used, as preferred. (Diagramming methods common to both new and old styles—and examples demonstrating them—do not have such added, differentiating labels.)

The primary differences between **QCD** and the traditional methods lie in these areas:

1. notation of compound sentences and phrases [§16.3.2]
   a. notation of correlative clauses [§16.3.2.3]
2. notation of the 'null' marker [§16.3.1.7]
3. notation of adverbial objectives [§16.3.5]
4. notation of limiting adverbs [§16.3.1.1]
5. notation of adverbs modifying entire phrases or clauses [§16.3.1.6]
6. notation of some conjunctions before predicate complements [§16.3.4.2]
7. notation of infinitives [§16.3.10]
   a. and of the subjects of infinitives [§16.3.10.7]
   b. and of split infinitives [§16.3.10.13]
8. notation of compound verbals
   a. compound infinitives [§16.3.10.2, §16.3.10.12]
   b. compound gerunds [§16.3.11.3]
   c. compound participles [§16.3.13.2]
9. notation of dependent clauses [§16.3.15*ff*]

Diagramming: Topics

•

16.3.1 The Simple Sentence

The root form on which all diagramming is based is the structure designed for the simple sentence.

This structure is a horizontal line on which the subject and verb are placed. A line perpendicular to the baseline is drawn through it, with the baseline dividing the vertical line in equal parts, above and below. This line splits the baseline into the subject portion on the left-hand side, and the predicate portion on the right.

Note that the first word of the original sentence is capitalized within the diagram; any punctuation is omitted.

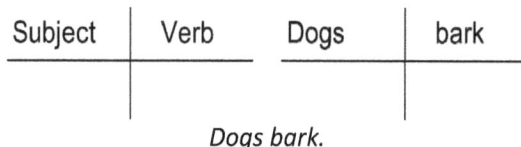

Subject | Verb   Dogs | bark

Dogs bark.

When the verb is abbreviated and joined in spelling to the subject itself, place the dividing line between the two parts, with those parts close to that vertical line. Otherwise, place the subject or the verb anywhere along the baseline that helps describe the structure of the sentence, and giving enough space to make the diagram as legible and balanced as possible.

Alternatively, an edit can be inserted to clarify the nature of the contraction.

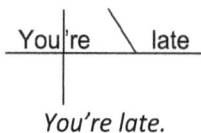

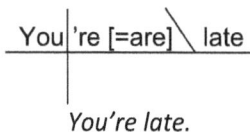

You|re \ late

You're late.

You |'re [=are] \ late

You're late.

16.3.1.1 The Simple Sentence: With Simple Modifiers

Simple, single word modifiers are placed each on a diagonal line, attached to the horizontal line beneath the word they modify, extending from there down toward the right. The text of the modifier is placed in alignment with that diagonal line. The modifiers to which this notation structure applies are *adjectives, adverbs* and *possessive nouns* and *possessive pronouns*.

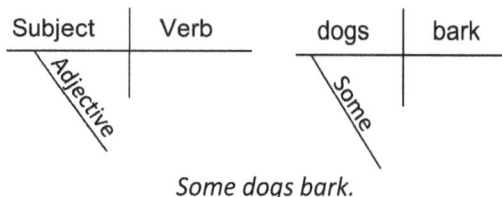

Subject | Verb   dogs | bark
Adjective   Some

Some dogs bark.

| Subject | Verb | Dogs | bark |

Adverb (on diagonal under Verb); *loudly* (on diagonal under bark)

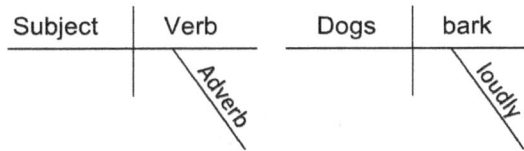

Dogs bark loudly.

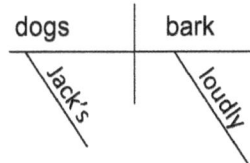

| dogs | bark |

Jack's (diagonal); *loudly* (diagonal)

Jack's dogs bark loudly.

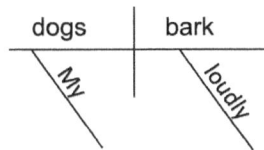

| dogs | bark |

My (diagonal); *loudly* (diagonal)

My dogs bark loudly.

When more than one simple modifier applies, they should be placed parallel to each other, in the order from left to right in which they appear in the sentence.

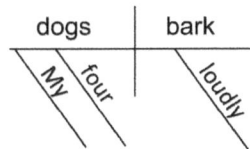

| dogs | bark |

My *four* (diagonals); *loudly* (diagonal)

My four dogs bark loudly.

When the verb is made up of more than one word, that is, whenever the verb form is itself made up of more than word, or when the verb is a phrasal verb, place all the words in the space reserved for the verb.

The length of the baseline, or the positioning of the subject-verb dividing line on the baseline can be adjusted to make room for larger or smaller subjects and predicates.

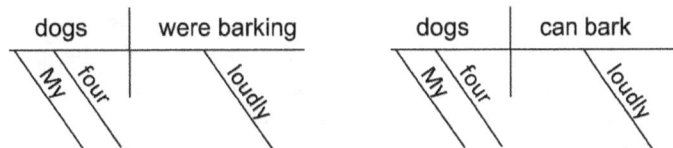

| dogs | were barking |

My *four* (diagonals); *loudly* (diagonal)

My four dogs were barking loudly.

| dogs | can bark |

My *four* (diagonals); *loudly* (diagonal)

My four dogs can bark loudly.

QCD: While traditional diagramming (and in some respects, traditional grammar, too) fails to pay attention to the differences between **limiting adverbs** and **attributive adverbs** [See §9.7] and incongruously uses the same diagram units for both, QCD provides a way of distinguishing this important difference in adverb usage. Because the limiting versus attributive usage of adverbs is distinguished by whether the adverb precedes or follows the modified word, this distinction also serves to portray adverb positioning as well as usage.

The *QCD* standard for diagramming attributive adverbs (those occurring to the right of the modified word) is the same as the traditional structure.

However, the *QCD* standard for diagramming limiting adverbs, as well as the **negative adverb *not***, is for the diagonal line bearing these adverbs to have a small line perpendicular it at the upper end, near the horizontal line to which it is attached. (This line is, in origin, a lower case 'L', for *limiting*.)

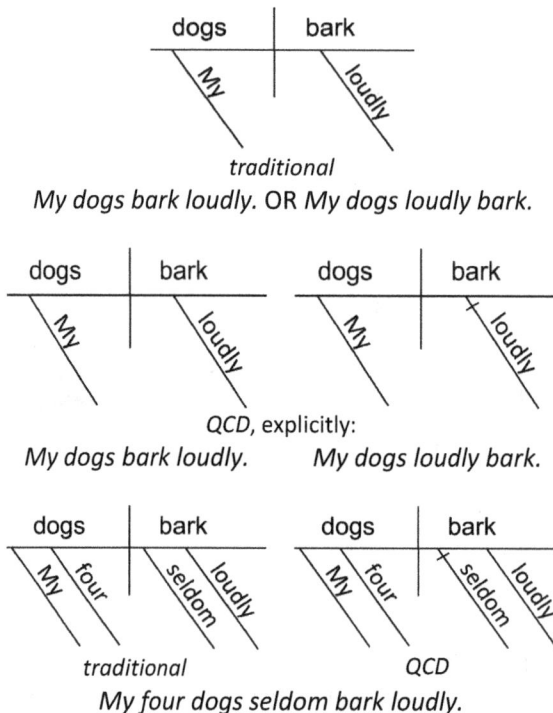

traditional
My dogs bark loudly. OR *My dogs loudly bark.*

QCD, explicitly:
My dogs bark loudly.   *My dogs loudly bark.*

traditional   *QCD*
My four dogs seldom bark loudly.

Because any adverb modifying an adjective or modifying another adverb is a limiting adverb [§9.7], its notation has the extra horizontal line built into its notation.

Note: When an abbreviated adverb is bound to the verb in a contraction, either place the entire contraction in the position for the predicate, or split the contraction and place the abbreviated adverb in its proper place unit, duplicating any letters in the contracted portion needed to make it sensible. For contractions such as "won't" it is best to leave the word whole and place it as part of the predicate.

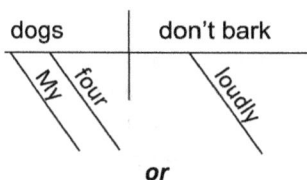

or

traditional   *QCD*

*My four dogs **don't** bark loudly.*

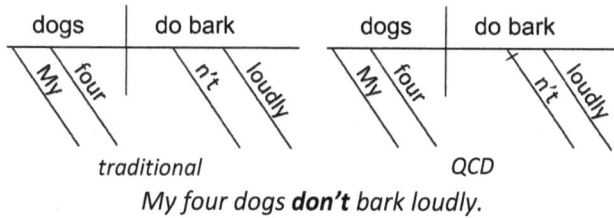

All three of these represent the uncontracted

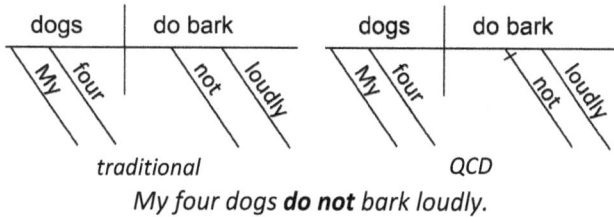

traditional   *QCD*

*My four dogs **do not** bark loudly.*

If the diagrammer, or teacher, wishes to give fuller, more explicit information, the following edit can be made to the diagram:

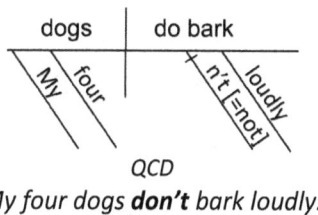

QCD

*My four dogs **don't** bark loudly.*

16.3.1.2   The Simple Sentence: Modifiers With Elided Modified

Adjectives, particularly in their comparative or superlative degree, and numbers, may be used in situations in which the word the modify is omitted because it can be understood from the context.

In these situations, traditional diagramming places an 'x' in the position that elided modified word would have appeared in. In *QCD* these can be marked either with the elided-word marker, Ø, or, more preferably, by placing the elided word within brackets: "[*elided word*]".

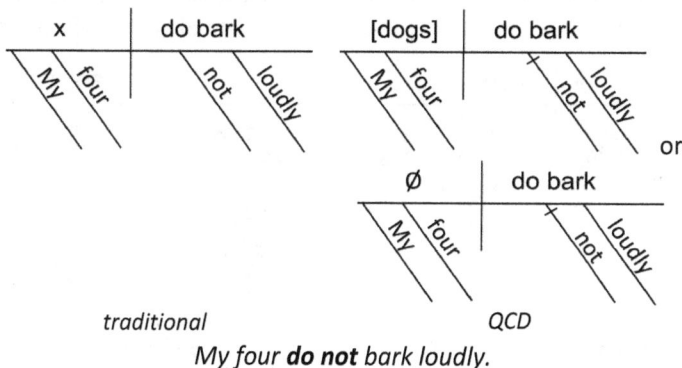

or

traditional   *QCD*

*My four **do not** bark loudly.*

16.3.1.3 The Simple Sentence: With Modifiers Of Modifiers

Modifiers of modifiers—usually limiting adverbs—are placed on diagonal lines to the left of the word they modify, connected to it by a line extending at a right angle from their lines to the line of the modified word. The line connecting the diagonal line of the modifier to that of the modified.

Because any adverb used in this way is a limiting adverb, in *QCD* the connecting right angle line segment serves as the 'L' used to distinguish limiting from attributive adverbs.

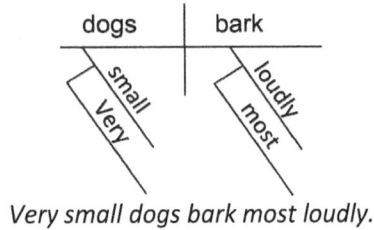

Very small dogs bark most loudly.

Reed/Kellogg uses a slightly different set of lines for the modifier of a modifier.

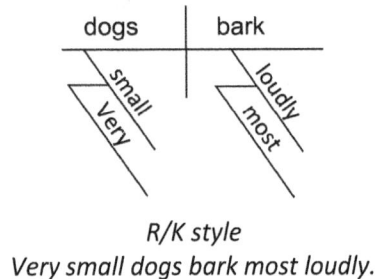

R/K style
Very small dogs bark most loudly.

However, this form causes problems in other situations in which it is used, such as single adverbs modifying other, compound modifier units [see §16.3.1.4]. Therefore, several traditional diagramming methods as well as *QCD* use the style given first in this section.

16.3.1.4 The Simple Sentence: With Modifiers of Compound Modifiers

Compound modifiers are modifiers joined by coordinate conjunctions. The manner of diagramming these conjunctions is different from that used with substantives because of the orientation of the lines on which the text is arranged.

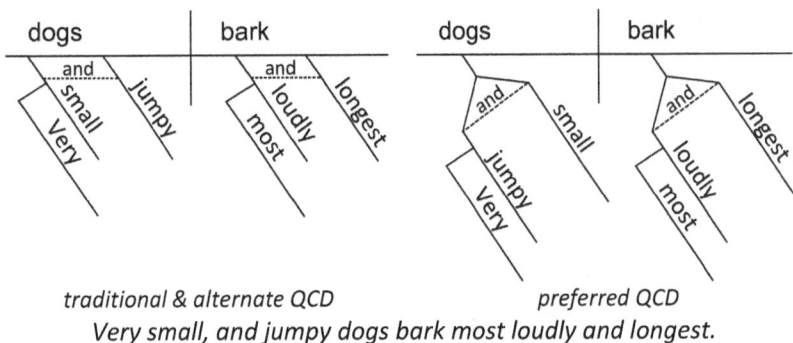

traditional & alternate QCD   *preferred QCD*
Very small, and jumpy dogs bark most loudly and longest.

The Simple Sentence: With Adverbs Modifying Compound Modifier Units

Compound modifiers may function as a single modifying unit. In such a case, the "preferred *QCD*" form given in §16.3.1.6 must be used to specify the exact nature of the phrase and the fact that the adverb modifies the compound modifier as a single unit, rather than merely the first part of the compound.

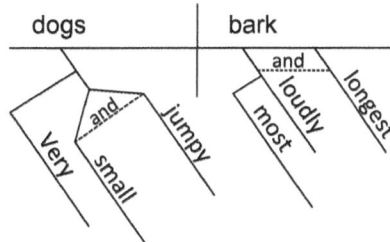

Very small and jumpy dogs bark most loudly and longest.
[***Very*** *modifies* ***small and jumpy*** *(and requires new structure), while, in the predicate,* ***most*** *modifies only* ***loudly*** *(so the older design can be used).*]

16.3.1.6 **The Simple Sentence: With Adverbs Modifying Phrases or Clauses**

Whenever an adverb modifies an entire prepositional or participial phrase, the design of its supporting branch is altered slightly. In traditional diagramming, solid lines are drawn from the diagonal of the word introducing the phrase and from the horizontal line containing the primary element of the phrase to the start of the diagonal line of the adverb modifying the phrase.

However, in *QCD*, in order to emphasize that modifying adverb's connection to the entire branch containing the modified phrase, the top section of the angled line on which the adverb resides is doubled, paralleling that original line segment.

In this example, the word "only" modifies the entire prepositional phrase "in the rainforest", and thereby establishes a contrast with other growing locations.

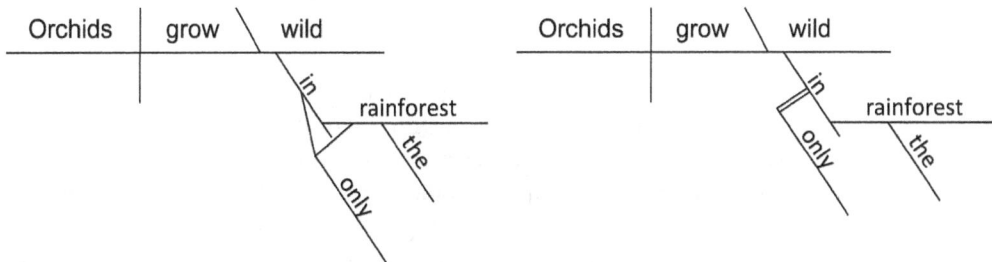

traditional   *QCD*
Orchids grow wild only in the rainforest.

If the phrase stood in contrast to other locations, or relationships, to the rainforest (such as "within the rainforest" or "on the rainforest"), the modifier would apply only to the preposition and would be diagrammed in the way specific for that usage.

16.3.1.7   The Simple Sentence: With Unexpressed Subject

An unexpressed subject is found in imperative sentences, and in some sentence fragments.

Traditional diagramming: There are four options. You can place the implied subject in position within parentheses; or you can place an 'x' in the unexpressed word's position; or you can place an 'x' within parentheses in its position; or you can leave that reserved area empty, which, however, makes the diagram look incomplete.

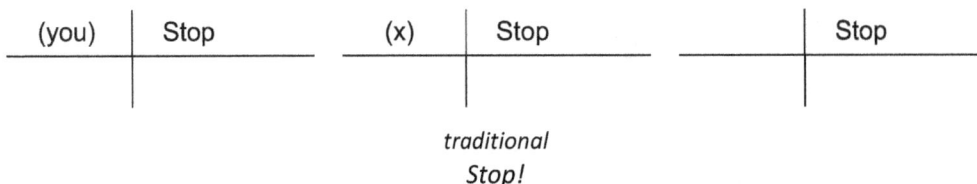

(you)	Stop		(x)	Stop			Stop

traditional
Stop!

QCD: ① You may place a character that looks like the mathematical 'null set' character, Ø, in that position, showing that an element has been omitted as part of the definition of the language.

Another character may have to be substituted: do not use a character native to the script of the language of the sentence you are diagramming. [Ø is Unicode U+00D8 {alt+0216 on Windows}; it is used by Danish, Norwegian, and some other languages.]

[On diagonal lines, this null sign is written as a hoop symbol, whose legs allow it to be attached clearly to the unit to which it applies.]

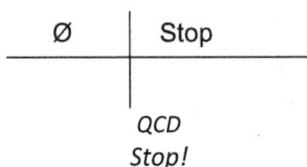

Ø	Stop

QCD
Stop!

② **However**, because it is clearer to reintroduce the elided text into its place, (other than of elided appositives) **in QCD the preferred way to mark elision is to insert the omitted word, or as much information as is discernible, within brackets**. Use of brackets in an editorial format [§15.13.1] is required because the insertion of any information that is not within the original sentence itself is an act of editorial expansion or explanation on the part of the diagrammer and must be evident. **Do not substitute parentheses** in this situation—these are specifically restricted in usage to provide the marking of appositives and appositive-like constructs.

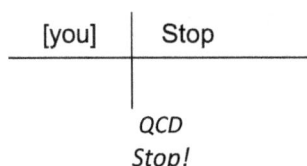

[you]	Stop

QCD
Stop!

16.3.1.8 The Simple Sentence: With Noun Appositive

An appositive is noted by enclosing it within a pair of parentheses and placing this unit directly after the noun to which it stands in an appositive relation.

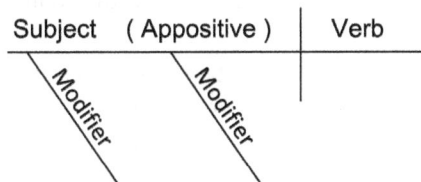

The point at which a modifier is attached to the baseline is extremely important with appositives, as its position reveals whether it modifies the substantive or the appositive.

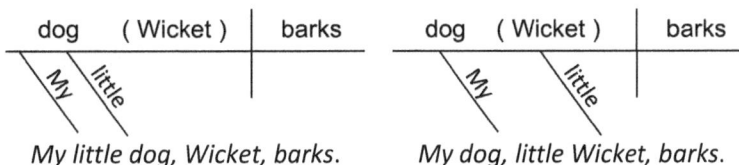

My little dog, Wicket, barks.　　　*My dog, little Wicket, barks.*

An appositive may also be introduced by the word *or*.

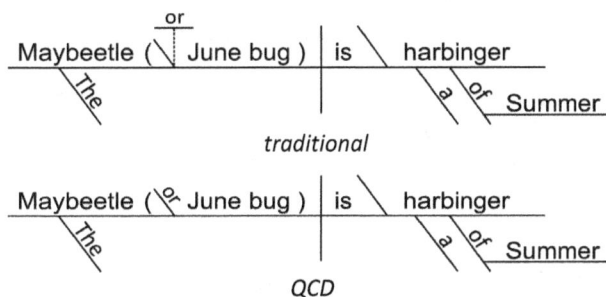

traditional

QCD

The Maybeetle, or June bug, is a harbinger of Summer.

16.3.1.9 The Simple Sentence: With Adjective Appositive

A noun may have an adjective used appositively. In this case, the lack of a noun appositive is noted by the empty slot marker of the diagramming style, and the adjective appositive displayed as modifying the missing noun

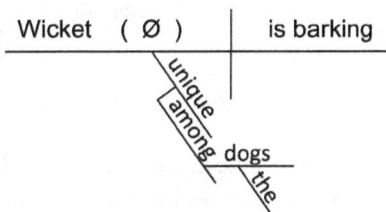

Wicket, unique among the dogs, is barking.
i.e., Wicket, unique [dog] among the dogs, is barking.

16.3.1.10 The Simple Sentence: With Compound Subject

A compound subject is placed on two or more horizontal lines, connected to the baseline by a triangular structure that also has room for the coordinating conjunction (usually *and* or *or*), rotated into a vertical orientation and placed on a dashed line that forms the long side of the triangle. The order of presentation is from top to bottom.

The dashed line and conjunction are placed on the right-hand side when the structure is to the left of the perpendicular line separating subject from predicate.

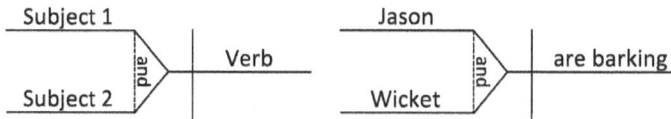

Jason and Wicket are barking.

When more than two subjects are joined in the same list, a horizontal line is inserted for each extra subject, and the conjunction is moved so that its position is between the two subjects it appears between in the original sentence.

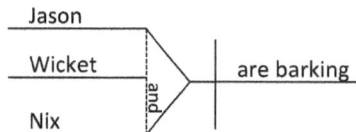

Jason, Wicket and Nix are barking.

Traditional diagramming will place an 'x' on the dashed line between the first and second subjects. However, this is not necessary as the presence of the conjunction between the second and third subjects shows that the vacant portion is correct.

However, if there is no conjunction joining any of the subjects, it is necessary to place the elided

16.3.1.11 The Simple Sentence: With Compound Predicate

A compound predicate is placed on two or more horizontal lines, connected to the baseline by a triangular structure that also has room for the coordinating conjunction (usually *and* or *or*). This triangle is reflected across the line dividing subject from verb, and the dashed line and conjunction are placed on the left-hand side of the structure because the unit is to the right of the perpendicular line dividing subject from Predicate. The order of presentation is from top to bottom.

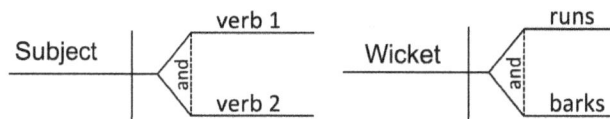

Wicket runs and barks.

When more than two predicates are joined in the same list, a horizontal line is inserted for each extra verb, and the conjunction is moved so that its position is between the two verbs it appears between in the original sentence.

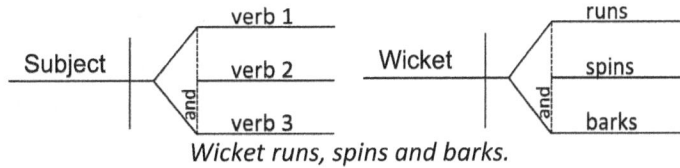

Wicket runs, spins and barks.

16.3.1.12 The Simple Sentence: With Compound Subject and Compound Predicate

In a sentence having both a compound subject and a compound predicate, the two methods of diagramming are simply connected through a unifying, single baseline segment bisected by the vertical subject/predicate divider.

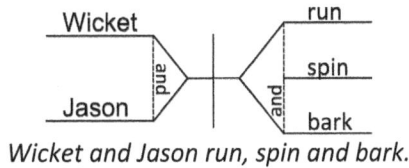

Wicket and Jason run, spin and bark.

Any element common to all parts of the predicate is placed on the baseline, as usual.

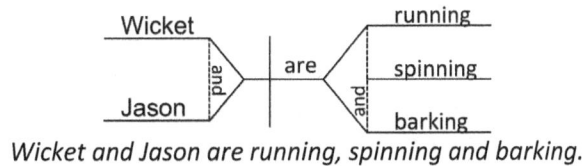

Wicket and Jason are running, spinning and barking.

NOTE: **A diagram must always include a section of the baseline that represents the "backbone" of the clause.** Failure to do so creates a very ugly diagram that is both missing an important graphic and informational element, and that resembles an electronics schematic more closely than a sentence diagram, or that may even look more like a spastic asterisk rather than the graphic representative of an independent or dependent clause:

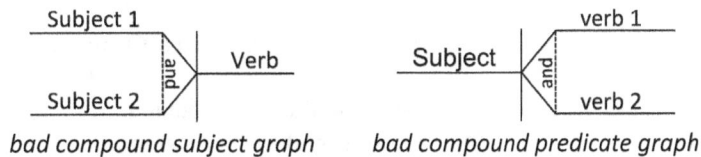

bad compound subject graph   *bad compound predicate graph*

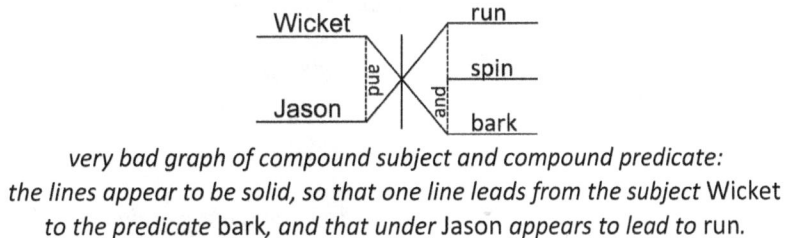

very bad graph of compound subject and compound predicate:
the lines appear to be solid, so that one line leads from the subject Wicket
to the predicate bark, *and that under* Jason *appears to lead to* run.

16.3.1.12.1 The Simple Sentence: With Common Modifier of Compound Subjects

The common modifier may be handled in either of two ways.

In one, the common line extending to the right from the compound subject toward the subject/predicate divider line is lengthened and the common modifier is attached to it on that common side.

In the other way, the structure holding the compound subjects is extended to the left and its lines are extended so that they merge on that left side into a single line.

From this line descend any modifiers that apply to all members of the compound subject in common.

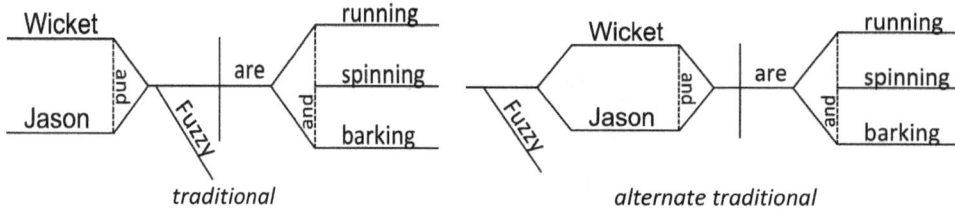

traditional   alternate traditional
(both forms are supported in QCD)

Fuzzy Wicket and Jason are running, spinning and barking.

16.3.1.12.2 The Simple Sentence: With Common Modifier of Predicates

A common modifier of a compound predicate is diagrammed by closing the verb units that are modified in common so that an extended, single horizontal line can be used as the shared attachment segment.

Note that modifiers of individual units within the compound are attached solely to the unit they modify, without change in layout.

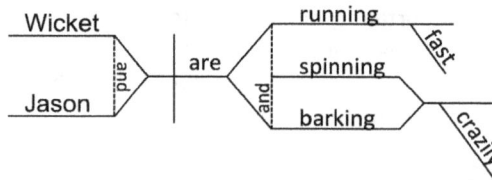

Wicket and Jason are running fast, spinning and barking crazily.

Notice the difference that adding a conjunction has on the structure of the following sentence, and of its diagram. In this instance we have a compound within a compound.

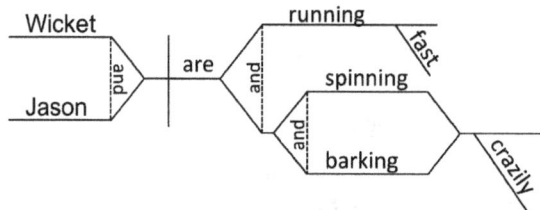

*Wicket and Jason are running fast, **and** spinning and barking crazily.*

16.3.1.13   The Simple Sentence: With Compound Appositive of Subject

Starting with the structure used with the compound subjects, a section of the base line is place to the left of the compound structure to hold the subject, then diagonal lines are drawn from that baseline segment to the ends of the horizontal lines on which the appositive entries have been placed.

That having been done, parentheses are either placed in the way they are in §16.3.1.8, or, larger parentheses are placed around the complete appositive structure, centered vertically above and below the main clause's baseline.

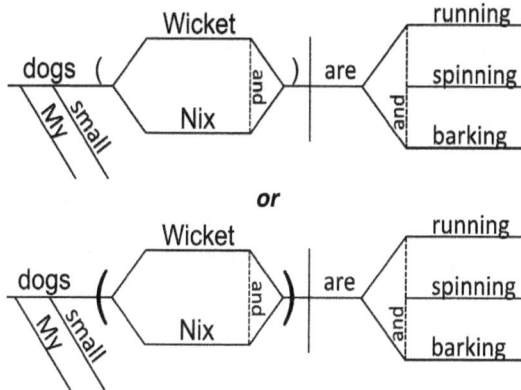

or

My small dogs, Wicket and Nix, are running, spinning and barking.

When more than two subjects are joined in the same list, a horizontal line is inserted for each extra subject, the conjunction is moved so that its position is between the two subjects it appears between in the original sentence, and a dashed or dotted line is placed on the left hand side, connecting the baselines of the appositives.

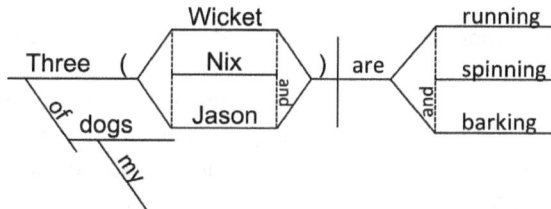

Three of my dogs, Wicket, Nix and Jason, are running, spinning and barking.

16.3.2 Compound Sentences

Simple sentences joined by a coordinating conjunction creates a structure called a Compound Sentence

This structure is unusual in that there are two ways in which it has been diagrammed in the past, as well as a new way suggested as the *QCD* method.

16.3.2.1 Two Independent Clauses

In traditional diagramming, a dashed line (often mislabeled as a *dotted* line) is drawn from the verb of the first sentence to the verb of the second sentence, with the coordinating conjunction placed on a horizontal, solid line segment between the sentences it appears between. Reed and Kellogg state that "the connecting line is drawn between the predicates merely for convenience", so we may assume its use was not clearly thought through.

As you can see from the diagram below, this method is clumsy at best, cluttered and messy at worst. It also suffers from an unfortunate assumption that conjunctions join the verbs rather than the entire clauses.

This method also minimizes the display of the fact that these clauses are, in fact, joined into a single sentence.

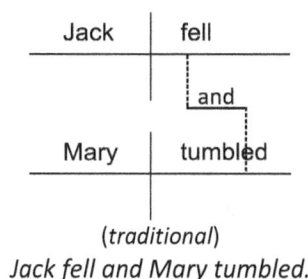

(*traditional*)
Jack fell and Mary tumbled.

In slightly more modern diagramming, a dashed line is drawn from the left hand side of the first sentence's baseline to the left hand, starting point of the second sentence's baseline, with the coordinating conjunction placed aligned with that dashed line midway between the two sentences. This method fixes the problem with diagramming conjunctions as joining verbs instead of clauses, but it is not well extendible.

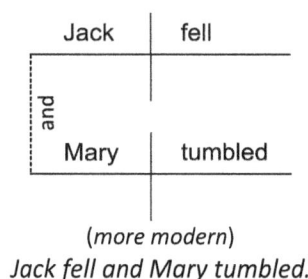

(*more modern*)
Jack fell and Mary tumbled.

In *QCD*, we simply re-use the coordinating, phrase-joining, construction for consistency and coherency. The reason for this, and its benefits, will become more apparent when considering its extension to diagramming other, particularly the correlative, conjunctions.

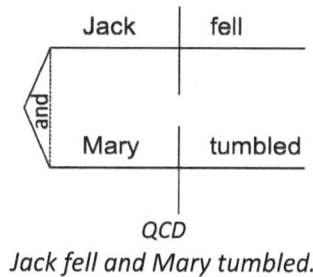

QCD
Jack fell and Mary tumbled.

16.3.2.2 More than Two Independent Clauses

When more than two sentences are joined by a coordinating conjunction, traditional diagramming connects the non-final pairs of clauses with its broken line, as above, then usually puts an 'x' in place of the conjunction to show that a conjunction has not been used there. The next to last and final independent clauses are then joined with the broken line and the conjunction used by the diagrammed sentence.

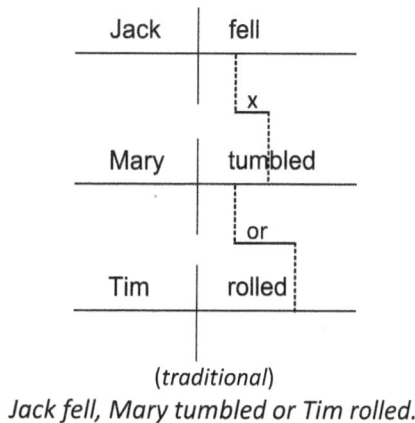

(traditional)
Jack fell, Mary tumbled or Tim rolled.

The slightly more modern method follows the traditional method's placement both of 'x' or '(x)' and of the conjunction, but moves the dashed line to the far left of all independent clauses.

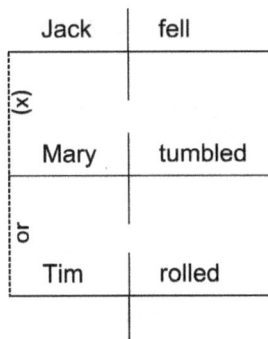

(*more modern*)
Jack fell, Mary tumbled or Tim rolled.

QCD simply extends the coordinating construction from two to more-than-two clauses. (There is no need to insert notation for non-existent conjunctions when the diagram is clear without them, which it will be if the conjunction is placed correctly .)

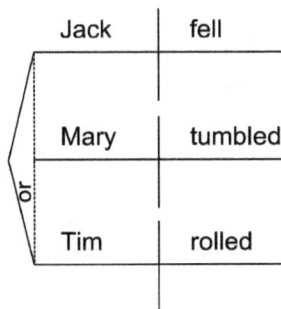

QCD
Jack fell, Mary tumbled or Tim rolled.

16.3.2.3   **Correlative Clauses**

Correlative conjunctions join two—and only two—independent clauses, phrases or words into either an alternate statement or into an emphasized pair of statements.

In both the traditional and the more modern ways of diagramming correlative independent clauses, the simple coordinating structure is simply extended, without purposeful or descriptive arrangement of the conjunctions.

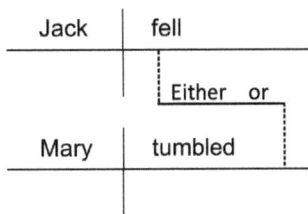

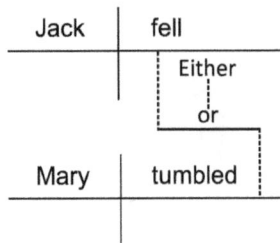

(*traditional*)   (*alternate traditional: R/K*)
Either Jack fell or Mary tumbled.

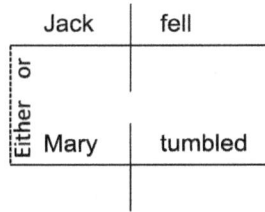

Jack | fell

Either or

Mary | tumbled

(*more modern*)
Either Jack fell or Mary tumbled.

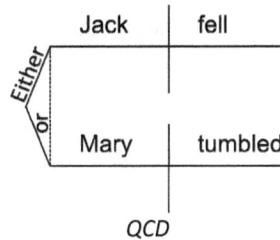

Jack | fell

Either / or

Mary | tumbled

QCD
Either Jack fell or Mary tumbled.

16.3.2.4   Correlative Phrases

Correlative conjunctions can join phrases or words that are smaller in form than independent clauses.

In traditional diagramming, the method used for joining independent, correlative clauses is not used for these smaller units; traditional usage switches instead to using the structure used both by traditional design and by *QCD* for all coordinate and correlative conjunctions. The difference between traditional and *QCD* diagrams is simply where the words are placed on the graphic.

In a *QCD* diagram, the second member of a correlative statement is placed in the middle of the dashed line within the triangle structure. This rule reiterates the fact that correlative conjunctions involve two, and only two, correlated units.

In both traditional and *QCD* diagrams the triangular graphic points in a specific direction: it is on the right hand side of the subject phrase and on the left of any predicate or object phrase.

16.3.2.4.1   Correlative Subject Phrases

The triangular graphic is on the right hand side of the construction. The arrangement of the words differs between traditional and *QCD* diagrams:

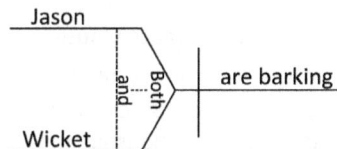

Jason

and *Both* are barking

Wicket

extremely poorly designed Reed/Kellogg format

Both Jason and Wicket are barking.

traditional (non-R/K)   *QCD*

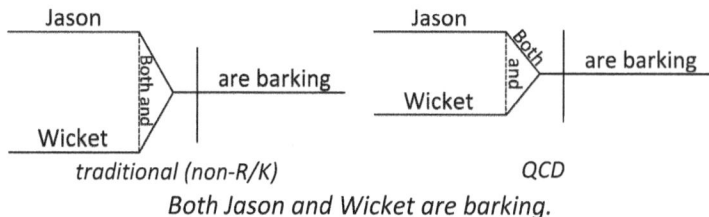

In this example, *Both* emphasizes the entire conjunct phrase, as do all the first members of the conjunctions uniting correlative conjunctive phrases. The *QCD* diagram is designed to show that emphasis more clearly. [Reed and Kellogg state that "the conjunction *both* is used to strengthen the real connective *and*..." {*One-Book Course in English* [1904], p. 77 *fn*}; however, this fact is secondary to its primary characteristic of modifying (by emphasis) the entire conjoined phrase that it precedes.]

16.3.2.4.2   Correlative Predicate Phrases

The triangular graphic is on the left hand side of the construction. The arrangement of the words differs between traditional and *QCD* diagrams:

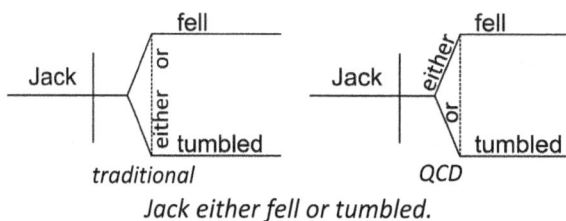

traditional   *QCD*

Jack either fell or tumbled.

The same arrangement as that for predicates themselves that are joined by coordinate conjunctions is used no matter where the phrase or words occur, when dealing with conjunct predicates or objects.

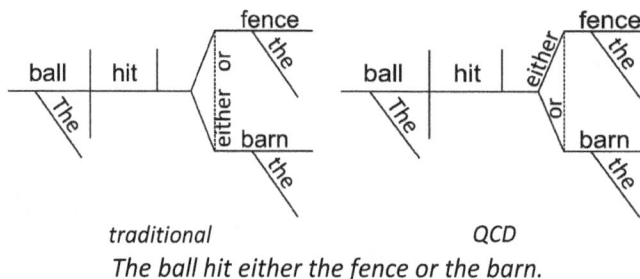

traditional   *QCD*

The ball hit either the fence or the barn.

16.3.2.5   Correlative Clauses Plus Coordinate Clause

When we come to the case of a sentence with a correlative clause joined to a following clause by a coordinating conjunction, both traditional and more modern methods fail to show the relationship between the clauses and between the internal units. With both these methods, the clauses simply appear to be in a list, which is an error of analysis.

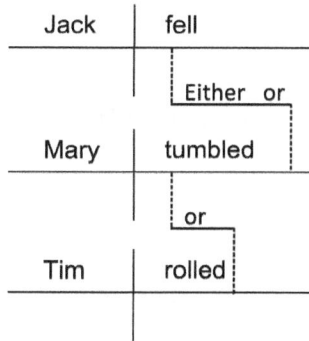

(*traditional: unclear*)
Either Jack fell or Mary tumbled, or Tim rolled.

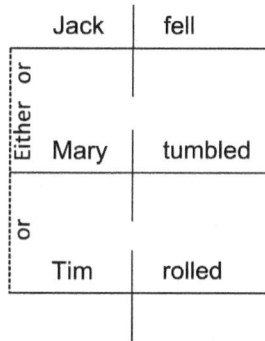

(*more modern, but still unclear*)
Either Jack fell or Mary tumbled, or Tim rolled.

The problem is that the second 'or' must be diagrammed showing that it is at the same level of structural importance as the entire first, correlative clause, while maintaining its separate nature. Neither of the older methods of diagramming can show this.

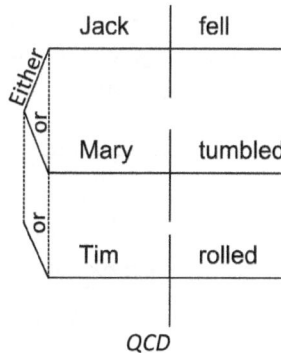

QCD
Either Jack fell or Mary tumbled, or Tim rolled.

16.3.3 Direct Objects

The direct object is separated from the verb by a line half as long as that which divides the subject from the predicate; this line rises from the baseline without a gap between it and the baseline.

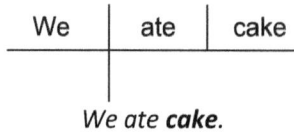

*We ate **cake**.*

16.3.3.1 Simple Predicate and Compound Direct Objects

The half-line of the direct object is placed on the baseline between the verb and the compound-triangle structure.

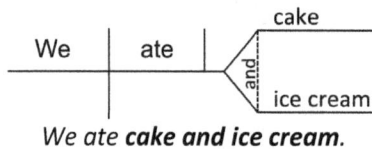

*We ate **cake and ice cream**.*

16.3.3.2 Compound Predicate and Single Direct Object

The half-line of the direct object is placed to the right, on the baseline extended from the point of the triangular structure rejoining the compound verb to a singular baseline that then holds the common direct object.

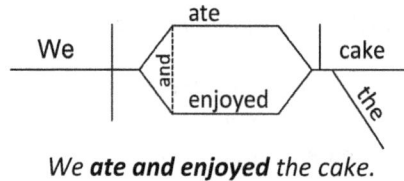

*We **ate and enjoyed** the cake.*

16.3.3.3 Compound Predicate and Compound Direct Objects

The half-line of the direct object is placed on each of the constituent baselines of each predicate, separating each verb from its particular direct object.

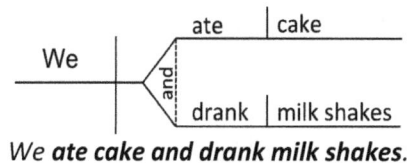

*We **ate cake and drank milk shakes**.*

16.3.4 Predicate Complements

The element distinguishing a predicate complement (a predicate nominative or a predicate adjective) from a direct object is the diagonal line leaning back towards the subject, as opposed to the upright (perpendicular) stance of the line dividing the verb from its object.

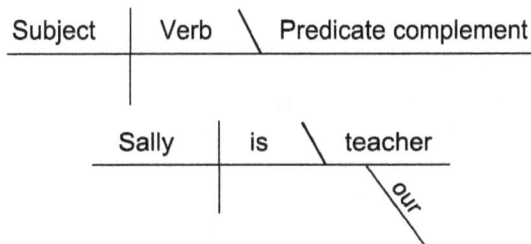

*Sally is our **teacher**.*
(***teacher*** is the predicate nominative.)

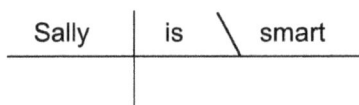

*Sally is **smart**.*
(***smart*** is the predicate adjective.)

Other verbs than just ***to be*** and ***to become*** function as linking verbs and govern predicate complements rather than objects. These must also use the left-leaning diagonal line as a separator.

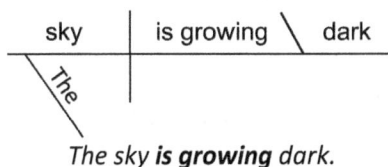

*The sky **is growing** dark.*

16.3.4.1 Compound Predicate Complement

Compound predicate complements are diagrammed in the same way that compound units in the predicate are formed. In this case, there is one verb with two predicate complements.

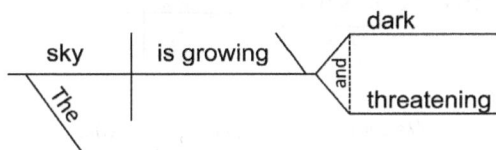

*The sky is growing **dark and threatening**.*

Compound predicates with predicate complements are diagrammed in a way similar to that above. The common part of the verb phrase is left on the sentence's baseline; the different parts of the verb phrase and their complements are placed on separate horizontal lines using the 'conjunction triangle'.

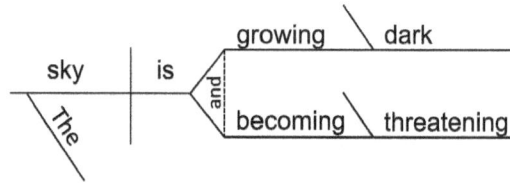

The sky is **growing dark and becoming threatening**.

16.3.4.2   Objective Complement

The special notation for an objective complement has to include two items to the right of the verb. One of these is the direct object of the verb, the second is another noun that extends the description of the direct object.

The original Reed/Kellogg notation for objective complements reversed the natural order of the words in the objective complement, making diagrams of this construct unwieldy and rather illogical in most situations.

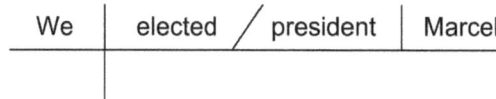

| We | elected | / president | Marcel |

obsolete Reed/Kellogg format
*We elected **Marcel president**.*

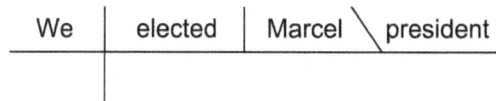

| We | elected | Marcel \ president |

post-R/K traditional, and QCD style
*We elected **Marcel president**.*

In one way of approaching it, the objective complement construction is an infinitive phrase from which the infinitive has been removed, leaving the infinitive's subject as the first noun of the predicate, and its object or complement as the second noun in the predicate. In this scenario, the example sentence would become "*We elected Marcel to be president.*" [Diagrammed in §16.3.10.7.]

The other way an objective complement may be perceived is as one in which the word "*as*" has been omitted, as demonstrated in this example:

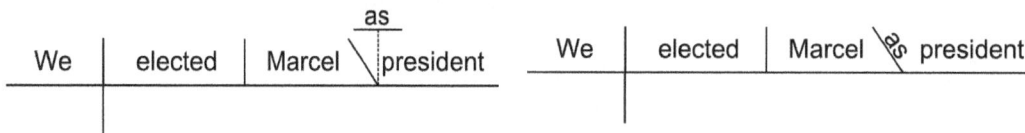

| We | elected | Marcel \ *as* president | | We | elected | Marcel \ *as* president |

traditional   *QCD*
*We elected Marcel **as** president.*

The traditional diagram has the word "*as*" floating above the main clause as it were a disembodied spirit, only vaguely connected to the structure, syntax or meaning of the sentence. *QCD* places it within the visual context of the sentence, where it belongs. This *QCD* notation also agrees with that used when "*as*" is used with other parts of speech.

16.3.4.2.1 **Compound Objective Complement**

The objective portion of the objective complement may be compound.

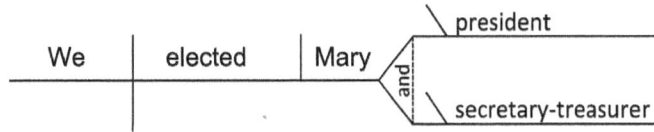

*We elected **Mary president and secretary-treasurer.***

16.3.4.2.1 **Compound Objective Complements**

The entire objective complement may be compounded, and the units within it may contain compounded subunits.

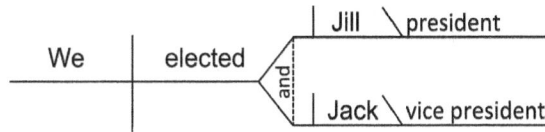

*We elected **Jill president and Jack vice president.***

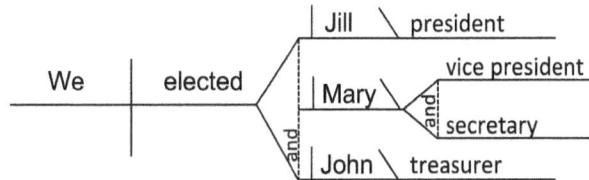

*We elected **Jill president, Mary vice president and secretary, and John treasurer.***

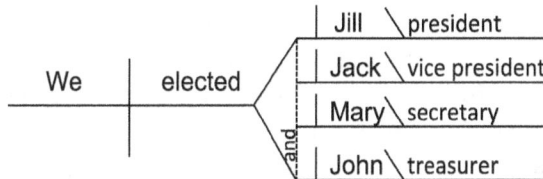

*We elected **Jill president, Jack vice president, Mary secretary and John treasurer.***

16.3.5 The Simple Sentence: With an Adverbial Objective

Here again, there is a difference between the traditional, the more modern and the QCD methods of diagramming. The traditional is minimal in its representation, and potentially confusing because, first, it leaves a blank opening along the diagonal, and, second, because it has the same layout and form as that for a prepositional phrase, it looks like it was left incomplete.

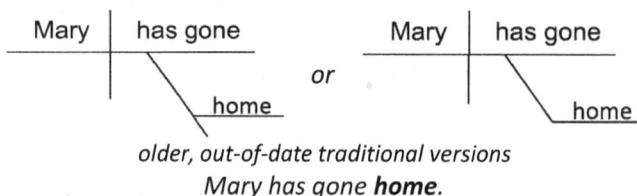

older, out-of-date traditional versions
*Mary has gone **home**.*

The more modern tries to remedy the shortcomings of the traditional method by using text to mark an unused portion of the structure used to hold an adverbial objective. This is potentially confusing because the reader must assume that this inserted text is not part of the input sentence, although there is nothing in particular that distinguishes it from the input text.

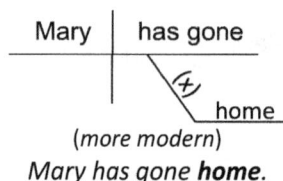

(more modern)
*Mary has gone **home**.*

QCD adds a specific graphic symbol (a variation of the null symbol used on horizontal lines) to the traditional structure; this symbol distinguishes this structure specifically as that of an adverbial objective and states plainly and unequivocally that nothing is to be inserted in the position it occupies.

Note that the diagonal line never extends below the horizontal line that holds the adverbial objective itself.

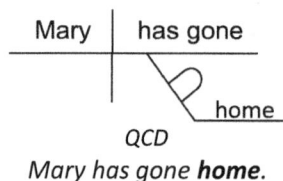

QCD
*Mary has gone **home**.*

16.3.6 The Simple Sentence: With Indirect Object

The indirect object is another kind of ***adverbial objective***, and as such, uses the same substructure to hold its information as that used by all adverbial objectives. It is also subject to the same problems with incompleteness or lack of clarity that the traditional and more modern diagramming methods impose on adverbial objectives.

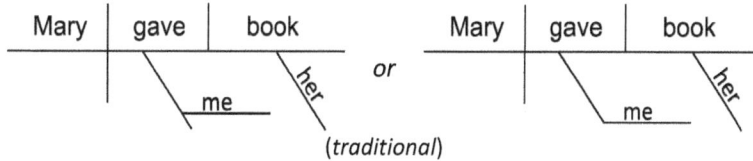

(traditional)
*Mary gave **me** her book.*

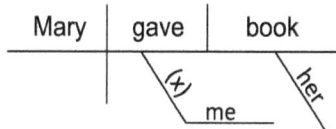

(slightly more modern traditional)
*Mary gave **me** her book.*

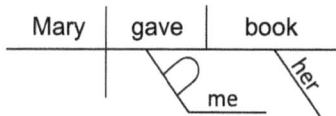

QCD
*Mary gave **me** her book.*

16.3.6.1 With Compound Predicate and Common Indirect Object

The positioning of the indirect object is the same in all three styles of diagramming.

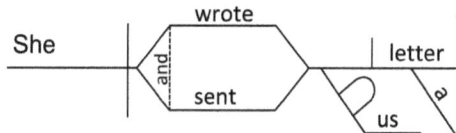

QCD
*She **wrote and sent us** a letter.*

16.3.6.2 With Compound Indirect Object

The traditional method of diagramming does not notate the indirect object as being distinct from other adverbial objectives. This creates inexactness of representation.

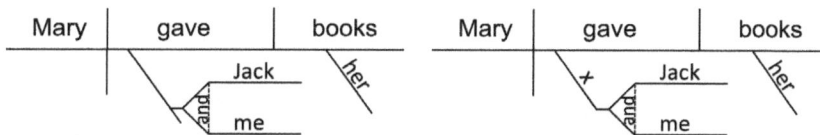

(old style)   (more modern style)
*Mary gave **Jack and me** her books.*

Unlike the traditional method, the *QCD* standard is consistent in its portrayal of indirect objects as a case of adverbial objective, and removes possible confusion with an incompletely written prepositional phrase.

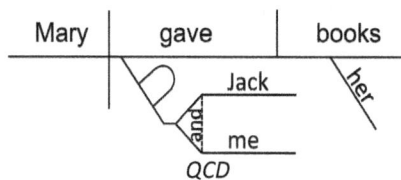

QCD

*Mary gave **Jack and me** her books.*

16.3.6.3 With Compound Appositives of the Indirect Object

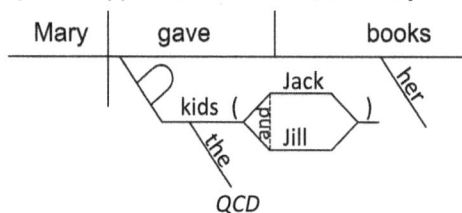

QCD

*Mary gave **the kids, Jack and Jill,** her books.*

16.3.7 The Simple Sentence: Elided Expressions

Some sentences have an elided subject, an elided predicate, or both.

Most often, these are independent units, termed **expletives** [see §16.3.14], but there are examples of an elided phrase having the structure, and being understood as, a complete sentence.

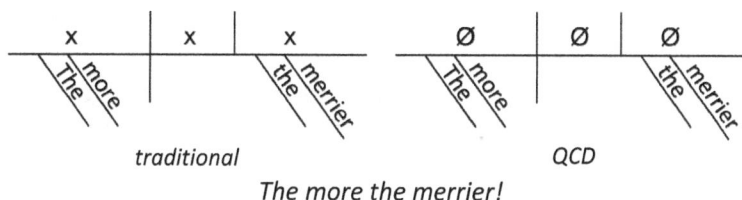

traditional   *QCD*

The more the merrier!

These are often independent units and are handled as such, but there are examples of an elided phrase having the structure, and being understood as, a complete sentence.

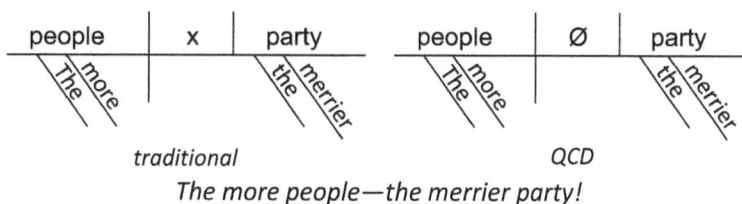

traditional   *QCD*

The more people—the merrier party!

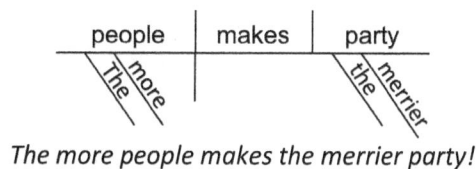

The more people makes the merrier party!

16.3.8 Prepositional Phrases

A prepositional phrase consists of a preposition followed by any modifiers of the phrase or object, then, finally, by its object. The object can be any part of speech that can be analyzed as being a substantive [as defined in §5.5].

Because prepositional usage is an extension of adverbial usage, the preposition itself appears on a diagonal line, in the same orientation as that of an adverb. Extending horizontally from that line is a line on which the object of the preposition is given.

Modifiers of the object of a preposition are attached beneath the object in the same way that they are attached to the baseline of the sentence whenever word or phrases modify items located on the baseline.

In some presentations of traditional diagramming, this horizontal line begins at the point the diagonal line ends; in others, it connects to the diagonal line above its end-point. The second method is preferred traditionally, and because of a need both for differentiation and for consistency, is the *QCD* standard for diagramming prepositional phrases.

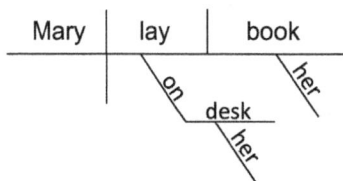

> Mary | lay | book
> on — desk — her
> her

(bad alternate traditional form)
[same form as, and confusable with, adverbial objectives]
Mary lay her book **on her desk**.

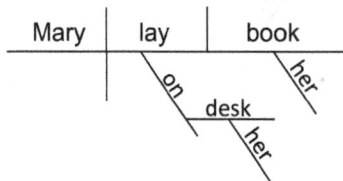

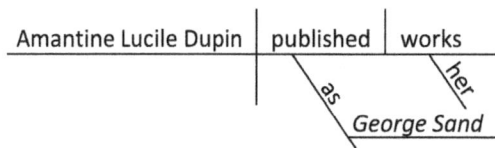

> Mary | lay | book
> on — desk — her
> her

normal traditional style, & QCD
Mary lay her book **on her desk**.

> Amantine Lucile Dupin | published | works
> as — *George Sand* — her

Amantine Lucile Dupin published her works **as George Sand**.

16.3.8.1 Prepositional Phrase Modifying a Modifier

A prepositional phrase that modifies another modifier is placed on an extended diagonal connector that shows what it modifies and leaves room for the preposition itself to be given in a modifier position.

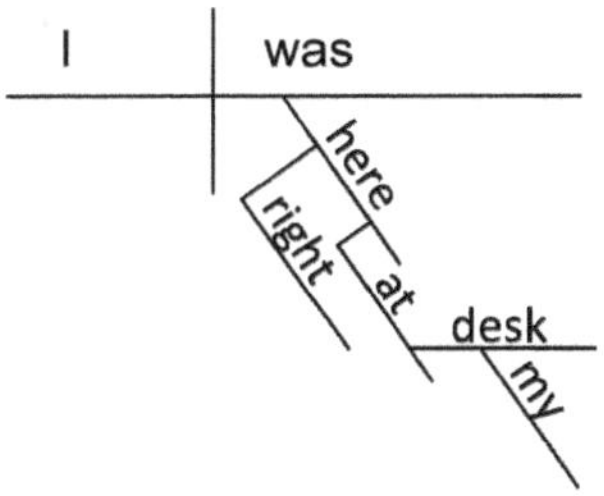

*I was right here **at my desk**.*

16.3.8.2 Prepositional Phrase With Compound Objects

A prepositional phrase with multiple objects is diagrammed just as the other compound substantives are diagrammed.

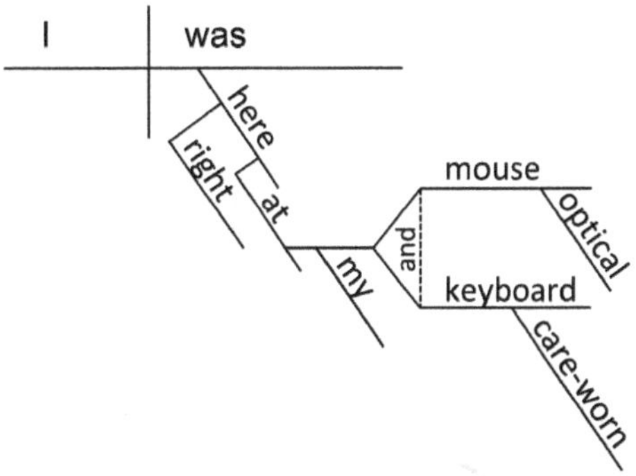

*I was right here **at my optical mouse and care-worn keyboard**.*

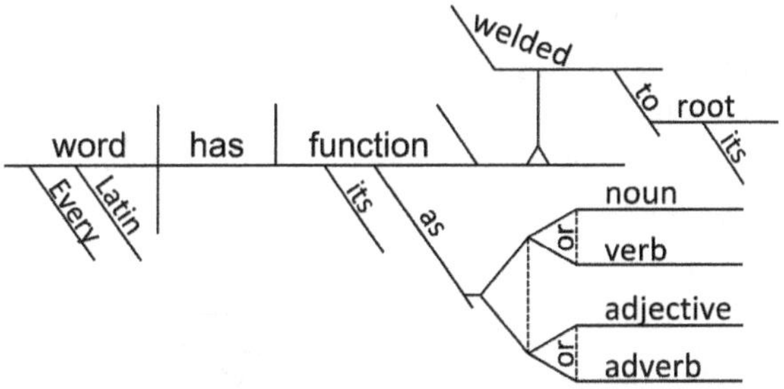

*Every Latin word has its function **as noun or verb, adjective or adverb** welded **to its root**.*

16.3.8.3 Prepositional Phrase With Compound Appositives of the Object

This diagramming construct is a combination of the standard structure for appositives, using parentheses, and that structure used for compound items appearing to the right of their connection to the main diagram.

Note that the lines of the compound structure holding the appositives themselves are extended diagonally, closed and a prepositional-object baseline is drawn to the right from their junction in order to provide a location for placement of the closing parenthesis.

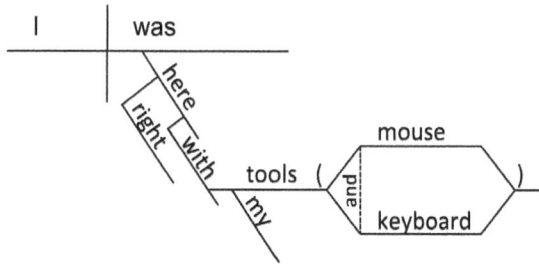

*I was right here **with my tools—mouse and keyboard**.*
(*Remember that punctuation is not represented in diagramming.*)

16.3.8.4 Prepositional Phrase Governed By a Compound Preposition

Compound prepositions are prepositions made up of two words governing a single phrase. There is a number of these—ones starting with *from, off,* and *over* in particular—that can be parsed as prepositional phrases imbedded within another.

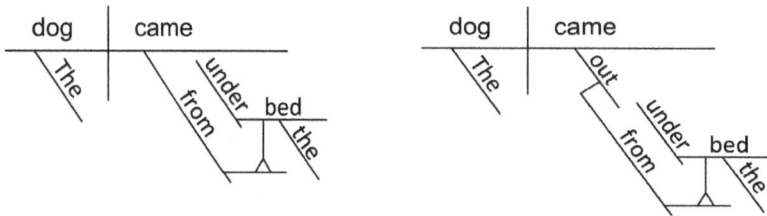

*The dog came **from under the bed**.*   *The dog came out **from under the bed**.*
(*fully parsed*)

However, because this is the normal way in which all compound prepositions are used, and because this depth of parsing does not reveal any truly useful information, it is also acceptable for the diagram of such a phrase to be done in a simpler manner.

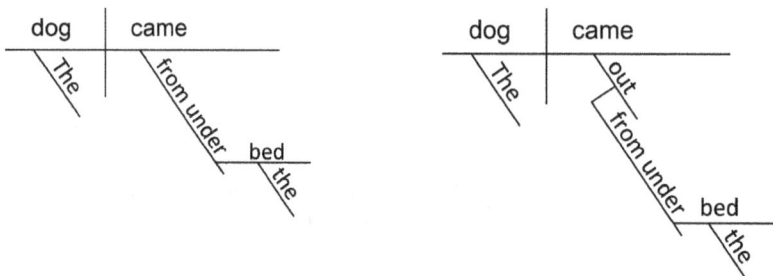

*The dog came **from under the porch**.*   *The dog came out **from under the porch**.*
(*alternate diagramming style of phrasal prepositions*)

Either way of diagramming this construct is considered to be correct.

16.3.8.5 Prepositional Phrase Governed By a Phrasal Preposition

Phrasal prepositions are diagrammed in the same manner as simple prepositions, with all parts of the phrasal preposition appearing on the diagonal line that is occupied by simple prepositions within their diagrams.

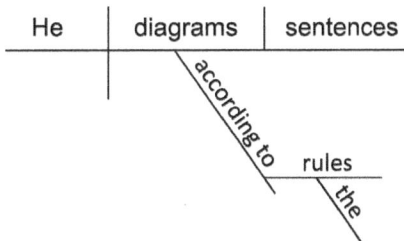

*He diagrams sentences **according to the rules**.*

16.3.8.6 Compound Prepositional Phrases With a Shared Modifier

Multiple prepositional phrases that share a common object have the object baseline extended to the right. From these diagonal lines are extended toward the bottom right from the top line, toward the upper right from the bottom line until they meet halfway, where the horizontal baseline is extended to the right from the intersection of the diagonal lines. On this baseline the shared modifiers are attached.

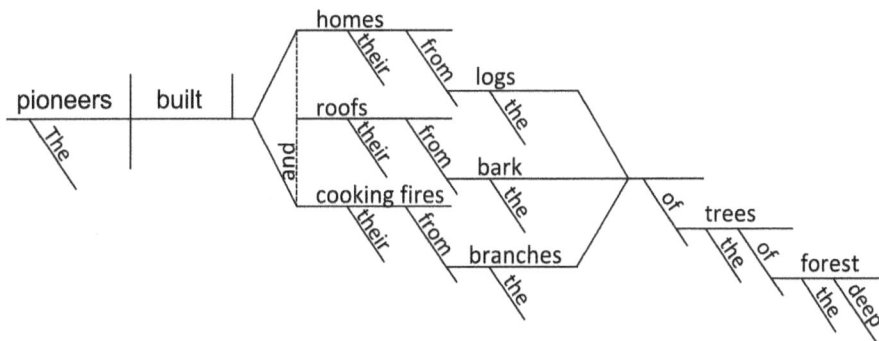

The pioneers built their homes from the logs, their roofs from the bark and their cooking fires from the branches of the trees of the deep forest.

Reed and Kellogg designed an alternate representation of such single modifiers of compound prepositional phrases, a design that can be used whenever one of the modified phrases needs room for its own modifiers that might require lines to cross or become too convoluted when using the form above.

In it, additional copies of the modifying construct are inserted, with only the top copy getting the fully spelled words. Any other copies have full diagrams, but each of the words is abbreviated to its first letter.

Re-working the example given above using that alternate form produces the following diagram:

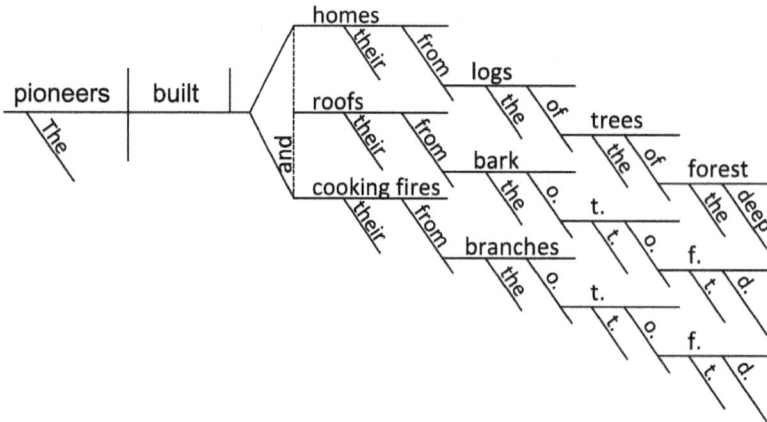

The diagram shows: pioneers / built, with "The" modifier. Branches: homes (their, from logs — the, of trees — the, of forest — the, deep); roofs (their, from bark — the, o., t., f., d.); cooking fires (their, from branches — the, o., t., f., d.). Connected by "and."

As should be obvious, this alternate method is far more cluttered and should not be used unless specifically required by the requirements of diagramming the sentence itself.

16.3.9 Verbals

Verbals—infinitives, gerunds and participles—have been given extremely inconsistent and incoherent treatment in traditional diagramming. Not only has each been given separate and unrelated structures, each requires special and specific treatment in its placement within a phrase, clause or sentence.

The *QCD* standard attempts to remedy these problems by introducing a new way of handling infinitives, one that is much closer to the representation of its kin, gerunds, than traditional diagramming could ever allow.

16.3.10 Verbals: Infinitives

In traditional diagramming, the infinitive is not differentiated from a prepositional phrase governed by *to*. This is unfortunate: the infinitive has nothing whatsoever to do with such a prepositional phrase: as stated in §7.24, that word has not had prepositional usage for over 1200 years. Because of this, **the traditional way of diagramming the infinitive should be avoided if at all possible**.

Which of the following two traditional representations is used is largely dependent on how prepositional phrases are diagrammed in the specific traditional guide one may consult.

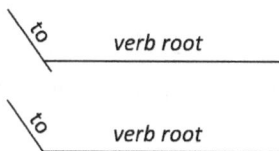

poorly designed, traditional diagrams of the infinitive

In *QCD*, the root of the infinitive is also placed on a horizontal line; and, to the left of the root is the **to** part of the infinitive, written in line with the diagonal on which it is placed.

However, in *QCD* there are two further changes to provide clear differentiation. First, the top of the diagonal bears a line segment that goes off toward the upper right at a ninety degree angle from the diagonal. Although this left portion of the infinitive subunit bears a resemblance to the structure for a *modifier of a modifier*, this upper portion is not used to attach the infinitive unit to another line or object. It is used solely as a mark of the infinitive, appearing to precede the **to** portion of the infinitive, or a symbol noting its elision. Second, the horizontal line bearing the root of the infinitive is extended to the left so that its left-hand extreme is at least as far left as is the angle in the lines above it.

QCD representation of the infinitive as noun

QCD representation of the infinitive as adjective or adverb

In certain situations, the **to** portion of the infinitive is elided and only the root is exposed. In these cases, traditional notation was not specific: the place normally holding the **to** portion was left blank, filled with an 'x' or '(x)', or marked with a hoop-like structure (which may have started life as half a zero). In QCD, only the hoop-like structure is used.

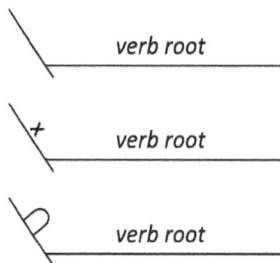

traditional representations of the infinitive with elided 'to'

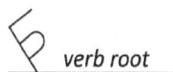

QCD representation of the infinitive with elided 'to'

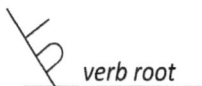

QCD representation of the infinitive with elided 'to' as adjective or adverb

In order to link infinitives either to the baseline of the sentence or to the object line of prepositions or adverbial objectives, a special, inverted 'Y' is used as a stand on which to place the infinitive subunit. In traditional diagramming this is required everywhere an infinitive occurs, though the places it occurs differ between infinitives and gerunds. In *QCD* the handling of infinitives and gerunds is coherent: the same structural arrangement applies to both in each situation in which they can occur.

The *QCD* notation of infinitives is also a closer representation of the historical forms and the use of infinitives in Anglo-Saxon.

In Anglo-Saxon, there were two forms of the infinitive, a single-word form (as in German), which was used in the same places that the elided infinitive is now found, and is diagrammed with the "elision hoop", and a two-word form marked by an initial *tō*, the form inherited by Modern English which occurs in all situations the full infinitive is used in Modern English. Traditional diagramming, erroneously, does not support such still-current distinctions.

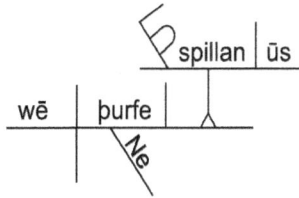

Ne þurfe wē ūs spillan.
We need not destroy each other.

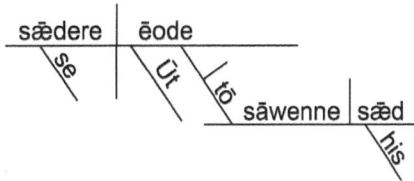

Ūt ēode se sǣdere his sǣd tō sāwenne.
Out went the sower, his seed to sow.

16.3.10.1 Infinitives as Subjects

As subjects, infinitives are hoisted onto the separating stand (mentioned above).

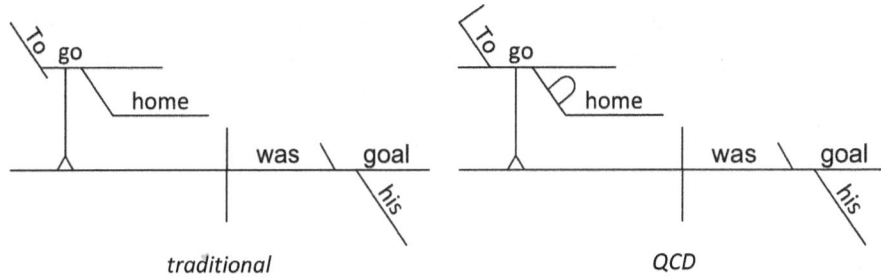

traditional

QCD

***To go home** was his goal.*

16.3.10.2 Compound Noun-Infinitives

It is in compound infinitives that *QCD* differs most from the traditional layout. In traditional diagramming, compound infinitives are laid out using a method more like that used for compound adjectives and adverbs than that used either for nouns or verbs, despite the fact that an infinitive is a verb form used as a noun.

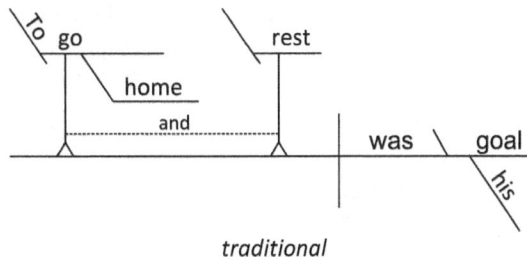

traditional
***To go home and rest** was his goal.*

More consistently, *QCD* uses the same style layouts for compound infinitives as that which is used for compound gerunds, whereas the traditional manner treats the two verbals differently. (The conjunction is on the left hand side, as is used with compound verbs, reflecting the fact that infinitives are verbals used as nouns, not themselves nouns.)

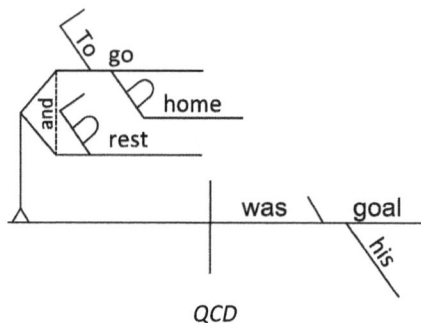

QCD

To go home and rest *was his goal.*

16.3.10.3 Infinitives with Modifiers

Traditional diagramming is incapable of making a distinction between types of adverb, that is of notating whether an adverb is attribute, limiting or negating. Traditionally, the diagonals holding adverbs are simply attached to the horizontal line of the modified infinitive in the order in which they appear in the source text.

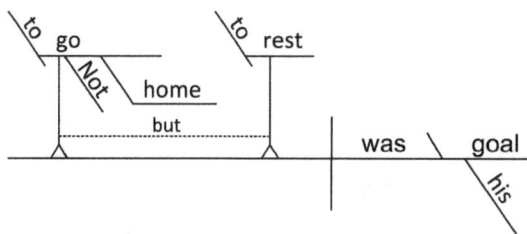

traditional

Not to go home but to rest *was his goal.*

In *QCD*, limiting and negating adverbs attach to the infinitive's horizontal line to the left of the diagonal, and use the *QCD* method of distinguishing themselves from attributive adverbs. Attributive adverbs and adverbial phrases attach to the right, beneath the root of the verbal. The benefit of this approach is that it reinforces the understanding both of adverbs, and of how and why not to split infinitives. There is a special notation in *QCD* for units that split an infinitive, described in §16.3.10.13.

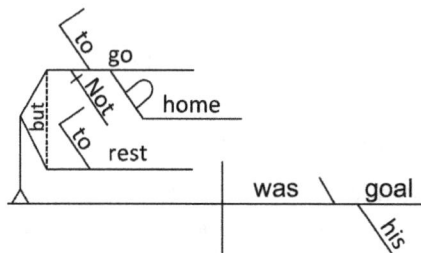

QCD

Not to go home but to rest *was his goal.*

The following diagram demonstrates a problem with traditional diagramming in that the first instance of the negating adverb **Not** in this example sentence applies to the entire compound subject. There is no easy way to represent this sentence:

attaching the leading **Not** as a modifier to the horizontal line of the subject area is nonsense, since **Not** is an adverb, and the subject area is reserved specifically for nouns, which cannot be modified by adverbs.

Attaching **Not** to the line of the conjunction is also unsatisfactory, as the adverb is not modifying the conjunction, but the entire compound infinitive phrase joined by the conjunction.

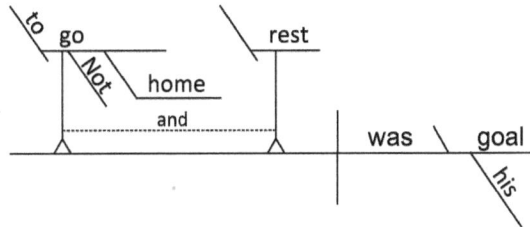

traditional, unclear
Not to go home and rest *was his goal.* **or**
Not to go home, and [to] rest *was his goal.*

However, the diagram structure supported by *QCD* allows easy representation of this sentence that causes problems for traditional diagramming.

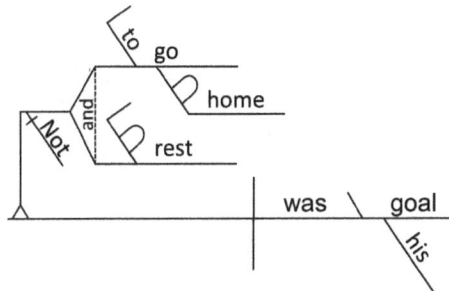

QCD
Not to go home and rest *was his goal.*

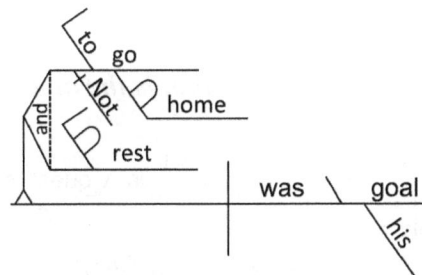

QCD
Not to go home, and rest, *was his goal.*

In this example the verb remains in the singular because, despite any commas, the compound infinitive phrase is a single unit, his unitary goal.

16.3.10.4 **Infinitives as Appositives**

Infinitives appear in an appositive usage in any of several positions within a sentence. They can occur in the positions usually thought of as appositive for nouns, or before or after the substantive they restate.

As appositives, infinitives appear in their normal, noun configurations, but with an enclosing pair of parentheses surrounding the base of the stand on which the infinitive structure sits.

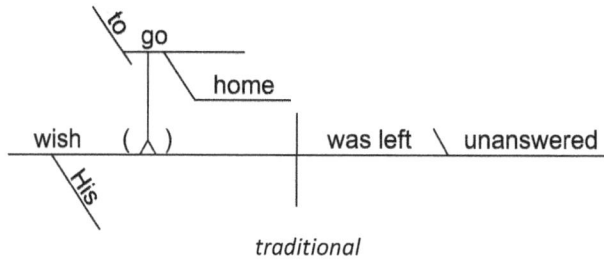

traditional

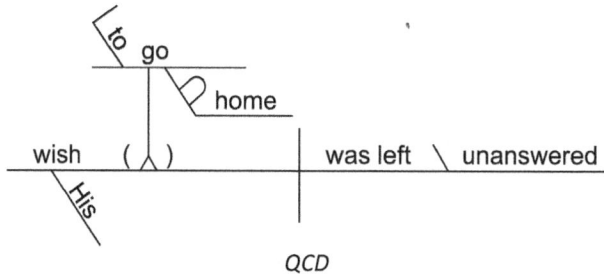

QCD

His wish, to go home, was left unanswered.
[*"To be left" (used in the past passive) is a verb phrase in this instance.*]

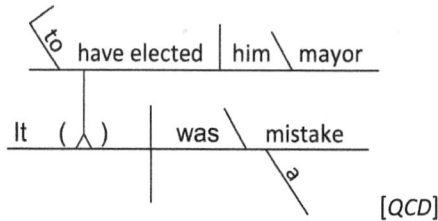

[*QCD*]

*It was a mistake **to have elected him mayor**.*

To be, or not to be—that is the question.

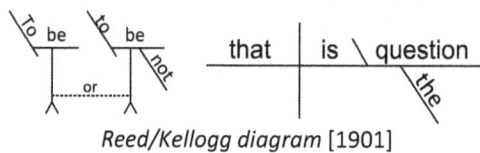

Reed/Kellogg diagram [1901]

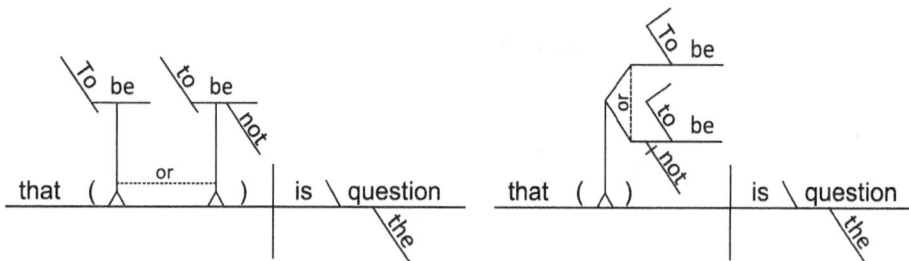

Reed/Kellogg's diagram of the sentence with the conjunct infinitives' being an aside or some absolute construction is incorrect. The infinitive construction is clearly an appositive, a restatement of the subject, simply moved forward of the subject for dramatic effect. The basic statement is *"To be or not to be is the question."*, which was transformed into *"That [i.e., That topic], to be or not to be, is the question."* before its being rearranged.

The traditional diagram of the appositive is imprecise, and could represent "to be or not to be", or " to be or to not be", or even " to be or to be not".

The QCD version is, however, the precise equivalent of the sentence. [See §7.24.15]

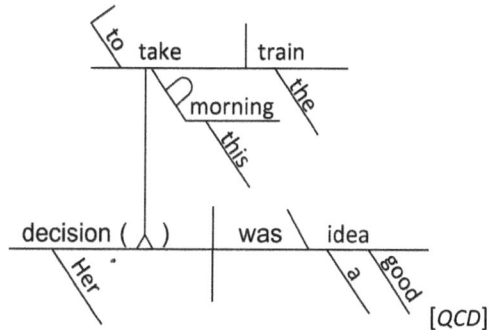

[QCD]

Her decision to take the train to work this morning was a good idea.
or *Her decision, to take the train to work this morning, was a good idea.*
Note that this infinitive could also be parsed as an adjective phrase. [See §16.3.10.10]

16.3.10.5 Infinitives as Direct Objects

As direct objects, infinitives appear in normal configurations, diagrammed much as when they appear as subjects.

He just wanted to go home.

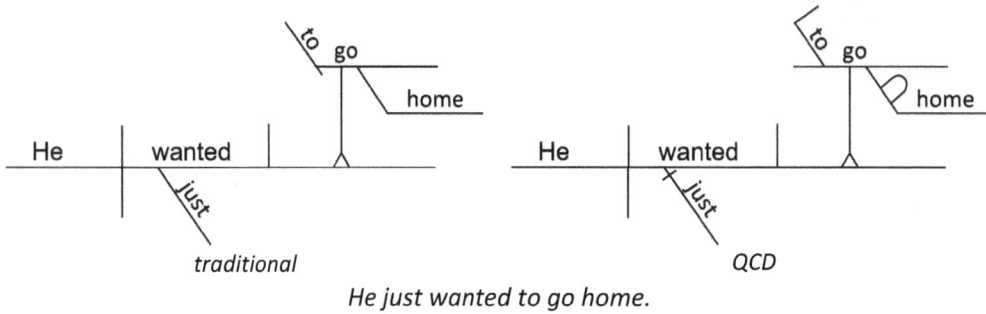

traditional   *QCD*

He just wanted to go home.

16.3.10.6 Infinitives as Objects of Prepositions

As the objects of prepositions, infinitives appear in their normal configuration, diagrammed much as when they appear as subjects.

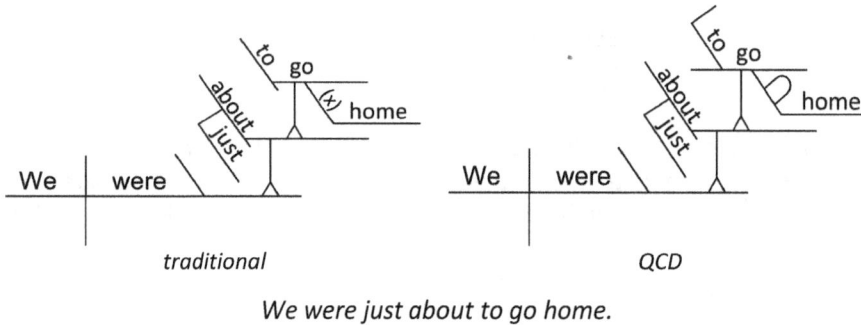

traditional   *QCD*

We were just about to go home.

However, because *QCD.* has a unique and unequivocal representation for infinitives, it has a second, optional pattern in which infinitives can be placed into the diagram in the same way other nouns (and gerunds) are placed, *i.e.*, in a manner that does not require the extra *y-stand* to hold up the infinitive phrase – only the stand for the prepositional phrase itself is required:

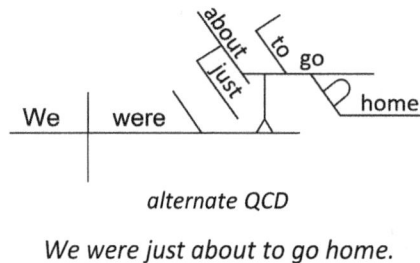

alternate QCD

We were just about to go home.

16.3.10.7 Infinitives: Subjects of Infinitives (1)

When infinitives have subjects, an additional level of structure is necessary in order to place the infinitive on the predicate side of its clause.

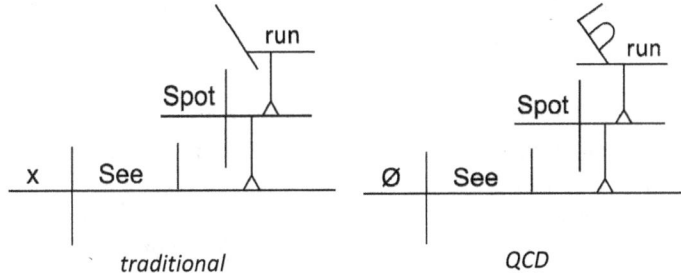

traditional   *QCD*

*See **Spot run**.*
(*The infinitive phrase is the direct object of the predicate **See**.*)

A predicate complement construction can be restated as an infinitive phrase containing both the subject of the infinitive and its complement, so that our original example

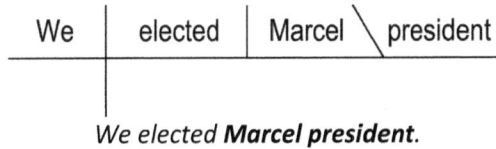

*We elected **Marcel president**.*

as rephrased becomes

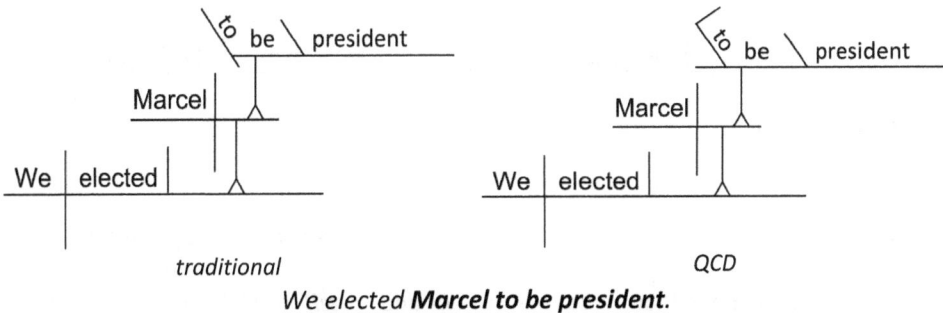

traditional   *QCD*

*We elected **Marcel to be president**.*

However, when the noun subject is replaced by its corresponding personal pronoun, the diagram has to change—the infinitive phrase has to be broken up—even though the sense of the sentence has not changed. (This faulty representation is remedied in the next section.)

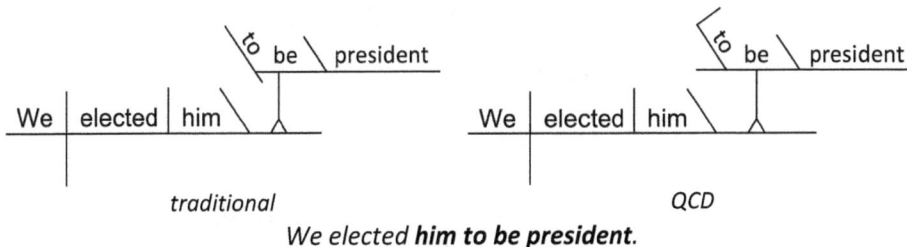

traditional   *QCD*

*We elected **him to be president**.*

16.3.10.8 Infinitives: Subjects of Infinitives (2)

QCD allows an optional second format for diagramming subjects of infinitives, a format that is more intuitive, and simpler, than the design given in the previous section. In this design, because the graphical notation of the infinitive is unique and distinctive, the infinitive phrase can be graphed as a single unit.

In this, the horizontal line on which the root of the infinitive sits is extended to the left to give room for holding the infinitive's subject.

Note that in the *QCD* version the support holding up the infinitive phrase is set up to end under the subject of the infinitive, which is the word heard as the object of the predicate because it is in the objective case. Remember, however, that it is the entire infinitive phrase that is the direct object, not just the infinitive, as the traditional diagramming constructs might suggest.

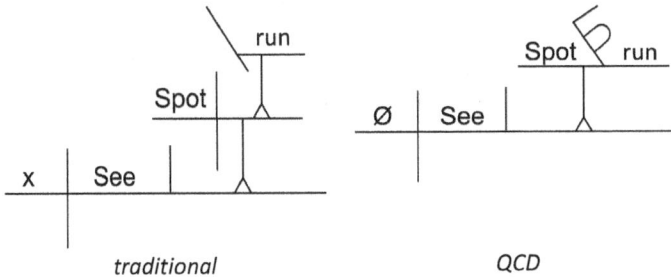

traditional   *QCD*

See Spot run.

The complement construction is also supported in this alternate format:

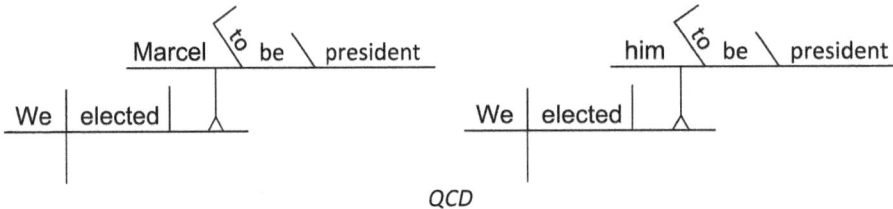

QCD

*We elected **Marcel to be president**.*   *We elected **him to be president**.*

> **NOTE**: Remember that verbs like *to help* and *to tell* are followed by indirect objects, which are optionally followed by direct object infinitives. [See NOTE in §5.12.3] Because they are indirect objects, they **cannot** be the subjects of the infinitives that might follow them.

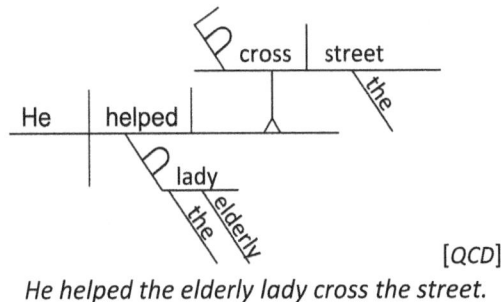

[QCD]

He helped the elderly lady cross the street.

[QCD]

He helped her cross the street.

[QCD]

She told Jack a story.   *She told him a story.*

[QCD]

She told Jack.
elision of the direct object can be diagrammed fully, as on the left,
or by omission, as on the right

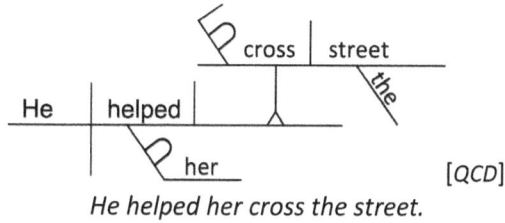

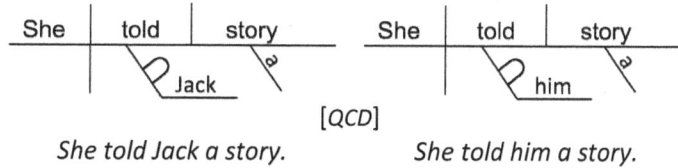

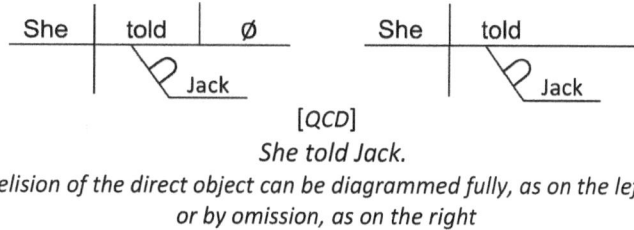

16.3.10.9   **Infinitives used with Causative Verbs**

Causative verbs express compelled or expected actions. Although associated with modal auxiliaries, they are not diagrammed similarly. The complete modal auxiliary phrase is diagrammed as part of the predicate itself.

In traditional diagramming, causative verbs are treated as normal verbs taking an infinitive as their direct object. In QCD, they are treated as an integral part of the verb.

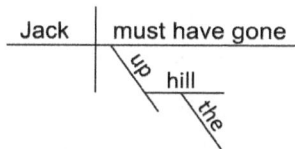

modal auxiliary: *Jack **must have gone** up the hill.*

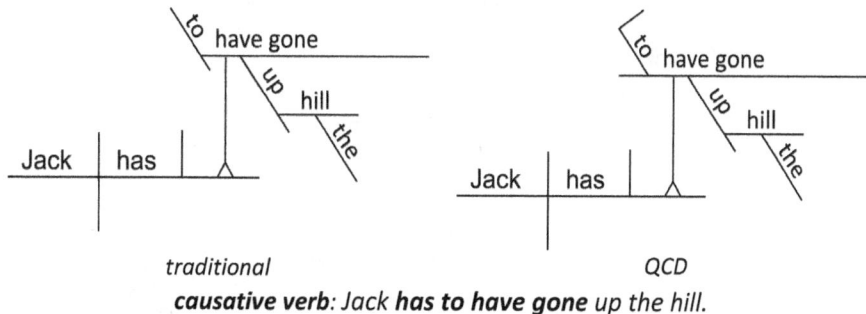

traditional   *QCD*

causative verb: *Jack **has to have gone** up the hill.*

16.3.10.10 Adjective Infinitives

When infinitives appear as adjectives, the diagonal on which the particle **to** appears is extended to attach to the baseline of the substantive the infinitive modifies. This process holds with both traditional and *QCD* diagramming, with the extra notational elements used in the *QCD* specification of infinitives retained in place.

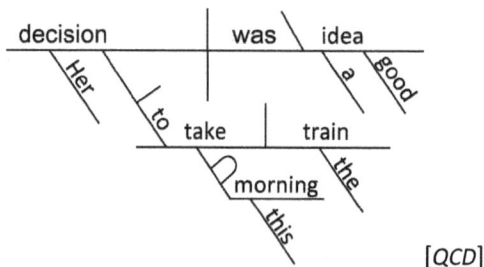

[*QCD*]

Her decision to take the train to work this morning was a good idea.
Note that this infinitive would be parsed as an appositive noun phrase if
it were separated from the mainline clause by commas.
[See the final example of §16.3.10.4.]

16.3.10.11 Adverb Infinitives

In diagramming, adverbial infinitive phrases are structured in the same way as infinitive adjective phrases. The only difference being the part of speech they modify and to which they are attached.

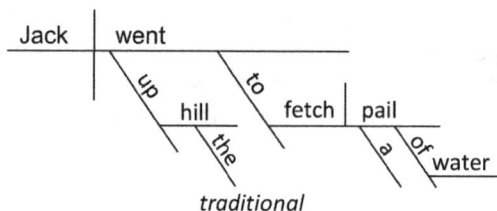

traditional
Jack went up the hill to fetch a pail of water.

The diagram above demonstrates the limitations—and bad influence—of traditional diagramming in not providing a complete differentiation between prepositional phrases governed by **to**, and infinitives. This shortcoming is remedied in the *QCD* version of the same diagram, below.

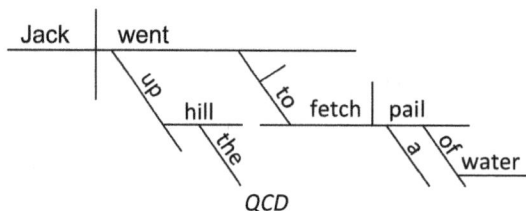

QCD
Jack went up the hill to fetch a pail of water.

The adverbial use of infinitives is often to present the purpose or goal for which something is done. They are sometimes called "final infinitives" because they express the end toward which the action is performed.

Final infinitives are often mixed with adverbial prepositional phrases, and those governed by the preposition *to* demonstrate very clearly the inferiority of the traditional manner of diagramming infinitives, for they erroneously show no differentiation between those prepositional phrases and the infinitives.

This next example demonstrates this, as it is confusing to see in the traditional diagram two of what appear to be prepositional phrases, although the second one has, illogically for a prepositional phrase, both a direct object and an indirect object phrase.

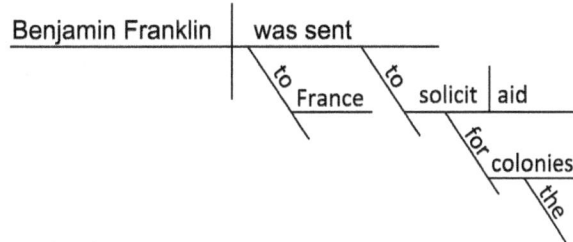

traditional
Benjamin Franklin was sent to France to solicit aid for the colonies.

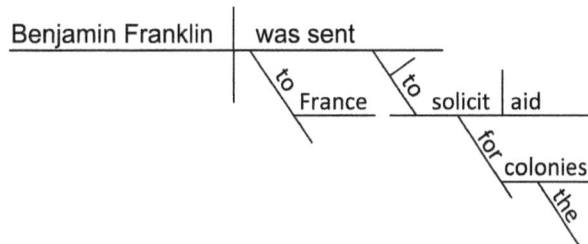

QCD
Benjamin Franklin was sent to France to solicit aid for the colonies.

16.3.10.12 Compound Adjective and Adverb Infinitives

Whenever a group of than one infinitive appears as in usage as adjective or adverb, the infinitives are joined by the conjunction or conjunctions, if any, in ways determined by the way such connected groups are diagrammed within the diagramming style in use.

Compound adjective infinitives:

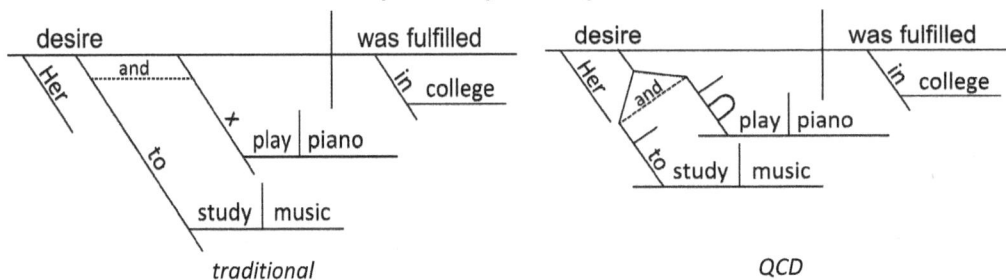

traditional   *QCD*

Her desire to study music and play piano was fulfilled in college.

Compound adverb infinitives.

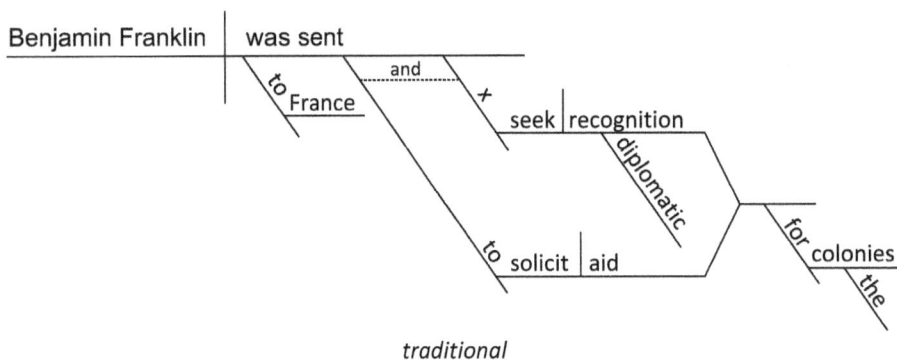

traditional

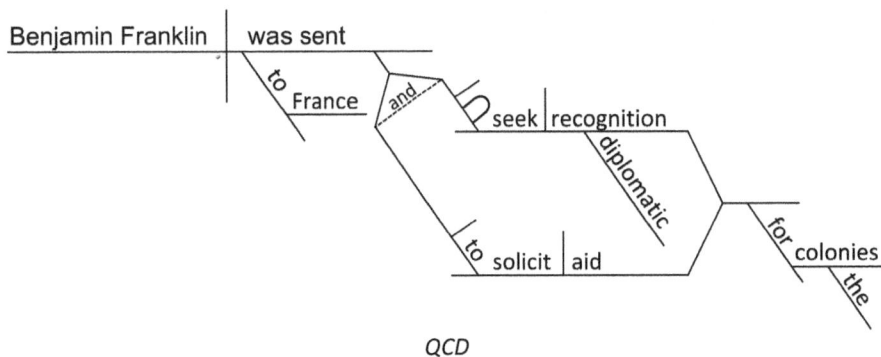

QCD

Benjamin Franklin was sent to France to solicit aid and seek diplomatic recognition for the colonies.

16.3.10.13 Split Infinitives

Traditional diagramming has no special way of distinguishing a split infinitive from a correctly formed one, just as it has no way of distinguishing the positions taken by modifiers in relation to the object modified. As pointed out below, traditional diagramming of the modifiers of infinitives leaves the positioning of those modifiers open to two, sometimes three, different arrangements, each of which has different implications.

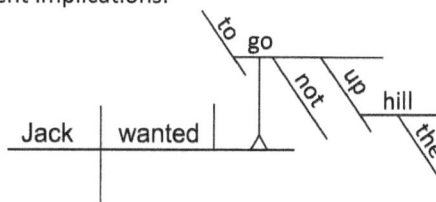

traditional
*Jack wanted **not to go** up the hill.*
*or Jack wanted **to not go** up the hill.*
*or even Jack wanted **to go not** up the hill.*

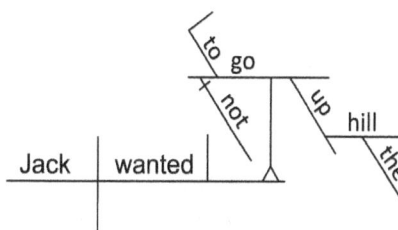

QCD has an extra mark that is applied to the diagonal line binding modifiers to the modified object, a mark that specifies the position of that modifier. If that a modifier splits the infinitive—a different this mark specific to this situation is applied to the diagramming structure of any object misused in this way.

That mark is an 'x' placed in line with the diagonal, at the top left of the diagonal itself. With this refinement, along with the other capabilities of QCD, all versions of the example given above are differentiable by using QCD rather than the traditional style:

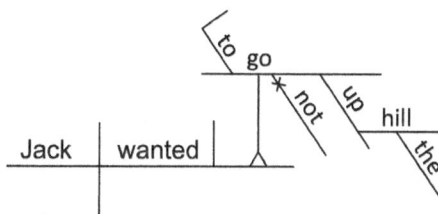

QCD

*Jack wanted **to not go** up the hill.*   *Jack wanted **not to go** up the hill.*

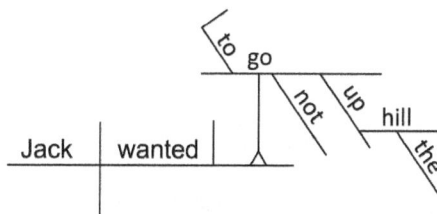

QCD
*Jack wanted **to go not** up the hill.*
[This placement of the negator is old-fashioned, or poetic, in use and
is found more often in the imperative style that doesn't use the emphatic *do*.]

16.3.11 Verbals: Gerunds

Gerunds are placed on a structure made of three straight lines (one horizontal, one vertical then another horizontal), with the gerund itself at an angle to the second of those lines. This structure uses the inverted 'Y' to hold it, above the horizontal, noun-holding line to which it belongs. (The height of the vertical line component is not indicative of any inherent quality: it should be as long as needed to provide clear indication that a gerund is intended by the person creating the diagram.)

In most traditional diagramming, as well as *QCD*, the different arrangements for diagramming gerunds are the same as those for infinitives used as nouns, except that the gerund structure is substituted for that of the infinitive.

In some variations of traditional programming, the structures used for gerunds are not differentiated from those used for denoting present participles. This is both academically slipshod. It is merely another example of how well poor traditional diagramming can discourage analytical rigor, grammatical conciseness and depth of understanding.

16.3.11.1 Gerunds as Baseline Nouns: Subjects, Complements or Direct Objects

As nouns positioned on the baseline, gerunds are hoisted onto the separating stand, exactly like that used to hoist infinitives.

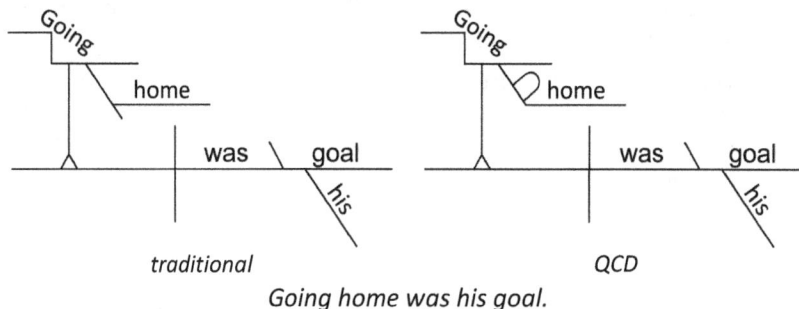

Going home | home | was | goal | his

traditional

Going home | home | was | goal | his

QCD

Going home was his goal.

Gerunds are always preceded by the possessive. [See §7.26.1]

16.3.11.2 Gerunds as Objects of Prepositions

When appearing singly as any part of speech that is not placed on the baseline of the sentence diagram, the "step" unit of the gerund diagram is connected directly to the diagonal line that is attached at the top to the modified item.

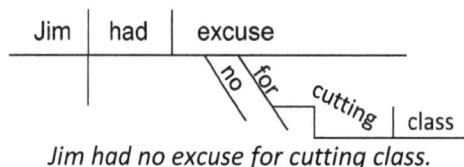

Jim | had | excuse | no | for | cutting | class

Jim had no excuse for cutting class.

16.3.11.3 Compound Gerunds

As it is in compound infinitives, *QCD* differs from most traditional layouts in how it diagrams compound gerunds. In most traditional diagramming, compound gerunds are laid out using a method more like that used for compound adjectives and adverbs than that used either for nouns or verbs, despite the fact that a gerund is a verb form always used as a noun.

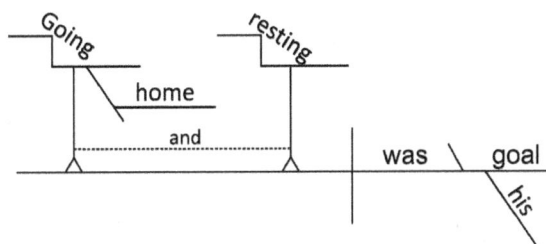

traditional
Going home and resting was his goal.

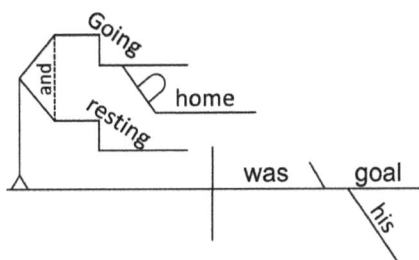

QCD
Going home and resting was his goal.

One benefit of the *QCD* method of diagramming compound nouns and compound noun-verbals is that they are dealt with as combined units, rather than as strung-out separate, only incidentally connected, entities.

The *y-stand* to which the conjunction is connected is always on the left side of the compound phrase because the conjunction connects verbals because of their essential identity as verbs, whose diagramming of compounds was given in §16.3.1.11.

One example of the problem with traditional diagramming is this example, also given using infinitives in §16.3.10.3.

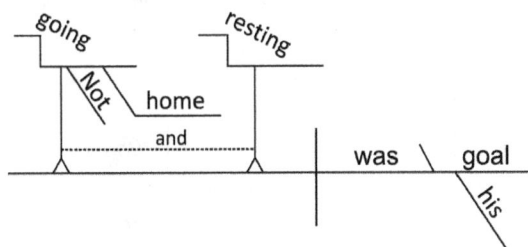

traditional
Not going home and resting was his goal.
or Not going home[,] and resting[,] was his goal.

The diagram structure supported by *QCD* allows easy and concise representation of this sentence. Moreover, it places the negation adverb correctly and specifically, so that it is shown to modify the entire compound gerund phrase and not merely the first part of it, a problem for traditional diagramming because it cannot distinguish the two cases:

Not(going home and resting) …

versus

Not(going home) and resting ….

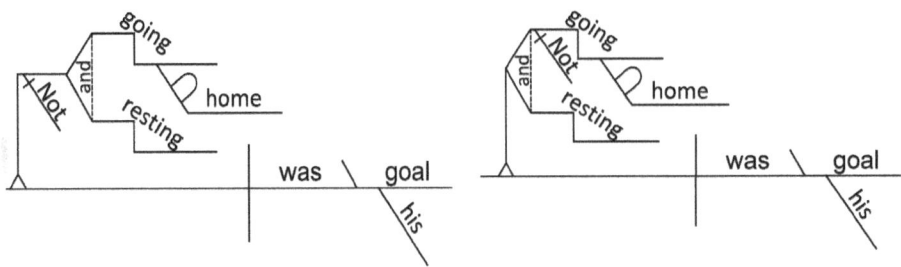

Not(going home and resting)…   *Not(going home) and resting…*

QCD

Not going home and resting was his goal.

In traditional diagramming, compound gerunds appearing as adverbial objectives or the objects of prepositions are always diagrammed in the same way as compound baseline-gerunds, using the inverted 'Y' stand as the connector between the conjunction structure and the horizontal line of their position.

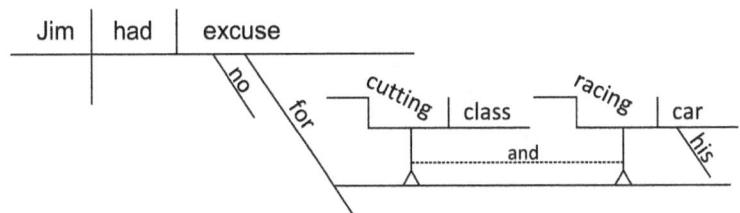

some traditional versions

Jim had no excuse for cutting class and racing his car.

In *QCD* diagramming, and in some versions of traditional diagramming, the notation for compound gerunds is the same conjunction-structure used by nouns that are not verbals.

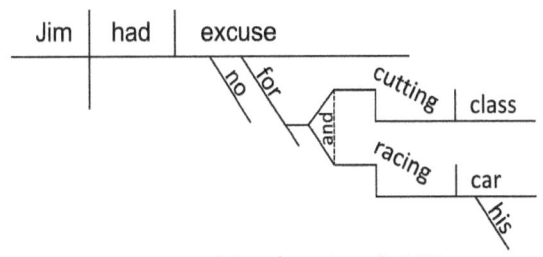

some traditional versions & QCD

Jim had no excuse for cutting class and racing his car.

16.3.12 Verbals: Present and Perfect Participles

The **present participle** is the other verbal with an "ing" ending, the first one being the gerund (covered above). Yet present participles are completely distinct from gerunds, because participles are only used as adjectives, whereas gerunds are always used only as nouns.

The linear structure used to diagram present participles is one that looks exactly like that used traditionally for adverbial objectives. [See §16.3.5] The differentiating aspect is the placement of the text that accompanies the graphic. The difference in *QCD* diagramming is more obvious, for the participle does not have the adverbial objective's 'hoop'.

Some traditional diagramming places the participle in a single line from upper left to lower right, stretching between the diagonal attachment branch to the horizontal line segment. In other traditional layouts, the root portion of the participle is placed in line with the diagonal, and the "-ing" of the participle (along with the other parts) is placed on the horizontal segment. Either is accepted in *QCD*, although the version that does not split off the "-ing" is easier to insert and handle in a computer graphics package like *Inkscape*.

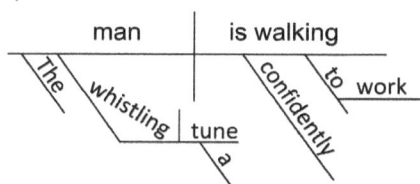

QCD & some traditional versions
The man whistling a tune is walking confidently to work.

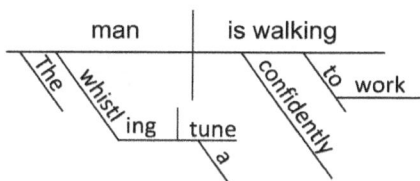

alternate traditional or QCD version
The man whistling a tune is walking confidently to work.

The **perfect participle** is formed using the present participle of the verb **to have** plus the past participle of the root verb. It is diagrammed with the word *having* in the participle position and the past participle placed horizontally on that line segment.

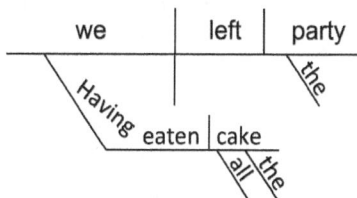

Having eaten all the cake, we left the party hoping not to be noticed.

16.3.13 Verbals: Past Participles

The **_past participle_** is the third principle part of English verbs. It is used to form all the tenses of the passive mode, as well as the perfect tenses of the active mode. It is also used by itself as an adjective. As an adjective it may take a complement if it performs the role of a linking, or state of being verb, or it may take adverbs, adverbial prepositional phrases, or an adverbial objective.

In traditional diagramming past participles can be handled in one of two ways. In one way, a past participle is consistently diagrammed in exactly the same way as present participles. In another traditional way, a past participle without modifiers could be placed on a diagonal line, exactly like any other simple modifier, while the diagram of a past participle with modifiers would change, to be diagrammed in the manner of a present participle.

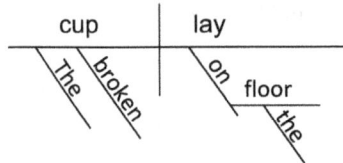

some traditional versions

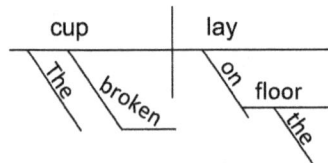

QCD & some traditional versions
The broken cup lay on the floor.

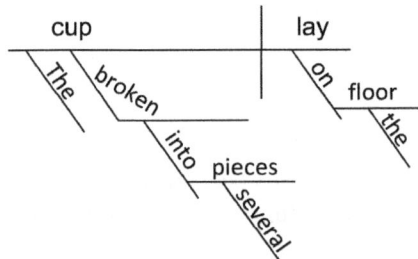

The cup, broken into several pieces, lay on the floor.

As a demonstration of the value of diagramming in making clear how important word order is to an analytical language like English, consider the too often misspoken way of expressing phrases like the previous example:

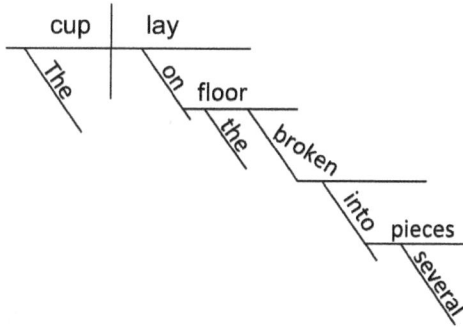

The cup lay on the floor broken into several pieces.

Diagramming shows unequivocally that placing the past participial phrase in that position causes it to modify **floor** rather than the intended **cup**.

16.3.13.1 Participles as Predicate Complements

When appearing as predicate complements (a.k.a., predicate adjectives), participles are placed on the inverted-y stand. This is then placed at the normal position for predicate complements within the diagram.

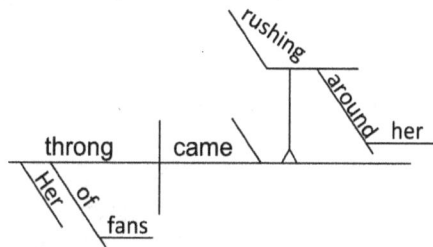

Her throng of fans came rushing around her.

16.3.13.2 Compound Participles

Compound participle are diagrammed as other compound modifiers are diagrammed in the set you have chosen to use: traditional or *QCD*.

16.3.13.2.1 Compound Participial Modifiers

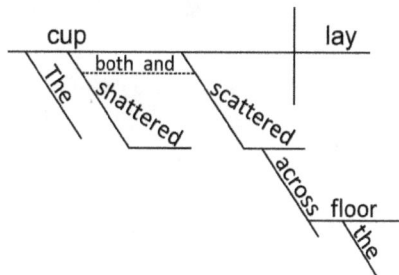

traditional

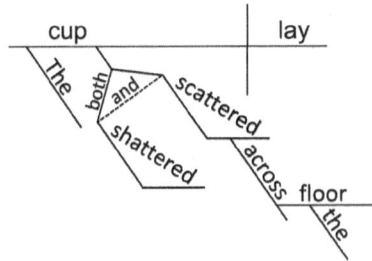

QCD

The cup lay both shattered and scattered across the floor.

16.3.13.2.2 Compound Predicate Complements

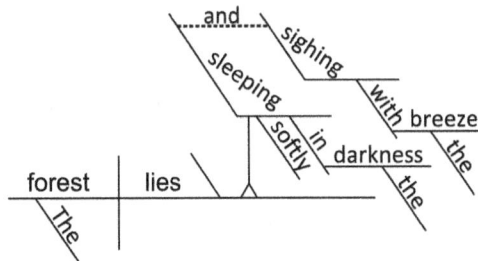

traditional

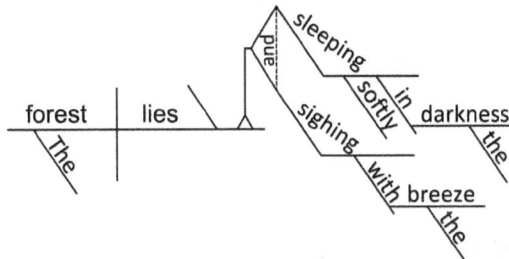

QCD

The forest lies sleeping softly in the darkness and sighing with the breeze.

16.3.14 Independent Elements

Interjections (exclamations, items of direct address, nominatives of exclamation, and responsives), parenthetical expressions and nominative absolutes are all independent elements: words or phrases external to the message of the sentence itself. [See §13.14]

Independent elements do not have any direct grammatical relationship to any part of the sentence itself, so they are diagrammed as floating apart from the graph of the sentence itself. Their placement is in the general area of their closest association within the sentence diagram, or their greatest relevance to the general meaning of the sentence.

16.3.14.1 Interjections

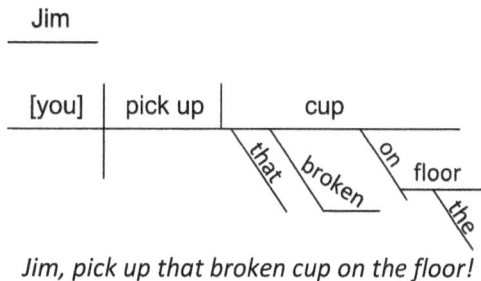

Jim, pick up that broken cup on the floor!

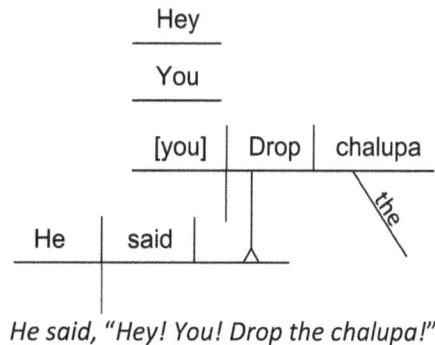

He said, "Hey! You! Drop the chalupa!"

16.3.14.2 Nominative Absolutes

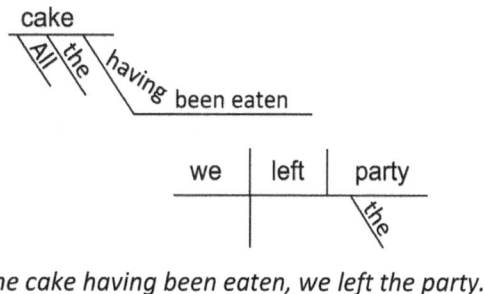

All the cake having been eaten, we left the party.

16.3.14.3 Parenthesized Expressions

All expressions within parentheses, along with parenthetical expressions (whether they are within parentheses or not) that are not appositives of particular parts of the sentence, but elucidate the entire sentence (or major clauses or phrases within it), are treated as independent objects. They are placed within parentheses in a position more or less relative to their position in the sentence, but outside the diagram of the sentence itself.

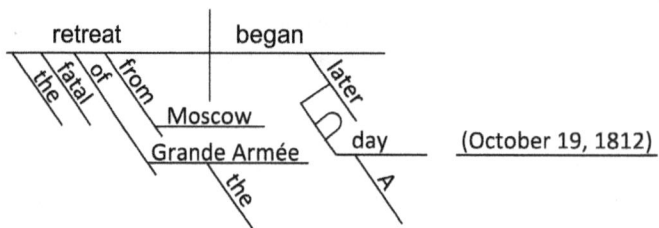

A day later (October 19,1812) began the fatal retreat of the Grande Armée from Moscow.

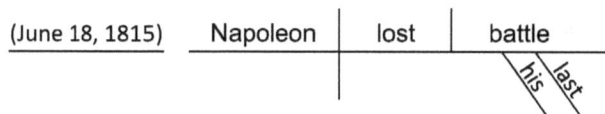

June 18, 1815: Napoleon lost his last battle.

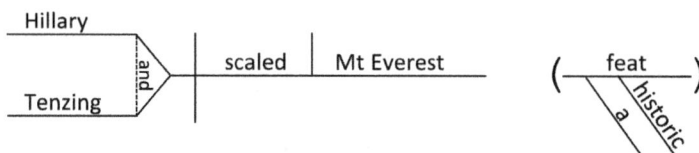

Hillary and Tenzing scaled Mt Everest—a historic feat.

16.3.15 Complex Sentences

Complex sentences are sentences made up of one independent clause and one or more dependent clauses.

While traditional diagramming shows the relationships between the independent clause and its dependents as tenuous arrangements, connected with dashed lines that may have to be drawn around or across other words and graphics, *QCD* uses a specific device that distinguishes all dependent clauses as such, while maintaining the facility of connecting the dependent clause with anything it may modify.

The traditional diagramming situation is based on the original Reed/Kellogg method, in which dependent clauses were placed on a baseline that had less thickness than that of the main clause, so its subordinate status was implied by that line's greater faintness. This has proved to be impractical, as the quill or steel-nib pens required for such ephemeral differences have not been common for over a hundred years. After drawing this reduced-visibility line, the dashed/dotted lines were used to establish a minimum indication of relatedness, or connectivity between the clauses. (Adding to the confusion, Reed/Kellogg erroneously diagrammed noun dependent clauses starting with *what* or *whatever* as if they were adjective clauses, but not in all situations.)

In *QCD*, **all dependent clauses have the same distinguishing characteristic**: the baseline on which they are diagrammed has two parallel diagonal lines at its far left that extend toward the upper left. These diagonal lines form the base on which conjunctions are placed, if the dependent clause is introduced by them. In the case of relative clauses, no mark is placed on these lines, but the relative pronoun or adverb is placed, on a double line, in its correct position within the dependent clause.

In the case of adjective and adverb dependent clauses, these lines are also extended from the dependent clause's baseline to the part of the independent, main clause the dependent clause modifies.

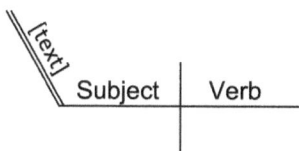

basic format for all dependent clauses in QCD, where
[text] *is replaced with a conjunction when there is one, or elided
when there is none, or when it goes in its normal position*

While traditional diagramming relies on placing one end of the dashed line near the connecting or relating word, *QCD* allows the diagrammer either to leave the word unmarked if unambiguous, or to place an asterisk at the start of the word or phrase to mark it unequivocally as the connector.

In *QCD*,

① Adjective dependent clauses do not have text on the double-diagonal part of their diagrams, excepting the word "that", if used. If this conjunction is elided, the elision-hoop is used to mark its absence, rather than the word "that" within brackets. Other conjunctions are inserted in their normal places as substantives or modifiers.

② Adverb dependent clauses have conjunctions on the diagonals when the adverbial connective modifies both the item in the modified clause and the predicate in the modifying clause.

③ Noun dependent clauses have the connector on the double-diagonal when the usage of the conjunction warrants its placement there. If the conjunction of a noun dependent clause is an adverb, it does not go on the double-diagonal, but is attached beneath the predicate of the dependent clause.

Beyond the samples in the following sections, there are examples in the Advanced Diagramming Examples that demonstrate this further.

16.3.15.1 Complex Sentences: Dependent Adjective Clauses

An adjective clause is a dependent clause that modifies a noun or pronoun.

Adjective clauses are introduced by relative pronouns: *that*, *which*, and *who*.

In traditional diagramming, a dashed line is drawn between the baseline of the noun or pronoun modified and the relative pronoun that acts to introduce the dependent clause. In, QCD a double-line diagonal of the same shape and angle as that of the simple adjective modifier connects the modified with the start of the baseline of the dependent clause.

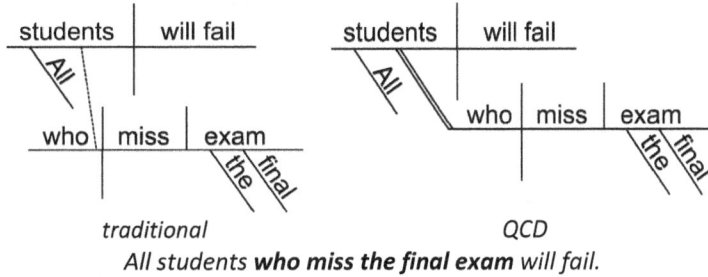

traditional   *QCD*

*All students **who miss the final exam** will fail.*

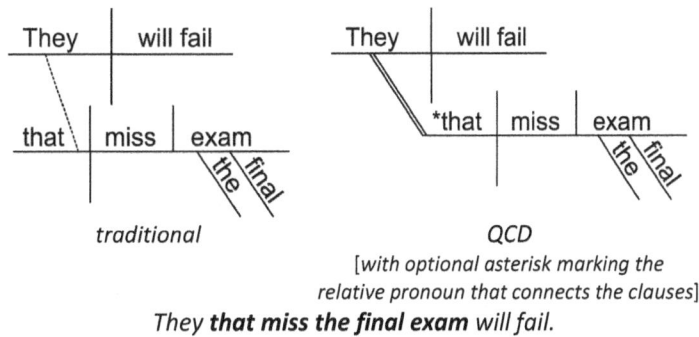

traditional   *QCD*

[with optional asterisk marking the relative pronoun that connects the clauses]

*They **that miss the final exam** will fail.*

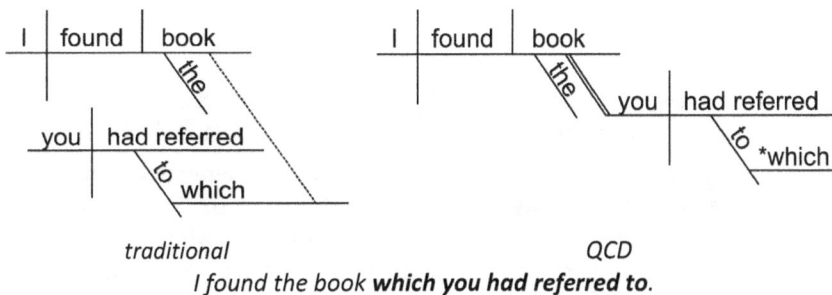

traditional   *QCD*

*I found the book **which you had referred to**.*

Note the use of the asterisk to denote the connecting word in the QCD version.

This compares to the following (and grammatically [but perhaps not stylistically] more preferred) version of the example, in which the prepositional phrase, rather than a single word, is used as the logical connector.

Traditional diagramming has no way to distinguish between these two cases.

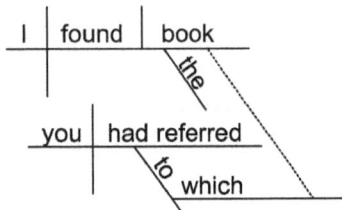

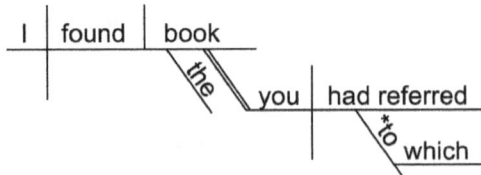

traditional
(undifferentiable from above)

QCD

*I found the book **to which you had referred**.*

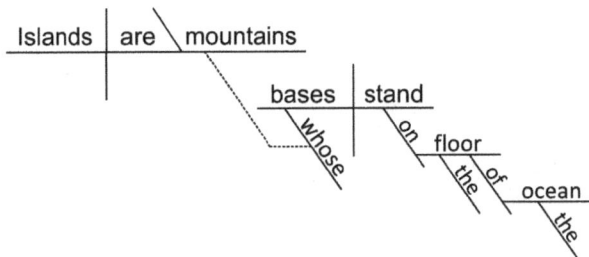

traditional

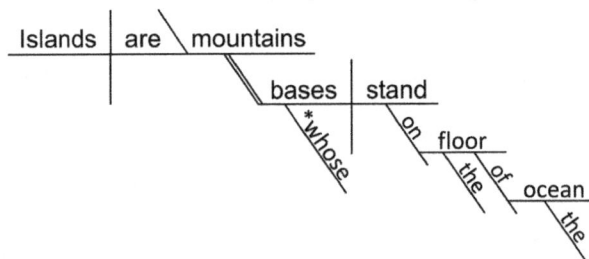

QCD

*Islands are mountains **whose bases stand on the floor of the ocean**.*

There is a problem in the examples in the Reed and Kellogg books that first define their way of diagramming. This incident arises because they have incorrect diagrams of dependent clauses that are introduced by *what or whatever*.

In those books, Reed and Kellogg diagram those dependent clauses as if they were adjective clauses. They apparently forgot the fact that (except in some *BE* dialects) adjective clauses cannot be introduced by *what or whatever*. This fact is obvious if you take their poorly chosen placeholder character "**x**" and use it as   word in the sentence, with correct punctuation:

> *She always did **x: what was expected**.*

In this sentence, you can see that the dependent clause is an appositive to the direct object "**x**". Because only nouns can act as appositives to nouns, the dependent clause must be a noun dependent clause.

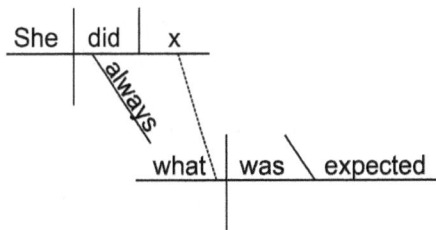

traditional – incorrect: Reed/Kellogg
She always did **what was expected**.

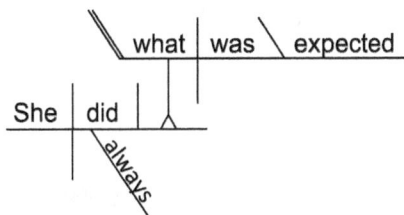

QCD
(with the dependent clause correctly diagrammed as a noun clause)
She always did **what was expected**.

Reed and Kellogg also diagrammed the compound predicate of an adjective dependent clause using both the special verbs *to help* and *to tell* [See the note of §5.12.3] within a single sentence.

Unfortunately, their diagram is wrong.

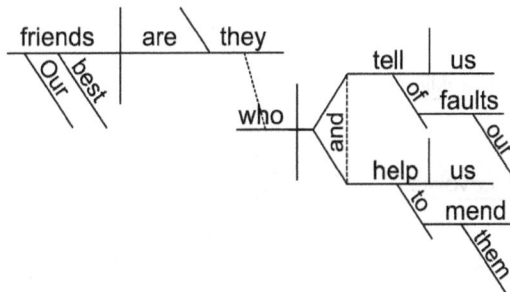

traditional – incorrect diagram of predicates: Reed/Kellogg

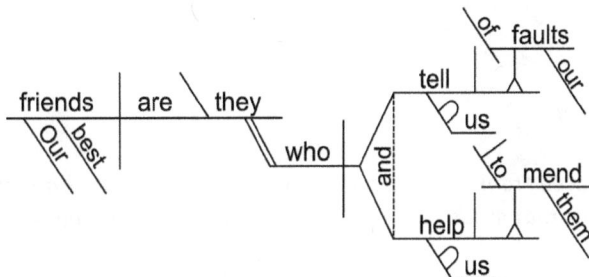

QCD
(**with corrections** to the parsing of the predicates of the dependent clause)
Our best friends are they who tell us of our faults and help us to mend them.

What do they tell? – *Of our faults*: direct object
To whom do they tell it? – *(To) us*: indirect object

What do they help? – *To mend them*: direct object
To whom do they render this help? – *(To) us*: indirect object

(*The root of their error is that R/K refused to accept the fact that prepositional phrases could be used as nouns.*)

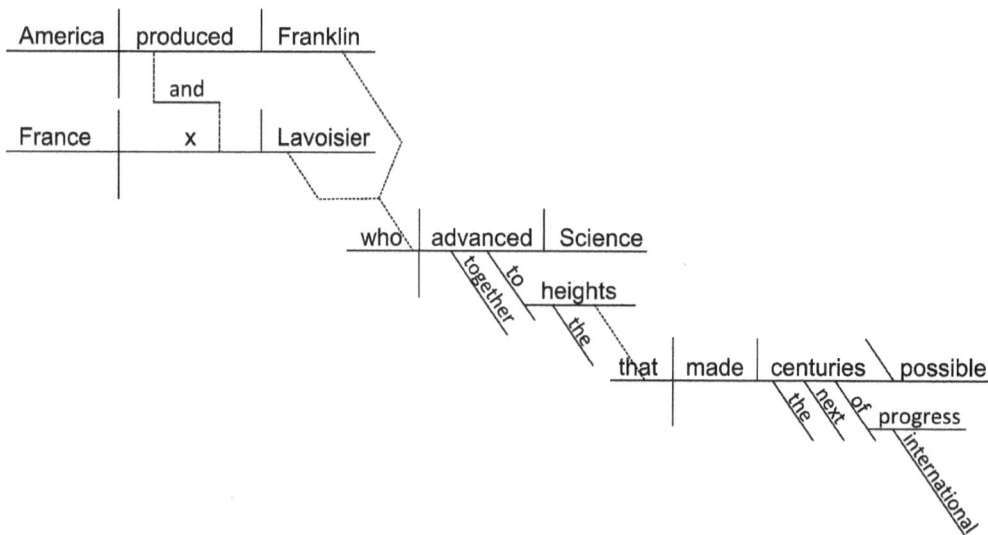

traditional

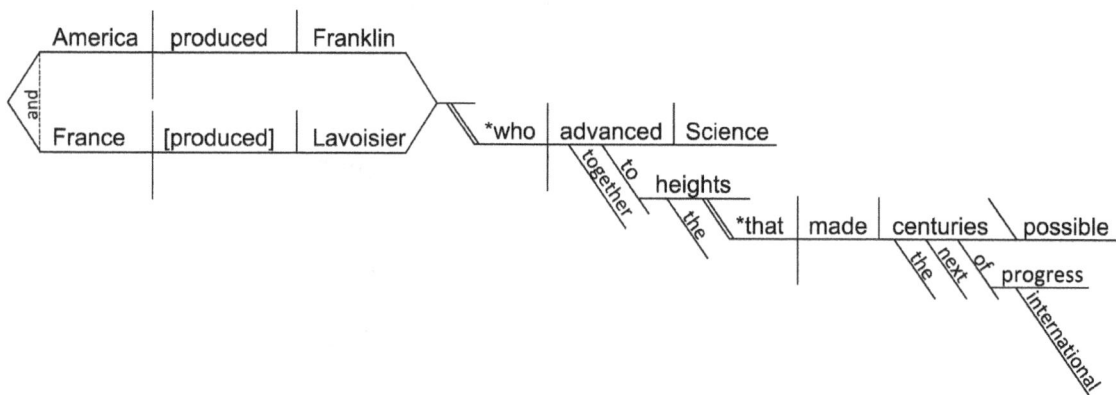

QCD

America produced Franklin, and France Lavoisier, **who together advanced Science** *to the heights* **that made** *possible the next centuries of international progress.*

traditional

QCD

King John was forced to sign the charter **which the English barons had written**.

16.3.15.2 Complex Sentences: Dependent Adverb Clauses

Dependent adverb clauses are dependent clauses that modify verbs, verbals, and adjectives. Because all dependent adverb clauses are attributive, *i.e.*, they always follow the unit they modify, they cannot modify other adverbs, conjunctions or prepositions.

Adjective clauses are introduced by relative adverbs, such as **when**, **where**, and **while**. [See §9.13]

In traditional diagramming, a dotted or dashed line is drawn connecting the modified word with the predicate of the dependent clause. Because the relative adverb that introduces adverbial dependent clauses modifies both units.

In the original definition of their diagramming specification, Reed and Kellogg say that the line joining the dependent clause to the clause containing the modified item should be solid for the first part of its journey, then dashed (or dotted) for the middle section, then again solid for the final part that connects to the dependent clause's predicate. They state that this is done in order to indicate the modifying relationships of the connector to the modified units.

However, as this multiply formatted line is nearly impossible to draw well, or to render at all in graphics editing programs, and because these relationships are actually part of the definition of an adverb clause, this redundant nicety is nowadays ignored.

In *QCD*, the connecting adverb is placed on the double-diagonal that descends from the modified, the that signifies a dependent-clause. **There is no need to indicate that it modifies the predicate of the dependent clause because** *that's an inherent part of the definition of an adverbial dependent clause*.

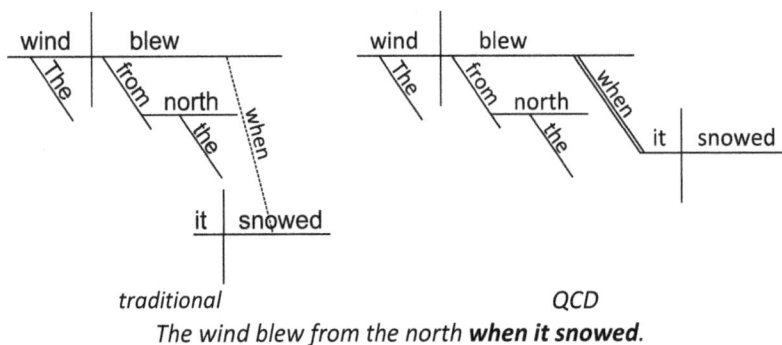

traditional   QCD

The wind blew from the north **when it snowed**.

In this example, the relative adverb *when* introduces the adverbial dependent clause "*when it snowed*". The entire adverbial clause (not just the adverb *when*) is the modifier of the predicate of the independent clause.

Because the connection between the modifying and the modified clauses are as strong as that between simple modifiers and the items they modify, that parallel relationship should be obvious from the diagram of dependent clauses. Yet traditional diagramming's method fails to do that clearly.

In *QCD*, all modifiers are rendered with elements that share a basic characteristic of form, that indicate shared properties of usage.

river | rose

the

After

it | rained

traditional

river | rose

the

After

it | rained

QCD

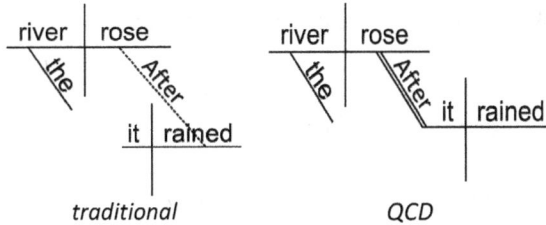

After it rained, *the river rose.*

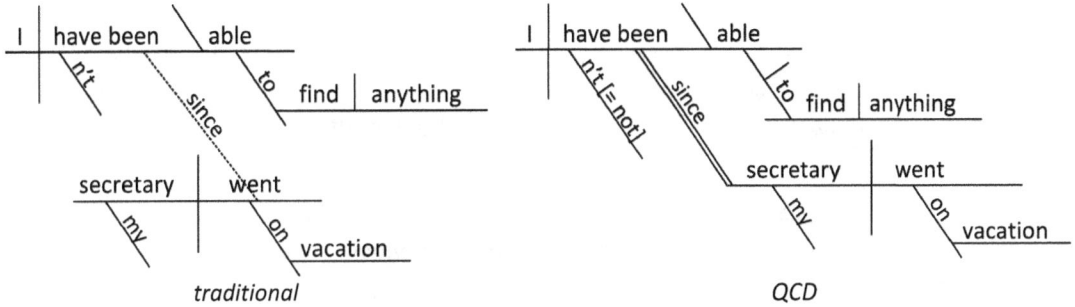

I | have been \ able

n't

since

to find | anything

secretary | went

my

on

vacation

traditional

I | have been \ able

n't [= not]

since

to find | anything

secretary | went

my

on

vacation

QCD

*I haven't been able to find anything **since my secretary went on vacation**.*

16.3.15.3 Complex Sentences: Dependent Noun Clauses

Dependent noun clauses are diagrammed with their baseline sitting atop the inverted-y pedestal, which is placed on the horizontal line that signifies the clause's usage within the sentence.

In traditional diagramming, an introductory that is placed on a short horizontal line above the dependent clauses' verb, with a vertical, dashed line descending to connect that short line to the baseline of the clause.

In *QCD*, however, the introductory conjunction is put into a position analogous to that occupied by conjunctions in other situations.

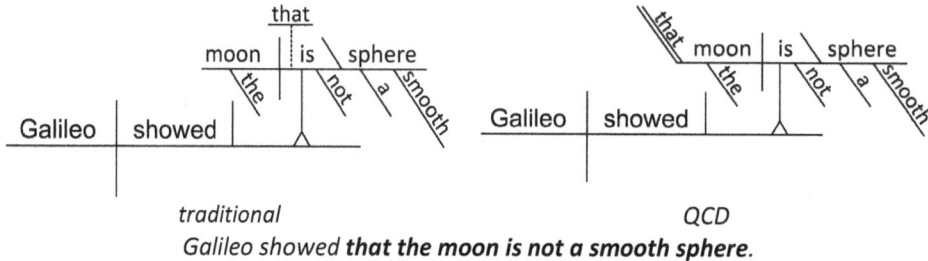

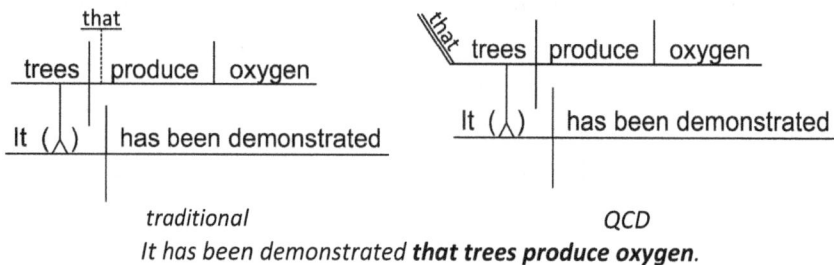

traditional   *QCD*

*Galileo showed **that the moon is not a smooth sphere**.*

traditional   *QCD*

*It has been demonstrated **that trees produce oxygen**.*

Note: "***It***" in this sentence is an expletive, without meaning except as a placeholder, as can be seen if the noun clause is put at the start of the sentence and used as the subject rather than as a virtual appositive, as shown below.

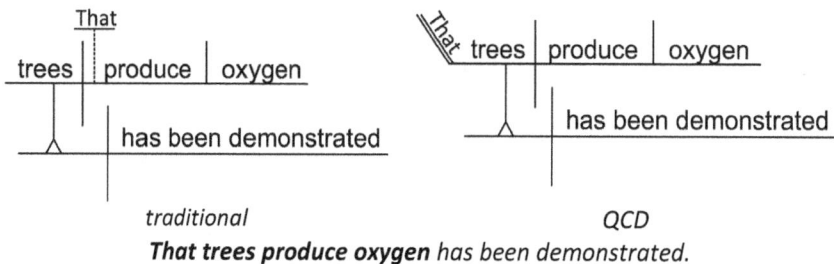

traditional   *QCD*

That trees produce oxygen *has been demonstrated.*

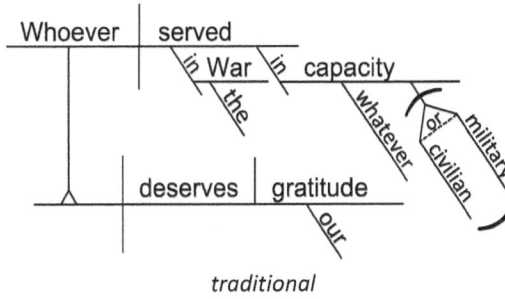

traditional

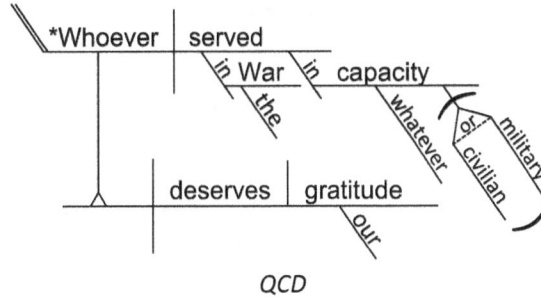

QCD

Whoever served in the War in whatever capacity, military or civilian, *deserves our gratitude.*

16.3.15.4 **Complex Sentences: With Comparatives**

Adjectives and adverbs in the comparative degree are used with adverbial dependent clauses that are headed by **than** to express complete comparisons as clauses. This may involve an adjective or adverb in its single word, **-er** form or in a phrasal comparative that uses the adverb **more** to create the comparative.

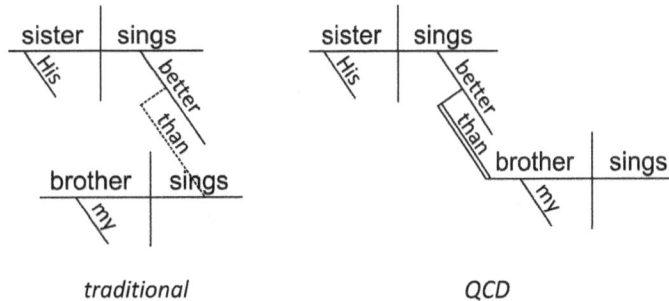

traditional   *QCD*

*His sister sings **better than my brother sings**.*

Either the subject or a portion of the predicate of the dependent clause may be elided whenever the elision will not cause confusion. However, in diagramming the entire clause is included, with the elision marked or editorially restored, in order to give the clearest possible description of the source sentence.

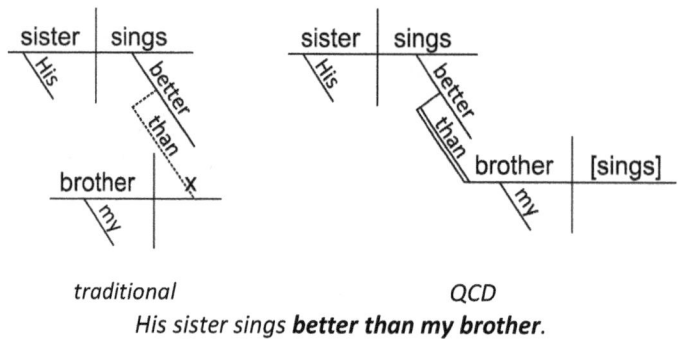

traditional   QCD

His sister sings **better than my brother**.

As stated in the Note of §8.14.3, the form taken by the word or words remaining after the predicate of the dependent clause has been elided can be very important to the meaning of the sentence.

Although traditional diagramming is good at showing where things have been elided, it is not designed to give information about what has been elided. In this case, the data provided by the *QCD* format carries more useful information. This is demonstrated in the following diagrams, using two of the example sentences from §8.14.3.

The elided version of *She likes you more than she likes me.* and of *She likes you more than I like you.* are distinguishable only from the case of the terminal pronoun, which reveals whether the subject and verb, or the complete predicate has been elided:

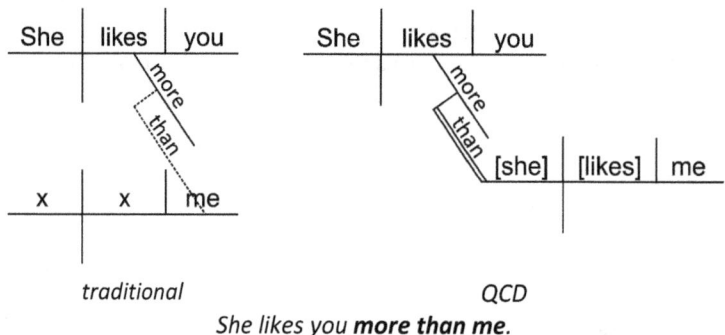

traditional   QCD

She likes you **more than me**.

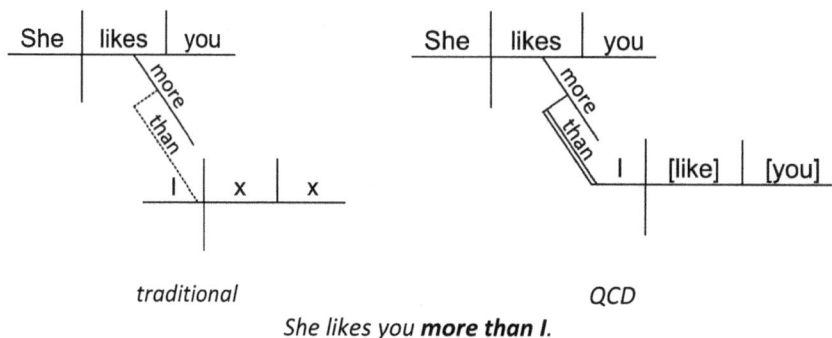

traditional   QCD

She likes you **more than I**.

16.3.15.5 Complex Sentences: With Correlative Conjunctions

Correlative conjunctions are used to encapsulate modifiers within the joining structures between clauses. Examples are *as ... as* and *so ... as*.

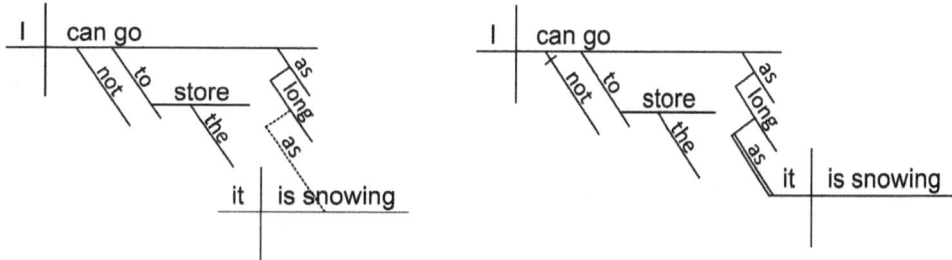

traditional   QCD

*I cannot go to the store **as long as** it is snowing.*

16.3.15.6 Complex Sentences: Compound Independent Clauses With Dependent Clause

The notation for compound clauses independent clauses is the same, whether they are modified by one or more dependent clauses. Thus, the diagrams for the following example sentence bear resemblance to the respective examples of compound independent clauses in either traditional or *QCD* representation.

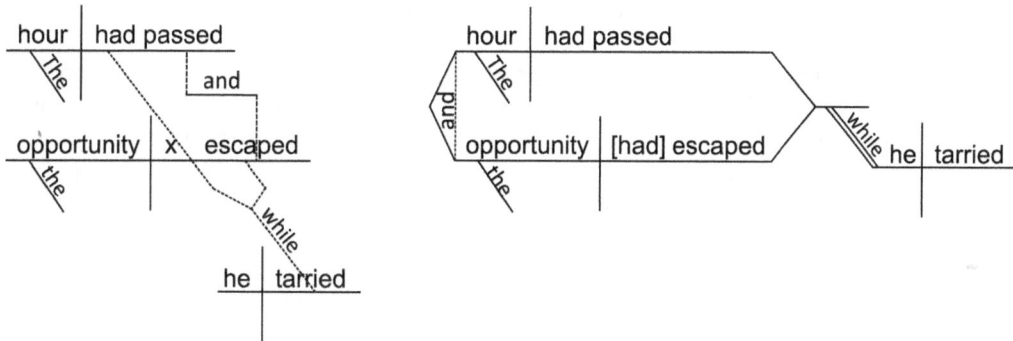

traditional   QCD

*The hour had passed and the opportunity escaped **while he tarried.***

16.3.15.7 Complex Sentences: Compound Dependent Clauses

In traditional diagramming, the notation for dependent clauses and the notation for compound clauses tend to conflict with each, so that there are multiple lines of thought running through a diagramming. These lines of thought can become rather unwieldy, or even spaghetti-like in more complicated sentences. In traditional diagramming, the notation for compounded clauses is different from that used for other compounded parts of speech, which seems to say that the two concepts are somehow different one from the other.

In *QCD*, the same constructs are used for compounding, whatever the compounded items. This creates a unified approach, expressing clearly that items share their essential concepts and behaviors whenever they form compounds.

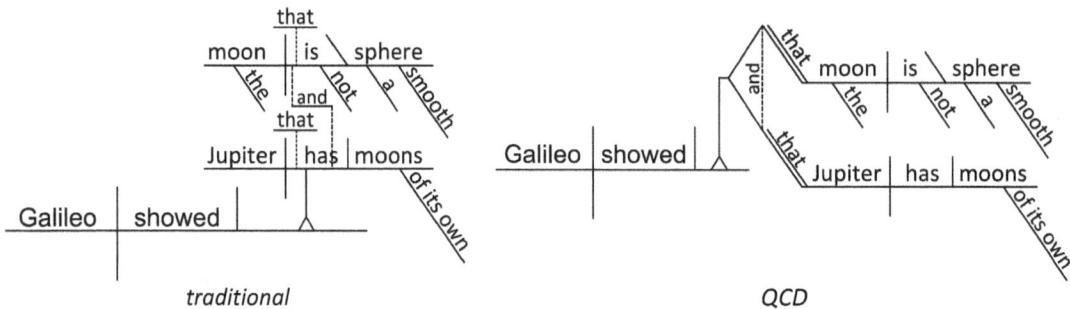

traditional   *QCD*

*Galileo showed **that the moon is not a smooth sphere and that Jupiter has moons of its own***.
(Note: "of its own" *is an idiom functioning as an adjectival modifier;*
it does not make sense to parse it to any deeper level.)

The following *Advanced Diagramming Examples* section has several good examples of how traditional diagramming precepts can result in spaghetti diagrams for sentences with compound dependent clauses, or for compound sentences with dependent clauses.

Advanced Diagramming Examples

1. Compound predicate; limiting adverb; present participle; prepositional phrase modifying adverb

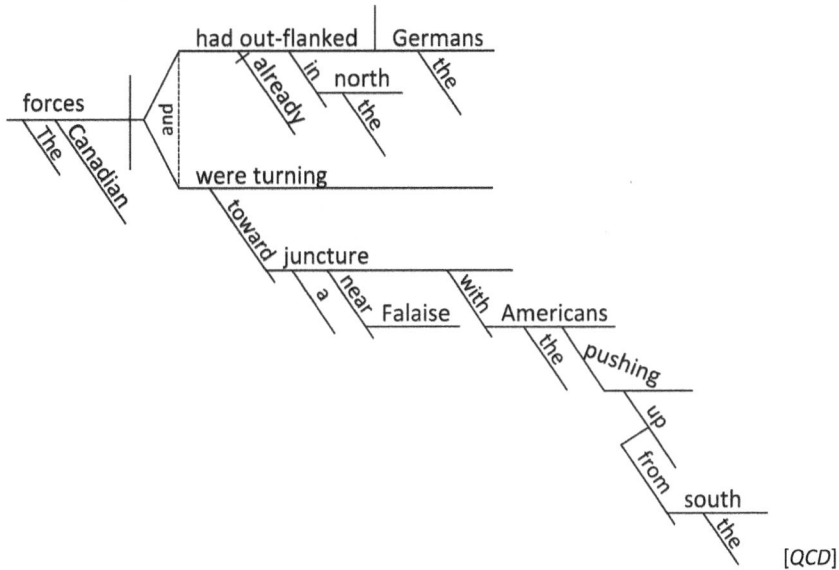

[QCD]

The Canadian forces had already out-flanked the Germans in the north and were turning toward a juncture near Falaise with the Americans pushing up from the south.
[*to convert to traditional format, remove limiting-adverb signal-crossbar from the line holding "already".*]

2. Compound adjectives modified by prepositional phrases

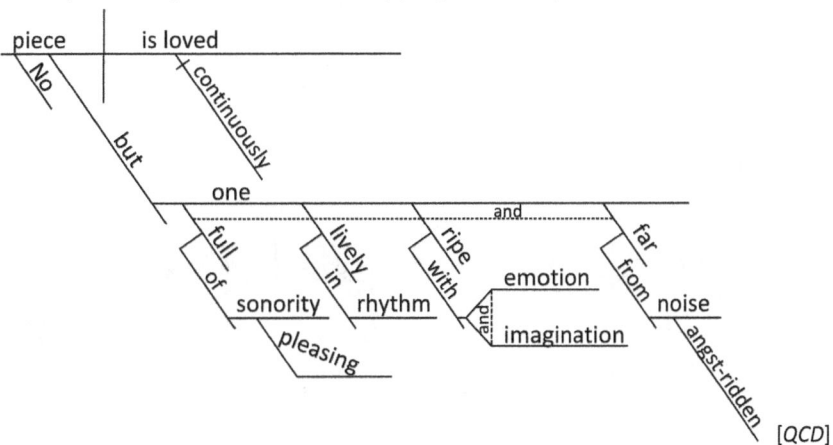

[QCD]

No piece of music is continuously loved but one full of pleasing sonority, lively in rhythm, ripe with emotion and imagination and far from angst-ridden noise.
[*to convert to traditional format, remove limiting adverb signal-crossbar from the line holding "continuously"*]
[*The alternate compound-modifier form supported by QCD is possible, but not recommended for this very complicated situation.*]

3. Compounded compound subjects; *"or"* used as connector of compound object of preposition

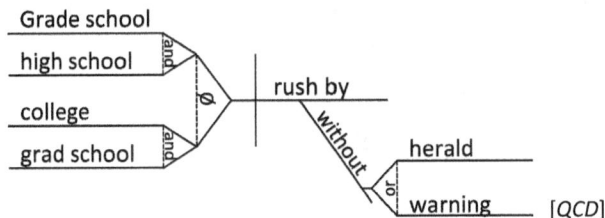

Grade school and high school, college and grad school rush by without herald or warning.
[*to convert to traditional format, replace "Ø" with an 'x'.*]

4. Compound-compound predicate; year-handling; preposition *"as"*

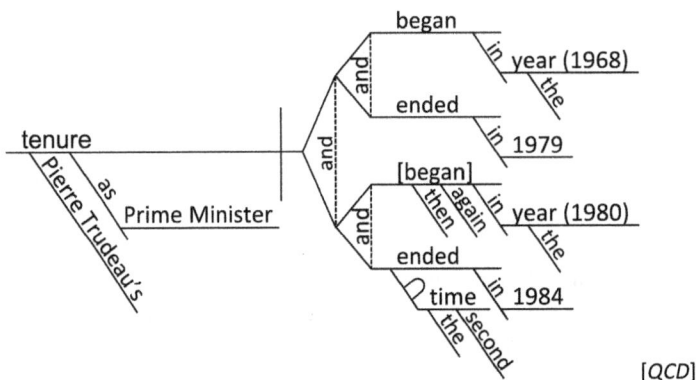

Pierre Trudeau's tenure as Prime Minister began in the year 1968 and ended in 1979, and then again in the year 1980 and ended the second time in 1984.
[*to convert to traditional format, replace "[began]" with an 'x', and remove the elision-hoop from the diagonal line of the structure holding the word "time".*]

5. Compound sentence using *"hence"*: elided conjunction in traditional style, normal conjunction in *QCD*

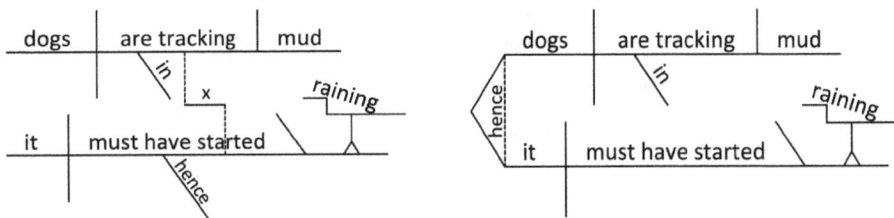

traditional   QCD

The dogs are tracking in mud; hence, it must have started raining.

6. Elided subject modified by prepositional phrase; compound predicate adjective; past participle with predicate adjective

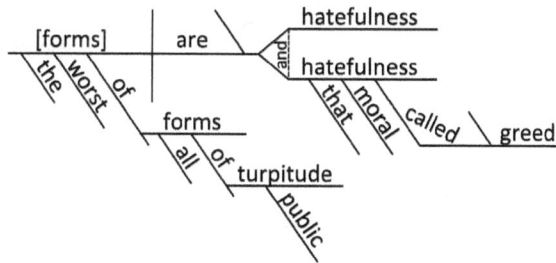

[QCD]

Of all forms of public turpitude, the worst are hatefulness and that moral hatefulness called greed.
[*to convert to traditional format, replace "[forms]" with an 'x'.*]

7. Elided compound subject; elided predicate complement

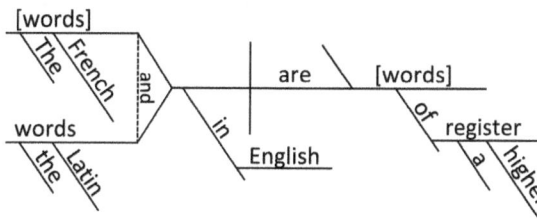

[QCD]

The French and the Latin words in English are of a higher register.
[*to convert to traditional format, replace each instance of "[words]" with an 'x'.*]

8. Noun infinitive; prepositional phrase as predicate objective; compound object of prepositional phrase

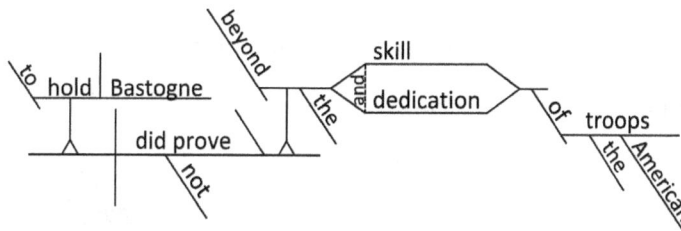

traditional

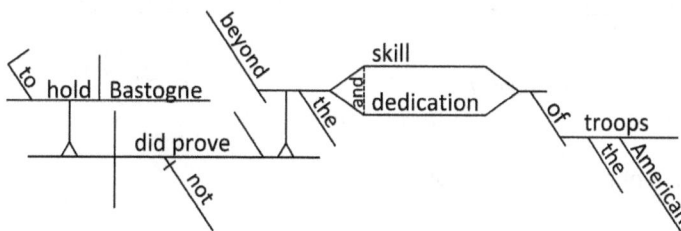

QCD

To hold Bastogne did not prove beyond the skill and dedication of the American troops.

9. Elided Infinitive with verbs of the senses [§7.24.8]

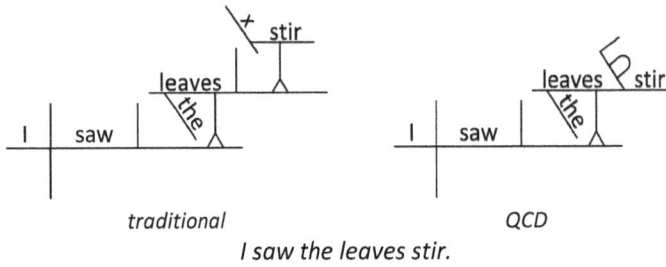

traditional   *QCD*

I saw the leaves stir.

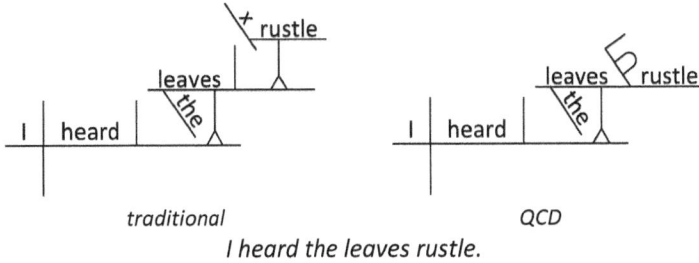

traditional   *QCD*

I heard the leaves rustle.

10. Infinitive with subject; infinitive as direct object

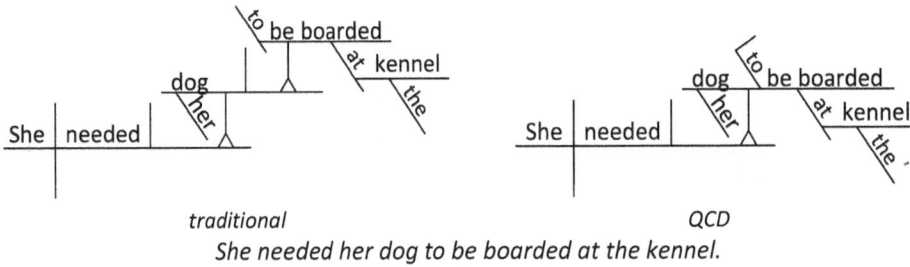

traditional   *QCD*

She needed her dog to be boarded at the kennel.

11. Elided infinitive with causative verb

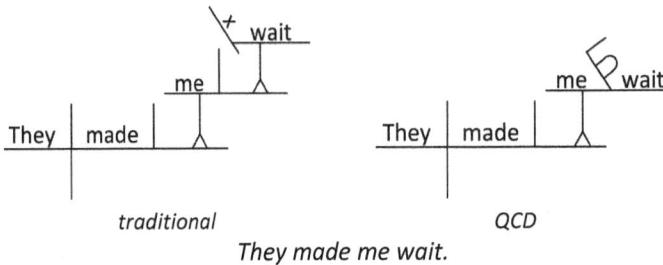

traditional   *QCD*

They made me wait.

12. Infinitive phrase as direct object

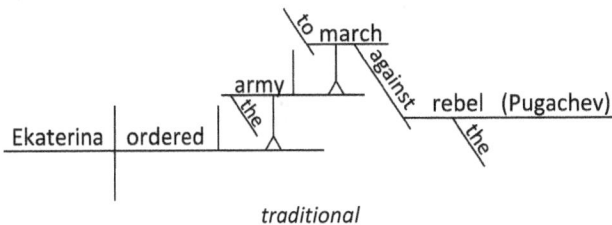

traditional

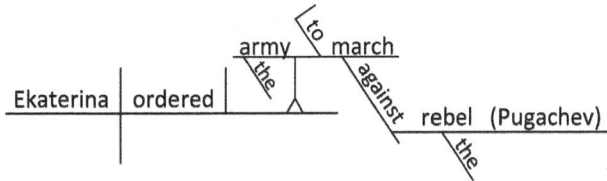

QCD

Ekaterina ordered the army to march against the rebel Pugachev.

13. Subject of infinitive with causative verb

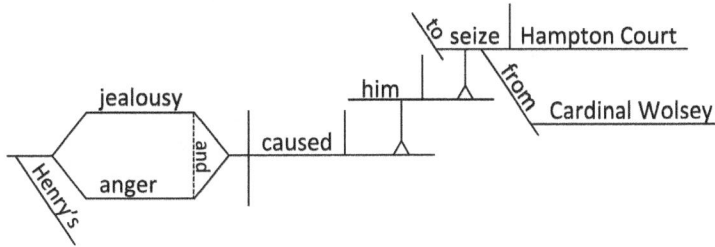

traditional

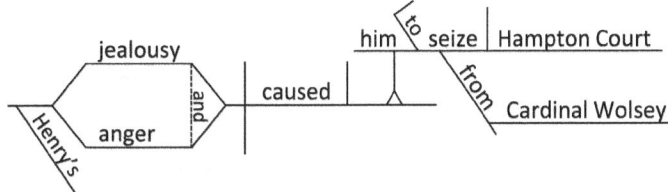

QCD

Henry's jealousy and anger caused him to seize Hampton Court from Cardinal Wolsey.

14. Infinitive object of preposition

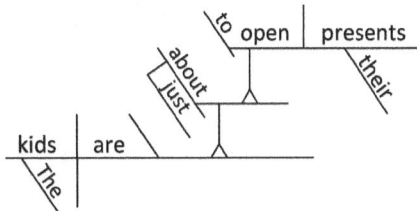

traditional

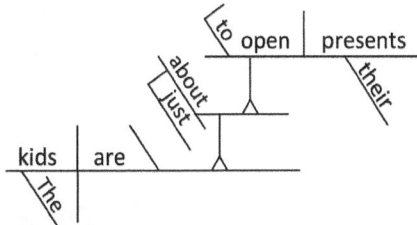

QCD

The kids are just about to open their presents.

15. Subject of infinitive; infinitive after the preposition "*for*": R/K traditional error in noting it as an adjectival infinitive – it is a noun infinitive with a subject, as shown if the noun "*man*" were replaced by the personal pronoun (which would be "*him*")

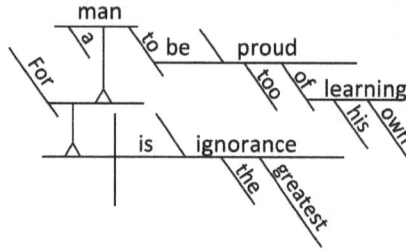

traditional: erroneous

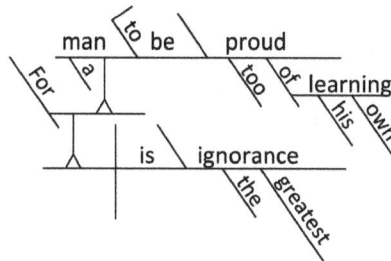

QCD

For a man to be too proud of his learning is the greatest ignorance.

16. Subject of infinitive; noun infinitive as object of preposition "*for*"; adverbial prepositional phrase modifying predicate adjective; subject of infinitive: same diagramming problem with traditional method as stated in no. 15

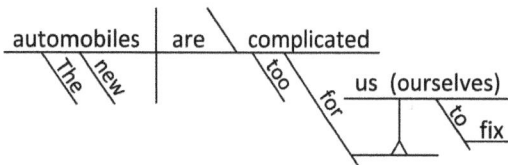 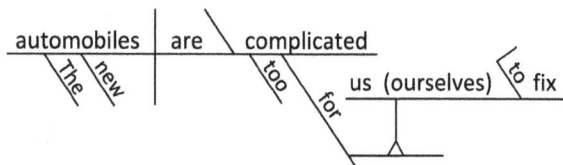

      traditional   *QCD*

The new automobiles are too complicated for us to repair ourselves.

17. Predicate appositive use of infinitive [§7.24.11]; adverbial dependent clause using **"than"** as conjunction.

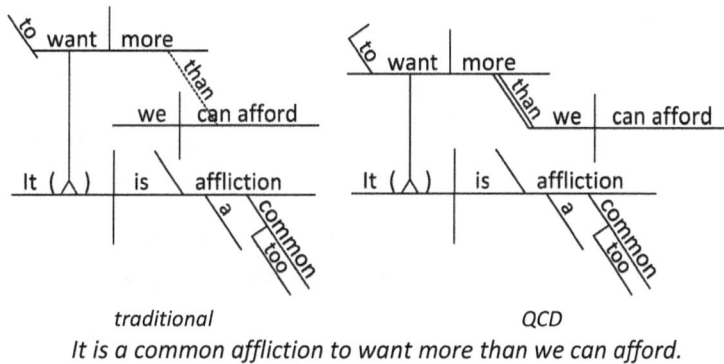

traditional   QCD

It is a common affliction to want more than we can afford.

18. Gerund object of preposition; possessive pronoun usage with gerund.

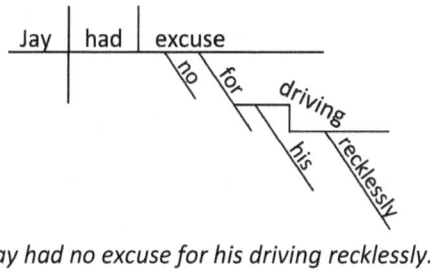

Jay had no excuse for his driving recklessly.

19. Gerund object of prepositional phrase; possessive with gerund; verb-idiom in gerund usage.

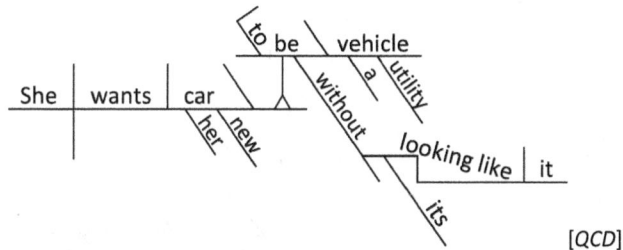

[QCD]

She wants her new car to be a utility vehicle without its looking like it.
[to convert to traditional format, replace the diagonal holding the "to" of the infinitive structure with its traditional form]

20. Present participle; infinitive object of present participle

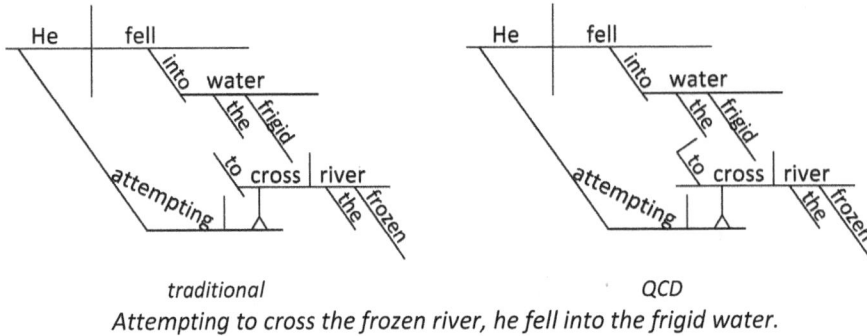

traditional   *QCD*

Attempting to cross the frozen river, he fell into the frigid water.

21. Present participle as predicate complement

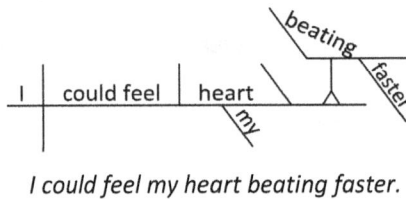

I could feel my heart beating faster.

22. Present participles as compound predicate complements

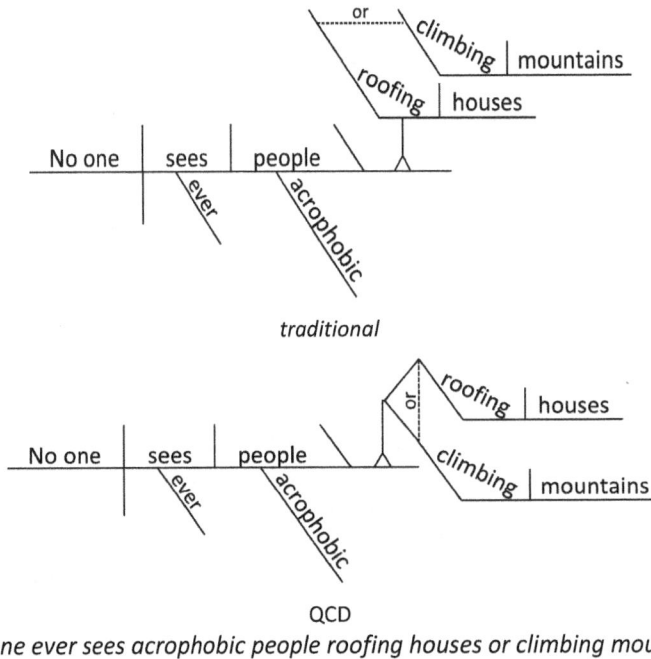

traditional

QCD

No one ever sees acrophobic people roofing houses or climbing mountains.

23. Effects of Adverb order: adverbial prepositional phrase

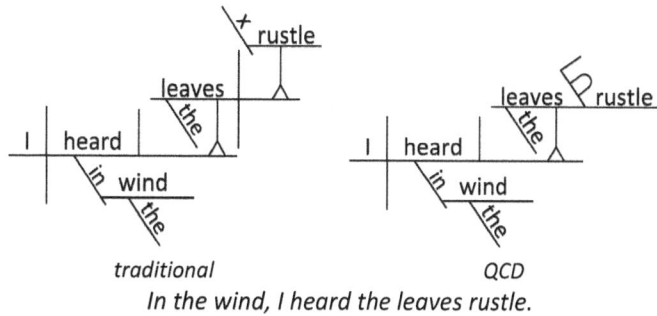

traditional   *QCD*

In the wind, I heard the leaves rustle.

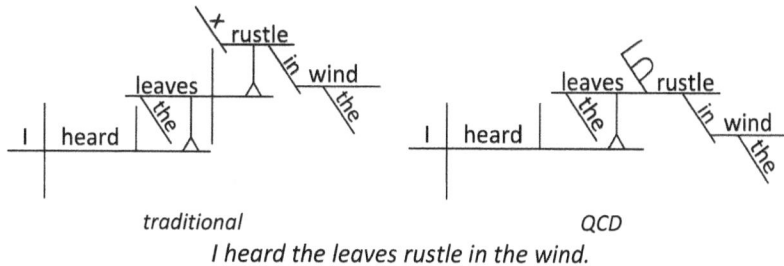

traditional   *QCD*

I heard the leaves rustle in the wind.

24. Infinitive phrase as direct object; adverbial objective; number as object of preposition.

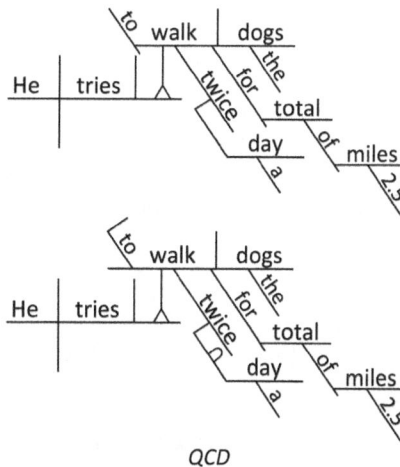

QCD

He tries to walk the dogs twice a day for a total of 2.5 miles.

25. Number as object of preposition

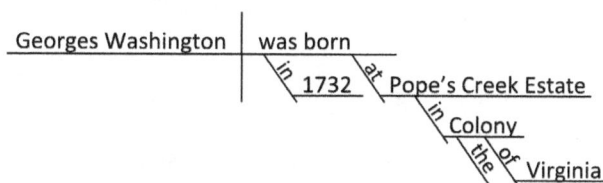

George Washington was born in 1732 at Pine's Creek Estate in the Colony of Virginia.

26. Independent Elements

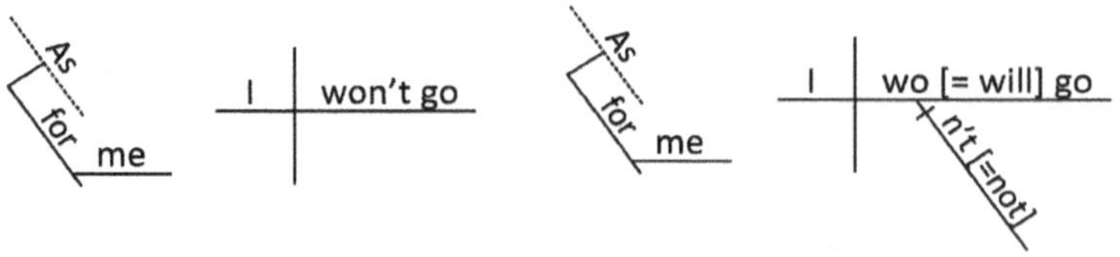

traditional　　　　　　　　　　　　*QCD*

As for me, I won't go.

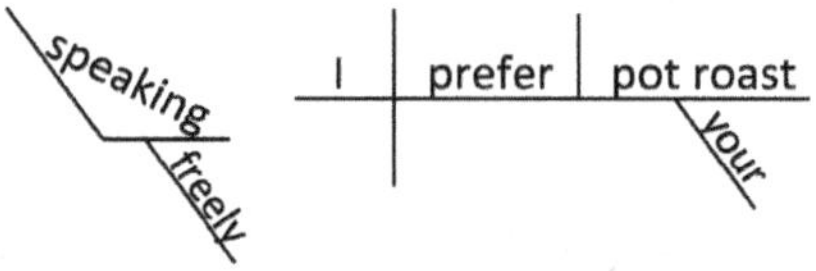

Speaking freely, I prefer your pot roast.

27. Modifiers of a (modifying) possessive noun; ***to seem*** as a state of being verb

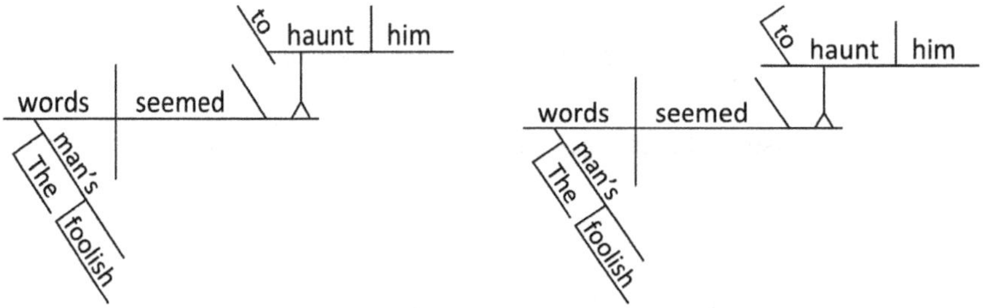

traditional　　　　　　　　　　　　*QCD*

The foolish man's words seemed to haunt him.

28. Past participle as predicate adjective; ***to stand*** used as a state of being verb

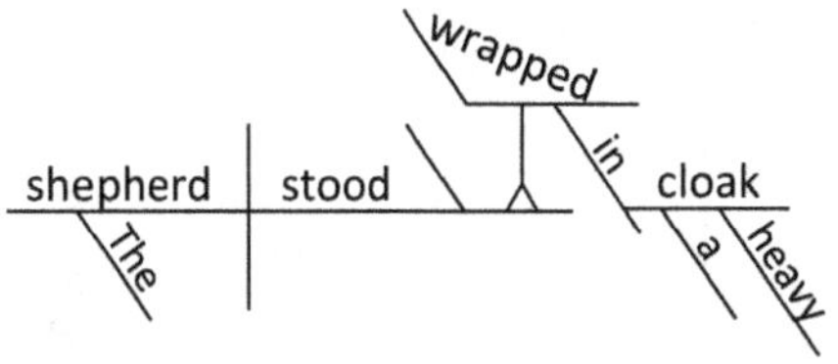

The shepherd stood wrapped in a heavy cloak.

29. Pronoun ***which*** versus pronominal adjective ***which*** (*cf.* no. 30, below)

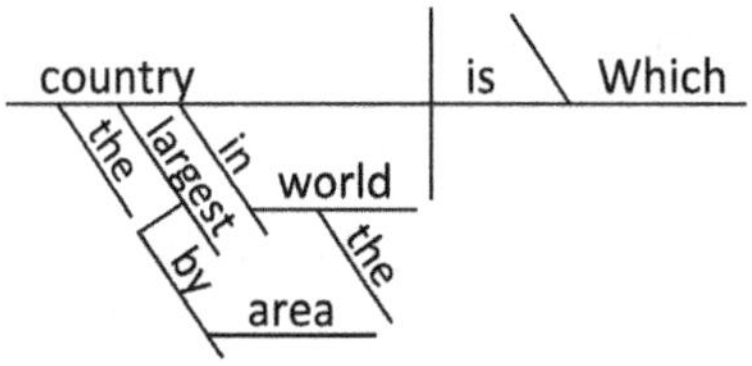

Which is the largest country by area in the world?

30. Pronominal adjective *which* versus pronoun *which* (*cf.* no. 29, above)

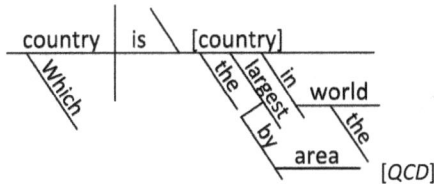

Which country is the largest by area in the world?
[*to convert to traditional format, replace "[country]" with an 'x'.*]

31. Noun dependent clause introduced by connecting phrase *that which*

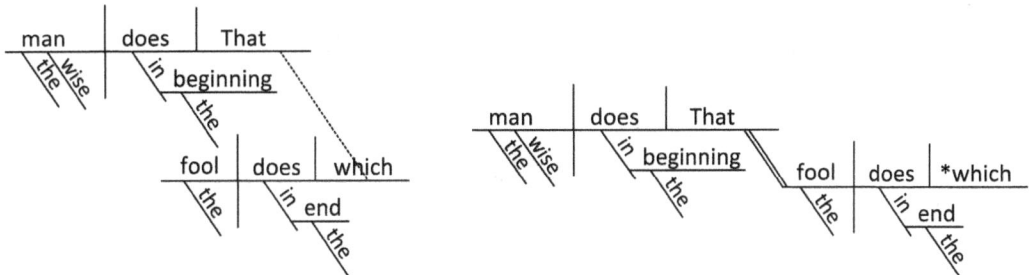

traditional   QCD

That which the fool does in the end, the wise man does at the beginning.
[*Parsed as "[the wise man does That at the beginning] [which the fool does in the end]."*]

32. Noun dependent clause as predicate appositive [§13.17.5.2]

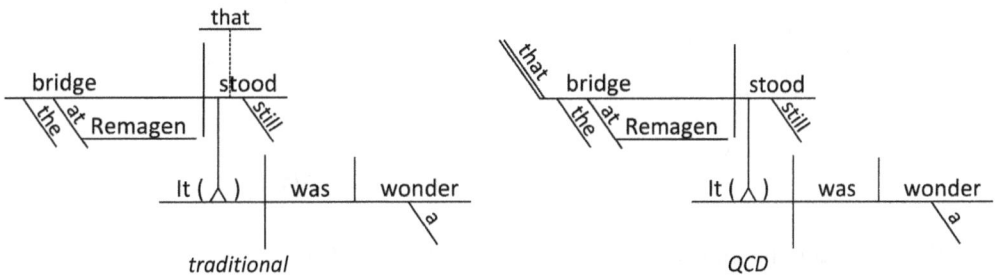

traditional   QCD

It was a wonder that the bridge at Remagen still stood.

33. Noun dependent clause as direct object of the predicate of the independent clause; conjunction as direct object or as modifier of direct object, of the dependent clause

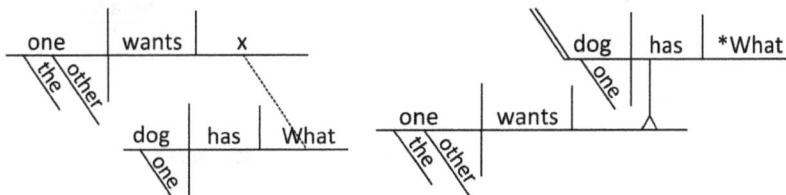

traditional   QCD

What one dog has the other one wants.

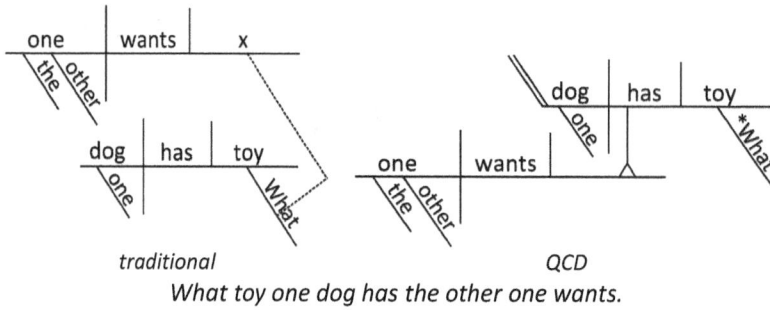

traditional   QCD

What toy one dog has the other one wants.

34.   Noun dependent clause as object of an infinitive

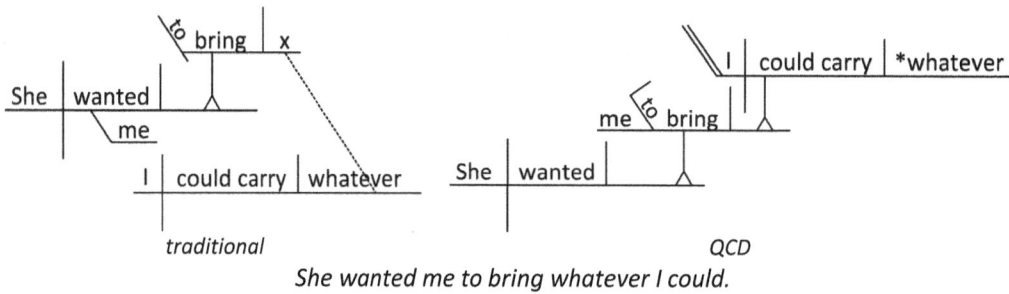

traditional   QCD

She wanted me to bring whatever I could.

35.   Noun dependent clause as subject of the independent clause

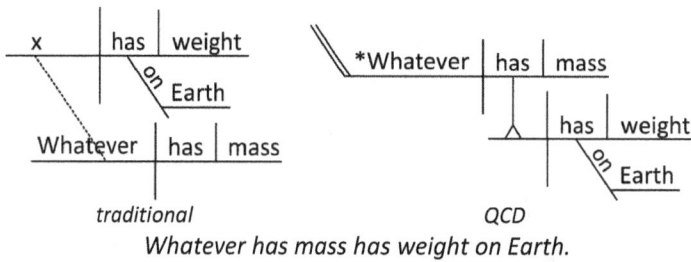

traditional   QCD

Whatever has mass has weight on Earth.

36.   Noun dependent clause used as object of a preposition

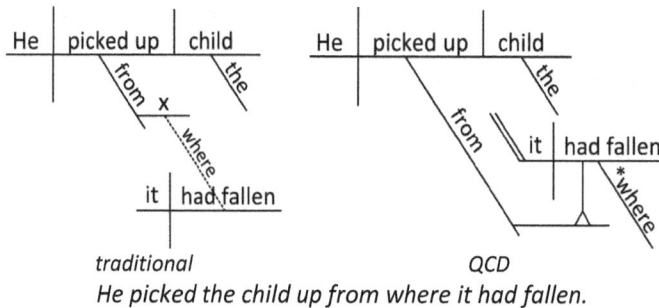

traditional   QCD

He picked the child up from where it had fallen.

37. Noun dependent clauses; compound independent clause; adverb dependent clause using "than"

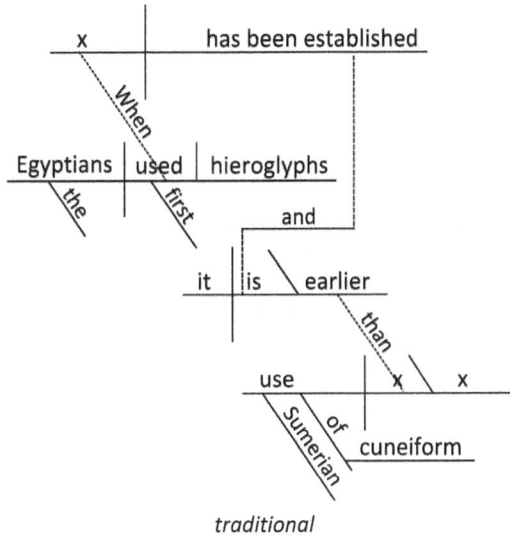

traditional

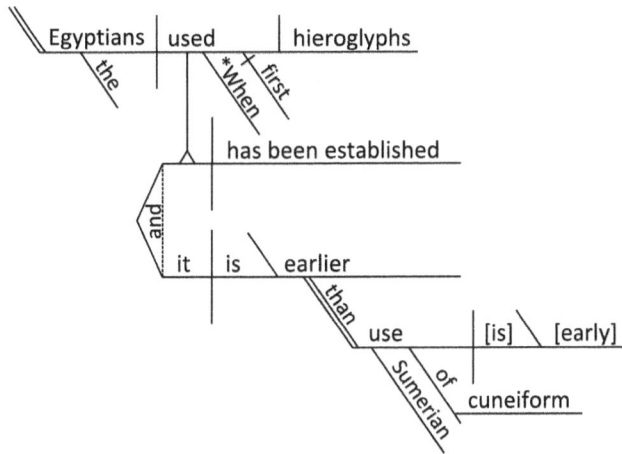

QCD

When the Egyptians first used hieroglyphs has been established,
and it is earlier than Sumerian use of cuneiform.
[When" modifies only the predicate of the noun dependent clause, as per §13.17.5.3]

38. Noun dependent clause with compound conjunction

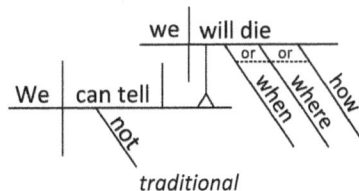

traditional

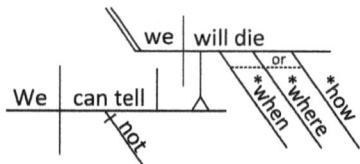 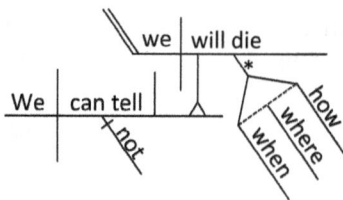

QCD: alternate   QCD: preferred

We cannot tell when or where or how we will die.

39. Comparative predicate adjective; elided adverbial clause of comparison using "than"

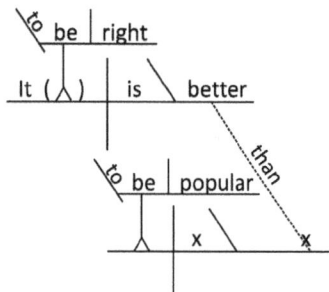 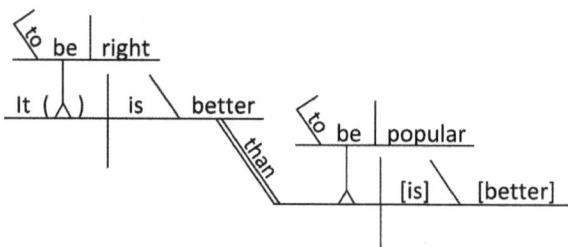

traditional   QCD

It is better to be right than to be popular.

40. Elided noun dependent clause after comparative conjunction *as ... as*

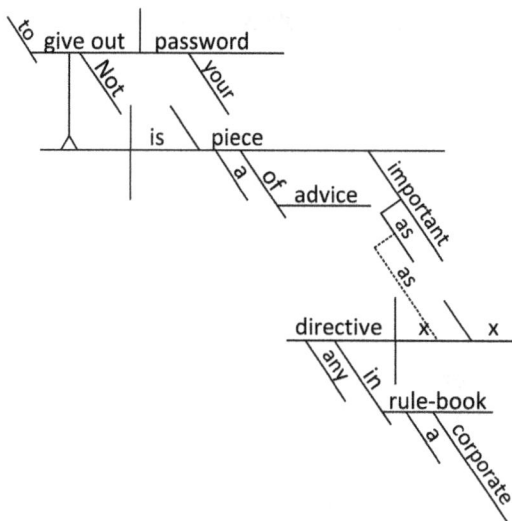

traditional

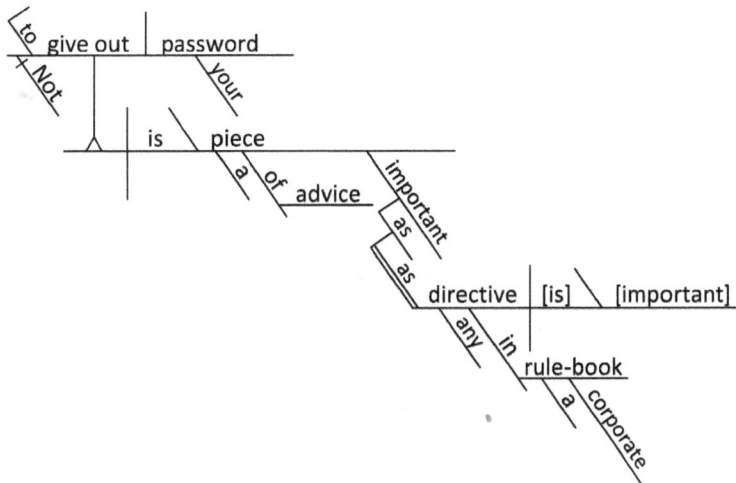

QCD

Not to give out your password is a piece of advice as important as any directive in a corporate rule-book.

41.   Adjective dependent clause; "***in which***" as conjunctive phrase

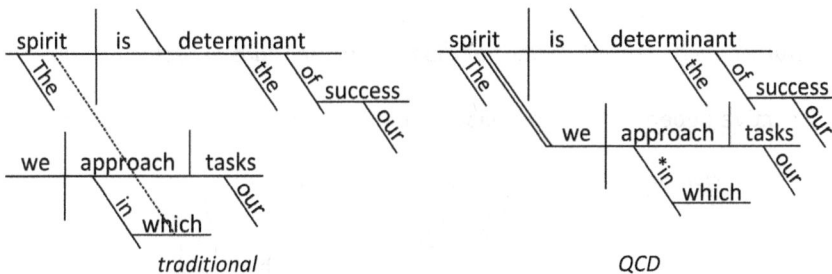

traditional   *QCD*

The spirit in which we approach our tasks is the determinant of our success.

[Note that the traditional diagram is almost impossible to render elegantly.]

42.   Adjective dependent clause

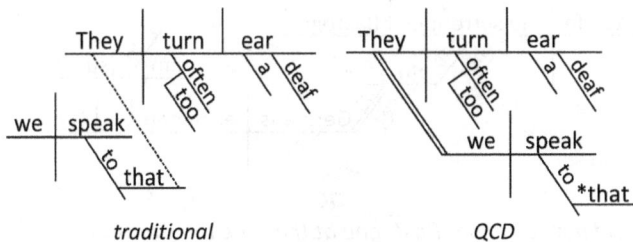

traditional   *QCD*

They that we speak to too often turn a deaf ear.

43. Adjective dependent clause; direct quotation with elided subject and verb.

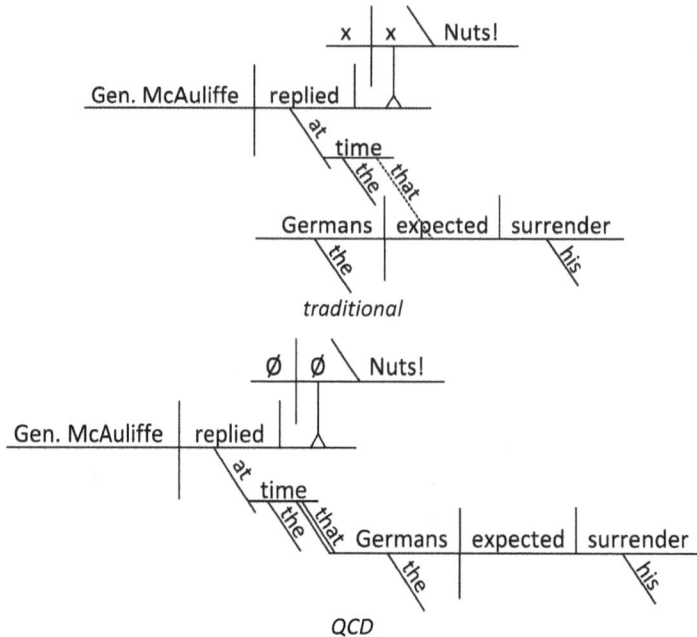

traditional

QCD

General McAuliffe replied, "Nuts!" at the time the Germans expected his surrender.

44. Adjective dependent clause; elided infinitive phrase.

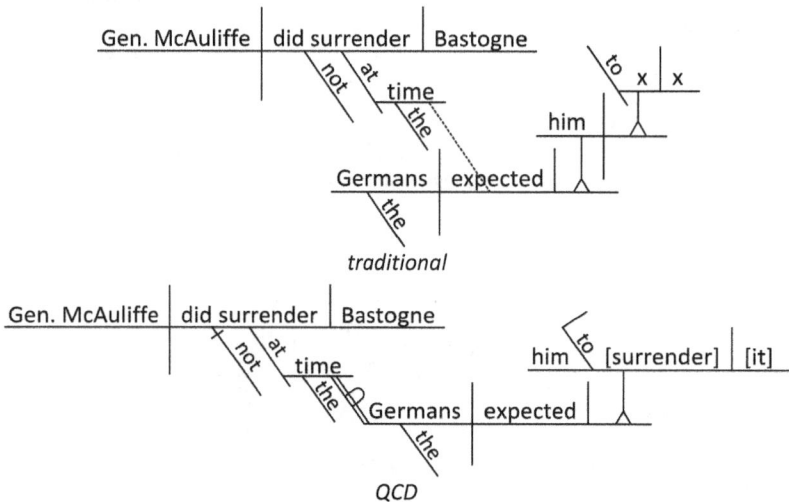

traditional

QCD

McAuliffe did not surrender Bastogne at the time the Germans expected him to.

45. Adjective dependent clause; placement of "*that ... to*" on diagram.

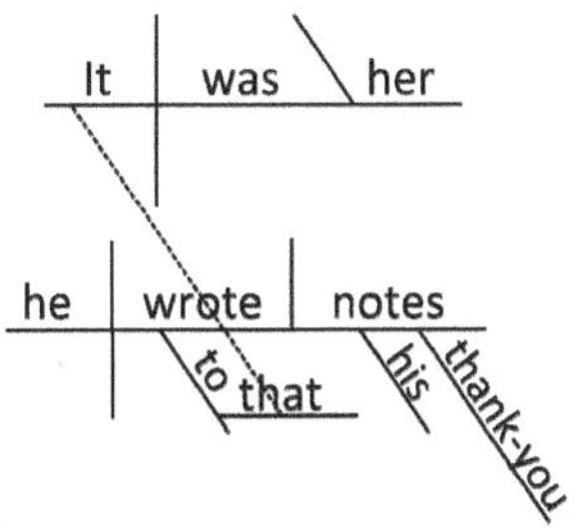

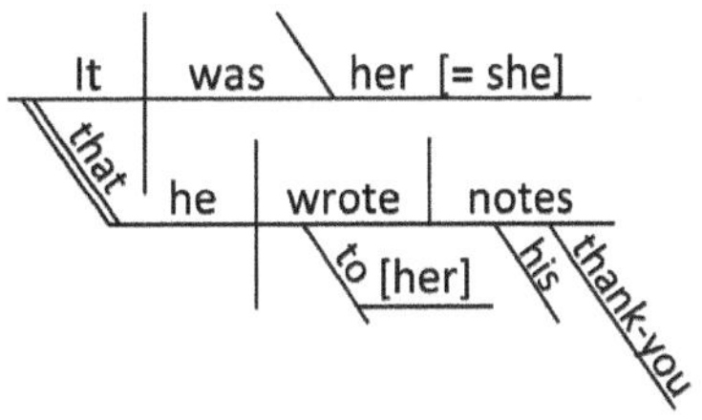

traditional   *QCD*

It was her that he wrote his thank-you notes to.

46. Adjective dependent clause

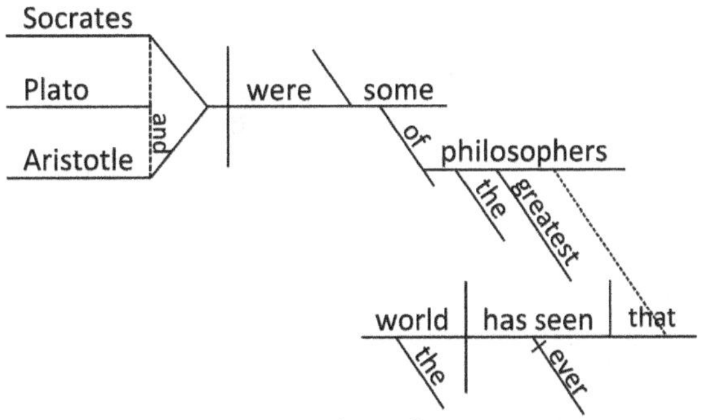

traditional

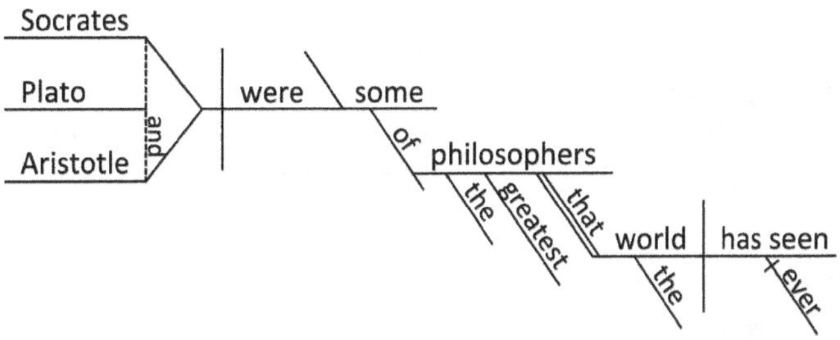

QCD

Socrates, Plato and Aristotle were some of the greatest philosophers that the world has ever seen.

47. Adjective dependent clause; elided conjunction

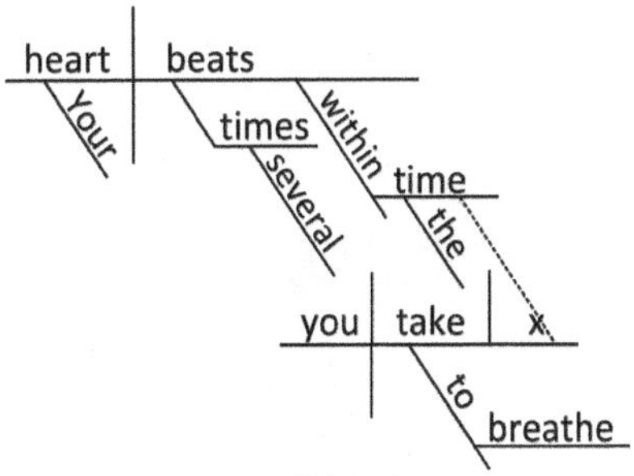

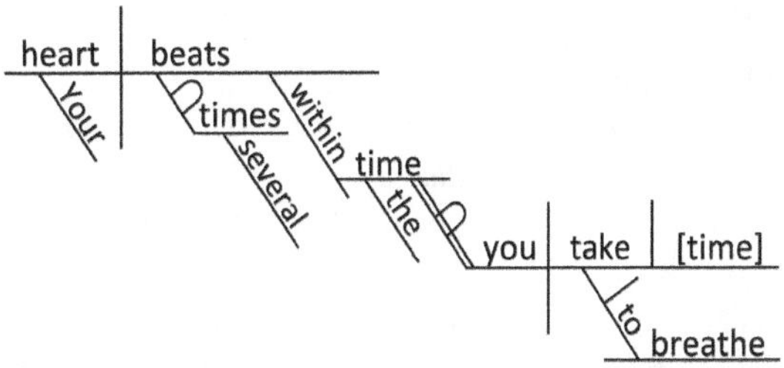

traditional   *QCD*

Your heart beats several times within the time you take to breathe.

48. Comparison of dependent clause diagrams:

Adjective dependent clause:

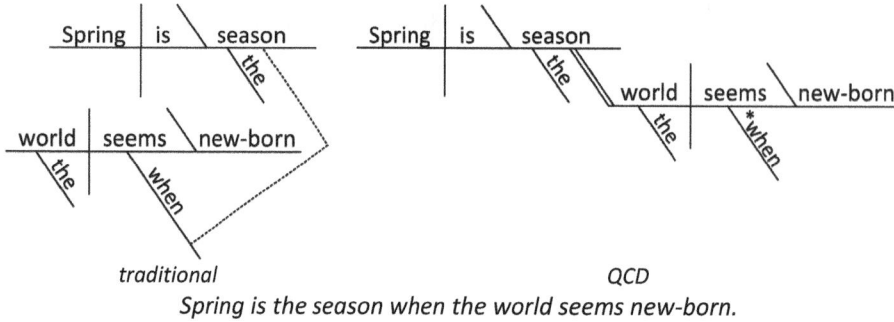

traditional

QCD

Spring is the season when the world seems new-born.

Noun dependent clause:

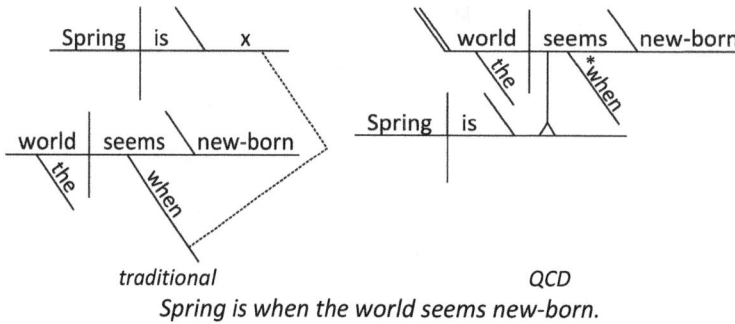

traditional

QCD

Spring is when the world seems new-born.

[Note that *QCD* uses the notation for noun dependent clauses, whereas *traditional* diagramming does not (and cannot) differentiate between noun dependent clauses, adjective dependent clauses and adverb dependent clauses.]

Adverb dependent clause:

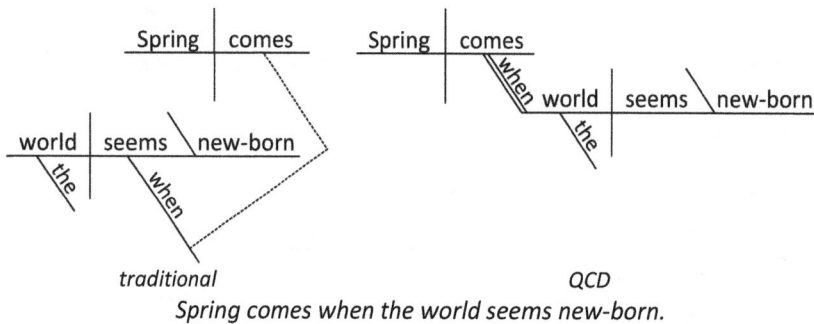

traditional

QCD

Spring comes when the world seems new-born.

49. Adjective dependent clause introduced by *"why"*

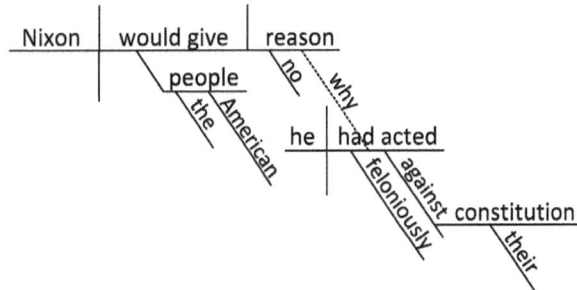

traditional

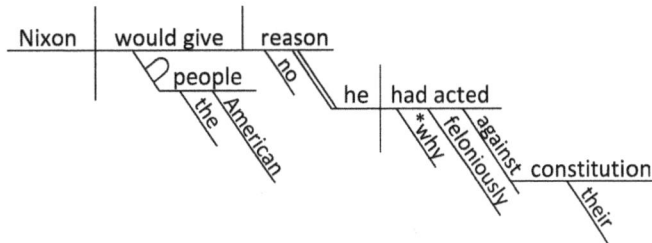

QCD

Nixon would give the American people no reason why he had acted feloniously against their Constitution.

50. Adjective clauses introduced by forms of *"who"*:

Adjective dependent clause introduced by *"who"*

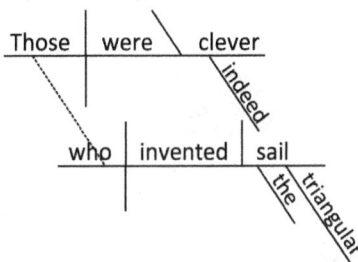

traditional

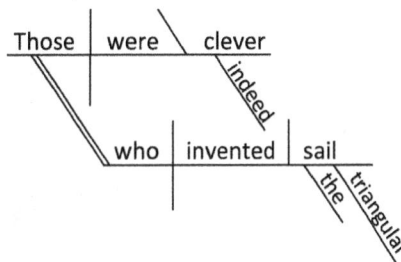

QCD

Those who invented the triangular sail were indeed clever.

Adjective dependent clause introduced by *"whose"*

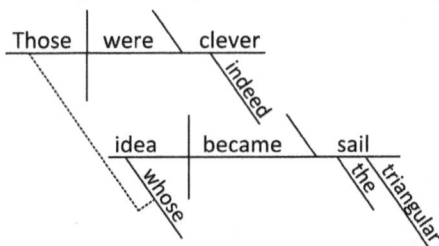

traditional

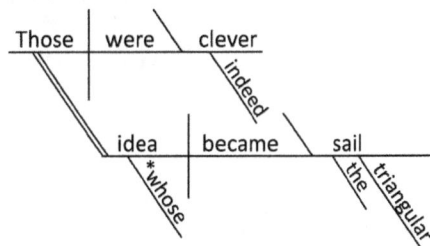

QCD

Those whose idea became the triangular sail were indeed clever.

Adjective dependent clause introduced by "*whom*"

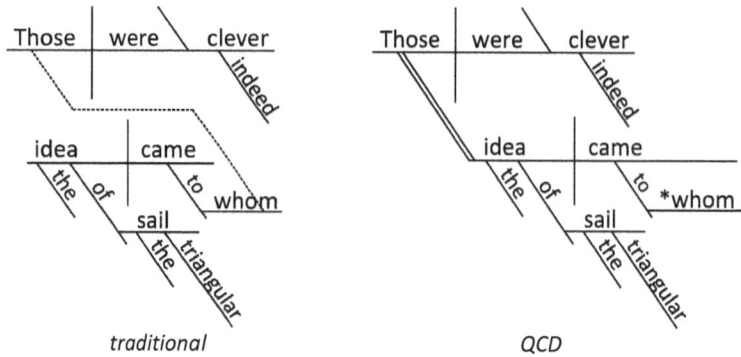

Those | were \ clever *indeed*

idea | came
the / of
sail
the / triangular
to / *whom*

traditional

Those | were \ clever *indeed*

idea | came
the / of
sail
the / triangular
to / *whom*

QCD

Those to whom the idea of the triangular sail came were indeed clever.

51. Compound adjective dependent clauses

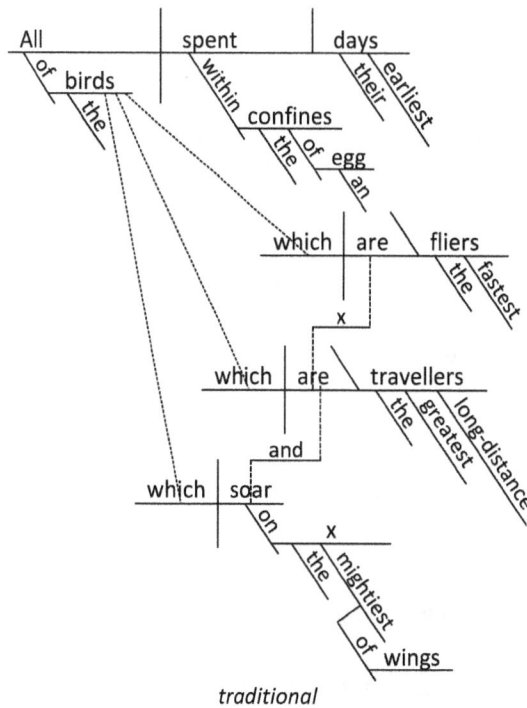

All | spent | days
of / birds
the
within
their
earliest

confines
the / of *egg*
an

which | are \ fliers
the / *fastest*

x

which | are \ travellers
the / greatest / long-distance

and

which | soar
on
the / mightiest
of / wings

x

traditional

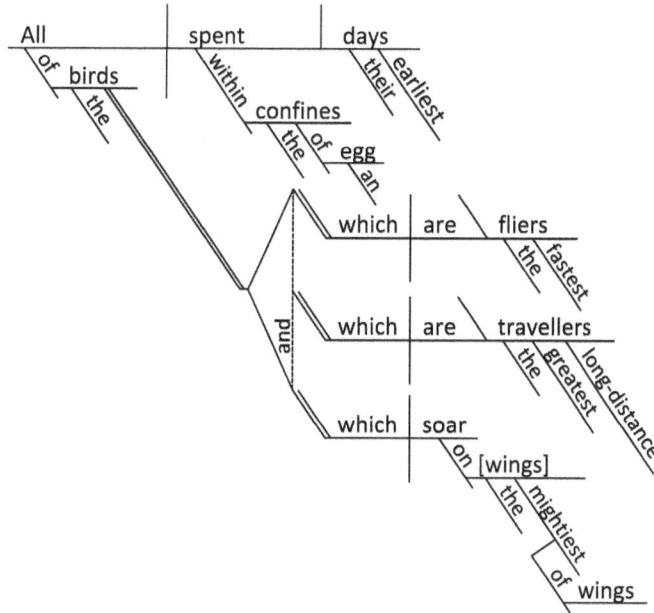

QCD

All of the birds which are the fastest fliers, which are the greatest long-distance travelers and which soar on the mightiest of wings, spent their earliest days within the confines of an egg.

52. Adjective dependent clauses modifying compound subjects; common adjective dependent clause modifying compound predicate nominatives.

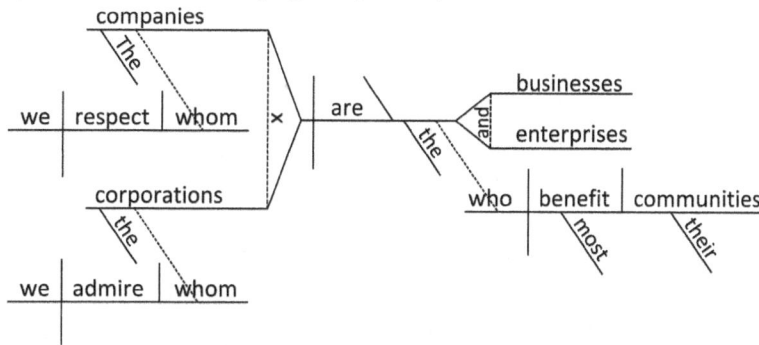

traditional

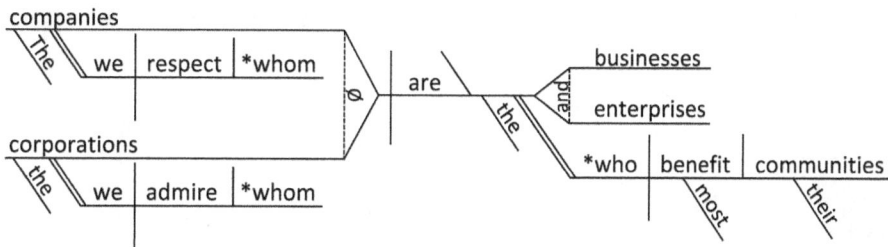

QCD

The companies whom we respect, the corporations we admire are the businesses and enterprises who most benefit their communities.

53. Adjective dependent clause; comparative usage with **"*than*"**; gerunds as subjects of both independent and dependent clauses

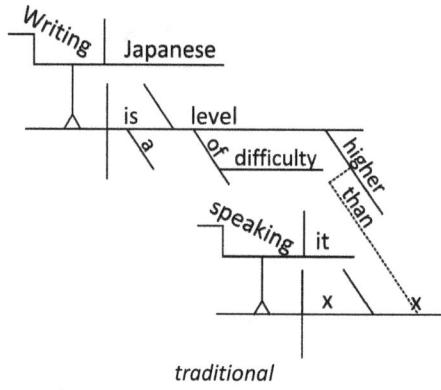

traditional

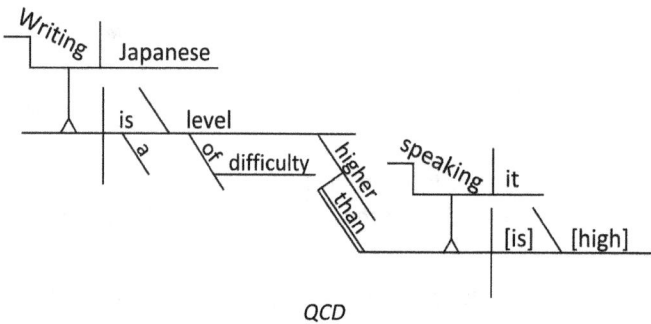

QCD

Writing Japanese is a level of difficulty higher than speaking it.

54. Adjective dependent clause; elided conjunction; gerund object of preposition

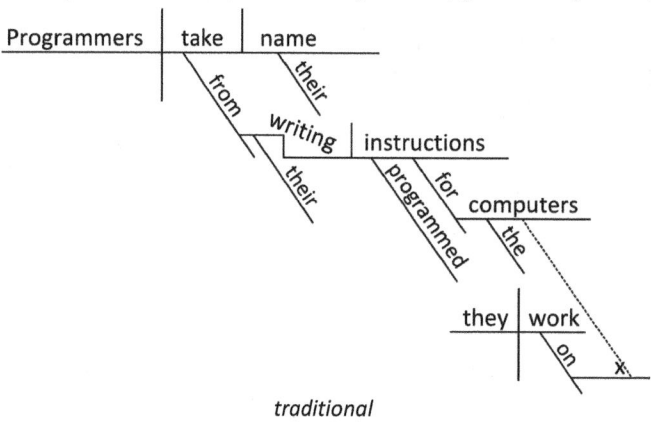

traditional

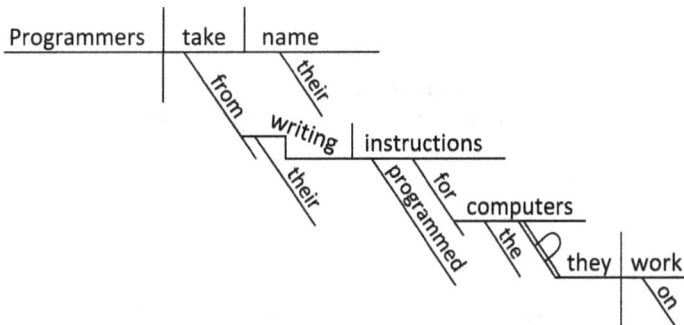

QCD

*Programmers take their name from their writing programmed instructions
for the computers they work on.*

55. Adjective dependent clause; correlative conjunction "**as … as**"
[The *QCD* diagram of the first "**as**" matches the diagramming method for appositives
introduced by "**as**".]

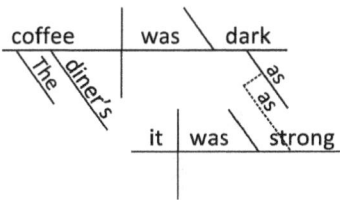

traditional

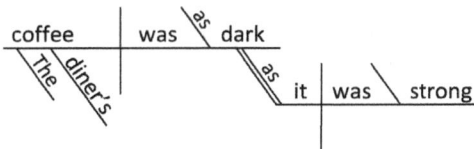

QCD

The diner's coffee was as dark as it was strong.

56. Adjective dependent clause; correlative conjunction "**as … as**"

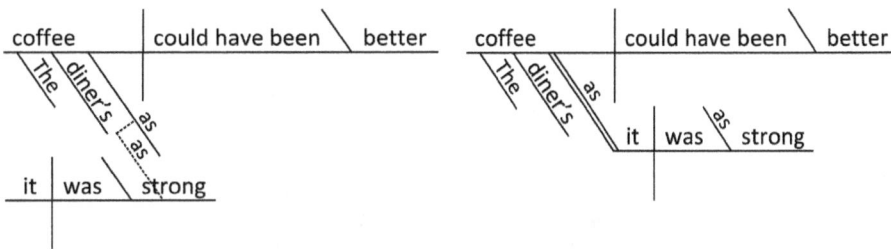

traditional   *QCD*

As strong as it was, the diner's coffee could have been better.

57. Adjective dependent clause; correlative conjunction "*so … as*"
    [Note that "*as … as*" and "*so … as*" are not equivalent (as shown in how "*so … as*" and "*so … that*" (in example 58) can parallel each other, yet "*as … as*" cannot parallel either of those two), so the *QCD* diagram of the two constructs are different.]

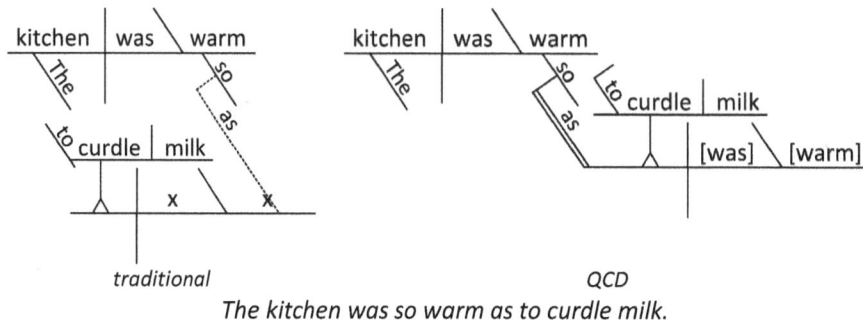

traditional   QCD

The kitchen was so warm as to curdle milk.

58. Adjective dependent clause; correlative conjunction "*so … that*"

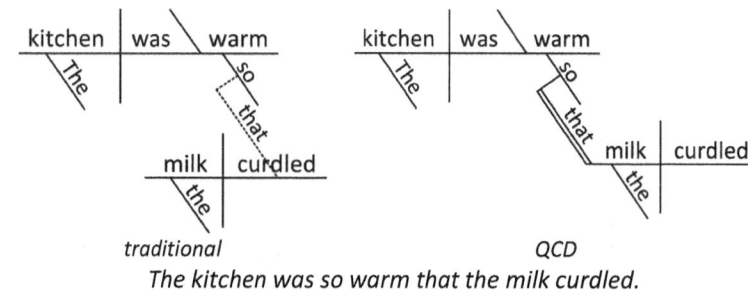

traditional   QCD

The kitchen was so warm that the milk curdled.

59. Compound-complex sentence; adverb dependent clauses; elided subjects and/or predicates of dependent clauses; comparative clauses using *"than"*
[*traditional format creates a "spaghetti diagram"*]

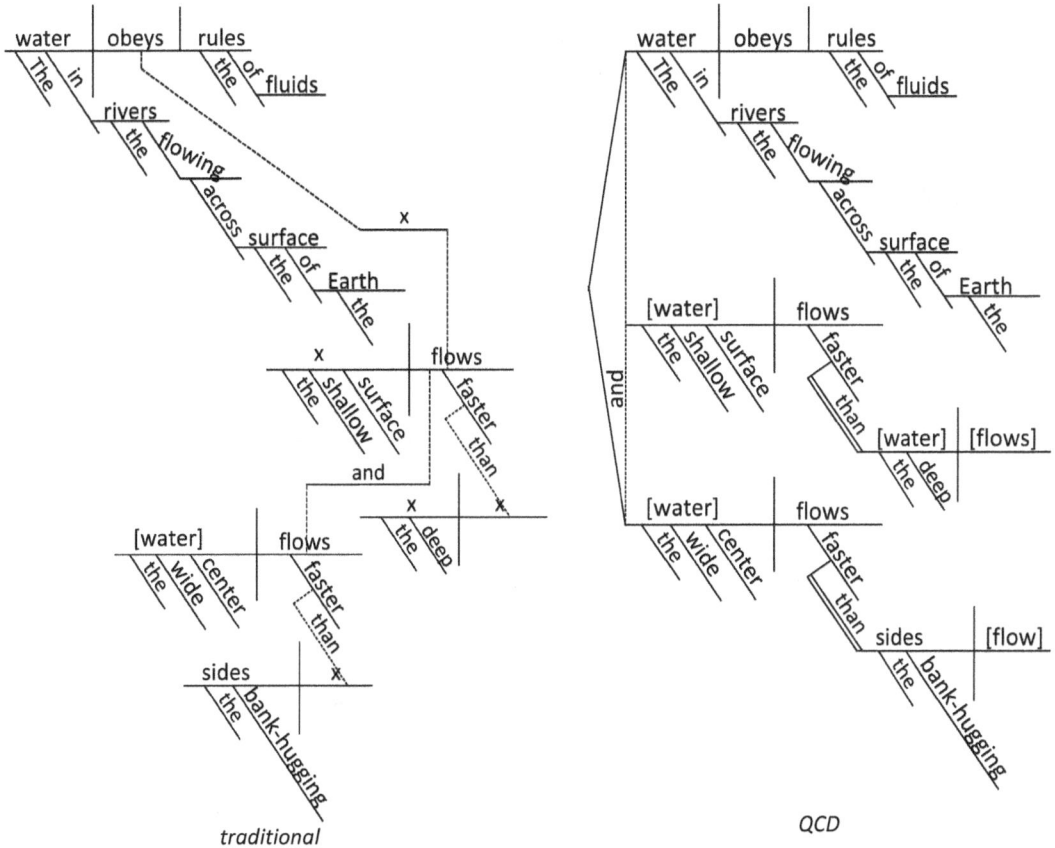

traditional

QCD

The water in the rivers flowing across the surface of the Earth obeys the rules of fluids; the shallow surface flows faster than the depths; and the wide center flows faster than the bank-hugging sides.

[The problem with the traditional diagram in this case is that the subordinate 'than' clauses seem to borrow, or to attempt to duplicate, the verb from their parent clauses, without notating change of number.]

60. Adverb dependent clause; single clause modifying compound predicate
(Compare with the diagrams of no. 61.)

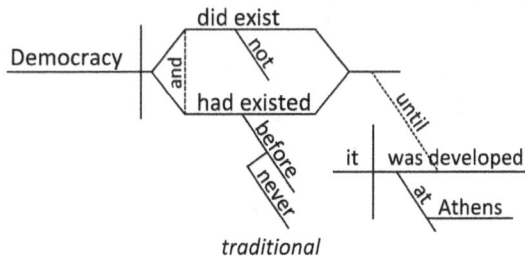

traditional

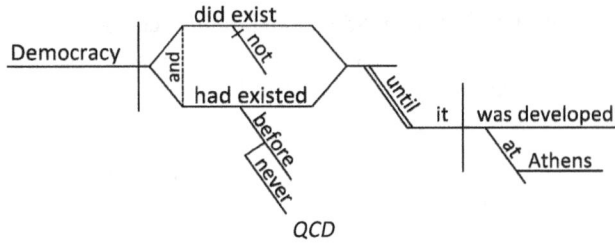

QCD

Democracy did not exist and had never existed before, until it was developed at Athens.

61. Adverb dependent clause; single clause modifying compound predicate; elision in compound predicate
(Compare to no. 60.)

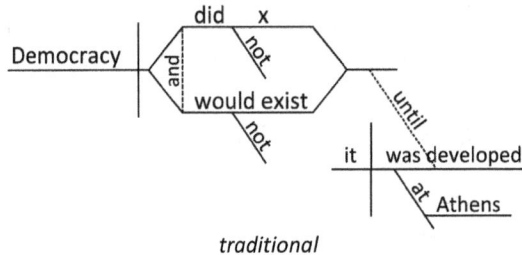

traditional

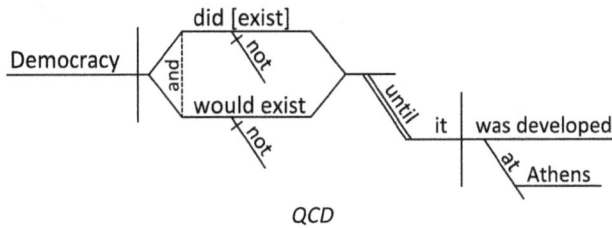

QCD

Democracy did not and would not exist until it developed at Athens.

62. Adverb dependent clause introduced by *"because"*; elided superlative in predicate complement; compound predicate construction in dependent clause joined by *"both … and"*

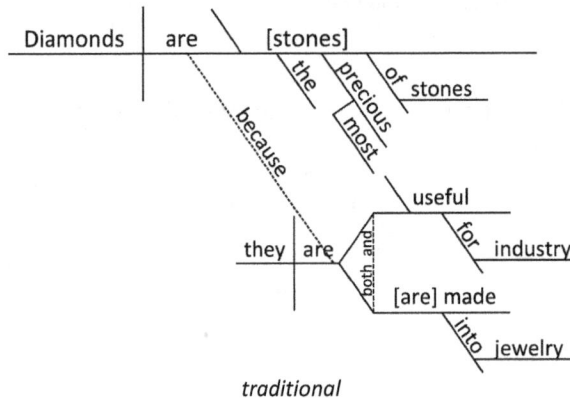

traditional

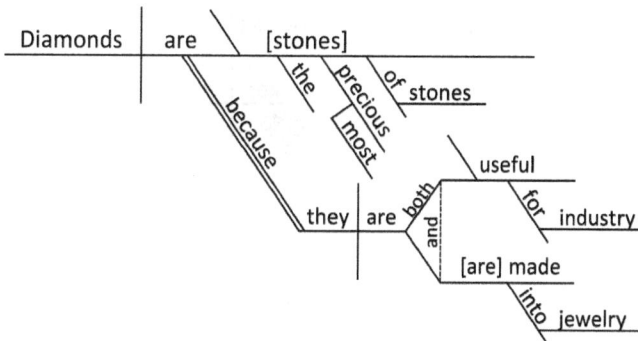

QCD

Diamonds are the most precious of stones because they are both useful for industry and made into jewelry.

63. Adverb dependent clause; elided predicate in dependent clause; predicate appositive use of infinitive; noun infinitive as subject of dependent clause

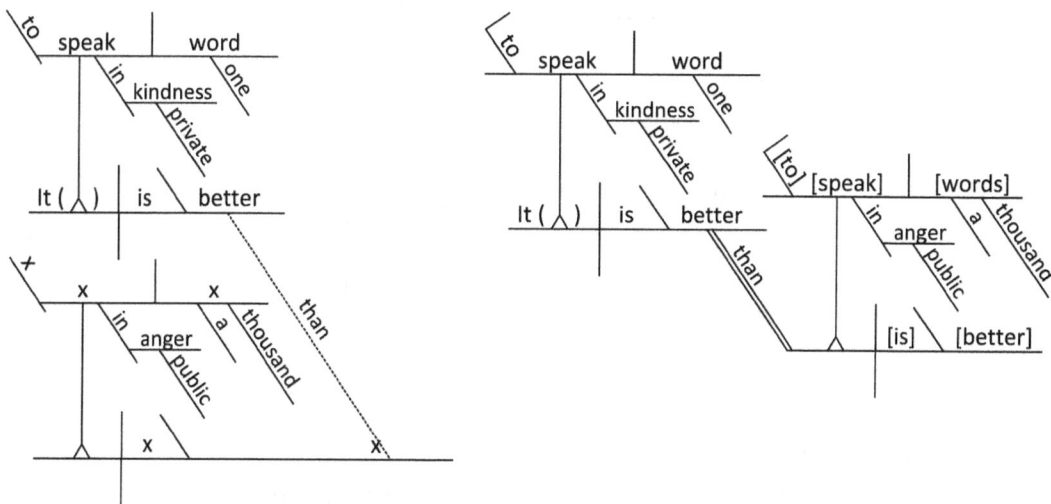

traditional   QCD

It is better to speak one word in private kindness than a thousand in public anger.

64. Adverb dependent clause introduced by *"where"*

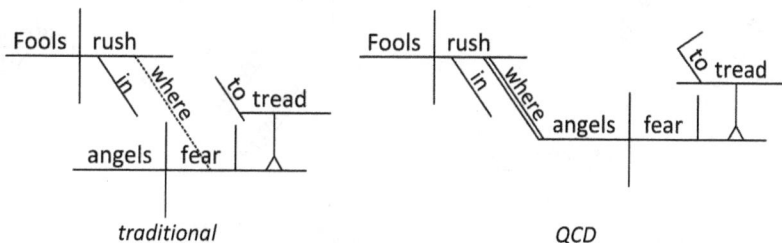

traditional   QCD

Fools rush in where angels fear to tread.

65. Adverb dependent clause introduced by "*as*"

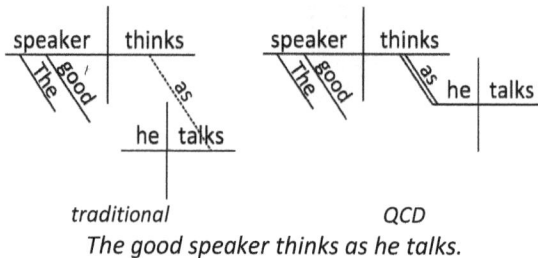

speaker | thinks
The good
as
he | talks

speaker | thinks
The good
as he | talks

traditional *QCD*

The good speaker thinks as he talks.

66. Imperative sentence with adverbial dependent clause

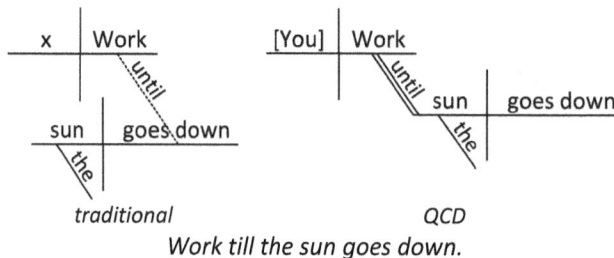

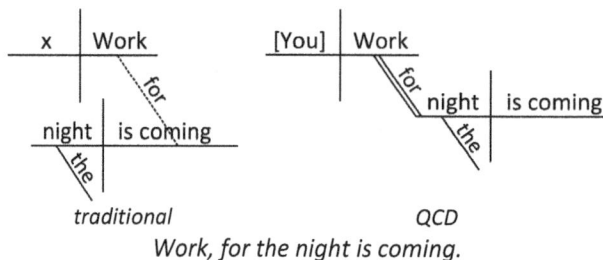

x | Work
until
sun | goes down
the

[You] | Work
until
sun | goes down
the

traditional *QCD*

Work till the sun goes down.

x | Work
for
night | is coming
the

[You] | Work
for
night | is coming
the

traditional *QCD*

Work, for the night is coming.

67. Adverb dependent clause with elided subject and partial predicate.
[The traditional format for the compound modifier "*downward, forward and sideways*" may be used in the *QCD* diagram.]

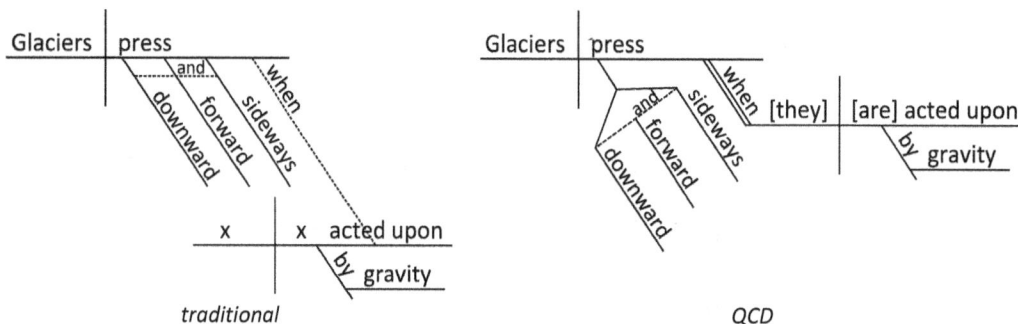

Glaciers | press
and
downward forward sideways when
x | x acted upon
by gravity

Glaciers | press
and sideways when
downward forward
[they] | [are] acted upon
by gravity

traditional *QCD*

Glaciers press downward, forward and sideways when acted upon by gravity.
[The traditional arrangement of the adverbs "*downward, forward and sideways*"
is also acceptable in *QCD*.]

68. Adverb dependent clause introduced by *"**because**"*; noun dependent clause as direct object of main clause's verb; noun dependent clause containing indirect quotation

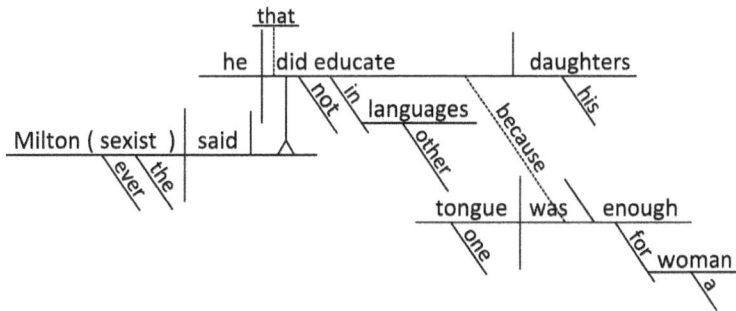

traditional

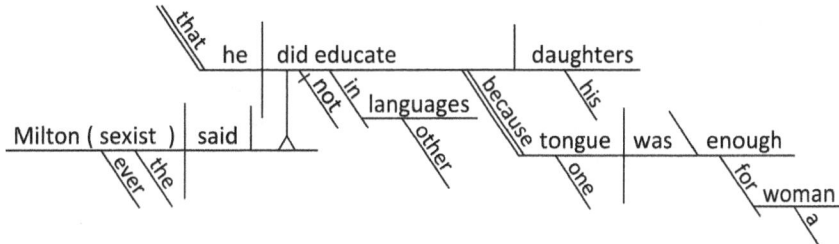

QCD

Milton, ever the sexist, said that he did not educate his daughters in other languages because one tongue was enough for a woman.

69. Adverb dependent clause; usage of *"**there**"* as a true adverb and not an expletive

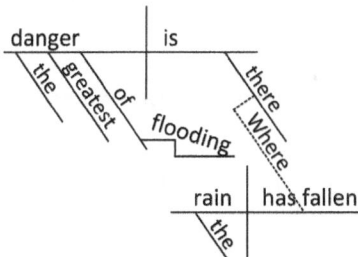

traditional

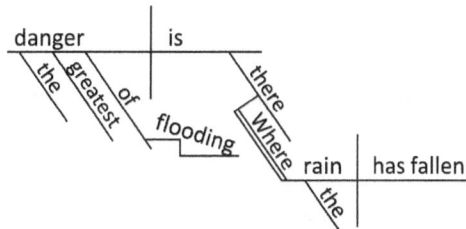

QCD

Where the rain has fallen there is the greatest danger of flooding.

70. Adverb dependent clause with "for"; noun dependent clause as predicate complement; compound noun dependent clauses as direct object of verb in a dependent clause

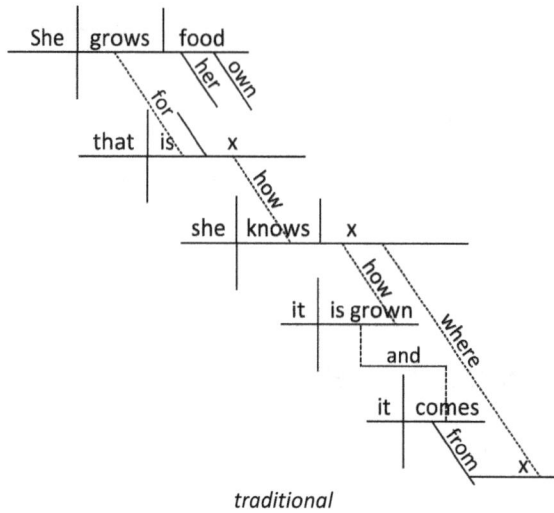

traditional

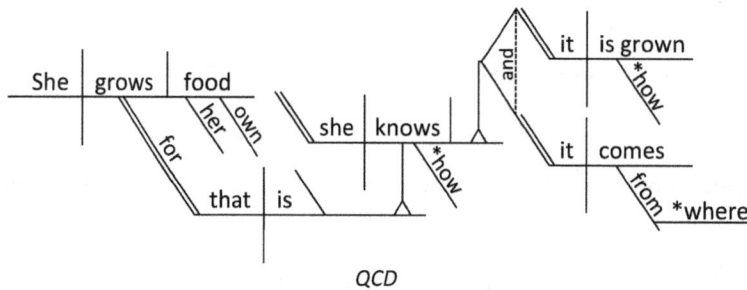

QCD

She grows her own food for that is how she knows how it is grown and where it comes from.

71. Adverbial dependent clause introduced by "*if*"; idiomatic use of "*with ... after ...*" forming substantive phrase

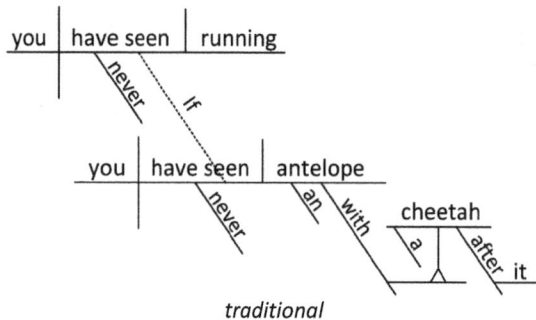

traditional

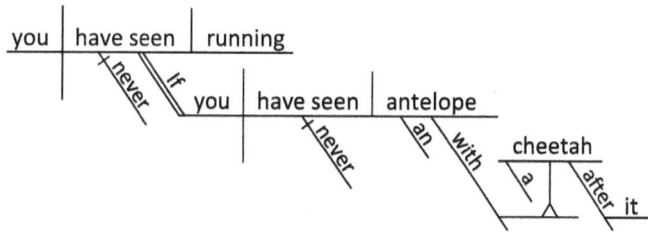

QCD

If you have never seen an antelope with a cheetah after it, you have never seen running.

72. Adverb dependent clause; phrasal conjunction "*so that*"; compounded compound predicate

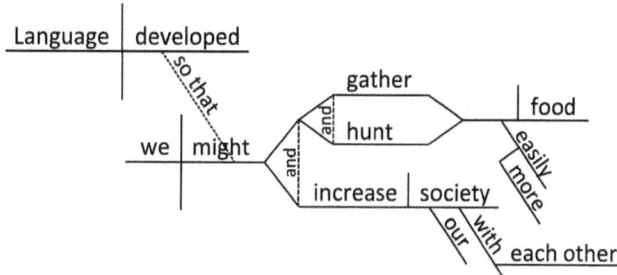

traditional

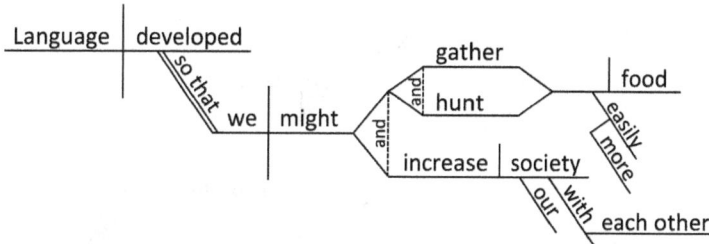

QCD

Language developed so that we might hunt and gather food more easily and increase our society with each other.

73. Compound adverb dependent clauses

[*traditional diagramming format requires that the phrase "**in order**" that is common to the conjunction introducing the compound clauses be marked as elided, although, in reality, it isn't*]

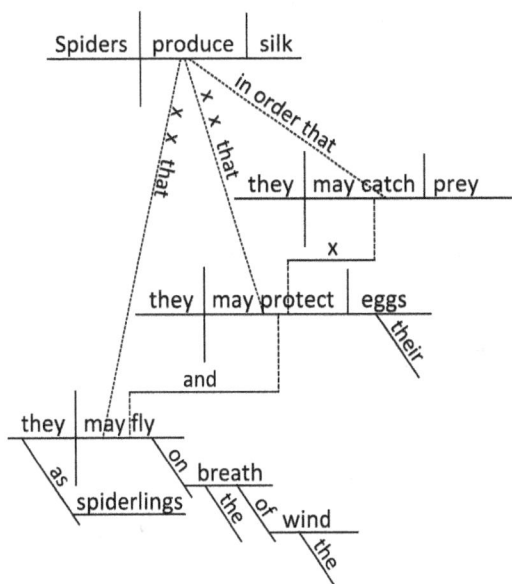

traditional

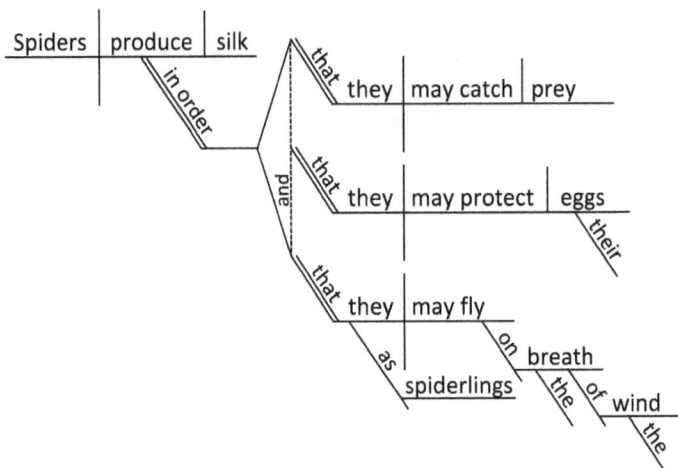

QCD

Spiders produce silk in order that they may catch prey, that they may protect their eggs, and that they may as spiderlings fly on the breath of the wind.

74. Adverb dependent clause introduced by "*if*"; elided subject and partial predicate of dependent clause

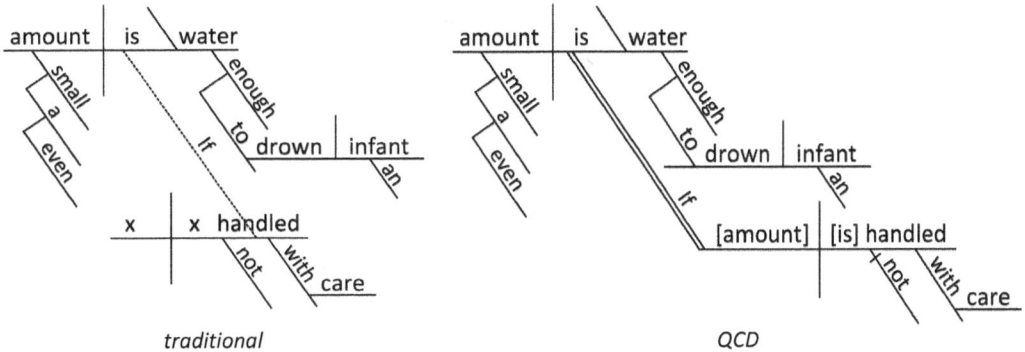

traditional   QCD

If not handled with due care, even a small amount is water enough to drown an infant.

75. Adverb dependent clause introduced by "*because*"

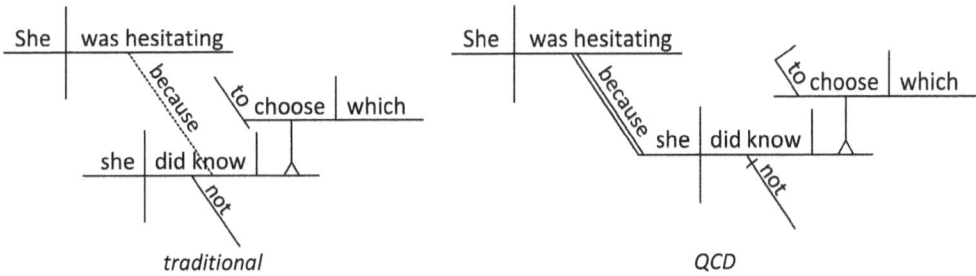

traditional   QCD

She was hesitating because she did not know which to choose.

76. Compound adverbial dependent clauses; use of singular verb with collective noun; proper use of the subjunctive mood in both dependent clauses

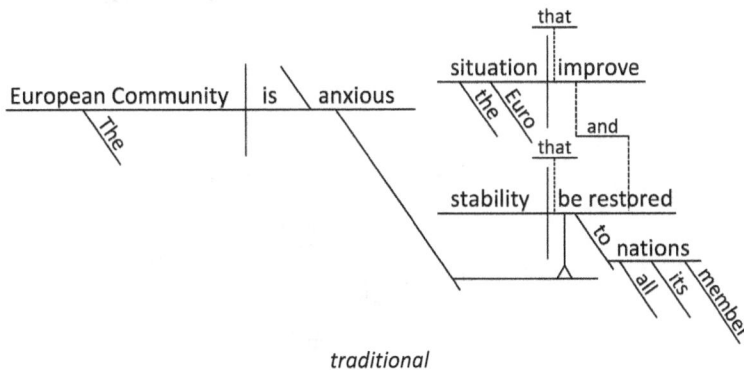

traditional

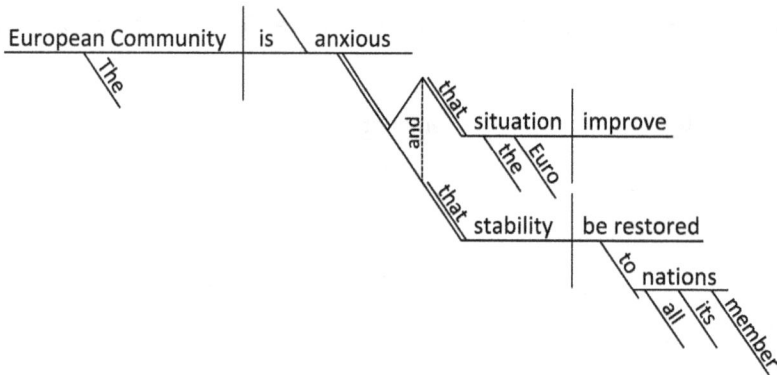

QCD

The European Community is anxious that the Euro situation improve and that economic stability be restored to all its member nations.

77. Compound-complex sentence: adverb dependent clauses; elided predicates and predicate complements in dependent clauses; compound sentence; usage of *"**more**"* as an adjective rather than as a comparative adverb

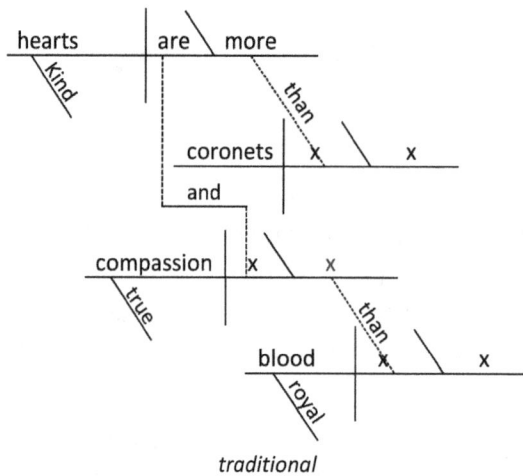

traditional

QCD

Kind hearts are more than coronets and true compassion more that royal blood.

78. Adverb dependent clauses; gerund as subject of independent clause; expletive usage of "*there*"

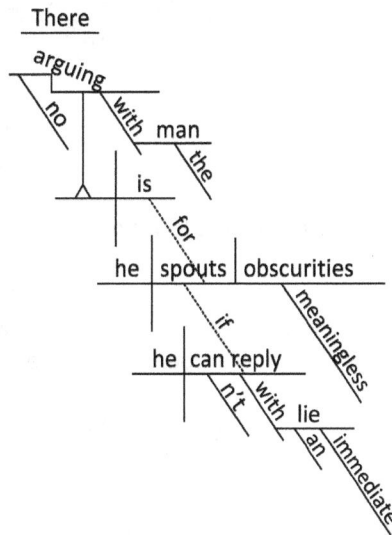

traditional

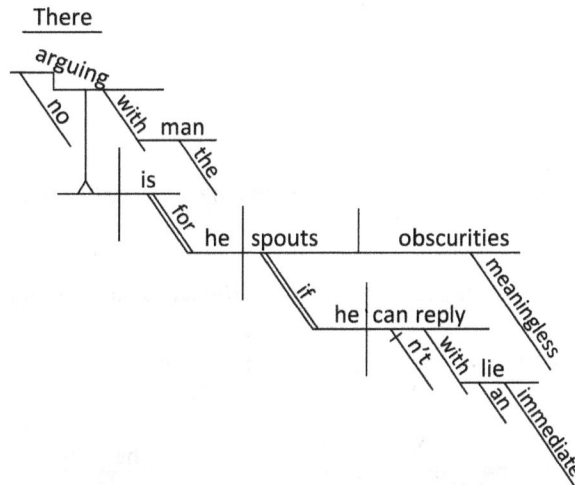

QCD

There is no arguing with the man, for he spouts meaningless obscurities if he cannot readily reply with an immediate lie.

79. Adverb dependent clause; elided subject and partial predicate of dependent clause

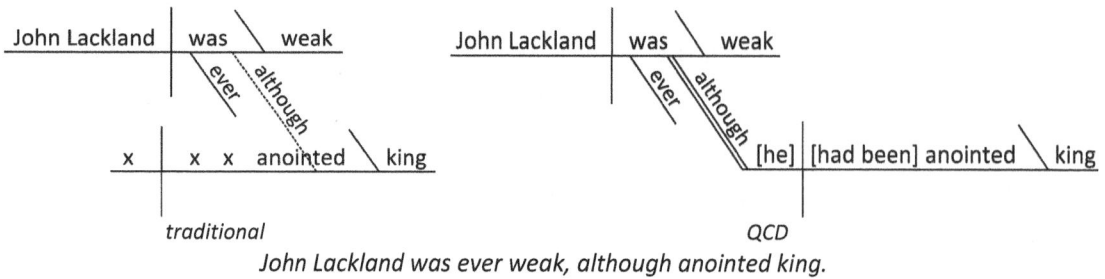

John Lackland | was \ weak

ever *although*

x | x x anointed \ king

traditional

John Lackland | was \ weak

ever *although*

[he] | [had been] anointed \ king

QCD

John Lackland was ever weak, although anointed king.

80. Adverb dependent clause; comparative clause using "***more than***" in modifying a verb; elision of subject and predicate of dependent clause

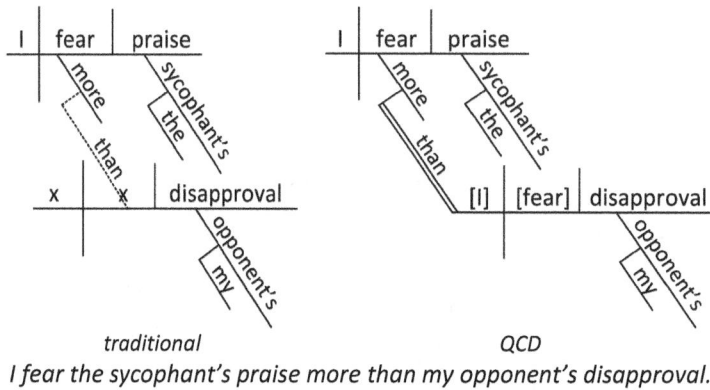

I | fear | praise

more *sycophant's* *the*

x | x | disapproval

opponent's *my*

traditional

I | fear | praise

more *sycophant's* *the*

[I] | [fear] | disapproval

opponent's *my*

QCD

I fear the sycophant's praise more than my opponent's disapproval.

81. Adverb dependent clause; use of "***the ... the ...***" as a conjunction

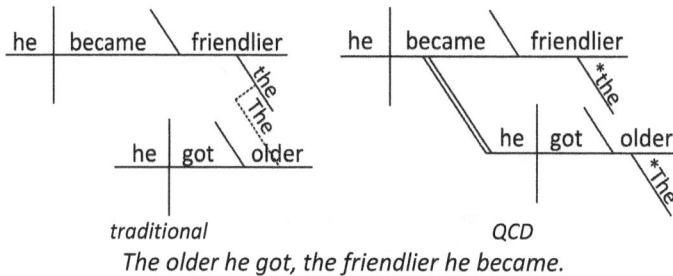

he | became \ friendlier

the *The*

he | got \ older

traditional

he | became \ friendlier

*the

he | got \ older

*The

QCD

The older he got, the friendlier he became.

82. Two adverb dependent clauses; adjective dependent clause; noun dependent clause as direct object of an infinitive; comparative clause using **"*more than*"** in modifying an adjective; elided verb and predicate complement in adverbial dependent clause.

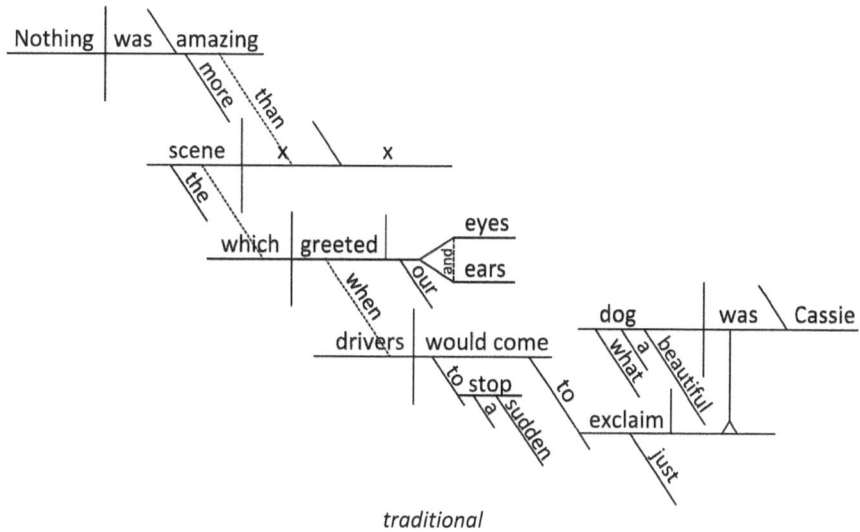

traditional

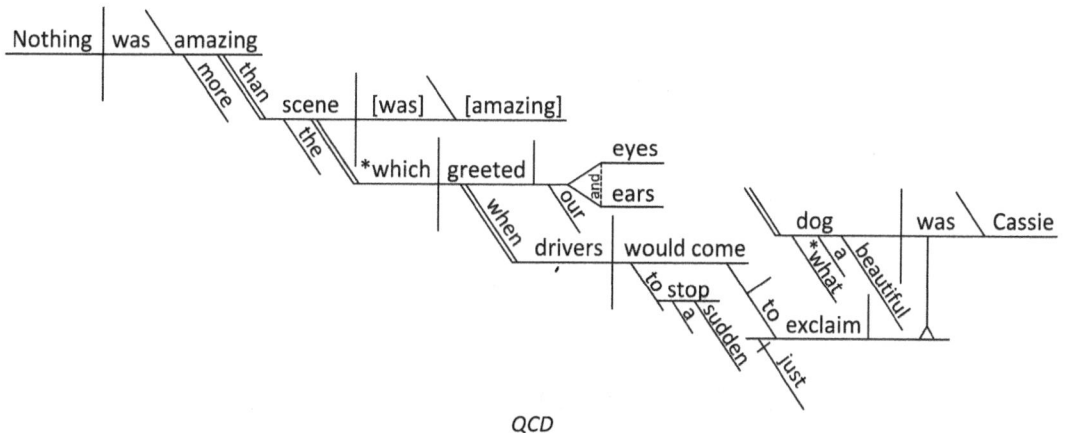

QCD

Nothing was more amazing than the scene which greeted our eyes and ears when drivers would come to a sudden stop just to exclaim what a beautiful dog Cassie was.

83. Adverb dependent clause; use of "*so ... that ...*" as a conjunctive phrase

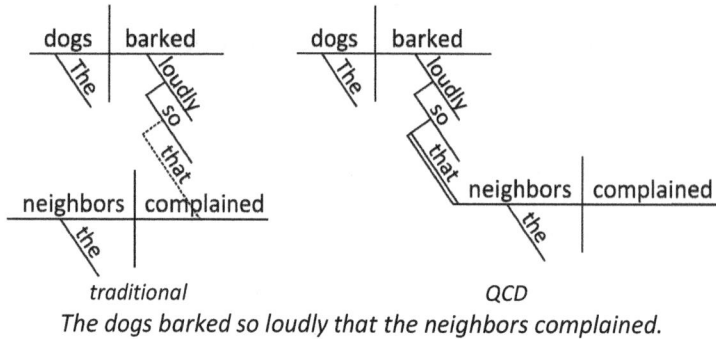

traditional   QCD

The dogs barked so loudly that the neighbors complained.

84. Adverb dependent clause; use of "***more than when***" as a conjunctive phrase.

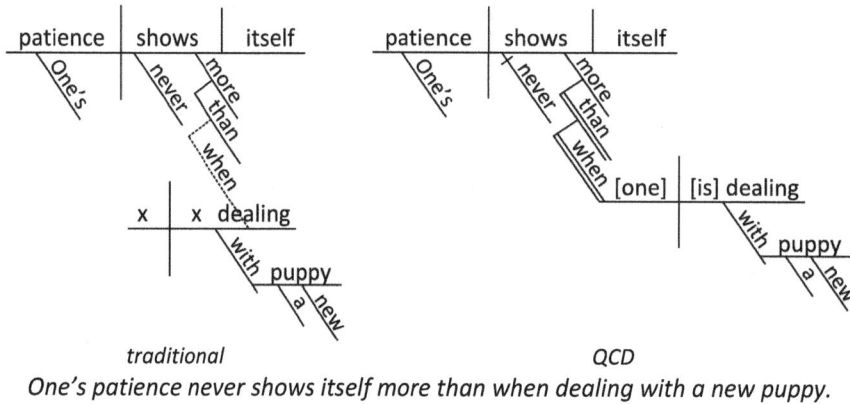

traditional   QCD

One's patience never shows itself more than when dealing with a new puppy.

85. Use of gerund phrase as replacement for adverb dependent clause (*compare to no. 84*)

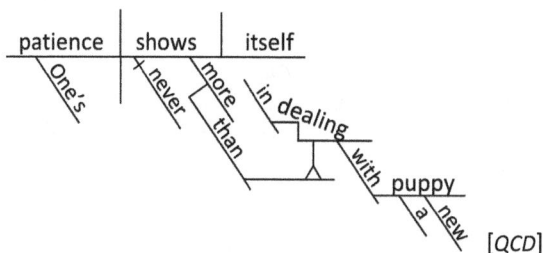

[QCD]

One's patience never show itself more than in dealing with a new puppy.
[to convert to traditional format, remove the "limiting adverb" mark
from the diagonal holding "[never]".]

86. Adverb dependent clause; "*as*" used as a conjunction

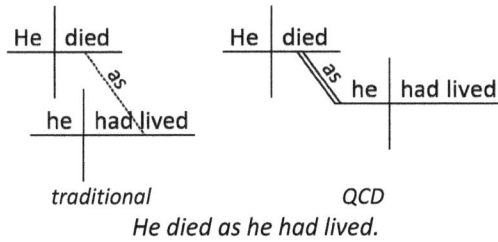

| He | died |

as

| he | had lived |

traditional

| He | died |

as

| he | had lived |

QCD

He died as he had lived.

87. Adverb dependent clause; "*as ... so ...*" used as a conjunction

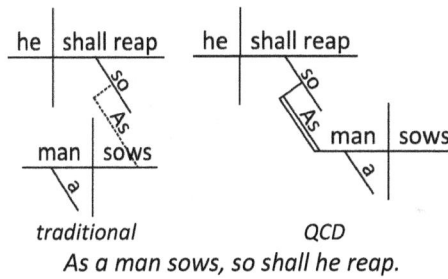

| he | shall reap |

so

As

| man | sows |

a

traditional

| he | shall reap |

so

As

| man | sows |

a

QCD

As a man sows, so shall he reap.

88. Adverb dependent clauses; adjective dependent clause; elision of conjunction "that" from adjective clause; use of "**so ... that ...**" as a conjunction

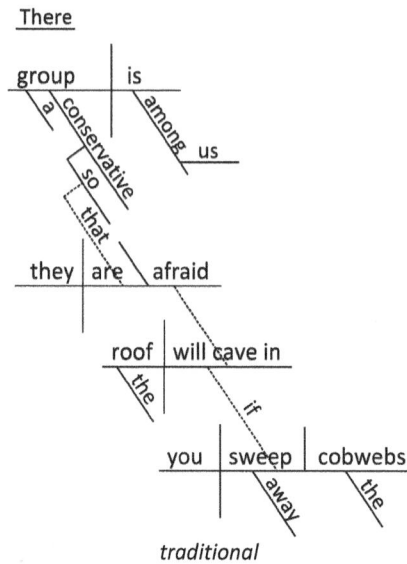

traditional

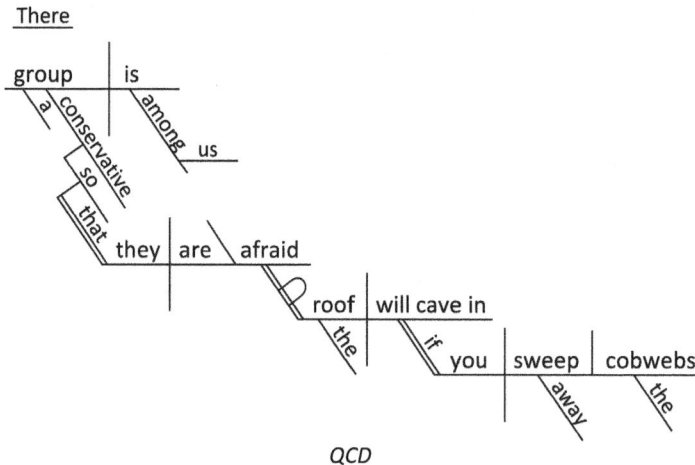

QCD

There is a group among us so conservative that they are afraid the roof will cave in if you sweep away the cobwebs.

[These diagrams detail the situation in which the emphasis is on existence or location of the subject; alternately, the prepositional phrase "among us" could modify "group" if that were determined to be the intent of the speaker.]

89. Compound-complex sentence: adverb dependent clause; partially elided predicate; compound independent clauses; expletive use of *"there"*

There

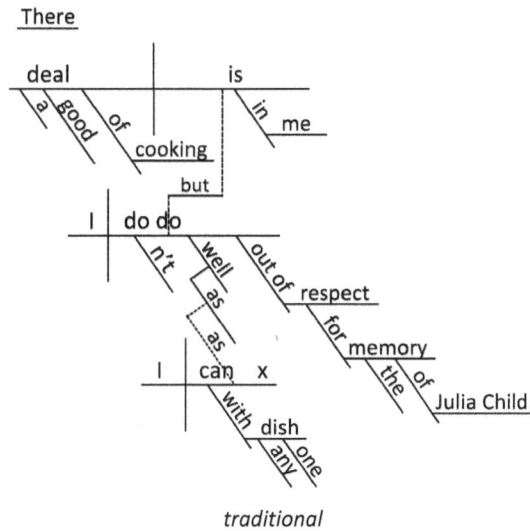

traditional

There

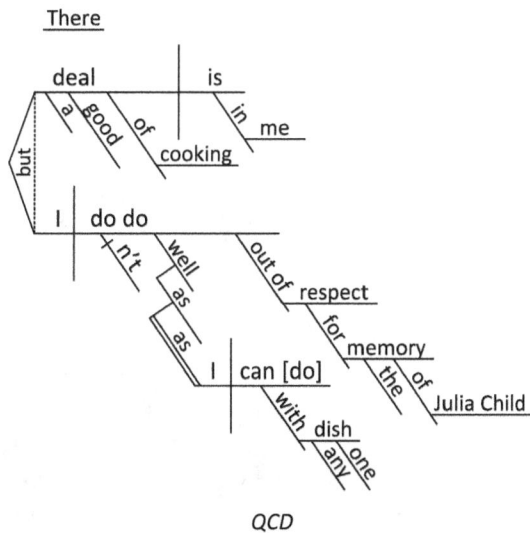

QCD

There is a good deal of cooking in me, but I don't do as well as I can with any one dish out of respect for the memory of Julia Child.

90. Infinitive predicate appositive with *it* + *form of to be* [§7.24.11]; *as...as* with .adverb; adverbial dependent clause; elision within dependent clause; elision of conjunction before dependent clause

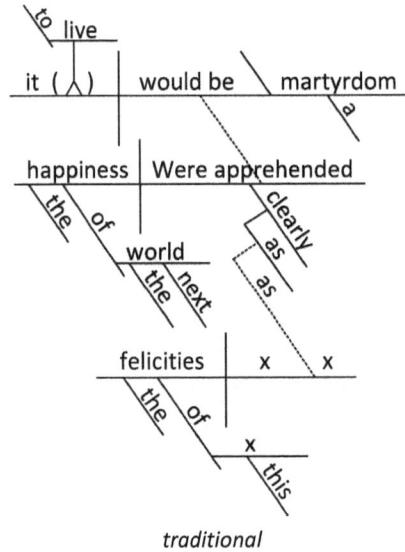

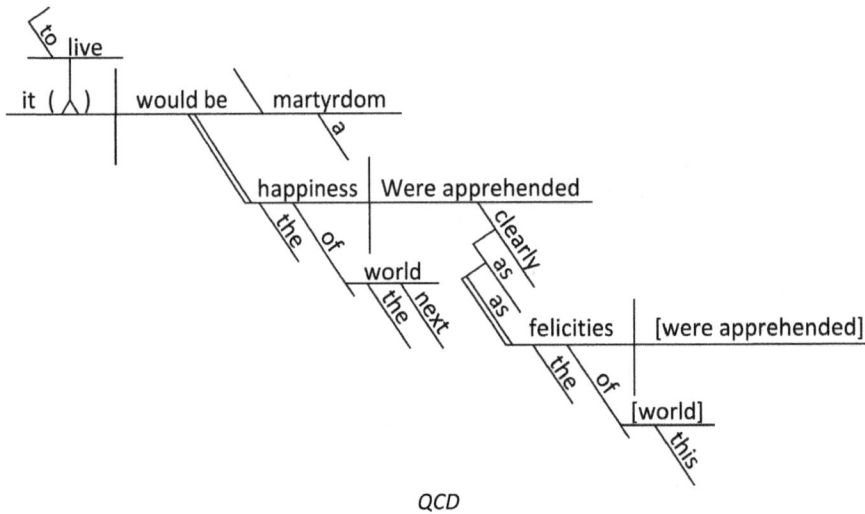

traditional

QCD
Were the happiness of the next world apprehended as clearly as the felicities of this, it would be a martyrdom to live.

91. Adverb dependent clauses; adjective dependent clause; direct quotation; imperative in direct quotation; gerund object of preposition

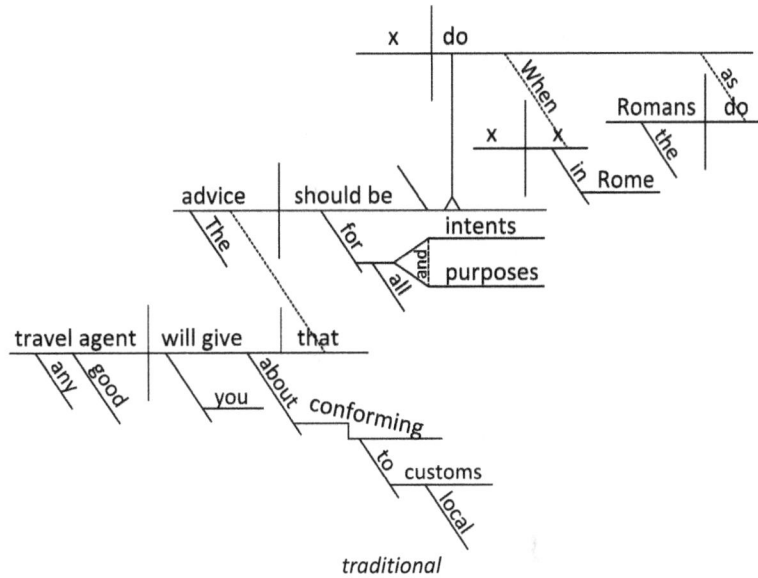

traditional

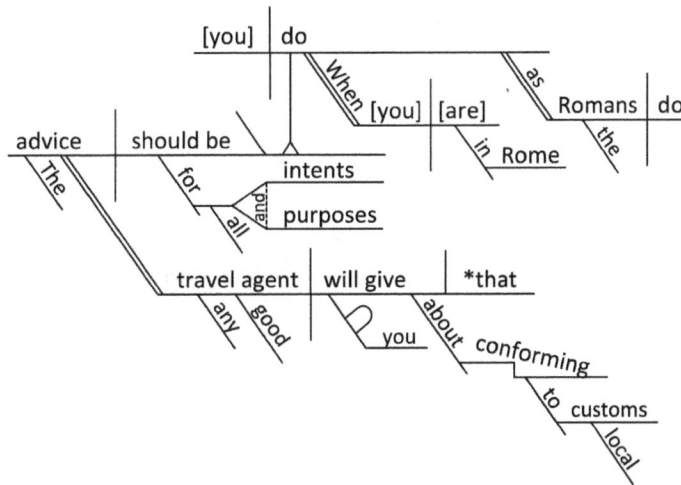

QCD

The advice that any good travel agent will give you about conforming to local customs for all intents and purposes should be, "When in Rome, do as the Romans do."

92. Subject infinitive; noun dependent clause as direct object of infinitive; infinitive as predicate complement.

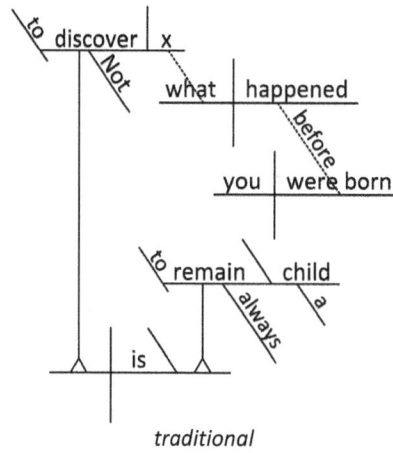

traditional

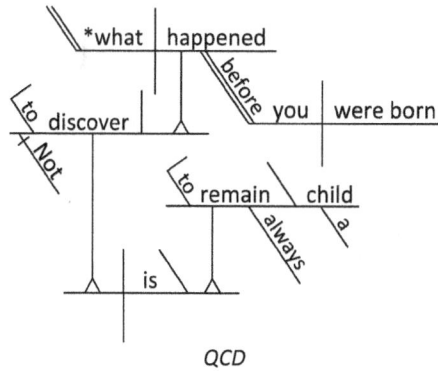

QCD

Not to discover what happened before you were born is to remain always a child.

17 Glossary

accusative case: *one of the names for the objective case in Modern English. In Anglo-Saxon it is specifically used for the direct object, the object of some prepositions, and a few other usages, such as the accusative of the duration of space or time.*

Anglo-Saxon: *the Germanic language of the three tribes, the Jutes, the Angles and the Saxons, that invaded Romano-Celtic Britain from the mainland of Europe in the early 5th century CE and settled in the area later known as the Kingdom of England. It is also known as Old English and was the spoken and literary language of folk and court until the Norman invasion of 1066.*

back-formation: *a word, suffix or prefix that is formed by removing a part or portions of another word to form a new word, or a vocabulary unit for word formation. An example is when the new word **pea** [plural = **peas**] was formed from the original singular **pease** [plural = **peasen**] because the original singular was mistaken for a plural.*

case: *a grammatical classification of nouns, adjectives and pronouns established by the usage of the word within the context of its phrase or sentence. In synthetic languages words change their forms depending on which case they are in. The number of cases, their exact usage and the forms they may take are specific to each language. There are three cases whose remnants appear in Modern English: the nominative, the possessive and the objective cases.*

Common English: *is a form of English that merges aspects of British English and North American English in order to emphasize their common elements and avoid the extremes of either dialect.*

conceptual derangement: *the inability to recognize, derive or maintain differences between unrelated concepts, based largely on confusion or misuse of names.*

An example of this is when residents of that area of the United Kingdom called England state, "I am English, so what I speak is English." They are confusing the geographic, topographic concept termed "England" or the idea of citizenship in, or residence within, the boundaries of a social organization labeled "England" with the unrelated nomenclature of the English language.

*Conceptual derangement is also operative when some residents of the Irish nation (or non-residents who identify themselves with that ethereal concept "Ireland") urge "[re-]unification of Ireland", confusing the topographic or geological concept of that island called "Ireland" with other cultural, organizational or government entities that just happen to have acquired the same name. The Republic of Ireland is already united; the island of Ireland is physically united by definition; those are each unitary concepts. What the users of the phrase "Unite/Reunite Ireland" actually mean is "Unite/Reunite the [English] Kingdom of Ireland", for only **that** was the item split into the Republic of Ireland and the area of Northern Ireland that chose to remain part of the United Kingdom.*

An extension of this has occurred in the U.S. among those Blacks who have taken the phrase "African-American" and extended it to mean that all occupants of the entire continent of Africa are, have been or should be "black" despite the fact that "Africa" is a geographic or geologic concept that has neither direct nor consistent relationship to race. ["Race" is itself a dubious concept, without basis in Biology.] As a result of this misconception, some believe that even those regions of Africa north of the Sahara were originally populated continually by members of the groups of people who are now limited to sub-Saharan regions, and that the only reason the nations from Egypt to Morocco don't have Negroid residents now is as a result of an overwhelming Arab invasion that swept away and supplanted those original, Negroid populations with people from the Arabian Peninsula. This derangement persists despite the fact that the Arabian Peninsula has never had sufficient population to have afforded such an ethnic-cleansing-style replacement; and despite genetic testing that, for example, proves that the current population of Egypt is made up of descendants of the very same people who built the pyramids, reaching back at least five thousand years ago.

This misunderstanding was the basis of the outrage expressed by American Blacks when the National Geographic Society had facial reconstruction experts recreate the face of King Tut-ankh-amun from his skeletal remains. That reconstruction, and all others done since, ended up looking very much like a modern Egyptian and not like a sub-Saharan African. Some blacks complained that National Geographic was "stealing their heritage," whereas, in fact, those angry individuals were merely victims of a culturally, biologically and historically uninformed, conceptually deranged theft by a few unschooled Black Americans of the heritage of the Egyptian people, based largely on racial profiling extrapolated from the feminized facial characteristics of the funerary masks of King Tut-ankh-amun.

*The fact is that **names, political concepts, or geographical or geological terms do not equal origin, society, government or language**. They do not automatically express historical veracity; they do not establish primacy; they do not confer ownership; they do not establish governmental regions nor societal boundaries.*

core vocabulary: *the set of words that form the basic group used by native speakers in everyday parlance, usually including the names of, descriptive modifiers for, and verbs used with everyday household items, family names and kinship terms, numbers, and basic environmental objects and manifestations (i.e., landscape and weather); along with basic pronouns used in referring to any of those.*

dative case: *one of the names for the objective case in Modern English, specifically when the word appears as the indirect object of the verb, a usage common to the same case in Anglo-Saxon. The objects of most prepositions in Anglo-Saxon also appeared in the dative case.*

deictic: *indicating or pointing out something from the perspective of the "pointer" or others forming an origin-point; used with demonstrative pronouns and adjectives, such as **this** and **that**.*

dysglossia: *use of language in ways that impede communication, or that place ulterior motives within the use of or form taken by language*

Erse: *the Celtic language of Ireland, also called **Irish**.*

Englandic: *the English language as specific to the inhabitants of England. This contrasts with "Canadian" or "American" as names given by the British to other dialects of English.*

expletive: *in grammar, a word that takes the place of another word or phrase, usually standing apart from the syntactical organization of the clause in which it appears; the most common such expletive in English is the word **there**.*

expletory: *adjective form of the noun **expletive**, q.v.*

finite verb: *a verb form that is marked for person, number, tense and mood; such a form stands in contrast to the **infinitive**, which is the verb form unrestricted by those distinctions*

Gaelic: *the Celtic language of Scotland*

genitive case: *an alternate name for the possessive case in Modern English, of the same usage it had in Anglo-Saxon.*

hypocorism: *a nickname, pet-name, or a euphemism*

idioglossia: *here used in its original, Greek-derived meaning of a private or personal [ἴδιος] form of speech [γλῶσσα]; in child psychology, a private language invented between closely associated* children, such as twins, or even by a lone child; in pathology, a situation marked by speech so distorted that it is unintelligible

London Pirate Dialect: *see p. 14*

Middle English: *the form of English current between the Norman Conquest (1066) and the late 15th century with the start of the Tudor era. This period of the language was the one in which the simplifications of grammar were manifested, with the extensive synthetic formations of Anglo-Saxon being replaced with a far more analytic organization.*

non-nativized: *of people having been sufficiently immersed in other cultures, or in this specific case, other languages, so that these individuals are able to stand apart or aloof from their native language, society or culture, to see it as if from afar.*

Old English: *another name for Anglo-Saxon, q.v.*

Old Norse: *the language of the Viking invaders of England during the 9th to 11th centuries, it was carried into England and became the dominant language of the wide backslash-shaped area called the Danelaw, stretching from London and East Anglia, north beyond York and west of York to the Irish Sea. Fairly closely related to Old English, it is suggested that the need of the peasants to communicate in either language caused a simplification of grammatical norms, with concentration on word roots without their grammatical endings, spurring the loss of complexity—a simplification that is a hallmark of English grammar.*

Predicate appositive use of infinitive: *see §7.24.11.*

protocol: *a set of rules and associated data that determines the order and organization of a signal – the format of the message – for successful transfer of information. Well-known protocols in use on the Internet are HTTP, FTP and TCP/IP.*

QCD: *Qualls Concise Diagramming, is the improved specification for Reed/Kellogg-style diagramming as put forth in this volume, starting in §16.3 (p. 207).*

QCG: *Qualls Concise Grammar, the title of this volume.*

register: *the social level at or situation in which grammatical forms or specific vocabulary items are considered to be proper. These are sometimes given numbers, at other times names, in which, for example, "1" could be set as "everyday" or "informal", "2" as "polite" or "conversational" and "3" as "formal". In Japanese, most grammars recognize five registers, with an "impolite" zero level, and registers higher than "formal" that continue the escalation of politeness.*

INDEX

This index covers topics only within the grammar sections. It does not include references to those topics when they may appear within the diagramming examples. To find the relevant location of matching items covered within the diagramming section, refer to the Diagramming Topics table on p. 209.

W

DANVM NE VEXATE

NEQVE DANAVM

www.ingramcontent.com/pod-product-compliance
Lightning Source LLC
Chambersburg PA
CBHW080659110426
42739CB00034B/3329